Cities in Crisis

In recent years, European societies and territories have witnessed the spatial impacts of a severe financial and socio-economic crisis. This book builds on the current debate concerning how cities and urban regions and their citizens deal with the consequences of the recent financial and socio-economic crisis.

Cities in Crisis examines the political and administrative implications of austerity measures applied in Southern European cities. These include cuts in local public spending and the processes of privatisation of local public assets, as well as issues related to the rescaling, recentralisation, or decentralisation of competencies. Attention is paid to the rise of new 'austerity regimes', the question of their legitimacy, their spatial manifestations, and in particular to the social consequences of austerity.

The contributions to this book lay the foundation for recommendations on how to improve and consolidate qualified governance arrangements in order to better address rapid economic and social changes. Such recommendations are applicable to cities and urban regions both within and outside Europe. It identifies possible approaches, tools, and partnerships to tackle the effects of the crisis and to prepare European cities for future challenges.

Jörg Knieling is Professor for Urban Planning and Regional Development at HafenCity University Hamburg, Germany.

Frank Othengrafen is Professor for Regional Planning and Governance at the Leibniz Universität Hannover, Germany.

T0347330

Regions and Cities
Series Editor in Chief
Susan M. Christopherson, *Cornell University, USA*

Editors
Maryann Feldman, *University of Georgia, USA*
Gernot Grabher, *HafenCity University Hamburg, Germany*
Ron Martin, *University of Cambridge, UK*
Martin Perry, *Massey University, New Zealand*

In today's globalised, knowledge-driven and networked world, regions and cities have assumed heightened significance as the interconnected nodes of economic, social, and cultural production, and as sites of new modes of economic and territorial governance and policy experimentation. This book series brings together incisive and critically engaged international and interdisciplinary research on this resurgence of regions and cities, and should be of interest to geographers, economists, sociologists, political scientists, and cultural scholars, as well as to policy-makers involved in regional and urban development.

For more information on the Regional Studies Association visit www.regional studies.org/.

There is a **30% discount** available to RSA members on books in the ***Regions and Cities*** series, and other subject-related Taylor & Francis books and e-books including Routledge titles. To order just e-mail alex.robinson@tandf.co.uk, or phone on +44 (0) 20 7017 6924 and declare your RSA membership. You can also visit www.routledge.com and use the discount code: **RSA0901**.

Cities in Crisis

Socio-spatial impacts of the economic crisis
in Southern European cities

**Edited by
Jörg Knieling and
Frank Othengrafen**

LONDON AND NEW YORK

First published 2016 by Routledge

2 Park Square, Milton Park, Abingdon, Oxfordshire OX14 4RN
711 Third Avenue, New York, NY 10017

Routledge is an imprint of the Taylor & Francis Group, an informa business

First issued in paperback 2018

British Library Cataloguing in Publication Data
A catalogue record for this book is available from the British Library

Library of Congress Cataloging in Publication Data
A catalog record for this book has been requested

ISBN: 978-1-138-85002-6 (hbk)
ISBN: 978-1-138-32911-9 (pbk)

Typeset in Times New Roman
by Wearset Ltd, Boldon, Tyne and Wear

This book is the result of an international conference funded by the German Academic Exchange Service (Deutscher Akademischer Austauschdienst) and the German Federal Foreign Office (Auswärtiges Amt).

Contents

Figures

Tables

Contributors

Jörg Knieling is Professor of Urban Planning and Regional Development at HafenCity University Hamburg. His academic background is spatial planning (Dr-Ing.) and social sciences (MA pol./soc.). As former 'Directeur de recherche' he is interlinked with the 'l'Institut d'études avancées' in Paris. His research is focused on sustainable urban and regional planning, territorial governance, communicative planning, and international planning cultures. Among his recent book publications are *Soft Spaces in Europe* (2015), *Climate Change Governance* (2013), *Planning Cultures in Europe* (2009), and *Metropolitan Regions* (2009). He is a member of the German Academy for Spatial Research and Planning and of the Advisory Board of the German Federal Ministry of Transport and Digital Infrastructure. As practitioner, he is partner of the consultancy KoRiS on communicative urban and regional development.

Frank Othengrafen is Professor of Regional Planning and Research at the Leibniz Universität Hannover (LUH). Before his appointment at LUH he was Visiting Professor of European Planning Cultures at TU Dortmund (2011–2012). He is co-editor of the German annual *City and Region* (*Jahrbuch Stadt und Region*) and a member of the editorial board of the *European Journal of Spatial Development*. His research covers a wide spectrum of issues including urban and regional planning and governance, planning culture and theory as well as comparative studies on planning systems. He has published various books and papers in international journals.

Joaquín Rodríguez Álvarez is a PhD candidate at the Autonomous University of Barcelona. His research is focused on the field of Science and Technology Studies as well as on urban studies. He has a master's degree in International Relations from Barcelona's Institute of International Relations (IBEI) and a Postgraduate degree in Project Management from the Center of High Academic Studies of the Organization of Ibero-American States. Currently, he works as a researcher and lecturer at the Autonomous University of Barcelona Foundation. Among his recent publications are *Migration und Integration in Europa* (2011) and *Jeder für sich oder alle gemeinsam in Europa? Die Debatte über Identität, Wohlstand und die institutionellen Grundlagen der Union* (2012).

Evangelos Asprogerakas is a regional and urban planner, holding a PhD from the National Technical University of Athens (NTUA) and a master's degree in Urban Economics from the University College London (UCL). He served as a teaching assistant at the NTUA and taught Regional Planning at the University of Thessaly as well as Spatial Planning and Development at the Hellenic National School of Public Administration. He is currently a tutor of Environmental Planning at the Hellenic Open University. His research activities include issues related to spatial planning and governance, spatial impact of IT, and development planning, mainly in the field of tourism and urban regeneration. His work has been published in renowned international journals.

Dimitrios Balampanidis is a PhD candidate in Urban Social Geography at Harokopio University, Athens (HUA). He holds a master's degree in Urban and Regional Planning (National Technical University Athens, NTUA) as well as a diploma in Architecture (Aristotle University Thessaloniki, AUTH). His research is focused on immigrants' settlement and ethnic residential segregation in the urban space, especially in Athens and Paris. His broader research interests lie in multiple divisions of space, segregation, and transcultural coexistence in neighbourhoods, as well as in housing policies, urban, and regional planning. He is an affiliated researcher of the Urban Environment Laboratory (NTUA) and has been a Visiting Research Fellow at the research department UMR Géographies-cités (Université Paris 1 Panthéon-Sorbonne, CNRS).

Angelo Besana has a PhD in Urban and Regional Geography. He is currently Assistant Professor of Economic and Political Geography at the Interuniversity Department of Regional and Urban Studies and Planning (DIST), Polytechnic University of Turin. He teaches a course on Geographical Information Systems and Territorial Development, and his research interests are applied geography, regional development, and GIS applications.

Josep Vicent Boira is Professor of Urban Geography at the Department of Geography, University of Valencia. His academic background includes urban studies, infrastructures geographies, and megaregional analysis of new urbanisation processes. Currently, he is Director of the Centre of Urban Research at the University of Valencia in collaboration with the City Council of Valencia. He is a member of the evaluation committee of different scientific Italian journals and a consultant for entrepreneurs associations. Among his recent book publications are *Valencia, la Ciudad* (2011) and *Valencia, la Tormenta Perfecta* (2013), an analysis of the socio-political situation of the crisis in the Valencian region. He is currently Secretary of the Urban Geography Group of the Association of Spanish Geographers (*Asociación de Geógrafos Españoles*) and Director of Communication at the University of Valencia.

Dolores Brandis is Professor of Urban Geography at the Complutense University of Madrid. Her research studies are focused on recent urban transformation events, new models of urban growth, and the values of landscape and urban image. Among her recent publications are: *Metropolitan Challenges:*

A Dialogue between Europe and Latin America (2014), *Cities and Urban System: Reflections on Times of Crisis* (2012), *Cities and Landscapes in the 21st Century* (2012), and *Functional Dynamics of Tourism and its Impacts on World Heritage Site Cities* (2010). Recently, she has participated in several research projects such as 'Assessment of landscape heritage and identity in Spain' and 'World Heritage cities of Spain and Mexico: comparative sustainable planning and management experiences'.

Nadia Caruso is postdoctoral research fellow at the Polytechnic University of Turin. Her academic background is spatial planning and her research is focused on the evolution of the planning field, housing policies and social housing, territorial governance, and planning education. She took part in an ESPON research and is currently working on an Italian research project, funded by the Italian Ministry of Education, Universities, and Research. She is a member of the Coordination Team of AESOP Young Academics.

Anastasia Chani holds a master's degree in Urban and Regional Planning (National Technical University Athens, 2012) and a diploma in Civil Engineering with specialisation in Transportation Planning (National Technical University Athens, 2010). She is a PhD candidate at the School of Architecture NTUA. Since 2011 she has participated in various research projects of the School of Architecture NTUA as a researcher and has attended many international conferences. Her interests are related to the impact of IT and innovation on urban space and the evolution of cities. Moreover, she is a certified property evaluator and works currently as a freelancer.

Helena Chuliá is a lecturer at the Department of Econometrics and Statistics at the University of Barcelona. She holds a PhD in Quantitative Finance from the University of Valencia and was Visiting Researcher at the Erasmus University of Rotterdam in 2006 and at Humboldt University in 2011. She has published in refereed journals including the *Journal of Banking and Finance*, *European Journal of Finance*, *Quantitative Finance*, *Journal of Futures Markets*, *European Financial Management*, and *Energy Economics* as well as in professional volumes. She has presented her work at different international conferences. Her current areas of research include applied econometrics, portfolio management, and international finance.

Susana Corvelo is an economist, holding a master's degree in Industrial Management and Strategy from the University of Lisbon and is currently a PhD candidate in Urban Studies at ISCTE–IUL, developing a thesis concerning urban governance and the development process and effects of participatory mechanisms in Lisbon's urban fabric. Her research interests are focused on urban studies and urban policy, participatory democracy as well as urban economic development and innovation. She is currently Director of the Department of Innovation and Strategic Sectors at Lisbon's Municipality. Previously, she was Vice Director of the Office for Strategy and Planning in the Portuguese Ministry of Labour and Social Solidarity and a researcher at the Institute for Innovation in Training.

Giancarlo Cotella is Assistant Professor of Spatial Planning at the Polytechnic University of Turin. His research is focused on European territorial governance and in particular on the interaction between European Spatial Planning and Member States' spatial planning systems. He has been Visiting Professor as well as a researcher in various institutions, including the Wroclaw University of Technology, the University of Tartu, the Polish Academy of Science, the University of Kaiserslautern. He has participated in several international research projects, mostly funded by the EU. He has published widely in international journals and has been actively involved in the Association of European Schools of Planning since 2007.

José Luís Crespo is Professor at the Faculty of Architecture of the University of Lisbon (FAUL). He is a researcher in the Centre for Research Architecture, Urban Planning and Design (CIAUD-FAUL). His main research interests are focused on the topics urban governance, urban geography, public participation in planning and projects, shared and participatory cities.

Ana Drago is a PhD candidate in Urban Studies at ISCTE-IUL/FCSH-UL in Lisbon. Her former research focused mainly on social movements and she published the book *Agitar Antes de Ousar* (*Shake it Before Daring*, 2004), concerning students' protest movements in Portuguese society. From 2002 to 2013 she was an elected member of the Portuguese National Parliament, working on education, health, and economic policies. Her current research is focused on critical urban theory and democratic urban governance.

Thomas Greve holds a diploma (1983) and a PhD (1993) in Architecture and Planning from Stuttgart University. He has been practising in Greece since 1983 as Managing Director of the planning companies Plan EE and Horodomi OE and is responsible for a wide range of projects (public and private buildings, urban and spatial planning). He has long-standing experience in consulting public bodies and local institutions. He is Vice President of the Board of Trustees of the German School of Athens. His scientific interest is focused on the 'Greek way of planning'.

Montserrat Guillen is Professor of Quantitative Methods in Economics and Business at the University of Barcelona (UB). She is also Visiting Professor of Insurance Econometrics at the Université de Paris Panthéon-Assas as well as Director of Riskcenter, a research group on risk analysis in finance and insurance based at UB. She is a senior editor of *Astin Bulletin*, the scientific journal of the International Association of Actuaries, and an associate editor of the *Journal of Risk and Insurance*. Her research covers a wide spectrum of issues related to health, ageing, and longevity, including risk quantification in policy decision-making. She has published papers in international journals and has developed many R&D projects, some jointly with leading insurance companies.

Umberto Janin Rivolin is Professor of Spatial Planning at the Polytechnic University of Turin, Italy. There he acts as Vice Head of the Interuniversity

Department of Regional and Urban Studies and Planning (DIST) and as Coordinator of the PhD Course in Urban and Regional Development. His research is focused on spatial planning systems and EU territorial governance. He has been a coordinator of national research units in the ESPON projects 'TANGO – Territorial approaches for new governance', 'Governance of territorial and urban policies from EU to local level', and 'Application and effects of the ESDP in the Member States'. Among his main book publications are *Governo del Territorio e Pianificazione Spaziale* (2013), *La Costruzione del Territorio Europeo* (2009), and *European Spatial Planning* (2004).

Ifigeneia Kokkali is an urban planner at the University of Thessaly, Greece. She holds a master's degree and a PhD in Urban Studies (2009) from the Institut Français d'Urbanisme (IFU), University Paris-Est. Her doctoral dissertation explored the patterns of socio-spatial inclusion of immigrants in Thessaloniki, Greece. She is an adjunct professor at the IFU since 2009. Currently, she is based at the Department of Architecture and Urban Studies, Polytechnic University of Milan, where she studies the dynamics and challenges posed by multi-ethnic coexistence in cities. Her further topics of interest are school segregation and its relation to urban segregation. Previously, she has held different positions at the University of Florence, the Robert Schuman Centre for Advanced Studies of the European University Institute, as well as the Department of Planning and Development at the Aristotle University of Thessaloniki.

Thilo Lang has studied and worked in Kaiserslautern, Hamburg, Berlin, Potsdam, Sheffield, and Durham before joining the Leibniz-Institute for Regional Geography (IfL) in Leipzig in 2009 where he is currently head of the department Regional Geography of Europe. Before that he worked in a regional development agency as manager of international innovation projects. His current research interests include socio-spatial processes of and responses to multiple forms of regional polarisation and peripheralisation, innovation outside agglomerations, economic regeneration, and regional development as well as return migration to east Germany and Central and Eastern Europe. He holds degrees in planning and in human geography. Major publications include an edited book on understanding new geographies of Central and Eastern Europe.

Teresa Marat-Mendes is an architect graduated at the Faculty of Architecture of the Technical University of Lisbon (1994). She holds a master's degree in Land Use Planning and Environmental Planning from the Faculty of Sciences and Technology of the New University of Lisbon (1999) and a PhD in Architecture from the University of Nottingham (2002). Currently, she is Assistant Professor at the Department of Architecture and Urbanism at the Lisbon University Institute ISCTE-IUL and a researcher at DINÂMIA'CET-IUL, Centre for Socioeconomic Change and Territorial Studies. She is also a member of the Scientific Council of the International Seminar on Urban Form and

President of the Portuguese Network of Urban Morphology. Moreover, she coordinates the research project 'MEMO – Evolution of the Lisbon Metropolitan Area Metabolism: Lessons towards a Sustainable Urban Future' at the DINÂMIA'CET-IUL, financed by the Portuguese Science Foundation.

Ramon Marrades is a PhD researcher at Econcult (Culture Economics Research Unit, University of Valencia). He holds a master's degree in Economics and Geography at Utrecht University and has been a guest researcher at PUCESE University (Ecuador). His work and research are focused on the interaction between economics, urban planning, and culture. He received an honourable mention in the International Young Planning Professionals Award (2012) and the Spanish Social Entrepreneur Award (2013). He is a founding member of the urbanism think-do tank '*La Ciudad Construida*' and a board member of URBEGO, the platform for young planning professionals of the International Federation of Housing and Planning.

Carme Melo has been Assistant Professor of Sustainable Development at the Hankuk University of Foreign Studies (South Korea) since September 2014. Prior to this appointment, she was a postdoctoral researcher at the University of Valencia (Spain). She has also been a guest researcher at the National University of La Plata (Argentina) as well as at Radboud University Nijmegen (The Netherlands). Her work mostly engages with the disciplines of environmental politics and green political theory. Her research is focused on issues of citizenship, democracy, and the state from an environmental perspective.

Maria Manuela Mendes is Professor at the Faculty of Architecture of the University of Lisbon (FAUL). She has also been a researcher in the Centre for Research and Studies in Sociology, University Institute of Lisbon (CIES-IUL) since 2008 as well as a member of the Centre for Research Architecture, Urban Planning, and Design (CIAUD-FAUL) and of the Institute of Sociology, Faculty of Arts of Porto (ISFLUP). Her main research interests are focused on the topics ethnicity, immigration, city and diversity, social and spatial exclusion, local development, relocation, and disqualified territories.

Joana Mourão is an architect graduated at the Department of Architecture of the Science and Technology Faculty at Coimbra University (2001). She postgraduated on Urban and Environmental Planning (2005) and holds a PhD in Urbanism from the Faculty of Architecture of Oporto University (2012). Her professional experience includes architectural training in Stuttgart (2000), architectural practice in Lisbon (from 2001 onwards), and research development on sustainable urban systems in Barcelona at the Polytechnic University of Catalonia (2007). As an expert on housing and urban ecological sustainability, she has taken part in several architecture and urban studies as well as in territorial assessment studies of policies and planning in Portugal and abroad. She is currently a researcher in the project 'MEMO – Evolution of the Lisbon Metropolitan Area Metabolism: Lessons Towards a Sustainable Urban Future' at the DINÂMIA'CET-IUL, financed by the Portuguese Science Foundation.

Jorge Nicolau is an architect and urban planner specialised in the field of urban regeneration. He is currently finishing a PhD in urban planning and works as a researcher in the Centre for Research Architecture, Urban Planning, and Design (CIAUD-FAUL). Since 2010 he has participated in a research line called 'The quarter and the city in question'. He has taken part in several conferences presenting scientific articles, some of which are published. His research interests are related to the city's microscale, stressing the importance of neighbourhood units in strengthening the sense of the residents' identity.

Christina Nikolakopoulou holds MEng (Distinction) in Urban and Regional Planning from the University of Thessaly and a master's degree from the University College London (UCL) with merit. Her research interests are focused on regional economics and urban regeneration. She is a management consulting professional and a domestic energy assessor.

Athanasios Papaioannou is Project Manager at the Professional School of the Leuphana University Lüneburg. Prior to this position he was responsible for various project developments in the private sector and was a PhD candidate at the HafenCity University Hamburg. He has an academic background in urban and regional planning. His research interests extend to various fields, such as urban planning, metropolitan regions, mega-events, as well as governance.

Elena Pede is a PhD candidate at the Interuniversity Department of Urban and Regional Studies and Planning at the Polytechnic University of Turin. She is currently a crisis mapper for the RUSH Crisis mapping service at the Information Technology for Humanitarian Assistance, Cooperation, and Action (ITHACA) and takes part in an Italian national research project called 'Post-metropolitan territories as emergent forms of urban space: coping with sustainability, habitability, and governance', financed by the Italian Ministry of Education, Universities, and Research (MIUR). Her research is mainly focused on cross-scale institutional linkages and building resilience in risk management policies.

Juan Romero is Professor of Human Geography at the University of Valencia. He was a visiting scholar at the School of Geography, Leeds University. His teaching and research activities are focused on political geography, public policy, state organisation, and new forms of territorial governance in Spain and in Europe. He was principal researcher and coordinator of a research project on 'Strategies of Territorial Cooperation in Spain', involving 54 researchers from 14 different Spanish universities. He participated in the Spanish LP team of the ESPON project 2.3.2 on Territorial and Urban Governance. Among his recent publications are *(Un)sustainable Territories: Causes of the Speculative Bubble in Spain (1996–2010) and its Territorial, Environmental, and Sociopolitical Consequence* (2012) and *Cities and Urban and Metropolitan Regions in Spain: A New Agenda in a Global Context* (2013).

Luís del Romero Renau is Professor of Human Geography and Spatial Planning at the University of Valencia. As a former researcher in Canada he is interlinked with the 'Observatoire des Conflits Urbains' of the University of Quebec in Montreal (UQAM). His research focuses on the study of conflicts linked to urban and regional planning issues: environmental, urban conflicts, and protest movements in cities. He is also a coordinator of the 'Recartografías' research unit at the University of Valencia, which studies planning issues and conflicts in shrinking regions. He has published different papers on this particular subject in international journals.

Carlo Salone is Professor of Regional Geography and Territorial Development at the Interuniversity Department of Regional and Urban Studies and Planning at the Polytechnic University of Turin. He is currently Visiting Professor at UPEC (Université Paris-Est Créteil), Paris and Lyon 2-Lumière (France). His research is focused on European spatial planning, innovations in territorial policies, and local development practices in the European Union and, more recently, on the cultural economy of cities. He authored, alone or with other scholars, a number of books on territorial policies as well as articles concerning the European territorial policies, the new regionalism, and the culture as a factor of urban cohesion and development.

Miguel Santolino is Senior Lecturer at the Department of Econometrics, Statistics and Spanish Economy at the University of Barcelona (UB). His research focuses on conflict resolution mechanisms, including Alternative Dispute Resolution (ADR) methods, quantification of risk and risk behaviour of agents, and the analysis of causes and consequences of motor accidents. His research is published in the international journals *Risk Analysis, Journal of Risk Research, Group Decision and Negotiation, International Review of Law and Economics, European Journal of Law and Economics, Accident Analysis and Prevention, Insurance: Mathematics and Economics*, and national insurance journals.

João Seixas is Associate Researcher at the Institute of Social Sciences of the University of Lisbon. His works are in the fields of urban studies, human geography, and socio-politics of territories. He is Visiting Professor at the Federal University of Rio de Janeiro and the Autonomous University of Barcelona. He was a commissioner of the Strategic Charter of Lisbon and is currently a consultant for the EU/URBACT programme. He has coordinated several projects in the fields of contemporary urban studies, urban politics, and urban regeneration. He is also administrator of the 'Ler Devagar' cultural centre in Lisbon and chronicler on urban themes in the *Público* newspaper. Most recent and forthcoming books are *Urban Governance in Southern Europe* (2012), *A Cidade na Encruzilhada* (2013), *Governação de Proximidade* (2014), and *Em Todas as Ruas* (2015).

Konstantinos Serraos is an architect, engineer, urban, and regional planner. He is Associate Professor of Urban Planning and Design in the School of Architecture of the National Technical University of Athens (NTUA). He has been scientific collaborator at the TU Wien, scientific associate of the Earthquake Planning and Protection Organization, Chairman of the Management Board of the Environmental Awareness Park 'Antonis Tritsis', and Chairman of the Management Board of the Public Law Entity 'Green Fund'. He worked as an associate lecturer in the Department of Planning and Regional Development of the University of Thessaly. Since 2001 he has been a tutor at the Hellenic Open University in the Postgraduate course 'Environmental Design of Cities and Buildings'. He has been involved in numerous research projects and publications, mainly in the fields of urban planning and urban growth, urban environmental planning, land use planning, open space planning, urban regeneration, systems and design methods, urban transformations, planning of metropolitan areas, institutional framework for urban planning, and impacts of socio-economic changes on urban space.

Simone Tulumello holds a PhD in Urban and Regional Planning from the University of Palermo and is currently a Postdoctoral Research Fellow at the Institute of Social Sciences of the University of Lisbon. Since October 2013 he has been an elected member of the Coordination Team of the AESOP Young Academics network. His main research project focuses on a critical analysis of urban security in spatial planning in the metropolis of Lisbon whereas his wider research interests lie at the border between planning research and critical urban studies: planning theory and planning cultures, conflict and power, neoliberal trends and insurgent practices, and Southern European cities and the crisis of the Eurozone.

Galya Vladova is a research associate at the Institute for Urban Planning and Regional Development of HafenCity University Hamburg. She holds a Bachelor Degree in Urban Planning from the University of Architecture, Civil Engineering and Geodesy Sofia and a master's degree in Urban Planning from HafenCity University Hamburg. Her main research interests lie in the field of European regional policy and territorial cooperation in large-scale areas, urban resilience, and austerity urbanism. She published about the process of regional cooperation in the Black Sea area and about new instruments of the EU cohesion policy.

Acknowledgements

The depth, duration, and global reach of the recent economic crisis, the severity of its manifold impacts on territories and societies, and the various implications of applied austerity measures have questioned existing institutional and decision-making structures, regulatory arrangements, and pre-crisis development models. The serious social, economic, and spatial challenges, faced by cities and regions today, require rethinking of urban policies. Addressing this need and building upon the current debate on how cities, urban regions, and their citizens deal with the various impacts of the crisis the current book studies possible approaches, strategies, and instruments for territorial development applied in Southern Europe.

This book is a result of the International Conference 'Cities in Crisis', financed by the German Academic Exchange Service within the programme 'Dialogue with Institutions of Higher Education in Southern Europe'. The individual chapters of the book originated as papers presented at the conference 'Cities in Crisis', which was held in Hamburg on 5 and 6 December 2013 and was organised by the Institute for Urban Planning and Regional Development of HafenCity University Hamburg and the Institute for Environmental Planning of Leibniz Universität Hannover. The book draws on the expertise and experience of academics from Greece, Italy, Portugal, Spain, and Germany and has an international coverage and interdisciplinary character. It aims at mapping up the diverse socio-spatial impacts and main challenges created or amplified by the financial and economic crisis and the strategies, approaches, and governance arrangements of Southern European cities and urban regions to deal with these.

The preparation of the book would have not been possible without the support and assistance of various institutions and individuals. We would like to thank the German Academic Exchange Service for the initial grant and funding of this publication. In particular, we thank the coordinators of the programme 'Dialogue with Institutions of Higher Education in Southern Europe' for their valuable institutional support during the whole project duration. Our thanks are also due to all the authors for their valuable inputs and contributions and for their positive responses to our frequent editorial requests. On behalf of all the authors we wish to thank all research assistants for their support in designing several maps, graphs, and tables included in this book. Furthermore, we owe a debt to the various publishers who provided copyright permission to use the images found herein. Finally, we would like to acknowledge here the support of our publishers, Routledge, who have been supportive throughout the project.

We would be glad if the book contributed to a better understanding of the complex challenges faced by European cities and urban regions as a result of the crisis. We hope that by offering innovative ideas to address these challenges further debates on the topic are encouraged opening up new channels of shared learning among scientists, practitioners, and decision-makers.

Jörg Knieling and Frank Othengrafen
Hamburg and Hannover
August 2015

1   Cities in crisis

Setting the scene for reflecting urban and regional futures in times of austerity

Jörg Knieling, Frank Othengrafen, and Galya Vladova

In recent years, the European countries and their citizens have witnessed the impacts of a severe financial and socio-economic crisis, caused by the interplay of a number of international and domestic factors (e.g. Werner, 2013). Economic recession, increasing unemployment rates, welfare cuts, and socio-cultural segregation are only a few of the diverse and wide-ranging consequences faced by nation states and cities across Europe (URBACT, 2010). The weak economic climate, often compounded by institutional and political mismatches, has meanwhile proved to have considerable negative impacts, most particularly in Southern European societies, where the crisis has hit particularly hard (e.g. Aalbers, 2009; Hadjimichalis, 2011).

The deep economic crisis has notably marked the end of a period of constant boom in the construction sector in many Southern European countries and cities. The increasing demand for housing, the provision of low-interest mortgages, the significant investments in major urban projects, and the extension of the welfare state have led to decades of massive urban sprawl and excessive dependence of the economy on the construction sector (Romero, Jiménez, & Villoria, 2012). This development has also been facilitated by the lack of adequate housing and social policies, as well as of complete and effective administrative control and mechanisms for coordination and territorial governance. The sudden bursting of the speculative property bubble and the ensuing cessation of large urban projects, leaving new housing developments uncompleted (mainly on the outskirts of cities), daily evictions from houses, and abandonment of offices and apartments due to the closure of enterprises and job losses, have had significant impacts on the real estate economy. The downswing has gradually spread to other sectors of the concerned national economies. This negative development has affected both the built environment in cities and the everyday life of citizens, thus revealing the first signs of a social crisis.

Taking the above into consideration, it can be concluded that Southern European cities and urban regions now have to deal with serious social, economic, and spatial challenges, such as the slowdown in employment and entrepreneurial economic dynamics, the worsening of the real estate economy, the discounting of functions in the urban fabric, the occurrence of new regional disparities, including spatial selectiveness and polarisation, increased levels of poverty, and even social unrest in certain areas (mainly in the urban peripheries). As a result, the set of tasks and functions that cities and urban regions need to fulfil increases drastically, while their political and fiscal revenue collection is curtailed or even collapsing. Facing impaired revenue collection and the need to set spending priorities, cities are challenged with regard to the provision of equal service coverage and living conditions, which inevitably affects the quality of life of their citizens.

As far as the political responses to the crisis are concerned, the implementation of austerity measures and financially driven policies have been put forward. Austerity here refers to government policies that seek to reduce budget deficits, public indebtedness levels, and spending by reducing or freezing labour costs, increasing taxes, and restructuring public services and the welfare state, or by a combination of these measures (Donald et al., 2014). This has, of course, manifold impacts on local self-government budgets, such as cuts in local public spending and reductions in local investments (Nunes Silva & Bucek, 2014a). In addition, municipalities are forced to become more entrepreneurial in order to promote economic development, often leading to 'the sale of ... municipal assets to reduce and relieve the public indebtedness' (Wollmann, 2014: p. 68; see also Donald et al., 2014). However, this can 'threaten the functioning of local government, and influence the quality and scope of the local services provided' (Nunes Silva & Bucek, 2014b: p. 182). This goes hand in hand with the fear of a widening gap between the demand for services and those offered, e.g. the provision of technical and social infrastructure, social cohesion policies, quality of life policies, which, in socio-spatial terms, can end in the emergence of uneven socio-territorial developments, resulting in the discontinuation of functions of the urban fabric and further inner segregation of the cities and their Metropolitan Areas.

At the same time, decision-makers have been put under pressure to fulfil the obligations imposed by the international donor community in cutting public expenditures and reforming the public sector. This means that the public bodies responsible for urban and regional development are currently in a phase of transformation and are, first and foremost, preoccupied with restructuring their tasks and competencies. In the majority of cases, the restructuring of the cities and municipalities is accompanied by a solid guidance from the state (Crespo, 2013). The current challenge is to rescale government levels and activities as part of a constant search for temporal-spatial fixes (Jessop, 2004) and as a contribution to relieve public budgets. The significant cuts in public expenditures thus lend increasing importance to new forms of governance and collaboration, service rationalisation, and public activation (e.g. Cohen, 2011; Fujita, 2013; URBACT, 2010).

In addition, the socio-economic and financial crisis has led to a strengthening of civil mistrust in public institutions and politician realms. This is mainly due to the development of semi-democratic forms of territorial governance and urban political regimes, which are often based on particularism, favouritism, and unclear relations between political and economic actors when implementing urban policies (e.g. policies connected with specific real estate developments, large development projects, public–private partnerships). This is particularly evident in cities where these social struggles and resistance become visible and where social protests, such as the recent instances in Istanbul, Athens and Madrid, take place (e.g. Uitermark, Nicholls, & Loopmans, 2012).

Drawing on the general debate outlined above and strongly linked to the most recent theoretical reflections and debates in the areas of urban politics, urban governance, and socio-economic crisis, it becomes clear that the complexity of the challenges faced by European cities and urban regions in crisis and the pressing need to master these abrupt changes call for new concepts, approaches, and solutions. These must be tailored to individual contexts and involve public, private, and civic stakeholders to enable adaptive governance, collaborative decision-making, and behavioural change towards more resilient and sustainable European cities (embedded within the built environment, the planning system, and the everyday activities of politicians, urban and regional planners, and civil society organisations).

Yet, crisis events are not a new phenomenon for Europe, but have happened throughout time in various forms, scopes, and intensities. Looking back over the last decades, important structural changes, geo-political transformations, and fundamental shifts in society can be traced back. The serious impacts of those crisis events have led to complex consequences in several policy fields, both at the national and the urban level. The demographic change in many European countries, for instance, has affected the labour, capital and housing markets, the social insurance schemes for health and long-term care, the system of financing pensions, and the provision of infrastructure (Fujita, 2013). In this context, both national and local authorities in Germany, for example, have been confronted with new and various challenges – how to maintain facilities in the light of declining and structurally modified demand, how to guarantee socio-territorial equity and integration, and so on (e.g. Hamm, Seitz, & Werding, 2008; Müller, 2013). Another 'crisis' experienced in many European countries has been the structural and economic transformation in former industrial regions, which has also led to changes in the development trajectories of many cities. This has caused pressure on the labour market and has led to increased migration flows, processes of decline, and regional disparities, *inter alia*, requiring new solutions, governance mechanisms, and innovative ideas to deal with these problems.

Despite the high degree of similarity in the evolution of crisis events, the recent financial and socio-economic crisis shows obvious unique characteristics related to its nature, prolonged duration, and widespread impacts. Starting as turbulence in the financial markets, it gradually evolved into a global crisis with diverse effects at the urban level. Southern European cities, which have extensively followed neoliberal policies over the last few decades and have largely focused on external financing, experienced the outburst of the crisis and the spread of its impacts particularly harshly. Austerity measures, applied in an attempt to lighten the impacts of the crisis, caused additional pressure at the local level. As a result, the current context in Southern European cities is mainly defined by the interplay of externally imposed and internally driven policies. This raises the question of how cities can adapt to this complex situation and which new concepts, approaches, and solutions for the future sustainable development of these European cities and urban regions and the living conditions of their citizens could be envisioned.

Purpose and main objectives of the book

The contributions in this book build upon the current debate concerning how cities and urban regions and their citizens deal with the various impacts caused by the recent financial and socio-economic crisis. Of particular interest here (see also Donald et al., 2014: pp. 6–10) are the political and administrative implications of austerity measures applied in Southern European cities. These include cuts in local public spending and the processes of privatisation of local public assets, as well as issues related to the rescaling, recentralisation, or decentralisation of competencies. In this regard, attention is paid to the rise of new 'austerity regimes', to the question of their legitimacy and their spatial manifestations, and in particular to the social consequences of austerity, here referring to the growing inter- and intra-urban inequalities.

While focusing on the analysis of the current situation in Southern European cities and Metropolitan Areas, the book recognises that the topic cannot be studied in isolation from previous developments and thus provides a critical overview of development models and strategies applied by Southern European cities prior to the crisis. This overview provides a better understanding of present-day problems and explains why models applied before the crisis (competition globally with large urban projects, the attraction of urban tourism with new airports and infrastructure, the reproduction of the same best practices and models in each city, especially with very real competition and no cooperation strategy, etc.) failed to work appropriately. Based on the insights gained, the questions of how to cope with the consequences of previous models (unfinished large urban projects or completed large urban projects but without a budget for their maintenance or commissioning) and how to apply new approaches in existing complex contexts are addressed.

In addition, the analysis of selected case studies from Southern Europe enables the identification of potential opportunities offered by the manifold impacts of the crisis for sustainable development of European cities and explores the extent to which the crisis could be seen as a motor of paradigmatic, institutional, and behavioural change. Hence, the book contributions discuss feasible approaches, tools, and partnerships to overcome the consequences of the crisis, study the need for the implementation of new governance models, and identify innovative approaches and possible new mechanisms for collaboration and public involvement in the process of urban development. Learning from past successes and mistakes is thus seen as the key to an adequate reaction to future challenges.

Viewed against this background, the focus of the book is on the following research questions: What new conceptualisations, approaches, and strategies are necessary – and possible – to enable European cities and urban regions to respond successfully and adapt to altered challenging conditions? Which paradigmatic changes must be confronted in the face of the various 'crash situations' in transformative fields such as those of energy, mobility, post-industrialisation, or sustainability? Does the current situation offer opportunities for cities to rethink existing decision-making structures and processes, to restructure the urban fabric, or to focus more strongly on integrated and sustainable development patterns (where, for example, social and environmental factors play a more significant role)? What is the role of urban and regional planning in this context and how can they contribute to necessary or possible transformations? What is the role of new forms of governance and participatory approaches in the qualification of urban politics and urban development?

The knowledge gathered lays the foundation for recommendations with regard to European cities and urban regions on how to improve and consolidate qualified governance arrangements, enabling them to be better prepared to address present and future rapid economic and social changes. In this sense, the book and its various contributions help towards overcoming the spatial impacts of the crisis, rethinking current governance structures, and exploring measures enabling adaptive governance and collaborative decision-making. The identification of possible approaches, tools, and partnerships to tackle the effects of the crisis and to learn from it thus provides a solid ground when preparing European cities for future challenges.

Furthermore, by assessing the driving forces and origins of the crisis and answering the questions on how the crisis affects urban development or how certain governance structures and new collaborations between public, private, and civic actors can be adapted or introduced to other national or regional contexts in order to provide solutions to minimise or overcome the impacts of the crisis, the book also contributes to the relatively new scientific discourse about planning culture (Knieling & Othengrafen, 2009; Othengrafen & Reimer, 2013; Sanyal, 2005). Against this background, the contributions in this book also address the role of different planning systems and local contexts for urban planning, looking at both the 'planning systems' and the 'role of planners', i.e. the planning professional culture and the ability of planners to act as a compact versus fragmented community of practice in lobbying for specific ways to respond to the crisis (Othengrafen, 2014).

This also includes a discussion on welfare states and welfare societies, which differ between countries and which are affecting the crisis and the potential solutions to deal with it in manifold ways. According to Santos (1993: p. 46), some Southern European countries have a welfare society, which can mitigate the effects of the decline of social benefits in the welfare state in the context of the fiscal crisis and its financial and social impacts. A welfare society can here be understood as forms of social organisation or relationship networks that are based on kinship and neighbourhood, in which small social groups exchange goods and services on a non-market basis or following other logics; such societies are characterised by inter-knowledge, mutual recognition, and self-help.

Against this background, the contributions in the book also address the role of different welfare models and contexts for spatial planning (see also Nadin & Stead, 2008). Bearing in mind the strong dependence on national contexts, this is crucial in order to understand how different cities within the affected countries are coping with the problems they face and the extent to which local government and governance are able to reinvent their social and economic fabric.

Outline of the book

The book comprises five main parts. The contributions in the first part (Cities in crisis: theoretical framework) aim to provide a theoretical framework for the analysis of the origins and impacts of the global financial and socio-economic crisis in relation to Southern European cities and urban regions. In Chapter 2, Helena Chuliá, Montserrat Guillen, and Miguel Santolino set the conceptual outline by providing insights into the roots of the economic recession of the late 2000s and its main socio-economic consequences. They analyse why particularly cities in Southern Europe have been affected by the economic crisis. Further, they argue that local level socio-economic indicators are needed in the future to analyse the inception and consequences of the current crisis. The socio-spatial and socio-political effects of the crisis are examined by Giancarlo Cotella, Frank Othengrafen, Athanasios Papaioannou, and Simone Tulumello in Chapter 3. They focus particularly on the challenges that the crisis poses for territorial govern-ance and spatial planning and their changing roles. They show that the crisis has geographically unevenly distributed impacts, which seem to be related to dif-ferent welfare state typologies, planning systems, and planning policies. Chapter 4, by Jörg Knieling, Umberto Janin Rivolin, João Seixas, and Galya Vladova, reflects on the possibilities the crisis offers for both institutional and societal change and looks at the role of planning in guiding – respectively facilitating – processes of change. The authors point out the need for changes in the under-standing of politics, governance, and the management of planning, and illustrate the complexity of transformative processes.

The second part of the book (Origins of the crisis and its socio-spatial impacts on Southern European cities) presents various case studies from Southern Europe. The contributions concentrate on the socio-spatial impacts of the eco-nomic crisis on selected cities and their experiences in dealing with these impacts. The overall aim of the part is to provide a better understanding of the current challenges faced by cities and urban regions and to explain why models applied before the crisis failed to work appropriately. The part starts with Chapter 5 by Juan Romero, Carme Melo, and Dolores Brandis, in which the authors discuss the neoliberal model of Southern European cities. They analyse the consequences of the neoliberal strategies applied in the Metropolitan Areas of Valencia and Madrid and their relation to the onset and effects of the eco-nomic and financial crisis. In Chapter 6, José Luís Crespo, Maria Manuela Mendes, and Jorge Nicolau look at the impacts of the crisis on the capacities of the local government in the provision of municipal services in the Lisbon

Metropolitan Area. The authors refer to recent reorganisation processes in the provision of public services and emphasise the need for new ways for managing public interests and property and new forms of governance. Konstantinos Serraos, Thomas Greve, Evangelos Asprogerakas, Dimitros Balampanidis, and Anastasia Chani in Chapter 7 focus on the spatial impacts of the crisis in the city of Athens. Making direct reference to the specific socio-spatial context of the city, the authors address the challenges faced by the local authorities and planners. Chapter 8, by Frank Othengrafen, Luís del Romero Renau, and Ifigeneia Kokkali, places particular emphasis on the increasing wave of public protests and urban unrest as a result of the crisis. The authors provide evidence from different Southern European cities, explaining the impacts of public protests on territorial governance arrangements and analysing the ways in which urban planning institutions and local politicians react to such protests.

In Part III (Urban planning and the economic crisis in Southern European cities), contributors from Portugal, Greece, and Italy provide insights into the complex interplay between the different implications of the crisis and spatial planning. Chapter 9, by Joana Mourão and Teresa Marat-Mendes, discusses the extent to which territorial planning and management in Portugal played a role in the onset of the crisis and the short- and long-term impacts on urban planning and development to which the crisis has led. Looking at trends from recent years, the authors argue that the crisis could be seen as a driver for low-carbon territorial planning and development. Athanasios Papaioannou and Christina Nikolakopoulou follow this theme in Chapter 10, putting particular emphasis on the crisis-related challenges spatial planning needs to address in the future. The authors make direct reference to the impacts of the crisis on the quality of urban life in Greek cities and examine how spatial planning could contribute to improving living conditions and urban resilience. Chapter 11, by Carlo Salone, Angelo Besana, and Umberto Janin Rivolin, takes up the topic of urban shrinkage as specific challenge of many Southern European cities which has even been intensified by the crisis. Introducing demographic and economic dynamics in Italian urban systems before and after the onset of the crisis, the authors discuss the role and challenges for domestic spatial policies.

Part IV of the book (Crisis as driver of change?) takes up the question of whether the crisis can be seen as a driver of change or not. The contributions in this part aim to present post-crisis scenarios for cities in Southern Europe, as well as new principles and approaches for the recovery of cities and urban regions after extraordinary events and external shocks. The discussion focuses on the exploration of new mechanisms for collaboration, new governance models, and different ideas and visions for the sustainable and resilient development of European cities in the future. In Chapter 12, João Seixas, Simone Tulumello, Susana Corvelo, and Ana Drago study the interlinks between the European crisis, its urban impacts, and the austerity measures applied following it, discussing selected innovative politics on different scales. Focusing on the Lisbon Metropolitan Area, the authors identify two main socio-political restructuring trends, financially driven central state policies, and more social and territorially driven urban political strategies, as well as a developing clash between the top-down austerity measures and bottom-up urban transformation. In Chapter 13, Joaquín Rodríguez Álvarez presents strategies, approaches, and policies applied by the city of Barcelona as a response to the crisis. He describes the main tendencies in terms of public participation and governance and critically discusses recent institutional changes, the new allocation of responsibilities, and budgetary priorities. Chapter 14, by Nadia Caruso, Giancarlo Cotella, and Elena Pede, looks at trends in the development of new governance arrangements in the Metropolitan Area of Turin. Discussing the changes in the framework conditions brought about by the crisis, the authors illustrate how these have affected the development of hard and soft forms of territorial governance in the Metropolitan Area. Focusing on the investigation of Valencia and its mega-region, Josep Vicent Boira and Ramon Marrades argue that the crisis questions existing territorial models of governance in Chapter 15. The authors point to the need for a new territorial vision for the role of cities and argue that future policies for economic reorientation should be accompanied by policies of reorientation and rescaling of territorial and urban governance. Chapter 16 by Thilo Lang ends the part with a critical reflection on the concept of resilience and a discussion of how cities and regions adopt to socio-economic crises and how urban and regional change happens under crisis conditions.

On the basis of the empirical material gathered, the concluding part summarises the findings concerning the socio-spatial impacts of the crisis across Southern European cities and urban regions. In Chapter 17, Jörg Knieling, Frank Othengrafen, and Galya Vladova discuss which lessons can be learnt from the experiences of various national and regional contexts with regard to the future planning of sustainable and adaptive cities and regions. The chapter thus represents considerations for both urban and planning theory and implications for policy-making and planning practice.

References

Aalbers, M. B. (2009) Geographies of the financial crisis. *Area*, 41, 34–42.

Cohen, M. P. (2011) Cities in times of crisis: The response of local governments in light of the global economic crisis: The role of the formation of human capital, urban innovation and strategic planning. *Institute of Urban and Regional Development, Working Paper 2011–01*, University of California, Berkeley.

Crespo, J. (2013) *Governance and territory: Tools, methods and management techniques in the Lisbon Metropolitan Area.* Doctoral dissertation in Urban and Regional Planning, Technical University of Lisbon.

Donald, B., Glasmeier, A., Gray, M., & Lobao, L. (2014) Austerity in the city: Economic crisis and urban service decline? *Cambridge Journal of Regions, Economy and Society*, 7 (1), 3–15.

Fujita, K. (2013) *Cities and crisis: New critical urban theory.* London, Sage Publishers.

Hadjimichalis, C. (2011) Uneven geographical development and socio-spatial justice and solidarity: European regions after the 2009 financial crisis. *European Urban and Regional Studies*, 18, 254–274.

Hamm, I., Seitz, H., & Werding, M. (eds) (2008) *Demographic change in Germany: The economic and fiscal consequences*. Berlin, Springer.

Jessop, B. (2004) Multi-level governance and multi-level metagovernance: Changes in the European Union as integral moments in the transformation and reorientation of contemporary statehood. In: Bache, I. & Flinders, M. (eds) *Multi-level governance*. Oxford, Oxford University Press, pp. 49–74.

Knieling, J. & Othengrafen, F. (2009) En route to a theoretical model for comparative research on planning cultures. In: Knieling, J. & Othengrafen, F. (eds) *Planning cultures in Europe: Decoding cultural phenomena in urban and regional planning*. Farnham, Ashgate, pp. 39–62.

Müller, B. (2013) *Demographic change and its consequences for cities*. Berlin, Deutsches Institut für Urbanistik (Difu).

Nadin, V. & Stead, D. (2008) European spatial planning systems, social models and learning. *disP – The Planning Review*, 172, 35–47.

Nunes Silva, C. & Bucek, J. (2014a) Introduction. In: Nunes Silva, C. & Bucek, J. (eds) *Fiscal austerity and innovation in local governance in Europe*. Farnham, Ashgate, pp. 1–6.

Nunes Silva, C. & Bucek, J. (2014b) Conclusion. In: Nunes Silva, C. & Bucek, J. (eds) *Fiscal austerity and innovation in local governance in Europe*. Farnham, Ashgate, pp. 181–186.

Othengrafen, F. (2014) The concept of planning culture: Analysing how planners construct practical judgements in a culturised context. *International Journal of E-Planning Research*, 3, 1–17.

Othengrafen, F. & Reimer, M. (2013) The embeddedness of planning in cultural contexts: Theoretical foundations for the analysis of dynamic planning cultures. *Environment and Planning A*, 45, 1269–1284.

Romero, J., Jiménez, F., & Villoria, M. (2012) (Un)sustainable territories: Causes of the speculative bubble in Spain (1996–2010) and its territorial, environmental, and sociopolitical consequences. *Environment and Planning C: Government and Policy*, 30, 467–486.

Santos, B. de Sousa (1993) O Estado, as relações salariais e o bem-estar social na semiperiferia: ocaso português. In: Santos, B. de Sousa (ed.) *Portugal: um retrato singular*. Porto, Afrontamento, pp. 15–56.

Sanyal, B. (ed.) (2005) *Comparative planning cultures*. London, Routledge.

Uitermark, J., Nicholls, W., & Loopmans, M. (2012) Cities and social movements: Theorizing beyond the right to the city. *Environment and Planning A*, 44, 2546–2554.

URBACT (2010) *URBACT cities facing the crisis: Impact and responses*. [Online] Available from: http://urbact.eu/fileadmin/general_library/Crise_urbact__16-11_web.pdf [accessed 20 February 2015].

Werner, R. A. (2013) Crises, the spatial distribution of economic activity, and the geography of banking. *Environment and Planning A*, 45, 2789–2796.

Wollmann, H. (2014) Public services in European countries: Between public/municipal and private sector provision – and reverse? In: Nunes Silva, C. & Bucek, J. (eds) *Fiscal austerity and innovation in local governance in Europe*. Farnham, Ashgate, pp. 49–76.

Part I

Cities in crisis

Theoretical framework

2 The economic and financial crisis

Origins and consequences

Helena Chuliá, Montserrat Guillen, and Miguel Santolino

Introduction

Financial and economic crises affect all segments of society, but the extent to which crises affect some regions more than others has remained largely unexplored. It is therefore worth carrying out some research into the effect of such crises on certain areas, notably cities, which increasingly accommodate much of the world's population.

For the purpose of evaluating the origins of crises and their consequences for cities, statistical information should be available at the municipality level. This level of detail would allow for the comparison between the pre- and post-crises situations, and also allow a contrast to be made between urban and rural environments. Unfortunately, analyses are often only carried out at the macroeconomic level.

The objective of this chapter is to give a general overview of the origins and consequences of economic crises. First, the role of economic indicators in detecting the inception of recessions is emphasised and the advantages and disadvantages of macroeconomic indicators are discussed. In order to assess the impacts of crises on cities, a system of economic indicators at a local level should provide more information than the typical information found at country level or regional level. A section is then devoted to describing the origins and causes of the current economic crisis from a broad perspective and then particular attention is paid to Southern Europe. In the final section, the effects of the economic crisis are discussed, namely the control of public debt, social consequences, and, in particular, the impacts on the labour market and the welfare state. The chapter outlines some brief conclusions, which point to the idea that cities may suffer more than rural areas from the consequences of a crisis in the short term and in the long term.

An economic crisis: definitions of a current phenomenon

The definition of the term 'crisis' as provided by the dictionary is 'a difficult or dangerous situation that needs serious attention' (Merriam-Webster, 2014). This is a generic definition that fits many contexts. In a complex system (e.g. the human body, an economy, a society), this term is applied to a prolonged period characterised by intense difficulty or danger. An economy is a highly complex network consisting of all activities related to the production, distribution, and consumption of goods and services in a society. An economic crisis can be then understood as a long-term state of poor performance in the economic system.

In fact, economic crises are complex and they share many similarities with human diseases. Treatments aim to palliate the consequences of disorders, but they may induce painful periods. In an economy, critical episodes are stressful, and cure options are seldom clear cut, but their prompt identification is always helpful. Agents who are involved in production, distribution, and consumption, together with public opinion, rumours, and expectations create an intricate framework that complicates the identification of an onset of a crisis. A good gauge to monitor economic stability is the statistical measures that summarise the whole range of activities carried out by enterprises, organisations, markets, and civil society. When statistical indicators point to a decrease in activities, economists interpret this fact as a symptom of economic weakness. Symptoms associated with weak economic performance are, among others, high unemployment rates, low prices, and low levels of trade and investment.

By definition, an economy experiences an economic crisis when it suffers from a fall in gross domestic product (GDP), a depletion of liquidity, and a persistent increase (inflation) or decrease (deflation) in prices (Besomi, 2013). Formally, an economic crisis can take the form of a recession. This is the case when GDP contracts for six consecutive months, i.e. it has a negative change for two consecutive quarters, but which can fail to extend over a year. In addition, it could also take the form of a depression, experienced when the negative cycle continues.

Occasional GDP falls are normal in Western economies, but when everyone realises that GDP has fallen one quarter after another, there is an air of discouragement and citizens stop having optimistic expectations about the future. Financial markets are generally extremely sensitive to the state of public opinion. They may anticipate imminent events and may also suffer from significant ups and downs, thus creating volatility. Volatility refers to fluctuations and turbulence, which is not appreciated by investors, who prefer stability. That is why it is difficult to disentangle whether turmoil in financial markets creates economic shakiness or the other way round.

Some researchers (see, for example, De Keulenaer et al., 2014) prefer to call a GDP decrease a 'negative growth' episode. However, even if euphemisms are used, it is clear that a decrease in economic activity leads to the most dangerous economic disease, namely, lack of confidence in the future. Uncertainty produces more caution in investment and this decelerates market dynamics which, in turn, refuels descent in economic activity. Lack of confidence is difficult to measure, if not impossible, so anticipating a crisis is a difficult task.

To sum up, an economic crisis is identified on the basis of a set of macroeconomic indicators (GDP, inflation, etc.). These indicators, which present the evolution of our society and economy, are based on estimate values, prepared by each national statistical agency responsible for the generation of public and official data. Most economic and social indicators are subject to sampling error and rely on strong statistical hypotheses. In addition, statistical trends that show correlation of indicators with economic performance do not necessarily indicate a causal relationship and so they may not be helpful in preventing the inception of a crisis. Moreover, economic crises have generally far-reaching economic and/or social impacts, which are not captured by general indicators. In the following section, an overview is given of economic indicators and how GDP and the Consumer Price Index (CPI) are computed. The presentation emphasises the limitations of studies of crises which are based exclusively on the evolution of general economic trends. Both the crisis and the impacts are measured in terms of indicators, which are defined in the following section, before the origin, causes, and qualitative consequences of the crisis are explained.

Statistical indicators: correlation does not equal causation

Several indicators play a central role in the diagnosis of a crisis. During a crisis, reduced purchasing power and increased unemployment is observed. In addition, there is an excess of supply over demand (for example, too many empty properties means a housing bubble). In times of crisis, the increase in prices is slower than normal, falling prices are observed, and wages do not rise. All symptoms, without exception, are measured from the databases of public statistical systems.

The main statistical instruments defining the existence of an economic crisis are likely to be GDP and the CPI but how are these calculated? The formula for GDP seems to generate a simple sum (Coyle, 2014), but it requires an assessment of how much has been produced in the economy or has been generated by the provision of informal services during one year. This assessment relies on existing models and hypotheses. The CPI is calculated based on a survey, which is conducted to estimate how much money is spent daily and also provides details about what goods have been bought by the survey participants. The participants are thousands of families, constituting a representative sample of the population, who record expenditures for a few weeks. This raw data is not intended to be made available to the public and, on top of that, the production of official figures takes a few weeks.

Having introduced the main macroeconomic indicators, it is worth exploring how these indicators and the economic crisis are linked. Indicators can be a measure of the existence and extension of a crisis or, rather, they can anticipate the beginning of a difficult period. GDP and other indicators can suggest or recognise a crisis but they track the phenomenon at the country level and not at the local level, which does not necessarily happen at the same pace. Furthermore, indicators do not explain why crises occur. Tracking the evolution of economic indicators is a useful tool in recognising an economic crisis, but it is a method that does not provide a rule to identify the origin of it. Most often the negative evolution of macroeconomic indicators is a symptom of the economic crisis rather than a cause.

In the nineteenth century, William S. Jevons became famous for a paper presented to the British Association at Bristol (1875). This was followed by numerous other contributions published in *Nature* (Jevons, 1878, 1879, 1882), in which he explained how the prices of cereals were determined by sunspots. According to Professor Jevons' theory if the periods of panic and of spots on the sun are the same, they are connected as cause and effect. This theory unleashed a debate about causality in economics that has lasted over 150 years. The lesson to be drawn from Jevons' conjecture is that an incorrectly diagnosed causal relationship without considering all facts may lead to the wrong conclusions.

Recently, Reinhart and Rogoff's work 'Growth in a Time of Debt' concluded that higher government debt is associated with slower economic growth. This conclusion terrified economic analysts and resulted in a complete reconsideration of the role of public debt in avoiding economic crises (2010; see Herndon, Ash, & Pollin, 2014 for a critique). However, the authors revealed later that their work contained calculations with errors and, perhaps, they had fallen into a trap similar to the sunspot economic theory of Jevons. Many lessons have been learned from those incidents, which showed that economic explanations and cure therapies must be taken with extreme caution.

These well-known examples show that the occurrence of two simultaneous phenomena does not necessarily mean that one causes the other. As mentioned before, a qualitative analysis of possible connections is essential to address the route to understanding why crises occur and how they can be avoided.

Cities and economic indicators: a long road ahead

Socio-economic indicators are usually country-level averages that may not exactly reflect city-level behaviour. Socio-economic information at the regional level and, even at the postcode level (i.e. detailed by municipality or even within a neighbourhood), is hard to find. Zip code refers to the postal identifier that differentiates one small part of a city from another. The average trend, however, does not necessarily mean that the local socio-economic activity, in a given city or in a small territory, is following the same path as shown by the general country-level or regional-level trend.

Disparities due to geographical location can be studied with statistical measures that are too little used in practice. The Herfindahl Index, also known as the Herfindahl–Hirschman Index, is one of these measures. It indicates whether a magnitude is uniformly distributed or whether it is rather unequal. Since inequalities in Europe have increased with the crisis it could be assumed that, as a result of the crisis, some economic measures would barely recover and get back to their pre-crisis position, but also that the disparities would seem to grow larger. The Herfindahl Index (see Rhoades, 1993) is a measure of the size of firms in relation to the industry and an indicator of the level of competition among them. For example, in a market with two firms that each have 50 per cent market share, the Herfindahl Index equals $0.50^2 + 0.50^2 = 0.5$, but if one firm concentrates all shares, it would equal 1.

As an example, market structure and competition in the banking sector have been measured with this Index. The relationship between unemployment and economic diversification in the United States over a 53-year period (1947–2009) has recently been investigated (Savitz, 2010). The model of unemployment as primarily a function of economic activity was extended by adding a variable for economic diversification. Economic diversification was measured by calculating the Herfindahl Index for GDP by sector. The author found that, where more economic diversification exists, lower unemployment rates are found. The implications of this finding are both important and wide-ranging. We suggest that a similar idea can be applied to characterising GDP by a classification of city-level areas. This would produce an assessment of the position of cities in the economic landscape.

Unfortunately, the available macroeconomic indicators in public domain statistical databases are predominantly at a country level and the system of economic indicators with details at the municipal level is still in a too early stage. Although indicators must always be interpreted cautiously, the lack of available data considerably limits an analysis of how cities experience crises, how they respond to them, and how inequalities evolve.

Origins and causes of the current economic crisis: a broad perspective

The financial and economic crisis

More than five years after the collapse of Lehman Brothers in September 2008, a failure that almost brought down the global financial system, stalled the economic growth of developed economies, and initiated the sovereign debt crisis in Europe, a miscellaneous collection of interpretations about what happened can be gathered. Essentially, there are two common narratives of the origins of this global economic recession (Rajan, 2012).

The first narrative focuses on the demand side and is based on the idea that governments and households have lived beyond their means. According to this narrative, after decades of declining ratios of economic growth, advanced economies entered a phase in which their capacity to grow by producing high value-added goods was reduced (IMF, 2014). This could be explained by reasons such as the rising of costs, industry offshoring, and the competitiveness of emerging economies. As a consequence, during the last decade of the twentieth century and the beginning of the twenty-first century, the search for growth in developed economies took different and unsustainable forms.

First, the governments of the United States and the Western European economies chose debt-fuelled spending policies, such as financing new economic sectors or spending increased amounts of money on the welfare state. Regardless of the high spending, this could not return the countries to a sustainable growth path because it did not stimulate competitiveness, productivity, or the production of value-added products (Rajan, 2012). Second, in front of this unreal scenario of economic 'bonanza', household and private debt rose faster than economic performance. The GDP of advanced countries during the pre-crisis decades was unsustainable because it was based on borrowing and unproductive jobs. At that time, private and public spending grew faster than GDP. After the crisis, GDP growth slowed down and, consequently, the ratio of the spending to GDP increased. A good example is Health Care Expenditures (HCE) in the European Union (EU) following the recession in 2008–2009. An increase in the ratio of HCE to GDP is reported by the European Commission's Public Finances Report in 2013 (European Commission, 2013). The significant amount of debt accumulated before the crisis and the loss of investor confidence resulted in the inability of households and countries to borrow needed funds, leading to the start of the economic crisis.

However, this narrative does not fit with the macroeconomic indicators of some European countries (Gros, 2011). For example, some countries with significantly higher fiscal deficits during the years preceding the crisis, such as Germany or the Netherlands, did not experience it as much as countries which had significant average surpluses, but were badly hit by the crisis, such as Spain or Ireland. The explanation might be found in the rather fragile structure and diversification of economic sectors.

The alternative narrative proposed by Rajan (2012) focuses on the supply side rather than on the demand side. When looking at the current financial system it could be said that it is one of the reasons for the financial crisis (Lo, 2012). The financial system acts as an economic engine because it provides borrowers with access to future income, to buy a house, or to run a new business, for example, and generates surplus earnings to current lenders. However, it can also create 'bubbles' based on unrealistic expectations, or a market crash by increasing the risk to unsustainable levels, leaving a legacy of unemployment and debt.

In line with this thinking, the financial crisis that has been inflicting chaos in markets since 2008 had its origins in an asset price bubble in the housing market of the United States. A boost in house prices interacted with new financial products, which reduced transparency and masked risk. All this was possible thanks to the previous dismantling of regulatory apparatus and the regulators' failure to restrain excessive risk-taking (Baily, Litan, & Johnson, 2008). The United States was not an exceptional case. The expectations of future price increases were disseminated across several national markets, such as Spain and Ireland, as a significant factor in inflating house prices. Subprime borrowers were made into attractive clients for mortgage lenders thanks to the continuous increase of house prices, together with the new financial products. In the end, the fall of Lehman Brothers unmasked the bubble and provoked its collapse.

The effects of this crash are still obvious in the world economy. Europe had its own internal imbalances and, in fact, the financial crisis evolved into the euro crisis. In addition to the above two narratives it should be noted that, in Europe, the origins of the crisis could be seen as a consequence of a capital flow bonanza. From a systemic point of view, during the post-euro adoption period (2000–2007), there were capital flows from the north of Europe to the south that provoked current account deficits in the southern countries. The launch of the euro prompted an extraordinary growth of the financial sector both within the euro area and in nearby banking hubs, such as the United Kingdom. Thanks to this capital flow, there was a credit boom in the banking sector that created jobs in low-skilled industries, such as construction. Moreover, it precipitated a consumption boom as people borrowed against overvalued houses. When capital flows suddenly stopped, due to the overall crisis, the credit boom also finished.

One of the first reactions generally displayed by worldwide policy-makers after the financial crisis was that a more regulated financial system was required. Interesting initiatives are currently being discussed in Europe in that direction (a unified European banking system, the Tobin tax,[1] etc.). A deep and rigorous analysis of these and other alternatives is required to avoid another global crisis in the future.

The region of Southern Europe

As outlined above, there are three narratives concerning the origins of the economic crisis: the depletion of capacity to grow in a sustainable form in advanced economies, a housing asset price bubble induced by the financial sector, and capital flow bonanza. All these narratives are not mutually exclusive. As argued at the beginning of this chapter, an economy is a complex system. The global economy is a profoundly complex network consisting of all national economies, which are highly complex systems themselves. All elements related to economic activity are closely interconnected. To some extent, all three narratives of the crisis have been observed in most countries' national economies. The depth and duration of the economic crisis in a particular country can be partly explained by how intense the causes are and, of course, once the crisis is a reality, by the decisions taken to deal with it. The 'perfect storm' happens when all these causes take place with significant force. The simultaneous occurrence of a multitude of causes in Southern European countries is the explanation of why these economies have been so badly hit by the crisis.

In the case of most Southern European countries, their economies are highly specialised in sectors with low productivity and high employment. In the early 2000s, there was a credit boom, initiated by Europe's capital flow bonanza, in which the price of money was very low.[2] In Spain, for example, the financial industry focused on the housing business as a strategy for growth. The ambition of Southern Europeans of purchasing their own property might also be among the reasons and also be a difference to the situation in Western Europe. Banks provided cheap mortgage loans to house purchasers, inflating house prices. Politicians did not act. The house price bubble was not anticipated by policy-makers and countermeasures were not launched. Even worse, tax deductions were applied to the purchase of a property, inflating the bubble. One of the sectors that benefited most was the construction sector. The building industry was very dynamic at this time and created a huge number of new jobs. The tourism sector, a primary sector of economic activity (particularly in Spain), may have helped to expand the demand for houses in coastal areas.

The dynamism of the housing market (loans, building societies, estate agents, etc.) provided a huge volume of resources to the public system. As a result, public spending increased very quickly. A significant part of public resources was allocated to financing public works, such as infrastructure programmes, public buildings, so public spending decisions also promoted the construction sector, rather than high-skilled industries. In parallel, important public policies were launched during the period of GDP growth, which increased public spending on the welfare state (e.g. long-term care reform, child financial support payments).

The growth of GDP was unsustainable in the long term because it was primarily based on borrowing and low-skilled industries. When GDP growth started to slow down and the housing market displayed signs of stagnation, a chain reaction of difficulties in other sectors happened. The construction industry and estate agent services were quickly affected by the stagnation of the housing market. It was followed by the financial sector. The large amount of private debt accumulated by agents and the loss of confidence resulted in an inability to return the money, which led to no more credit being extended. Saving banks stopped lending money to individual citizens and enterprises. Thus difficulties spread from the financial sector to all economic activities. The ratio of public spending to GDP quickly increased and, as a consequence, levels of public debt grew. Cities may have been hit particularly hard as construction takes place primarily in large agglomerations of population and in the outskirts of Metropolitan Areas. The situation was similar in many Mediterranean countries, such as Portugal, Italy, and especially Greece.

Effects of the recent economic crisis

Control of public debt

Traditionally, in a financial crisis situation, a part of the financial system, for example a bank, investor, or asset, is vilified and then banned or regulated (*The Economist*, 2014). There is much discussion about the part played by the financial system, which has been mainly responsible for the recent crisis, and some consensus in this regard has also been reached. In the United States, some investment banks and the subprime mortgages were proclaimed as the cause by most economist analysts (Lo, 2012). In Europe, bad governmental public spending has been identified as the major problem.[3] In most Southern European countries, public spending and saving banks were particularly blamed. Remarkably, another part of the financial system, the private market, received public backing when it needed to be rescued.

As a consequence, the crisis made the financial system more dependent on state support. In Southern European countries, this led to a rise in public deficit as related to GDP, partly due to falling GDP figures, but also because government deficits worsened. At the end of 2013, some countries can still be seen in the high debt group: Greece, whose level of debt-to-GDP peaked at 175.1 per cent, Italy at 132.6 per cent, Portugal at 129 per cent, Ireland at 123.7 per cent, and Spain at 93.9 per cent. All of these countries had more than the average debt-to-GDP ratio in the Eurozone, which was 92.6 per cent (*The Economist*, 2014).

The European sovereign debt crisis started in 2009 when the Greek government admitted its situation was uncontrollable. It was the first European country to receive a bailout from other European countries. Yet it was not the only one; soon Portugal, Ireland, and Cyprus received public help via this mechanism. The diagnosis was clear: to stabilise an economy it was necessary to control public debt. To deal with this situation and to control public deficits, the European countries hit by the crisis were subject to mandatory austerity measures imposed by the European Commission, the European Central Bank, and the International Monetary Fund. As a result, most Southern European governments announced cuts in expenditure and increases in taxes to ensure governmental solvency. The cuts affected the creation and maintenance of infrastructure, social welfare, education, and research. There is much debate about the efficiency of these measures (Krugman, 2013). What is clear is that the austerity measures have affected the welfare state through the dramatic reduction of public expenditure and have contributed to the increase in socio-economic inequality.

Socio-economic consequences

Past economic crises had a negative impact on employment and the salaries of the population during and immediately after in the recessions that followed. The global financial crisis of the late 2000s was no exception. It drew attention to Europe, where the rise in the unemployment rate in the crisis years has been dramatic, especially in the Southern European region. The unemployment rates in Greece and Spain, for example, were 27.5 and 26 per cent in 2013, respectively, while, at the beginning of the crisis in 2007, they were around 8 per cent (Eurostat, 2014). Although there are few reasons for optimism, an encouraging sign is that the unemployment rates in these countries seem to have reached their peak in 2013, and falls in unemployment rates can be faintly detected in 2014. These two economies show positive growth of GDP in 2014 which seems to indicate that the worst of the crisis is over.

Economic specialisation is among the reasons for the high impact of the financial crisis on employment in the Southern European countries. The lack of tradition of human resource mobility is a disadvantage for the dynamics of labour market, as individuals prefer to stay in their home town, even if they are unemployed, rather than seek better opportunities elsewhere. However, Southern European countries have cultural particularities, compared to the Northern European countries, which can make them more resistant to high unemployment rates. In particular, the role of family links is strong and natural solidarity between relatives and family members is not only common, but is also a tradition in the Mediterranean region. During periods of economic depression, families may act as a mechanism mitigating the impacts of the economic and

financial crises on individuals. Unfortunately, this hypothesis has not been verified and the difference between urban and rural habits still remains unexplored.

Except for Germany, all EU member states faced a rise in unemployment rates
in the years 2007–2013, but this was less intense in magnitude. The duration of the
effects on unemployment was also different. For example, the peak in the unemployment rate in the United Kingdom was reached in 2011. The divergent impact
of recession on national labour markets has widened the differences in the unemployment rates between Northern and Southern European member states from the
beginning of the financial crisis (FUNCAS, 2014; Katsimi et al., 2013).

The unemployment rate only provides a partial portrait of the labour market
in a given country. A wider range of indicators should be considered for a fuller
understanding of the market. These should include the number of people in temporary work who could not find permanent jobs and people in part-time work
who want a full-time job. A further indicator is the number of people earning a
living wage, or who are paid even less than that. Analysing all labour indicators
together it could be concluded that unemployment rates are particularly high in
Southern European member states. Labour markets in Northern European
member states are also suffering the consequences of the crisis. For example,
according to the last available data for the United Kingdom, the rise in the
number of part-time workers looking for a full-time position and the number of
workers paid below the living wage had not decreased by the first half of 2013
(MacInnes et al., 2013). Another example is the reduction in working hours and
salaries, applied by the short-time working programme (*Kurzarbeit*) in Germany,
with the aim of preserving jobs. Similar programmes aimed at reducing the
number of hours worked were intended by the latest labour market reform legislation in Spain, with little success. The new regulation allows managers to automatically reshape the number of hours worked according to production demand,
but this procedure has not been implemented in many industrial sectors, which
have suffered drastic reductions in the number of employees rather than redefinition of contracts. It is not therefore surprising that the annual number of working
hours was reduced much more in Germany (3.1 per cent) than in Spain (2 per
cent) in 2009, but the unemployment rates of both countries in the same period
were 7.5 and 18.1 per cent respectively (Laparra & Pérez-Eransus, 2012).

Labour market data seems to indicate that divergences in employment in the
European regions could not be exclusively explained by the economic specialisation of the individual countries. A major role is being played by the national
labour market features as well. In the Southern European member states, whose
economies are more specialised towards low productivity activities and are characterised by more segmented labour markets, the economic deceleration strongly
impacted employment, primarily the chance of finding a job. In contrast, the rise
of underemployment in Northern European member states seems to indicate that
the lesser impact of recession was primarily expressed in the reduction of the
number of working hours and salaries of the population. A first conclusion to be
drawn in this regard is that the economic recession had an impact on the labour
markets in all European countries. This, however, differed across the individual

regions in terms of intensity, as well as elements mostly affected, such as the number of jobs and working hours or annual income.

A direct consequence of high unemployment and insufficient wages and salaries is the fact that a part of the population has no or low income. This, however, does not automatically imply an increase in the number of people living in poverty. The mitigation of inequalities is addressed by redistribution policies of individual countries and their social protection systems. In the context of the increasing number of people in need, as well as the increasing demand for welfare benefits and services, larger resources are required by a state to extend the levels of social protection while having limited public resources. Yet countries often have difficulties in sustaining the levels of pre-crisis social protection. During an economic recession, public income is reduced, since the impact of the crisis on economic activity and employment causes a drop in tax collection (e.g. income reductions in taxes from revenues, incomes, and consumption). An immediate after-effect is an increasing level of public debt of countries, forcing national governments to restore the balance in public financial accounts.

Important differences can be observed between countries in how they design their social protection policies. For example, similar expenditures in labour market policies were carried out by Denmark, Belgium, Ireland, and Spain in the year 2011 in terms of their GDP, even though their annual unemployment rates were quite different, namely 7.2, 7.7, 14.9, and 22 per cent, respectively (FUNCAS, 2014). However, a revealing sign is observed when the aggregated data is broken down. For Denmark and Belgium, the largest percentage of expenditures was addressed to active labour market measures (i.e. improving employability), but around 80 per cent of the expenditures in Ireland and Spain were addressed to passive interventions (i.e. unemployment benefits and subsidies). The consequence of those strategies is slower recovery in countries, which implemented passive actions, where unemployment rates remained high.

A commonly used measure to analyse the degree of inequality of a society is the Gini Index, which measures the extent to which the distribution of income of individuals deviates from equal distribution (World Bank, 2014). The Index is ranged between zero and one. Intuitively, the larger the Index value is, the higher the distance between rich and poor in a society. Looking at the evolution of that indicator from the beginning of the global crisis, at least three different patterns can be observed across EU member states. EU-12 new member states[4] show a fall in the Index value, but their pre-crisis levels were relatively high in comparison to other EU members. In the remaining EU member states, the dispersion in the income distribution of individuals increased after the crisis. Unlike Northern European member states with relatively low pre-crisis levels, inequalities in Southern European member states increased after the crisis, while the initial levels were already high. In 2012, the highest values of the Gini Index in the EU were observed in Spain (0.35), Greece (0.34), Portugal (0.35), and Latvia (0.36). In contrast, the associated coefficients of Finland and Sweden were 0.25 and 0.24, respectively (Eurostat, 2014). A high and increasing inequality indicator means that the social gap is increasing, so poverty affects more citizens than before the crisis.

The increase in the divergence between rich and poor in most of the EU member states indicates that the effects of the global crisis were accentuated for the most vulnerable strata of society. The rise in inequality in income distribution for individuals suggests an increase in the proportion of population at risk of poverty. Poverty has many faces, such as financial exclusion, deprivation, social exclusion, and it limits the access of individuals to resources and opportunities; people in vulnerable situations are pushed to areas of marginality. This has not been welcomed: poverty is perceived by three-quarters of European citizens as widespread in their countries (European Commission, 2010).

There is not a simple definition of poverty. At the EU level, poverty is divided into absolute poverty and relative poverty. The former is when an individual lacks the basics for survival. The latter is when people have much lower incomes than the general standards of living in their country, which is generally measured as income lower than 60 per cent of the median income for the country (European Commission, 2011). Although the EU is one of the richest areas in the world, poverty inside the EU is a very real problem, particularly in the Southern and Eastern European member states. According to the latest definition of poverty, in 2011, 17 per cent of the population in the EU (84 million people) lived below the poverty line. The poverty rate in Spain, Greece, and Eastern Europe has reached over 20 per cent (European Commission, 2011).

The eradication of poverty is one of the major challenges for modern societies. The extent of poverty reflects the inefficiency of society in redistributing wealth fairly. This problem is particularly serious for the most vulnerable groups of society, such as children, older people, and immigrants. The long-term risk is that the high levels of inequality in income distribution become structural and so a large percentage of the population in Europe will be condemned to live below the general standards of living without any option of breaking the vicious circle of misery.

The rise of euro-scepticism in Europe and of extreme right-wing parties with populist ideologies (extreme nationalism, xenophobia, etc.), which gained significant support across most of the EU member states, cannot be understood as a phenomenon which is isolated from the economic context. The ascension of new political parties is an expression of the lack of trust by a part of the population in their political institutions. Discontented individuals feel that traditional parties are not able to react to emerging problems of the society and therefore pursue alternative options. This discontent about institutions is particularly notable across classes less favoured by the economic circumstances and among individuals in vulnerable situations, who are deeply affected by the negative consequences of the global crisis.

Conclusion

The reasons for, and impacts of, the crisis in Southern European countries are mostly related to the economic and social structure of their societies, based on services such as tourism, rather than on industries which employ highly skilled workers. The low productivity and the volatility of demand impact these economies more than those with solid industrial networks.

The need for local-level socio-economic indicators to analyse the inception and consequences of the current crisis is highly recommended. Even if indicators must always be interpreted cautiously, they can be very useful in comparing the evolution of cities in crises and to establish the evolution of inequalities that country-level macroeconomics indicators are unable to capture. It seems plausible that cities have been hardest hit by the consequences of the crisis simply because population agglomerates in urban areas, but this has not been confirmed.

The simultaneous occurrence of multiple causes of economic crisis in Southern European countries is the explanation of why these economies were so badly hit. Some of the most important causes are: an economy based on tourism and volatile housing demand; a fragile banking system that was a victim of financial turbulence; an accumulation of public debt; and limited governmental capability to enforce and implement active and practical policies to mitigate the crisis. Their social structure may be the primary reason why these economies have strong resilience.

Notes

1 The Tobin tax was originally suggested in 1972 by the Nobel laureate economist James Tobin and refers to a sale tax on currency trades across borders.
2 In fact, real interest rates, which are the difference between the nominal and actual inflation, have decreased significantly in Spain since the 1990s (Ayuso, Blanco, & Restoy, 2006).
3 As noted above, the government chose debt-fuelled spending policies, which did not stimulate competitiveness, productivity, or the production of value-added products.
4 Bulgaria, Cyprus, Czech Republic, Estonia, Hungary, Latvia, Lithuania, Malta, Poland, Romania, Slovakia, and Slovenia.

References

Ayuso, J., Blanco, R., & Restoy, F. (2006) *House prices and real interest rates in Spain.* Documentos Ocasionales No. 0608, Banco de España.

Baily, M. N., Litan, R. E., & Johnson, M. S. (2008) *The origins of the financial crisis.* Initiative on Business and Public Policy at Brookings, Fixing Financial Series, Paper 3.

Besomi, D. (ed.) (2013) *Crises and cycles in economic dictionaries and encyclopaedias* (Vol. 130). New York, Routledge.

Coyle, D. (2014) *GDP: A brief but affectionate history.* Princeton, NJ, Princeton University Press.

De Keulenaer, F., De Neve, J. E., Kavetsos, G., Norton, M. I., Van Landeghem, B. G., & Ward, G. W. (2014) *Individual experience of positive and negative growth is asymmetric: Evidence from subjective well-being data.* Centre for Economic Performance, London School of Economics.

Economist (2014) The slumps that shaped modern finance. *The Economist.* 12 April 2014. [Online] Available from: www.economist.com/news/essays/21600451-finance-not-merely-prone-crises-it-shaped-them-five-historical-crises-show-how-aspects-today-s-fina [accessed 9 May 2014].

European Commission (2010) *Poverty and social exclusion report.* Special Eurobarometer 355.

European Commission (2011) *The measurement of extreme poverty in the European Union.* Directorate-General for Employment, Social Affairs and Inclusion.

European Commission (2013) *European Commission public finances report.* [Online] Available from: http://ec.europa.eu/economy_finance/publications/european_economy/2013/pdf/ee-2013-4-04.pdf [accessed 15 May 2014].

Eurostat (2014) *Gini coefficient of equivalised disposable income.* [Online] Available from: http://epp.eurostat.ec.europa.eu/tgm/table.do?tab=table&language=en&pcode=tessi190 [accessed 15 May 2014].

FUNCAS (Fundación de las Cajas de Ahorros) (2014) *Focus on Spanish society.* Social Studies Office of FUNCAS. [Online] Available from: http://epp.eurostat.ec.europa.eu/tgm/table.do?tab=table&language=en&pcode=tessi190 [accessed 16 May 2014].

Gros, D. (2011) Debt and taxes in the eurozone. *Project Syndicate.* May.

Herndon, T., Ash, M., & Pollin, R. (2014) Does high public debt consistently stifle economic growth? A critique of Reinhart and Rogoff. *Cambridge Journal of Economics*, 38 (2), 257–279.

IMF (International Monetary Fund) (2014) *World economic outlook.* April.

Jevons, W. S. (1875) *Influence of the sun-spot period on the price of corn.* A paper read at the meeting of the British Association, Bristol.

Jevons, W. S. (1878) Commercial crises and sun-spots. *Nature*, XIX, 14 November, 33–37.

Jevons, W. S. (1879) Commercial crises and sun-spots. *Nature*, XIX, 24 April, 588–590.

Jevons, W. S. (1882) The solar–commercial cycle. *Nature*, XXVI, 6 July, 226–228.

Katsimi, M., Moutos, T., Pagoulatos, G., & Sotiropoulos, D. (2013) *Growing inequalities and their impacts in Greece.* GINI Country Reports from AIAS, Amsterdam Institute for Advanced Labour Studies.

Krugman, P. (2013) How the case for austerity has crumbled. *New York Review of Books*, 6 June 2013. [Online] Available from: www.nybooks.com/articles/archives/2013/jun/06/how-case-austerity-has-crumbled/ [accessed 9 May 2014].

Laparra, M. & Pérez-Eransus, B. (2012) Crisis y fractura social en Europa: Causas y efectos en España. *Obra Social 'La Caixa', Colección Estudios Sociales*, 35 (In Spanish).

Lo, A. W. (2012) Reading about the financial crisis: A twenty-one book review. *Journal of Economic Literature*, 50 (1), 151–178.

MacInnes, T., Aldridge, H., Bushe, S., Kenway, P., & Tinson, A. (2013) *Monitoring poverty and social exclusion 2013.* Joseph Rowntree Foundation, New Policy Institute.

Merriam-Webster (2014) [Online] Available from: http://Merriam-Webster.com [accessed 9 September 2014].

Rajan, R. G. (2012) The true lessons of the recession: The west can't borrow and spend its way to recovery. *Foreign Affairs*, May/June. [Online] Available from: www.foreignaffairs.com/articles/134863/raghuram-g-rajan/the-true-lessons-of-the-recession [accessed 9 May 2014].

Reinhart, M. & Rogoff, K. (2010) Growth in a time of debt. *American Economic Review*, 100 (2), 573–578.

Rhoades, S. A. (1993) The Herfindahl-Hirschman index. *Federal Reserve Bulletin*, March, 188–189.

Savitz, R. (2010) The relationship between unemployment and economic diversification. *International Journal of Business Research*, 3. [Online] Available from: www.freepatentsonline.com/article/International-Journal-Business-Research/243957226.html [accessed 9 September 2014].

World Bank (2014) *GINI index.* [Online] Available from: http://data.worldbank.org/indicator/SI.POV.GINI [accessed 10 May 2014].

3 Socio-political and socio-spatial implications of the economic crisis and austerity politics in Southern European cities

Giancarlo Cotella, Frank Othengrafen, Athanasios Papaioannou, and Simone Tulumello

Introduction

This chapter focuses on the social, cultural, political, and geographical implications of the economic crisis and the applied austerity politics in, and for, Southern European cities. It does so by adopting an approach that progressively unravels challenges for and the changing role of urban planning and territorial governance. The idea underlying this chapter is that the local dimension, and especially the dimension of cities, offers a privileged perspective to understand crisis and austerity for two reasons. First, crisis and austerity concern the cities, especially in the European context, where urbanisation is at a very advanced stage. Cities are the places where (most) people live; this means that capital, power, and wealth are accumulated here on the one hand; but on the other hand they are also the place where the most vulnerable classes are concentrated. Second, because of their role in global economic networks, cities are a significant level for understanding the linkages between the local and the global, hence the political and social implications of the crisis and the policies applied in response to these.

Therefore, the chapter provides an understanding of the relations between economic crisis and austerity and gives an overview of the way crisis and austerity have had different effects on different European member states: the spatial manifestation of the crisis, effects for local political regimes, and the variegated geographical distribution of impacts in the current and past crises. Second, the chapter engages with the role of different contexts for, and cultures of, spatial planning in order to explore the way the variegated versions of the crisis clash with a landscape of administrative, political, and territorial contexts. Third, it depicts the emergence of new and alternative models for territorial and urban governance, and their implications for legitimacy and accountability in decision-making processes.

Crisis and austerity

In its etymological roots, 'crisis denoted the turning point of a disease, a critical phase in which life or death was at stake and called for an irrevocable decision'

(Roitman, 2014: p. 15). As far as the current European crisis is concerned, the way the financial breakdown turned into one long-lasting economic recession shall be addressed analysing what (political) decision was taken in order to deal with the (economic) turning point. Put in other words, the European crisis cannot be understood without understanding its relations with austerity.

It is thus crucial to unravel the relations between the moment of crisis and the anti-crisis decisions. Several scholars (e.g. Lapavitsas et al., 2010; Krugman, 2012; Blyth, 2013) offered in-depth explanations of how the crisis was the culminating point of neoclassical macroeconomics of the last few decades: transference of wealth from labour to rent; retrenchment of the welfare state; liberalisation of financial sectors; and economic financing. The connections between urbanisation economies and the crisis provide significant insights in this regard. Schwartz (2012) unravels these connections looking at the case of housing policy. The erosion of welfare and public housing since the 1980s, together with financial support for homeownership, have been boosting private debt and recurrent housing bubbles, which allowed enormous leverage in financial markets, hence triggering the financial burst.

As a consequence of the economic crisis and the increasing public debts, austerity policies came into force in all Southern European countries. Austerity is a political economy grounded on a neoclassical understanding of macroeconomics. According to it, when a state is suffering economic retrenchment, emphasis is put on the supply side (i.e. restoring business confidence) with measures that aim at (i) adjusting a state's fiscal balance (reduction of public expenditure and/or increase of taxes) and (ii) restoring competitiveness through internal devaluation, that is the reduction of wages and prices. However, outside neoclassical circles, austerity is said neither to adjust national budgets, nor to foster economic recovery (Krugman, 2012; Blyth, 2013).

As a matter of fact, different degrees and typologies of austerity policies are reflected into different capacity for economic recovery. Put in other words, the relevance of national contexts for economic performance of cities during the crisis – which we will present in detail below – can be explained, beyond patterns of development in the pre-crisis period and the specific forms of national capitalism (Musil, 2014), by different implemented national anti-crisis policies. Hints from urban regions studied in this volume (e.g. Seixas et al.) suggest thus to look at consequences of the crisis from a double perspective, distinguishing the direct effects of the economic burst from the impacts of national political decisions. These preliminary insights call for a deeper understanding of the relations between crisis and austerity. Focusing on the local and mainly urban perspective, the next section starts exploring how the crisis has affected the local spatial and social fabrics.

Socio-spatial manifestations of the crisis in the city

Not all European countries and not all cities are suffering from the same consequences (Nunes Silva & Bucek, 2014a: p. 182). Nevertheless, it is possible to highlight specific impacts of the European economic crisis and austerity measures. In order to do so, this section focuses on the urban territories of Southern European countries, where the cumulated effects of the economic recession and austerity policies can be discerned with stronger evidence, although they are not qualitatively different from those on cities all around Europe and Northern America (e.g. Lang, 2012; Donald et al., 2014). The austerity impact has been especially strong in those countries under international bailout (Greece, Portugal, and, to a lesser extent, Spain) by the so-called Troika made of the International Monetary Fund, the European Central Bank, and the European Commission.

In Greece, 'such has been the depth of the crisis that the rate according to which forces of production have been destroyed in the country is only comparable to societies at war or going through major political transformation' (Gialis & Herod, 2013: p. 101). The case of Greece is an extreme exemplification of the link between economic crisis, austerity measures, and social effects. The national GDP decreased by 25 per cent between 2008 and 2013 whereas unemployment has more than tripled from 7.7 per cent in 2008 to 27.5 per cent in 2013.[1] The successive bailouts and structural reforms – i.e. cutbacks in public spending, tax increases, reduction of public services, massive layoffs, and wage cuts in public jobs – which should have promoted fiscal adjustment, have been accompanied by a sustained growth of national debt (Gialis & Herod, 2013). Moreover, the cuts of public services have strongly affected the population, the most evident example being the breakdown of the national health system (Kentikelenis et al., 2014).

Another (early) impact of the economic crisis is, due to the crucial role that urbanisation economies played in these countries before the crisis, to be found in the real estate and construction sectors (Garcia, 2010; Ferrão, 2013). This, in a first step, raised intra-urban polarisation, inasmuch as some urban contexts especially dependent on urbanisation economies (i.e. districts where more low-skilled workers reside) suffered growth of unemployment and loss of purchasing power. Although quantitative data about the distribution and variation of inequalities at the local scale are not available, it is worth noting how most Southern European countries have experienced increases in income inequalities, after a decade of convergence (Carmo & Matias, 2014). Additionally, the impacts among social groups are unevenly distributed – it has been the youth and the poor who suffered most from income loss and unemployment growth (OECD, 2014).

In a second phase, austerity policies are accompanied by an accelerated increase of polarisation and territorial inequality (Seixas et al., this volume). The case of low-income neighbourhoods in Athens indicates how the uneven distribution of austerity policies get inscribed in already existing inequalities, reinforcing 'inequalities among places, between women and men, locals and migrants, big and small employers, secure and precarious workers – and, most importantly, intersections of these' (Vadiou, 2014: p. 2).

The urban polarisation of the economic crisis is especially evident in relation to the housing crisis and issues of mobility. As for housing, the combination of the burst of the housing bubble, together with the loss of purchase power of low- and middle-class households, has brought about the paradoxical coexistence of enormous stocks of unoccupied houses[2] on the one hand, often concentrated in specific areas of the city, such as in new peripheries or historic centres, and of foreclosures of households due to mortgage insolvency on the other hand. In Spain, for example, more than 400,000 households have been foreclosed (Lamarca, 2013) and in Greece the term 'neo-homelessness' has been introduced to describe a new wave of homeless populations (Theodorikakou, Alamanou, & Katsadoros, 2013). As for mobility, the growth of fuel prices, together with the increase of public transport fares – promoted by austerity measures – have brought about significant reduction of travels, both with private and public means, in cities.[3]

It is also possible to discern potential future impacts on the urban environment, not least because of spatial planning laws promulgated in Greece, Italy, and Portugal with the purpose of relaunching real estate and construction.[4] What these laws have in common is the simplification of procedures for land-use change and construction in exception to urban and landscape planning, as well as the acceleration of procedures for public works. As exposed by non-governmental environmental organisations (WWF, 2014a, 2014b) and planners,[5] these laws, and the waves of unregulated construction which may follow, constitute serious threats to the already fragile planning and environmental legislations in these countries (see also Mourão & Marat-Mendes, this volume).

Beyond social and spatial effects, crisis and austerity have been impacting local political regimes, in between local government actions and bottom-up reactions. The next section will explore these impacts in more detail and, at the same time, will highlight the relevance of the local scale for understanding the current European crisis.

Impacts of the crisis on local political regimes

The most evident consequence of the crisis and austerity on local governments is the sharp decline in budgets, because of economic downturns and cut of transfers from the national level. Hence, lower spending levels in social services (education, health, etc.) or local tax increases happened at the same time as the demand for service provision was growing, because of increasing unemployment and poverty rates (Chuliá, Guillen, & Santolino, this volume).

The specificities of Southern European austerity policies have brought about further, more structural, impacts. The Troika has strongly pushed countries in rushes towards privatisation 'through the sale of public, not least municipal, assets to reduce and relieve the public indebtedness' (Wollmann, 2014: p. 68). Hadjimichalis (2014) focuses on the case of Greece, where massive 'dispossession' of land and natural resources, that is, privatisation, took place – under the Hellenic Republic Privatisation Programme, a fund (the Hellenic Republic Asset Development Fund) has been created, whose sole mission is 'to maximize the proceeds of the Hellenic Republic from the development and/or sale of assets'.[6] Greece became a target for international and local speculative capital for two reasons: first, the de-valorisation of exchange-value of land (diminished by

15–30 per cent depending on the areas when compared with the year 2005) resulting from the economic crisis; second, the special legal status, imposed by the Troika after the economic bailout, which has been 'facilitat[ing] the trespassing, privatisation or selling off of public land' (Hadjimichalis, 2014: p. 505).

The critical connections between national or European policies, on the one hand, and the challenges for local governments and communities, on the other hand, can be ultimately understood through the concept of 'transference of vulnerability' (Sapountzaki, 2012: p. 1283). According to Sapountzaki, it can be argued that austerity policies increase (or are expected to increase) national resilience to the debt crisis while, at the same time, transfer vulnerability to the local level. This entails social losses and risks as well as budget constraints for regional and urban authorities (ibid.). This means that the current round of austerity 'is peculiarly local in nature' (Donald et al., 2014: p. 5). The cuts by national governments affected local budgets and boosted 'reforms', that is, retrenchment of competences, privatisation, or cuts to services (Nunes Silva & Bucek, 2014b; Donald et al., 2014). This has implications for the legitimation of local political regimes such as democratic deficits in implementation of austerity measures and the rise of new 'austerity regimes' in the relations between austerity, recentralisation, and reduction of governmental proximity (Bolgherini, 2014; Donald et al., 2014). Colomb and Santinha (2014) argue that the economic crisis, and also austerity, have exacerbated problems already entrenched in EU state aid rules and liberalisation policies. These had already affected the state's ability to support subnational territories and provide public services, especially in peripheral regions.

It is nonetheless important to highlight that cities are not only the places where crisis and austerity are experienced, but also the places where they are contested and debated. Recent years have seen the emergence of the so-called 'new-new' social movements, a term that refer to the organisational characterisation of new social movements, the use of ICTs as mobilisation tools, the establishment of horizontal and direct forms of decision-making (Accornero & Pinto, 2014). The connection between these new forms of mobilisation and austerity goes beyond the simple reaction to the effects of the crisis experienced especially by youths. With more evidence in Italy and Greece, with the downfall of governments and the establishment of technocrat-friendly ones based on wide parliamentary 'supermajorities' (Verney & Bosco, 2013), electoral volatility and general disaffection to politics have been one of the shortcomings of austerity measures.

The growing complexity of parliamentary politics has been mirrored by the emergence of a plurality of practices at the local level. Urban protests, which spread all around Southern European countries, have been accompanied by new forms of local organisation, resounding with specific problems or traditions. Spain has experienced a strong link between the *Indignados* movement and anti-foreclosure organisation (Lamarca, 2013). In Portugal, the cycle of anti-austerity protests has seen a strong connection between new-new movements and traditional actors such as unions and left-wing parties (Accornero & Pinto, 2014). In Greece, a spatialisation of democratic and post-democratic policies took place around the confrontation of indignant squares and social initiatives (alternative currencies, time banks, cooperatives, social services), on the one hand, and anti-immigrants, sciovinist protests, and actions by the neo-nazi Golden Dawn movement, on the other (Kaika & Karaliotas, 2014). Italy has experienced a set of local protests and actions that have been focusing on the commons as ways to promote new means of management of public heritages such as environment, public spaces and places, or cultural facilities (Vianello, 2015).[7]

Against this background of renewed growth of inter- and intra-urban inequality, and tension between top-down and bottom-up policies and politics, the next section will explore how the geographic distribution of the crisis at the local level shall be understood in relation to supra-local (regional, national, European) relations.

Variegated geographical distribution of the crisis impacts

Dominant explanations of crises rely on macroeconomic and financial issues and neglect spatial and geographical ones (Hadjimichalis, 2011), insofar as 'economic models have not been primarily concerned with the question of spatial distribution of economic activity, since they often implicitly assume that markets ensure a geographically well-distributed economy' (Werner, 2013: p. 2789). The lessons from the ongoing crisis suggest that this may not be the case, as we shall detail on a geographical and temporal perspective.

As for a geographic perspective, data from available studies about the economic performance of cities during the crisis period helps us understand how crucial the national dimension for the distribution of impacts of crisis on European cities is. The following remarks are grounded on Musil (2014) and data from the European Metromonitor of the London School of Economics' Cities lab.[8] According to this data, urban typologies, absolute population, or economic size seem to have not affected economic performance of cities during the crisis. On the contrary, wealthier cities performed better, increasing economic polarisation inside states. And, despite significant variations inside countries, a strong correlation is found between performance of metropolitan regions and national contexts. Hence, the way cities were affected by the crisis was shaped, more than by their specific characterisations, by pre-existing economic disparities, both at the European and national scale – and this is a first explanation of why Southern European cities have been suffering the most. At the same time, the economic crisis acted as a multiplier of polarisation effects.

Looking at the geography of long-term development trends and regional convergence/divergence patterns in Europe is thus a second necessary step in order to understand present trends. Between the 1990s and early 2000s, endogenous development of less developed regions – also supported by EU Structural Funds – was expressed into a period of convergence and reduction of regional and national polarisation (Pinho, Andrade, & Pinho, 2011; Bouyad-Agha, Turpin, & Védrine, 2013). However, convergence interrupted during the 2000s and new divergence and polarisation patterns characterise the years after the 2007 financial crisis (Pinho, Andrade, & Pinho, 2011; Chuliá, Guillen, & Santolino, this volume). Accordingly, Lapavitsas et al. (2010) and Hadjimichalis (2011) provide an interpretation to the crisis, especially in Southern Europe, based on uneven geographical development among European states.

Against this background, a brief comparison with the challenges for ex-industrial cities during the 1990s will furnish some insights useful to generalise insights so far grounded mostly on the experiences of Southern European cities. Among the cases of post-industrial transition, the case of eastern Germany is especially interesting. Here, the severe urban crisis was the result of the combination of rapid deindustrialisation and migration to western Germany. The specificity of that crisis was that it 'clashed with the expectations and standards of an advanced capitalist welfare state established in West Germany' (Rieniets, 2009: p. 246). Beyond significant economic transfers at the national level, the discourse about the regeneration of eastern German cities was grounded on the need for a shift towards knowledge-based economy, creative cities, and the attraction of creative classes (Bontje & Musterd, 2009; Wademeier, 2010), a discourse that has taken a dominant role in the benchmarking of 'best-practices' and policy lessons for further cities in crisis (Burdett et al., 2013).

However, further analyses show a more complex picture. Bernt (2009) reconsiders the entrepreneurial urban governance, highlighting patterns of uneven development and institutional fragmentation. On these grounds, Bernt and Rink (2010) understand the renewed difficulties of eastern German cities to deal with the current crisis, arguing that regions considered 'not relevant to the system' have suffered the most from the crisis and have less capacity to 'mobilise power' in order to solve their problems. Lang (2012) thus explores discursive socio-spatial patterns of peripheralisation in recent times. This may also explain the increasing regional polarisation during the crisis in Germany, which is evident despite the successful recovery from recession achieved already in 2010 (OECD, 2013: p. 15).

The comparison between the urban crises of the 1990s and the present one in Southern Europe shows significant differences: the former were characterised by regionalised decline despite national growth, whereas the current one is extremely dependent on national contexts and policies. However, some crucial analogies, namely the processes of polarisation and peripheralisation, could be said to be a general characterisation of recurrent urban (economic) crises. This reinforces the need for a structural understanding of the present crisis, and especially the relation between local crisis experience and national/European 'anti-crisis' policies. It is against a twofold background, (i) peripheralisation and regionalisation of impacts and (ii) strong national dependence, that the challenges for spatial planning and territorial governance, to be explored in the next section, shall be understood.

Urban planning and the economic crisis: causes and effects

As already indicated, the economic crisis, in combination with austerity policies, has strong socio-political and socio-spatial implications such as unemployment, increasing household indebtedness, spatial polarisation, and so on. But what is the role of urban planning in Southern European countries in this context? How far has urban planning or urban development patterns been responsible for the emergence of the crisis? What are the impacts of the economic crisis on urban planning?

To start with, there are various comparative studies and taxonomies of national planning systems trying to identify similarities and differences across European countries (e.g. Newman & Thornley, 1996; CEC, 1997; Larsson, 2006). Following the *Compendium of Spatial Planning Systems in the European Union* (CEC, 1997: p. 37), for instance, the Mediterranean countries all belong to the urbanism tradition which has a strong architectural focus, including urban design, townscape and building control, and where various laws and regulations exist without a coherent system or general public support (see also Lingua & Servillo, 2014: p. 128). The latter aspect is also stressed by Newman and Thornley (1996: p. 57) when summarising that laws and policies in the Mediterranean countries, all belonging to the *Napoleonic planning family*, 'undergo regular change as there is no political consensus over planning and each change of government brings shifts in approach and laws'. They conclude, that the legal context has been built up over time and is 'therefore piecemeal and complex, involving a labyrinth of amendments, exemptions and special laws, and has not been properly codified' (ibid.).

Nevertheless, the planning traditions in Southern Europe are highly formalised (e.g. Oliveira & Breda-Vázquez, 2011: p. 64; Janin Rivolin, 2008) and often follow a 'command and control' planning style (Getimis, Reimer, & Blotevogel, 2014: p. 296). However, as developments such as uncontrolled urban sprawl, illegal parcelling of land, or illegal housing in the Mediterranean countries indicate, the reality of urban development does not necessarily relate to the legal framework (Newman & Thornley, 1996; Oliveira & Breda-Vázquez, 2011). One reason for this is the absence of programming capacities, i.e. strategic and comprehensive urban (and national) strategies (Cotella & Janin Rivolin, 2011: p. 43; Lingua & Servillo, 2014: p. 128); additionally, in countries such as Portugal urban master plans have only slowly been developed or implemented even if this is requested by law (Oliveira & Breda-Vázqez, 2011: pp. 66–67). Moreover, the formal regulation reaches its limits in Portugal as, for example, the distinction between urban and rural areas drawn in urban or regional plans is not followed in reality (Mourão & Marat-Mendes, this volume); something which can also be observed in other Mediterranean countries (e.g. Wassenhoven et al., 2005). As a result, construction activities in several municipalities grew very intensively even where it was restricted by plan dispositions. In consequence, the development of built land and housing plots (either legitimised or not) expanded enormously in the two decades before the outbreak of the crisis, opening the possibility for the construction sector to increase rapidly. Furthermore, the banks granted generous loans to households and investors to finance housing projects which have also contributed to the speculative housing bubble and the eruption of the crisis

A second reason for the gap between formal planning and implementation is to be found in the 'ratification' of urban plans, which, in general, appears to be a highly complicated, centralised, and political process, which takes such a long time that it might be that projects are realised without the context of approved wider spatial policies or regulatory plans. Additionally, in countries such as Greece and Portugal, the urbanisation process of the last decades took place at a very fast rate, meaning that 'planning authorities proved unable to plan ahead of urban development and provide agglomerations with the necessary urban infrastructure' (Getimis & Giannakourou, 2014: p. 151). Urban planning is thus not leading urban development but only responding to it (CEC, 2000, p. 29; Wassenhoven et al., 2005: p. 5)

According to Leontidou (1993: p. 953), the lack of state control, the comprehensive rights for landowners to build houses, and the speculative housing market, combined with land fragmentation, result in piecemeal urban development and a large informal housing sector which is unique in Europe. These, often unauthorised, settlements are generally accepted and retrospectively legitimised by planning authorities (Getimis & Giannakourou, 2014: p. 151), which leads Leontidou (1993: p. 953) to the conclusion that 'cities have developed within a peculiar context of benign neglect by governments, or sometimes corruption'. This also indicates that many politicians regard urban planning as a means to serve their voters' private interests. This might help explaining why large-scale urban projects, technical infrastructure projects, and the integration of unauthorised settlements into statutory plans 'are the most popular spatial interventions and those most likely to be given political priority' (Wassenhoven et al., 2005). However, as particularly large-scale urban projects or technical infrastructure projects often unexpectedly charge the public budget with their high costs, this might help explain why the impacts of the crisis in Southern European cities are more serious and why the 'room for manoeuvre' for municipalities is limited in times of crisis. This seems to be intensified through the establishment of informal relationships and clientilistic relations or 'exclusive networks' between politicians and other (economic) actors which is an expression of political localism that is mainly to be found in Southern European countries whereas legal localism, that is a high degree of administrative regulation from above, prevails in North-western European countries (Loughlin, 2001).

Furthermore, the demand to live in one's own house or flat seems to be a fundamental Mediterranean societal value, expressing a high degree of independence and helping explain the ongoing urban sprawl and sometime illegal settlements in Metropolitan Areas in Southern Europe. As one expression of the 'anti-planning attitudes of the population' (Leontidou, 1993: p. 951), people do not expect the state – in terms of public administration and other public bodies – to take care of them; they have more confidence in their family and neighbourhood to provide them with social services and facilities. Owning a property can thus be understood as a strategy to be independent from the state:

> In essence, it is a substitute for the Welfare State in many areas of social policy: relief from poverty, unemployment, homelessness, illness, defective

education and care for pensioners are based on informal strategies, and especially family businesses, income-sharing, mutual support and unpaid female
labour within the family.

(Leontidou, 1993: p. 956; see also Vettoretto, 2009)

Together with the inefficiency of the state, the centralised (planning) institutions
and the favourable loans granted by banks, this might help explain the housing
bubble and its eruption. It also indicates why Southern European countries have
been hit hard by the crisis as the economic crisis led to an increase of unemployment, foreclosures, and mortgage insolvencies as individuals, households, or
families were no longer able to repay their loans.

However, urban planning did not only intensify the economic crisis; Southern
European countries 'hit by the global economic crisis are under strong pressure
to move towards "market-led" planning, in order to facilitate private investments
and to overcome planning burdens through outsourcing specific planning services' (Getimis, Reimer, & Blotevogel, 2014: p. 298). As indicated above, this
results in 'market-led' and pro-growth strategies, including privatisation, outsourcing, or facilitating investments. At the same time, this also includes the
'weakening of strict environmental and planning regulations and "bypassing" of
planning burdens through specific planning regulations' (ibid.).

A second major shift or consequence of the economic crisis impacting on
urban development is to be found in processes of state rescaling (e.g. Brenner,
2004). Even if these processes, mainly in terms of decentralisation or downscal-
ing, started before the crisis occurred, it becomes apparent that the decentralisation processes are combined with the 'recentralization of power on the central
level concerning important policy areas such as major infrastructure investments,
protection of environment and water resources, retail planning or coastal zone
management' (Getimis, Reimer, & Blotevogel, 2014: pp. 300–301). As a consequence of the crisis, we can then summarise that decentralisation leads to an
increase of tasks and duties at the local level while, at the same time, local
budgets are cut due to austerity policies. Additionally, the possibility of cities
and municipalities to act are restricted in some policy areas as the nation state
still retains most of the competences. However, it has to be emphasised that,
with regard to state rescaling processes, there is no recognisable uniform pattern
across Southern European countries (Oliveira & Breda-Vázquez, 2011: p. 67).
On the contrary, there exists a variety of different approaches, ranging from
more centralised structures to more decentralised structures or pragmatic governance approaches.

Furthermore, the economic crisis has intensified the development of new
planning modes and more strategic and proactive planning tools. In almost all
Southern European countries, strategic spatial plans have been introduced alongside regulative planning modes and styles (Cotella & Janin Rivolin, 2011: p. 44).
On the one hand, these strategic planning approaches aim at a better horizontal
and vertical coordination of spatial planning in general; on the other hand, they
can also be seen as an attempt of a 'market-led' planning approach to increase

the visibility and competitiveness of a city adequately. However, there are further distinctions across Southern European countries. Whereas strategic planning approaches in Greece concentrate on the 'promotion of economic growth, social cohesion and sustainability, along with the implementation of major infrastructure projects (e.g. Athens international airport, motorways, etc.)', the shift to strategic planning in Italy 'is mainly connected to territorial governance ... including multi-actor planning actions, public-private coalitions and participatory networking for strategic local and regional development' (Getimis, Reimer, & Blotevogel, 2014: p. 283; see also Cotella & Janin Rivolin, 2011). As it will be further explored in the following section, the emergence of alternative territorial governance models represents indeed one of the major shifts in Southern Europe over the last two decades (Oliveira & Breda-Vázquez, 2011: p. 64); whereas, in times of the economic crisis, this intensifies the challenge for urban planning to open up to negotiations with public and private stakeholders, on the other hand, it raises new challenges in relation to the actual legitimacy and accountability of the decisions taken.

The emergence of new and alternative territorial governance models

The new urban dynamics caused by the crisis, outlined more in detail in the previous sections of the chapter, clearly demanded the introduction of new approaches to urban planning and policies to tackle them, while triggering various consequences for traditional models of governance at the same time. All this occurred in the context of Southern European cities, where urban planning and policies had proved to be a highly inertial field that resists change as a potential threat to those actors detaining power, competences, and resources. Between un-experienced socio-political reconfiguration tendencies and the risks of fragmentation of urban politics itself, local authorities and administrations found themselves all of a sudden faced with a new set of challenges that led to different, not always coherent, reactions. The latter range from conservative attempts to maintain former powers and responsibilities in the hands of the public sector to the development of alternative models of governance, featuring higher flexibility and the incremental involvement of non-public actors into the decision-making process.

This coexistence of inertia and will of innovation is symptomatic of the sense of disorientation that rose in most local authorities and administrations as a consequence of the framework changes that the crisis had on the equilibrium of urban systems. In particular, whereas it appeared clear that traditional territorial (urban) governance, in Southern European cities consisting of a mix of rigid regulatory planning tools often bypassed by episodic decisions taken to the benefit of exclusive, clientelistic networks, was not able anymore to deal with the urban phenomena in the time of crisis, the initiatives to deal with the challenges these changes have caused are very different and depend very much on contextual conditions and opportunities. May they be 'harder' or 'softer' in nature, more institutionalised, or taking the shape of ad hoc responses to critical challenges and to emerging opportunities, the new models of territorial governance that emerged move away from traditional territorial governance tools grounded on the existing administrative jurisdictions without replacing them. Rather, they call for the introduction of new, overlapping scales of governance often delimited by fuzzy boundaries, that aim at increasing the efficiency of territorial governance processes by focusing on the real geographies of issues under consideration as well as opening the decision-making arena to the private sector and the civic society (Haughton & Allmendinger, 2008; Allmendinger & Haughton, 2009, 2010; Haughton et al., 2011).

As it is not difficult to understand, the introduction of new, semi-democratic forms of territorial (urban) governance contributed to substantially reshape traditional urban political regimes. In a context of perceived or real 'state failure', as the one generated from the global economic and financial crisis, new practices that draw heavily on a greater involvement of individuals or actors from both the economy and the civil society were viewed as empowering, democracy enhancing, and more effective forms of governing compared with the sclerotic, hierarchical, and bureaucratic state forms that conducted the art of governing during much of the twentieth century. This is particularly true in Southern European countries where, as mentioned in the sections above, an anti-planning, anti-state feeling has increased since the beginning of the crisis, also due to the incapacity of the public sector to effectively react to the latter and to counteract its impact in terms of increasing inequalities and pauperisation of large strata of the population.

However, whereas their capability of bringing together different and dispersed actors and aims surely opens new possibilities, often linking statements concerning greater economic effectiveness of the proposed interventions to promises of greater democracy and grass-root empowerment, they also exhibit a series of contradictory tendencies.[9] Various studies on the matter show how the new innovative institutional or quasi-institutional arrangements of governance often act *beyond-the-state*, being organised as blurred, horizontal associational networks of public, private, civil society actors (for an overview see: Swyngedow, 2005; for concrete examples see Caruso, Cotella and Pede & Seixas et al., this volume). These apparently polycentric ensembles in which power is dispersed are increasingly prevalent in rule-making, rule-setting, and rule implementation at a variety of geographical scales (Hajer, 2003b: p. 175), being particularly relevant at the local/urban level (in various forms, such as development corporations, ad hoc committees, stakeholder-based formal or informal associations dealing with social, economic, infrastructural, environmental, or other matters, strategic coalitions, urban fora, etc.). This is evident, for instance, in the case of Turin, where the construction of a public–private metropolitan governance model, has been pursued since the development of the First Strategic Plan approved in 1999 (Caruso, Cotella, & Pede, this volume).

The urban scale has indeed been a pivotal terrain where these new arrangements of governance have proliferated in the context of the crisis. For instance, the above-mentioned strategic turn that interested the planning activity of some of the main Italian municipalities (cf. also: Cotella & Janin Rivolin, 2011; Sartorio, 2005; Caruso, Cotella, & Pede, this volume), led to the proliferation of such heterogeneous networks of actors, often providing them with a strong influence on decision-making. Similarly, as it will be shown more in details in some of the following chapters, various cities located in Southern European countries saw a growing influence of the private sector (and, partly, of the civic society) over decision-making. Due to this reason, it is interesting to address and problematise these emerging regimes of (urban) governance with a particular emphasis on the tension between the stated objective of inclusion, on the one hand, and their often authoritarian character, on the other hand, as well as to reflect on their implications on terms of legitimacy and accountability. This is particularly pertinent as the inclusion of civil society organisations (like NGOs) in systems of (urban) governance, combined with a greater role of 'local' political and economic arrangements, is very often presented to the general public as potentially empowering and democratising (Le Gales, 2002; Hajer, 2003a).

These forms of governance may indeed contain germs of ideas that permit greater openness, inclusion, and empowerment of hitherto excluded or marginalised social groups. However, there are equally strong processes at work pointing in the direction of a greater autocratic governmentality (Swyngedouw, 1996, 2000; Harvey, 2005). As a matter of fact, the new governance arrangements often ended up being based on particularism and unclear relations between the political and the economic actors when implementing urban policies (e.g. policies connected with specific real estate developments, large development projects, public–private partnerships). As far as Southern European cities are concerned, this situation is exacerbated by the importance that traditionally characterise urban elites and clientelistic networks, and by the fact that these arrangements often take place within an 'institutional void', as there are no clear rules and norms according to which politics are to be conducted and policy measures are to be agreed upon. Whereas traditional urban governance processes are pivoted around a rigid legislation that clearly distribute power, competences, and responsibilities between the various (mostly public) authorities, the new configuration brings along with it serious accountability and legitimacy issues in the decision-making processes, with more and more planning-related decisions that came into power through legislative acts that do not require any particular form of consultation, and often substantially lack consistency when one examines the broad picture.

In particular, the mechanisms and lineages of accountability are radically redrawn in the new arrangements as, while traditional urban governance characterising Southern European cities has, despite its already mentioned drawbacks, more or less clear mechanisms for establishing accountability, the new stakeholders' representation fundamentally lacks explicit lines of accountability, with the latter that is assumed to be internalised within the participating groups through their insertion into (particular segments) of civil society (Rhodes, 1999; Rakodi, 2003). However, given the diffuse and opaque systems of representation, accountability is generally very poorly, if at all, developed. In other words, effective representation has to be assumed, is difficult to verify, and practically impossible to challenge (Swyngedow, 2005).

Furthermore, these new forms of governance face considerable internal and external problems with respect to establishing legitimacy. In fact, this has been a long-running problem for many of these new, soft forms of governance, particularly as coercion and the legitimate use of coercive technologies remain largely, although not exclusively, with the state (Swyngedow, 2005). On the contrary, legitimacy depends here more crucially on the linguistic coding of the problems and of strategies of action and, more in details, on the formation of discursive coalitions and constructions that produce representations of desirable options while, at the same time, ignoring or silencing alternatives (see Hajer, 2003a; Adams, Cotella, & Nunes, 2011). These discursive strategies have become powerful mechanisms for producing hegemony and, with it, legitimacy. The latter, of course, remains extremely fragile as it can be continuously undermined by means of counter-hegemonic discourses and the mobilisation of a deconstructionist apparatus for deciphering the coding of power that are embedded in legitimising discourses (for more detailed insights on the consolidation of hegemonic concepts see Servillo, 2010; Adams, Cotella, & Nunes, 2011).

Finally, one should remind that, in parallel to the new governance models, aiming at 'unboxing' the 'container view' that characterises traditional spatial planning (Faludi, 2011) through the institution of new, project-based governance arrangements insisting on soft spaces and fuzzy boundaries, also new, 'hard containers' for governance, featuring well-defined boundaries, are being instituted as an answer to the crisis. These new administrative layers often group and recentralise traditional administrations, in order to show public opinion the state's will to make the system more 'efficient' through a rationalisation of public expenditures. This occurs particularly in those countries where, despite the opening up negotiations with public and private stakeholders and the introduction of the new principles of governance (coherence, participation, accountability) in planning systems and practices, the rigidity of hierarchical planning systems prevails (e.g. Italy and Greece; see Getimis, Reimer, & Blotevogel, 2014: p. 279 and the introduction of metropolitan cities in Italy as described in Caruso, Cotella, & Pede, this volume). Once more, the role of different planning culture and contexts appears indeed crucial in influencing the way the various cities react to the crisis.

Conclusions

In order to provide a sound and coherent background against which to read the case studies presented in the following parts of the volume, this chapter provided a preliminary overview of the heterogeneous implications of the crisis and of the austerity measures put in place in various Southern European countries as an answer to the latter. It did so by unravelling the multi-dimensional nature of the crisis, exploring its socio-spatial manifestation in cities, its unequal geographical impacts, as well as its consequences for the stability of local political regimes. Through the analysis, it was possible to reflect on the role played by the peculiar Southern European approaches to urban planning in contributing to the manifestation of the crisis, as well as, conversely, on the changes that the crisis stimulated in the urban planning field. Similarly, the incremental introduction of new, alternative models of governance as a potential answer to the crisis situation was taken into account, together with its implications in terms of accountability and legitimacy.

Above all, the chapter highlights a strong conjugation of economic and social polarisation stemming from both the occurrence of the global financial and economic crisis and of the austerity policies caused by the latter. At the same time, it shows that logics of path-dependency that influenced the patterns of change followed by urban planning and territorial governance in Southern European countries (for a detailed analysis see Getimis, Reimer, & Blotevogel, 2014) contribute to reinforce the mentioned trends. The clientelistic praxes that often characterise Southern European local planning cultures have contributed indeed to push forward further deregulation interventions within the general austerity framework. This occurred through a discursive process in which, rather than acknowledging and attempting to tackle the actual causes of the crisis, the promoted, growth-oriented interventions risk to set out the grounds for further crises to come.

More in detail, whereas the new models of governance *beyond the state* may appear, at a first sight, capable of dealing more effectively with the economic and social emergencies stemming from the crisis, they present, on the other hand, several questions marks in terms of their actual potential for reducing spatial polarisation trends. Within the new, weaker planning frame, power relations are reshaped according to the capacities of local communities, this influencing, in turn, the quality of the decisions taken their impact. Furthermore, the possibility for the private actors to influence these decisions to their own advantage, often at the expenses of the public good, is inversely proportional to the strength and resources of the local public actors, this contributing to reinforce polarisation trends (for a comparison with the debates about the relations between localism and polarisation in UK planning see Deas, 2013).

All in all, shifting from the local to the national dimension it was possible to observe the dynamics generated from the crisis from a privileged perspective. As already mentioned in the introduction, European cities, due to the role they play in the global economy, are indeed a significant level for understanding the linkages between the local and the global, hence the political and social implications of the crisis and of its policies for the European continent. The experiences of Southern European cities that will be presented in the various contributions in this volume will show how the crisis and its impacts on countries and cities risk threatening the so-called 'European model of society' (Rifkin, 2004; Faludi, 2007), in so doing striking the process of European integration at its very heart.

Notes

1 Own elaboration on data from the Hellenic Statistical Authority, retrieved from www. statistics.gr/portal/page/portal/ESYE/PAGE-themes?p_param=A0704&r_ param=SEL84&y_param=TS&mytabs=0 (GDP) and www.statistics.gr/portal/page/ portal/ESYE/PAGE-consumerworks?inputA=2 (unemployment) [accessed 25 February 2015].

2 Still in 2013, 5.6 million of houses (20 per cent of total assets) were unoccupied in Spain (Lamarca, 2013).

3 In Greece, a reduction of 30 per cent of traffic on main metropolitan motorways between 2009 and 2013 is observed, also because of new tolls introduced (Egnatia Motorway Observatory, 2014) and decreases of 15–20 per cent in travels in public railways and trams between 2008 and 2010 (our elaboration on data Hellenic Statistic Authority, retrieved from www.statistics.gr/portal/page/portal/ESYE/PAGE-themes?p_ param=A1105&r_param=SME21&y_param=TS&mytabs=0 [accessed 25th February 2015]). For some data about Lisbon, cf. Seixas et al., this volume.

4 Greece: Law 4269/2014 about 'Spatial and urban planning'. Italy: Decree-Law 133/2014 about 'Urgent measures about launching of construction works, building of public works, digitalization, bureaucratic simplification, hydrogeological instability, and recovery of production activity', also known as Sblocca Italia (Unjam Italy). Portugal: Law 31/2014 about 'Guidelines for public policy about land, regional and urban planning'.

5 For the Italian debate, see www.eddyburg.it/.

6 From the institutional website (www.hradf.com/en/the-fund/mission [accessed 25 February 2015]). In the fund's portfolio, key infrastructures (like Athens' international airport), real estate assets, and several land parcels of naturalistic, environmental, and landscape value. With Syriza's success in the January 2015 polls, the privatisation process is expected to slow down, however.

7 At the politico-electoral level, recent elections or rounds of polls have seen the emergence or consolidation of new and less new coalitions and parties, which have explicitly challenged austerity, from a plurality of perspectives, left- or right-wing, anti-Euro or European reformist, like: Syriza in Greece, Podemos in Spain, and Tempo de Avançar in Portugal on the left-wing; Golden Dawn in Greece, Front-Nationale in France, UKIP in the UK on the right-wing; and movements hard to locate in the traditional spectrum like the moVimento 5 Stelle in Italy. The recent victory of Syriza in Greece and the polls assigning the leadership to Podemos in Spain show how these trends may actually bring about a restructuring of the European political landscape in the short term.

8 The European Metromonitor (available at http://labs.lsecities.net/eumm/home/) ranks European metropolitan regions according to annual growth rates of employment and gross value added (GVA) in the period 2008–2012. Comparisons are made in relation to some features of the Metropolitan Areas: typology, population size, absolute GVA, GVA per capita, capital city status.

9 One should note that concerns on this matter are not new: for at least 20 years, several authors attempted to theorise and substantiate empirically the emergence of new formal or informal institutional arrangements that engage in the act of governing in parallel to the traditional public sector routines (Rose & Miller, 1992; Mitchell, 2002; Jessop, 1998; Pagden, 1998; Hajer, 2003a; Whitehead, 2003; Swyngedow, 2005). In particular, they focused on the emergence and proliferation of governance arrangements which give a much greater role in policy-making, administration, and implementation to private economic actors on the one hand and to parts of civil society on the other in self-managing what until recently was provided or organised by the national or local state.

References

Accornero, G. & Pinto, P. R. (2014) 'Mild mannered'? Protest and mobilisation in Portugal under austerity, 2010–2013. *West European Politics*, 38 (3), 491–515.

Adams, N., Cotella, G., & Nunes, R. (eds) (2011) *Territorial development, cohesion and spatial planning: Knowledge and policy development in an enlarged EU*. London and New York, Routledge.

Allmendinger, P. & Haughton, G. (2009) Soft spaces, fuzzy boundaries, and metagovernance: The new spatial planning in the Thames Gateway. *Environment and Planning A*, 41, 617–633.

Allmendinger, P. & Haughton, G. (2010) Spatial planning, devolution, and new planning spaces. *Environment and Planning C: Government and Policy*, 28, 803–818.

Bernt, M. (2009) Partnerships for demolition: The governance of urban renewal in East Germany's shrinking cities. *International Journal of Urban and Regional Research*, 33 (3), 754–769.

Bernt, M. & Rink, D. (2010) 'Not relevant to the system': The crisis in the backyard. *International Journal of Urban and Regional Research*, 34 (3), 678–685.

Blyth, M. (2013) *Austerity: The history of a dangerous idea*. New York, Oxford University Press.

Bolgherini, S. (2014) Can austerity lead to recentralisation? Italian local government during the economic crisis. *South European Society and Politics*, 19 (2), 193–214.

Bontje, M. & Musterd, S. (2009) Creative industries, creative class and competitiveness: Expert opinions critically appraised. *Geoforum*, 40 (5), 843–852.

Bouayad-Agha, S., Turpin, N., & Védrine, L. (2013) Fostering the development of European regions: A spatial dynamic panel data analysis of the impact of cohesion policy. *Regional Studies*, 47 (9), 1573–1593.

Brenner, N. (2004) *New state spaces: Urban governance and the rescaling of statehood.* Oxford, Oxford University Press.

Burdett, R., Colantonio, A., Rode, P., & Taylor, M. (2013) *Policy lessons and opportunities from metros in the EU*. LSE Cities Next Urban Economy series. [Online] Available from: http://files.lsecities.net/files/2013/04/Policy-Lessons.pdf [accessed 25 February 2015].

Carmo, R. M. & Matias, A. R. (2014) *Income inequality in Portugal and in Europe: The impact of austerity?* Inequality Watch. 11 June. [Online] Available from: www.inequality watch.eu/spip.php?article192&id_groupe=13&id_mot=48 [accessed 25 February 2015].

Colomb, C. & Santinha, G. (2014) European Union competition policy and the European territorial cohesion agenda: An impossible reconciliation? State aid rules and public service liberalization through the European spatial planning lens. *European Planning Studies*, 22, 459–480.

CEC (Commission of the European Communities) (1997) *The EU compendium of spatial planning systems and policies*, Luxembourg, Regional Development Studies, Office for Official Publications of the European Communities.

CEC (Commission of the European Communities) (2000) *The EU compendium of spatial planning systems and policies: Greece*, Luxembourg, Regional Development Studies, Office for Official Publications of the European Communities.

Cotella, G. & Janin Rivolin, U. (2011) Europeanization of spatial planning through discourse and practice in Italy. *disP – The Planning Review*, 186, 42–53.

Deas, I. (2013) Towards post-political consensus in urban policy? Localism and regeneration under the Cameron government. *Planning Practice and Research*, 28 (1), 65–82.

Donald, B., Glasmeier, A., Gray, M., & Lobao, L. (2014) Austerity in the city: Economic crisis and urban service decline? *Cambridge Journal of Regions, Economy and Society*, 7, 3–15.

Egnatia Motorway Observatory (2014) *Δελτίο ΑποτελεσμάτωνΔείκτη TRA01: Κυκλοφοριακός Φόρτος. Απρίλιος 2014* [Indicator results factsheet TRA01: Traffic volume. April 2014]. [Online] Available from: http://observatory.egnatia.gr/factsheets/fs_2014/TRA01_factsheet_2014.pdf [accessed 25 February 2015].

Faludi, A. (2007) *Territorial cohesion and the European model of society*. Cambridge MA, Lincoln Institute of Land Policy.

Faludi, A. (2011) *Cohesion, coherence, cooperation: European spatial planning coming of age?* London and New York, Routledge.

Ferrão, J. (2013) Território. In: Cardoso, J. L., Magalhães, P., & Machado Pais, J. (eds) *Portugal Social de A a Z: TemasemAberto*. Paço de Arcos, Expresso, pp. 244–257.

Garcia, M. (2010) The breakdown of the Spanish urban growth model: Social and territorial effects of the global crisis. *International Journal of Urban and Regional Research*, 34, 967–980.

Getimis, P. & Giannakourou, G. (2014) The evolution of spatial planning in Greece after the 1990s: Drivers, directions and agents of change. In: Reimer, M., Getimis, P., & Blotevogel, H. H. (eds) *Spatial planning systems and practices in Europe: A comparative perspective on continuity and changes*. London, Routledge, pp. 149–168.

Getimis, P., Reimer, M., & Blotevogel, H. H. (2014) Conclusion: Multiple trends of continuity and change. In: Reimer, M., Getimis, P., & Blotevogel, H. H. (eds) *Spatial planning systems and practices in Europe: A comparative perspective on continuity and changes*. London, Routledge, pp. 278–305.

Gialis, S. E. & Herod, A. (2013) *Human Geography*, 6, 98–115.

Hadjimichalis, C. (2011) Uneven geographical development and socio-spatial justice and solidarity: European regions after the 2009 financial crisis. *European Urban and Regional Studies*, 18, 254–274.

Hadjimichalis, C. (2014) Crisis and land dispossession in Greece as part of the global 'land fever'. *City*, 18, 502–508.

Hajer, M. (ed.) (2003a) *Deliberative policy analysis: Understanding governance in the network society*. Cambridge, Cambridge University Press.

Hajer, M. (2003b) Policy without polity? Policy analysis and the institutional void. *Policy Sciences*, 36, 175–195.

Harvey, D. (2005) *Neoliberalism: A short history*. Oxford, Oxford University Press.

Haughton, G. & Allmendinger, P. (2008) The soft spaces of local economic development. *Local Economy*, 23, 138–148.

Haughton, G., Allmendinger, P., Counsell, D., & Vigar, G. (2011) *The new spatial planning: Territorial management with soft spaces and fuzzy boundaries*. London, Routledge.

Janin Rivolin, U. (2008) Conforming and performing planning systems in Europe: An unbearable cohabitation. *Planning Practice and Research*, 23, 167–186.

Jessop, B. (1998) The rise of governance and the risks of failure: The case of economic development. *International Social Science Journal*, 50 (155), 29–46.

Kaika, M. & Karaliotas, L. (2014) The spatialization of democratic politics: Insights from indignant squares. *European Urban and Regional Studies*, doi: 10.1177/0969776414528928.

Kentikelenis, A., Karanikolos, M., Reeves, A., McKee, M., & Stuckler, D. (2014) Greece's health crisis: From austerity to denialism. *Lancet*, 383 (9918), 748–753.

Krugman, P. (2012) *End this depression now!* New York, W.W. Norton & Company.

Lamarca, M. G. (2013) Resisting evictions Spanish style. *New Internationalist Magazine.* 1 April 2013. [Online] Available from: http://newint.org/features/2013/04/01/sparks-from-the-spanish-crucible/ [accessed 25 February 2015].

Lang, T. (2012) Shrinkage, metropolization and peripheralization in East Germany. *European Planning Studies*, 20 (10), 1747–1754.

Lapavitsas, C., Kaltenbrunner, A., Lindo, D., Michell, J., Painceira, J. P., Pires, E., Powell, J., Stenfors, A., & Teles, N. (2010) Eurozone crisis: Beggar thyself and thy neighbour. *Journal of Balkan and Near Eastern Studies*, 12, 321–373.

Larsson, G. (2006) *Spatial planning systems in Western Europe*. Amsterdam, IOS-Press.

Le Gales, P. (2002) *European cities: Social conflicts and governance*. Oxford, Oxford University Press.

Leontidou, L. (1993) Postmodernism and the city: Mediterranean versions. *Urban Studies*, 30, 949–965.

Lingua, V. & Servillo, L. (2014) The modernization of the Italian planning system. In: Reimer, M., Getimis, P., & Blotevogel, H. H. (eds) *Spatial planning systems and practices in Europe: A comparative perspective on continuity and changes*. London: Routledge, pp. 127–148.

Loughlin, J. (2001) *Subnational democracy in the European Union: Challenges and opportunities*. Oxford, Oxford University Press.

Mitchell, K. (2002) Transnationalism, neoliberalism, and the rise of the shadow state. *Economy and Society*, 30, 165–189.

Musil, R. (2014) European global cities in the recent economic crisis. *TijdschriftvoorEconomischeenSocialeGeografie*, 105, 492–503.

Newman, P. & Thornley, A. (1996) *Urban planning in Europe: International competition, national systems, and planning projects*. London, Routledge.

Nunes Silva, C. & Bucek, J. (2014a) Conclusion. In: Nunes Silva, C. & Bucek, J. (eds) *Fiscal austerity and innovation in local governance in Europe*. Farnham, Ashgate, pp. 181–186.

Nunes Silva, C. & Bucek, J. (2014b) Introduction. In: Nunes Silva, C. & Bucek, J. (eds) *Fiscal austerity and innovation in local governance in Europe*. Farnham, Ashgate, pp. 1–6.

OECD (Organisation for Economic Co-operation and Development) (2013) *The economic crisis and recovery in OECD regions and cities*. [Online] Available from: www.oecd.org/regional/ministerial/Monitoring-the-Crisis.pdf [accessed 25 February 2015].

OECD (Organisation for Economic Co-operation and Development) (2014) *Rising inequality: Youth and poor fall further behind*. Insights from the OECD Income Distribution Database. June 2014. [Online] Available from: www.oecd.org/els/soc/OECD2014-Income-Inequality-Update.pdf [accessed 25 February 2015].

Oliveira, C. & Breda-Vázquez, I. (2011) Territorial governance in Portugal: Institutional change or institutional resilience? *disP – The Planning Review*, 186, 64–76.

Pagden, A. (1998) The genesis of 'governance' and enlightenment conceptions of the cosmopolitan world order. *International Social Science Journal*, 50, 7–15.

Pinho, C., Andrade, C., & Pinho, M. (2011) Regional growth transition and the evolution of income disparities in Europe. *Urban Public Economics Review*, 13, 66–103.

Rakodi, C. (2003) Politics and performance: The implications of emerging governance arrangements for urban management approaches and information systems. *Habitat International*, 27, 523–547.

Rall, E. L. & Haase, D. (2011) Creative intervention in a dynamic city: A sustainability assessment of an interim use strategy for brownfields in Leipzig, Germany. *Landscape and Urban Planning*, 100, 189–201.

Rhodes, R. (1999) *Understanding governance: Policy networks, governance, reflexivity and accountability.* Buckingham, Open University Press.

Rieniets, T. (2009) Shrinking cities: Causes and effects of urban population losses in the twentieth century. *Nature and Culture*, 4, 231–254.

Rifkin, J. (2004) *The European dream.* Cambridge, MA, Polity Press.

Roitman, J. (2014) *Anti-crisis.* Durham, NC, Duke University Press.

Rose, N. & Miller, P. (1992) Political power beyond the state: Problematics of government. *British Journal of Sociology*, 43, 173–205.

Sapountzaki, K. (2012) Vulnerability management by means of resilience. *Natural Hazards*, 60, 1267–1285.

Sartorio, F. (2005) Strategic spatial planning: A historical review of approaches, its recent revival, and an overview of the state of the art in Italy. *disP – The Planning Review*, 162, 26–40.

Schwartz, H. (2012) Housing, the welfare state, and the global financial crisis: What is the connection? *Politics and Society*, 40, 35–58.

Servillo, L. (2010) Territorial cohesion discourses: Hegemonic strategic concepts in European spatial planning. *Planning Theory and Practice*, 11, 397–416.

Swyngedouw, E. (1996) Reconstructing citizenship, the re-scaling of the state and the new authoritarianism: Closing the Belgian mines. *Urban Studies*, 33, 1499–1521.

Swyngedouw, E. (2000) Authoritarian governance, power and the politics of rescaling. *Environment and Planning D*, 63–76.

Swyngedouw, E. (2005) Governance innovation and the citizen: The janus face of governance-beyond-the-state. *Urban Studies*, 42, 1991–2006.

Theodorikakou, O., Alamanou, A., & Katsadoros, K. (2013) 'Neo-homelessness' and the Greek crisis. *European Journal of Homelessness*, 7, 203–210.

Vadiou, D. (2014) Tracing aspects of the Greek crisis in Athens: Putting women in the picture. *European Urban and Regional Studies*, doi: 10.1177/0969776414523802.

Verney, S. & Bosco, A. (2013) Living parallel lives: Italy and Greece in an age of austerity. *South European Society and Politics*, 18, 397–426.

Vianello, M. (2015) New rights and the space of the practices: Italian contributions to a theory of the urban commons. Footprint. *Delft Architecture Theory Journal*, 16 (forthcoming).

Vettoretto, L. (2009) Planning cultures in Italy: Reformism, laissez-faire and contemporary trends. In: Knieling, J. & Othengrafen, F. (eds) *Planning cultures in Europe: Decoding cultural phenomena in urban and regional planning.* Farnham, Ashgate, pp. 189–204.

Wademeier, J. (2010) The impact of the creative sector on growth in German regions. *European Planning Studies*, 18 (4), 505–520.

Wassenhoven, L., Asprogerakas, V., Gianniris, E., Pagonis, T., Petropolou, C., & Sapountzaki, P. (2005) National overview Greece. *ESPON Project 2.3.2, Governance of Territorial and Urban Policies from EU to Local Level*, Work Package 2, Athens, National Technical University of Athens.

Werner, R. A. (2013) Crises, the spatial distribution of economic activity, and the geography of banking. *Environment and Planning A*, 45 (12), 2789–2796.

Whitehead, M. (2003) 'In the shadow of hierarchy': Meta-governance, policy reform and urban regeneration in the West Midlands. *Area*, 35, 6–14.

Wollmann, H. (2014) Public services in European countries: Between public/municipal and private sector provision – and reverse? In: Nunes Silva, C. & Bucek, J. (eds) *Fiscal austerity and innovation in local governance in Europe*. Farnham, Ashgate, pp. 49–76.

WWF (World Wildlife Fund) (2014a) *Environmental legislation in Greece: Tenth annual review – summary*. [Online] Available from: www.wwf.gr/crisis-watch/crisis-watch/governance/7-issue-20-november-2013/download/1_9e5e18a8fd7e37d681b63c3d751c 811d [accessed 25 February 2015].

WWF (World Wildlife Fund) (2014b) *Sblocca Italia, unaManovracontrol'Ambiente*. [Press release] 6 November 2014. [Online] Available from: www.wwf.it/?11760 [accessed 25 February 2015].

4 Crisis and urban change

Reflections, strategies, and approaches

Jörg Knieling, Umberto Janin Rivolin,
João Seixas, and Galya Vladova

Introduction

The global reach of the recent economic and financial crisis, the depth and duration of its manifold impacts, and the massive default in finance, employment, consumption, and trust have called for new approaches and developments for the years ahead. While some authors assume that we have entered 'another lost decade' (Leigland & Russell, 2009), others recognise the fact that each crisis contains the seed of change and that it might be perceived as an accelerator of processes of change that are already in train (Shiller, 2008). Understanding the crisis also as a driver for change and seeing the change not only as a threat and a source of uncertainty but also as an opportunity allows the search for new solutions to the emerging challenges and altered circumstances.

The growing complexity, the increasing interdependence, and financial scarcity form 'the new "normal" with which we will have to live in the near future' (Cohen, 2011: p. 4). The times of crisis are precisely 'the times for questioning, reflection and system improvement' (Martinez, Smoke, & Vaillancourt, 2009: p. 16) that enable us to rethink our values as human beings, the organisation of our society, and the territory we are living in. Considering this, it could be argued that the recent economic and financial crisis with its numerous social, economic, spatial, and environmental impacts has changed conditions we have been used to for years and has led to a new understanding of the organisation of our territory (Romero, Jiménez, & Villoria, 2012). Meanwhile, it has called for the need to rethink existing governance structures and urban policies as well as to identify new instruments, strategies, and approaches for territorial development.

A look back to the pre-crisis decades enables the identification of certain models of development, applied and reproduced in many cities. Analysis of spatial politics developed in Europe reveals that these politics are the outcome of specific forms of political-economic interventions and of the application of state spatial strategies that often neglect space (Brenner & Elden, 2009). While being a reflection of the dominant modes of production and the endeavour for economic growth (Lefebvre, 1992), urban space has also witnessed the interest of national and local governments for intensified competition on the global scene.

All this found its expression in the implementation of large urban projects and the attraction of enterprises or tourism, with new airports and infrastructures, for instance. In line with this argumentation the recent crisis could be interpreted as an indicator for a lack of sustainability in dominant modes of territorial development and as a sign of a lack of socio-political comprehension of these modes. It helps to better understand the roots of present day problems, makes us question the properness of existing, as well as recently proposed development pathways and governance regimes, and calls for the need of the identification of new ones.

The interpretation of the crisis and what it actually means to cities has been largely framed, as argued by Oosterlynck and González (2013), through the existing organisational settings. An overview of the impacts of decline, as well as the pathways of recovery from the crisis, reveals that these vary considerably throughout Europe. A major role in this regard is being played by the specific institutional environment and the existing decision-making structures of each concrete place. Therefore, the crisis offers cities and regions the potential for institutional reform that could provide a stronger framework for future action – 'no matter how powerful and technologically sophisticated the train, it is only as good as the track on which it runs' (Shiller, 2008: p. 11). In this context the crisis opens the opportunity to research current decision-making structures and processes and to search for new sustainable development patterns.

Yet, it should not be underestimated that differences in the pathways of recovery also result from the specific political culture and socio-political power formations in the individual countries. This correlates with the contemplation that it is not the (institutional) city itself, but the actions of individual and collective actors that constitute change (Lang, 2010). This illustrates that institutional reforms go hand in hand with societal change and emphasises the role of the civil society, bringing it more to the fore than it has been in the past years. 'Don't waste the crisis' has been the call of the Organisation for Economic Co-operation and Development (OECD) as an appeal to respond to the crisis with local leadership and purpose (Clark, 2009), emphasising the importance of local action.

With the above thoughts taken into consideration the current chapter studies the potential, offered by the recent crisis, for both institutional and societal change, and what new approaches are thinkable and necessary in times of crisis. The next section of the chapter starts with a theoretical reflection on crisis as a driver of change. This touches upon Holling's Adaptive Cycle and the transition theory, studying their contribution to understanding how change happens and which factors favour and constrain (social) transformation, experimentation, and innovation. Based on conceptual insights, in the third section, the authors discuss possible strategies and approaches for cities and regions to adopt in order to overcome the impacts of the crisis, adapt to the altered circumstances, and reduce their vulnerability to future external shocks. Addressing the recognised need for a new way of understanding politics, governance, and management of planning, the fourth section of the chapter proceeds with a subsection on the role of spatial planning in the face of crisis, particularly on how a planning system can be more or less counteractive, and on whether the crisis could trigger change in Southern European planning systems, which are less mature. Based on the gained insights, a concluding section rounds off the contribution by summing up the main findings achieved, thus laying the foundation for further discussion on open questions.

Theoretical reflection on crisis and urban change

Cities and regions are complex systems, composed of dynamic relationships between their physical, natural, and socio-cultural environments. In this context, the core of the discussion on how crises trigger urban development lies in a better understanding of change in complex systems. An overview of the available body of literature on the topic enables the identification of several theoretical approaches, which could be used to obtain both general and in-depth insights into how change happens and which could provide a framework of thinking about the various dimensions of change.

A basic aspect in the discussion of change in complex systems is the definition of these systems as being interlinked in 'never-ending adaptive cycles of growth, accumulation, restructuring, and renewal' (Holling, 2001: p. 392). This so-called Holling's Adaptive Cycle communicates change as one of four phases of development each system undergoes, when its components interact and the connections between them alter. Upon its establishment, each system undergoes a period of rapid growth, characterised by the accumulation of resources and the existence of a range of opportunities. When, over time, the resources start decreasing due to the concentration of actors and the connections between them, the system's capacity for rapid growth starts diminishing until at some point the system reaches a state of stagnation, uncertainty, and vulnerability to disturbance. The occurrence of even a small disturbance could lead to the collapse of the system and to further loss of resources. Apart from negatively affecting the functions of the system's components, however, the loss of resources also opens ways for renewal, allowing the establishment of a new order that could either be similar or significantly different from the existing one (Walker & Salt, 2012).

In an attempt to illustrate the above cyclical process Walker and Salt (2012) propose differentiation between two modes – the development mode, characterised by stability and the accumulation of capital, and the back mode, characterised by uncertainty, but at the same time by novelty and experimentation. The potential for change in the system, be it destructive or creative, proves to be highest in the back mode (ibid.). If it is assumed that the recent economic crisis has been preceded by a period of growth, the concentration of resources and competition between actors, the crisis itself has pushed cities and regions as complex systems into a back mode. They now have to deal both with inherent problems and new challenges, such as scarcer resources and increasing uncertainty. The altered conditions, however, offer potential for innovation, space for novel solutions, and creative change.

Touching upon the above discussion on how change happens, Burkhalter and Castells (2009) argue that changes in the old system mainly happen when it has ceased to function properly. It could be argued that this statement is particularly true for urban territories and urban societies as complex systems, whose overall function highly depends on the ability of their individual components to function. The presence of external shocks and emergent hazards could cause pressure on urban systems and might challenge their ability, or in certain cases even reveal their inability, to function properly. This might result in delinking established norms, rules, and mechanisms and in altering their individual components (Pelling & Navarrete, 2011 on change of social systems). Fundamental changes in times of vulnerability at multiple levels are, however, rather rare and several developments need to occur simultaneously to create space for the creation of fundamental new opportunities (Holling, 2001). This coincides with Burkhalter and Castells' conviction that urban change 'does not follow an orderly rationale but rather it results from multiple mutations in various dimensions of the urban system that, in their convergence, end up modifying the overall dynamics of urban space' (2009: p. 3).

Following the line of the above argumentation it could be assumed that the economic and financial crisis of the late 2000s and the subsequent serious economic downswing have been perceived by European cities as external shocks and have necessitated differentiated change in the individual components of urban systems. Due to the multifaceted character of the crisis (economic, financial, urban, social, energy, etc.) and the variety of effects it has simultaneously caused on the provision of infrastructure, services, and on the built environment in urban systems, the crisis has increased the chance for changes in all these fields. In this regard, it has facilitated the initiation of changes in planning practices, the promotion of innovation in governance and institutional domains, the rethinking of current lifestyles and values, and the identification of new future development paths for cities and regions.

The development paths following on from the outburst of the economic crisis and the extent to which these could be considered new when compared to previous ones vary significantly. On the one hand, this demonstrates evident differences in the cities' and regions' ability to absorb externally induced disturbance or stress. On the other hand, however, it shows that internal policies justified by the crisis have also affected urban systems (see Seixas et al., this volume). Useful insights into the debate about the stability of urban systems against interference, the extent to which these recover from external shocks, and the nature of the responses facilitating such recovery, have been provided by the concept of resilience. Applied initially in psychological studies, the concept has also been introduced in an urban context, referring to the capacity of cities and regions to avoid and manage natural and human-induced hazards (Bosher & Coaffee, 2008), establishing their former state of equilibrium or entering into a new one.

Today, in times of commonly perceived high uncertainty and vulnerability, the question of what makes an urban system more resistant to external influence, adaptable to altered circumstances, and capable of absorbing positive change, gains increasing importance. In this respect Walker and Salt (2012) argue that the capacity of a system to absorb disturbance decreases over time if the system is held unaltered and explain this by the fact that the system's history in dealing with disturbances is the basis for its capacity to deal with future shocks. This understanding points to the notion that changes of some of the system's components might be meaningful, both to increase the resilience of and, in some cases, to even avoid the collapse of the whole system. Furthermore, the purposeful organisation of processes in such a way that they lead to the demolition of the system might result in the system's reorganisation and its modernisation.

Along with the above considerations, analyses in the field of urban resilience emphasise that resilience depends highly on a number of factors, such as the prevailing economic conditions and sectoral structure of the place, the governance structure, and the level of fiscal and legislative autonomy, and highlight the significant positive role played by the level of social capital, informal institutions, and network capital (ESPON, 2013). In this regard 'resilience is ... conceived as a place-based capacity shaped both by a territory's inherited resources and structures, as well as its people and the agency of its individuals, businesses and institutions' (ibid.: p. 7). Such a conceptualisation imposes the need to link the study of the structural determinants of the place under observation to its social processes of and institutional framework for decision-making (Lang, 2010, 2012).

Since decision-making is defined within the framework of an existing place and time-specific institutional and governance environments and is embedded in prevailing social and cultural structures, the initiation of particular forms of action is highly determined by dominant norms, routines, practices, and perceptions, which, as argued by Lang (2012: p. 288), 'constitute institutionalized forms of behaviour, which tend to make local policy and responses to change path dependent'. The notion of 'path dependence' refers to the 'interaction patterns between economic, political and institutional actors that affect the ability to react to changed circumstances' (van Grunsven & Smakman, n.d.). Considering this, it should be assumed that the performance of individual cities and regions during the crisis has to be seen in the light of path-dependent developments. These and the presence of institutional thickness (Amin & Thrift, 1994) could in many cases lead to functional or political lock-ins (Olson, 1982; Grabher, 1993). Grabher (1993) defines political lock-ins as thick institutional tissues, which, as proposed by Edquist (1997), consist both of organisations and of norms, rules, and laws, and argues that they could slow down restructuring processes and indirectly hamper the development of indigenous potential and creativity. At some point these could even hinder new forms of development. Therefore, it could be assumed that the change in established practices and associated rules is the very foundation of change in the existing system and a key milestone for the establishment of new development paths.

The above understanding lies at the core of the studies about change in socio-technical systems, the so-called 'socio-technical transitions'. Defined as long-term processes comprising multiple actors, transitions are theoretically explained as the result of the interplay between developments in three different analytical levels: niches, regimes, and landscape (Geels, 2011). Niches are described as small protected spaces, where new practices can develop and radical innovation can emerge, protected from the resistance of the prevailing regimes (Westley et al., 2011). Regimes are the dominant sets of rules, such as cognitive rules and shared beliefs, institutional arrangements and regulations, competences and user practices, that coordinate the activities of social groups (Geels, 2011). The landscape provides the structural context for both the regimes and the niches and includes processes such as environmental change, broad economic restructuring, or cultural developments (Smith, Voß, & Grin, 2010).

By their nature transitions are defined as the shifts from one stable regime to another (Geels, 2011). On the one side, changes in the regime could be triggered by landscape developments, which cause pressure on the dominant regimes, undermine satisfaction with their performance, and destabilize them (Smith, Voß, & Grin, 2010), thus generating opportunities for promising niches to recombine with elements of previously prevailing regimes into a new configuration (Rotmans & Loorbach, 2009). This process is partly governed by economic and political powers. In this context, powers might cause resistance to change or even social conflicts, resulting either in productive developments or in counterproductive and even destructive reactions (Van den Bergh, Trufferc & Kallis, 2011). On the other hand, shifts from one regime to another might occur when competitive niche innovations gain high internal momentum and at moments of tension on the dominant regime break through and replace the latter (Geels, 2011). As noted by Geels (2011), niches could gain momentum in a case where the expectations that guide innovation activities become precise and more broadly accepted or if different learning processes align in a new stable configuration and social networks become larger, involving more (and powerful) actors and resources. In this sense, innovation might be facilitated by encouragement of experimentation and exploration, support for bottom-up responses, promotion of norms of learning and memory, and the connection of innovative ideas to institutional resources to guarantee durability (Westley et al., 2011: p. 771). All this supports the assumption that the mobilisation of actors and resources in the context of instability and dissatisfaction caused by the economic crisis as well as the creation of framework conditions for the promotion of experimentation are essential prerequisites to facilitate change in existing norms and practices.

The presented concepts of urban resilience, change in complex systems, and socio-technical transitions, provide useful theoretical tools to contextualise the discussion on how a crisis could trigger urban change and establish new development paths. Bearing in mind the above theoretical reflections, the following section proposes some insights into new approaches and strategies that are thinkable and necessary so that European cities and regions, particularly in southern countries as the most affected ones, could overcome the consequences of the crisis and reduce their vulnerability to future ones.

Strategies and approaches for cities and regions in crisis

The urban socio-political flection

The new city positioning and dynamics, with a growing political and cultural relevance for the urban spheres and the large-scale socio-territorial pressures, in particular the pressures caused by the economic crisis and the reactions to it, are demanding new urban policies, maybe even new urban politics, and a general-ised change in urban regimes (Seixas & Albet, 2012). At the same time, the frac-talisation and hyper-positioning of human geographies and quotidianities (Agamben, 2008), combined with the 'triple crunch' of global economies,[1] are also bringing a complete set of new dilemmas and challenges, again most par-ticularly in the urban realms.

This crossroad situation is particularly evident in most Southern European cities and regions. In fact, and despite clear path-dependent socio-political land-scapes, paradoxically most evident in countries where democracy is just a few decades old, long-established socio-political urban regimes in several European Mediterranean urban areas, particularly when established throughout semi-organic governance cultures, are now under clear pressure for change. Between high socio-political reconfiguration exposure and the risk of deeper fragmenta-tion of urban politics themselves, city governance and its capability of bringing together different and dispersed actors and strategies might open new possibil-ities as well as new uncertainties. In this context, several open questions could be raised. Are Mediterranean urban societies adequately aware of the pace of changes taking place, or do their cultural perceptions and socio-political struc-tures remain to the side of contemporary risks and challenges? Are their respec-tive structures and cultures of governance efficiently and democratically adapting to the crisis pressures and to the new realities and challenges, or is there signi-ficant path-dependency prevalence, causing limited change capabilities?

The paradoxes and possibilities underlying change processes in the urban socio-political landscapes are particularly relevant when considering their inher-ent transversal characteristics. Territory is clearly a transversal dimension, com-bining different political arenas in areas such as environment protection, spatial planning, regional and urban development, spatial cohesion, transport and mobil-ity, water, waste, and energy management. These transversal characteristics cut across the classical borders of institutional and technical domains, as well as classical political arenas, thus turning integration and subsidiarity into main knowledge and political challenges.

Insights into a better understanding of the questions raised could be gained by the analysis of selected policies, strategies, and approaches developed and applied since the outbreak of the economic crisis, and not only those directly formed in response to its manifold impacts. While many of these strategies have proved a high degree of innovation, providing urban as well as politico-administrative qualification, others raise doubts upon equitable results or effective public deliverance. A closer look at the developments over recent years clearly shows that new types of urban projects and urban policies are being consolidated – from consumption and mobility to cohesion and participation. In addition, varied institutional structures are being reframed or even created – from the smaller scale of neighbourhoods to the meta-regions of metropolises and the wider polycentric regions. Several processes of administrative and political decentralisation, some against established historical path dependencies, are slowly being raised and different arrays of principles and tools for urban planning and civic participation are being introduced. If some of these policies have been thought and tailored according to pre-crisis reflections, models, and tendencies, it now seems considerably clear that most new developments have been strongly influenced by the impact of the crisis.

The pace of change is, undoubtedly, making its way on what concerns European urban politics and governance. However, the overall scenarios on what directions these changes are to take still remain unclear. On the one hand, reactions seem to differ considerably from city to city, showing that the capacity for innovation, particularly in the political and governance realms, is most dependent on inner and endogenous capabilities mostly concerned with local autonomy, social capital, and specific leadership (ESPON, 2013). On the other hand, the regional and urban policies of the European Union, particularly the Europe 2020 strategy and the regulations for cohesion funds, make relevant exigencies in terms of territorial governance changes requiring relevant aspects, such as more polycentric policy integration and wider community policy compromises. Therefore, and notwithstanding a growing tendency towards change, both in urban policies as well as in urban administration and even urban government structuring and procedures, it looks as if several if not most of the changes occurring in established practices are still predominantly 'niche' situations, framing a considerable although fundamental initial stage for vaster urban socio-political changes.

City empowerment paradoxes

Attention should be paid to the fact that several of the political developments raised by the crisis have created difficulties for overall urban politics and for local capacitation. Even for some of the seemingly most necessary political developments, such as the creation of metropolitan political authorities configuring stronger governance commitments at recognised scales of the most relevant urban collective regulation and action, or the need for new accountability enforcements in the face of the risks of resource deviation, many urban European Mediterranean societies seem to show that the pace of their 'real cities' is not being adequately followed by the pace of their 'socio-political cities'. This perspective is particularly relevant in times of deep socio-economic and political crisis.

The vision of cities as local societies (Bagnasco & Le Galés, 2000) mostly configured by governance (formal and informal) networks turns out to be highly relevant for the cities of the Mediterranean. This represents one of the most (if not *the* most) triggering paradox of these cities. The conjunction of the strength of their socio-cultural complexities, with the deep fractalities – or spontaneous alternative dynamics – inherent to their spatial and political projections (now even more expanding due to the crisis), and the development of democratic principles and new citizen exigencies on most recent decades, might reveal after all a vast potential of Mediterranean cities to break with inertias and particularisms and to create innovative and socially responsible proposals. As some researchers have proposed, the growing fractality of contemporary urban life might ultimately well prove to be one of the most interesting metabolical bases for new types of urban socio-political challenges and opportunities (Rhodes, 1997; Kooiman, 2003).

It is relevant to note that besides the roles of local and regional governments, in most of Mediterranean Europe the national state still preserves a major role in defining a city's positioning and evolution through urban governance configurations and dynamics. In many Mediterranean countries the weaknesses of local administrations, coupled with chronic issues regarding fiscal and financial support for their existence, have by and large conditioned their autonomy and political competences in terms of drawing up their own policies and thus local empowerment. This seems to be true even in such decentralised states like Spain, or in cities with a powerful economy like Paris or Milan. For most, 'La République contre la Ville' as expressed by François Ascher (1998), still seems to be the major framework by which the national, regional, and urban governance networks structure themselves. And this is also the case even when, as still happens in vast urban Mediterranean territories, the dominant role of the national governmental institutions seems to play a distant and even demissionary role in what concerns more detailed forms of strategic urban planning and urban development policies. This situation restricts relevant resources and capacities as well as main planning regulatory functions at the local level (Chorianopoulos, 2002; Seixas & Albet, 2012), and develops relevant distortions between urban needs, particularly in times of changing paradigms, and each city's governance capacities.

Over the last 30 years, some Mediterranean countries have initiated regional decentralisation processes of varying scopes, which have brought about, with debatable success, a greater focus on intermediate and local territorial scales. These decentralisation processes have not quite hit the right expression on the local level yet and have sometimes even proven detrimental. On the other hand, and to a considerable manner influenced by the EU regional and urban policies, territorial planning and administration systems have been changing towards much more integrative and operational approaches. The main tendencies seem therefore to depend on the conjugation of European-wide tendencies, with the potentials, limitations, inner forces, and dilemmas underlying the socio-cultural, political, and administrative structures existent in each city. This growing importance of the transnational interlinks, somewhat surpassing national governments, leaves to the local levels a great deal of responsibility or capability to shape their own future.

Strategies towards new socio-political dynamics

The European Commission itself proposed (2011), with regard to aims, objectives, and values, that a clear shared vision of the *European city of tomorrow* as a
place of advanced progress, with high degrees of socially and economically
cohesive and healthy habitats, should be developed encompassing an 'education
for all' service provision; as a place of green, ecological, or environmental
regeneration; as a place of intelligence attraction and enhancement, and an
engine of economic growth; as a hub for democracy, cultural dialogue, and
human diversity. Among other political vectors, the materialisation of these
visions would imply, for every urban project, the assumption of some basic principles on the qualification of urban life, regarding main dimensions such as: (a)
the shape of the urban fabric, and the dilemmas between compactness and
dispersion throughout the territories where urbanisation has long been developed;
(b) the functionalities and opportunities of urban life, and the dilemmas between
complexity and specialisation; (c) the social inclusion and cohesion in the city,
and the tensions of a deeper social integration or a continuous socio-spatial
segregation; (d) the recognition and identity of the city, and the choices between
the deepening of our complicity with it, or the moving towards a fearful cognitive fragmentation.

In political terms, this would imply directing the political administration
boundaries and strategies much more towards the diverse scales of contemporary
urban problems. Bringing more importance to each cost–benefit analysis, to
balance sheets, and to correspondent political decisions, the building of social
and environmental values; expanding small-scale sources of finance as well as
more secure and accessible local banking systems, including the enhancement of
local bonds; developing a tax/fiscal system more connected with the social, energetic, and environmental impacts on the urban fabric, on urban (re)production,
and on urban consumption; creating time banking systems in the territorial communities; developing a housing policy protecting families from speculation and
crash-related evictions.

New forms of governance are obviously essential to tackle these vast and new
challenges, particularly for the Southern European urban territories and societies.
This requires more integrated, holistic, and evolving governance models that
include the construction of shared and compromised strategies; combining multi-
sectoral visions with a politically variable geography; permanent structures for
citizen empowerment (thus also permitting here social and informal innovation);
good foresight and monitoring capacity (namely considering the 'managing
transition'). In a certain sense the territorial and community strategic articulation, understood in the operational frameworks for the materialisation of
Europe 2020, has the potential to follow these socio-territorial dynamical perspectives. The recent charter for multilevel governance in Europe approved by
the Committee of the Regions also follows these approaches.

Against this complex background, it seems important to develop a new type
of questioning and to open new conceptual and analytical perspectives – both on

the interpretation of the new political attitudes in the cities facing crisis and change, and on scientific capabilities to conveniently interpret and conceptualise them. Questions that have been raised in recent years through several fields of analysis include: the place and scope of city politics, the political economy, and its urban projections; urban governance debates; urban regime approaches; social capital and cultural capital in the cities; the actors strategies; and the socio-political systems.

Recognisably, the governance focusing on the urban politics realms has been establishing new mechanisms and institutional procedures that can be driven both top-down and bottom-up. More autonomous and empowering agents appear in the face of the traditional political parties and political institutions, policies needing to be increasingly developed through constant negotiation between the diverse agents and through consensuses built by a state that, in itself, also becomes more polycentric. In South European societies, where the power and the role of the state has been traditionally strong but not so participative-driven, and where most recent changes are shown to occur in knowledge and civic capacitation, democratic governance becomes, therefore, an undoubted opportunity to manage change in different ways, in the fields of urban politics.

In this context, the apparently more specific question on what might be the role of spatial planning systems provides one fundamental pillar for the development of proper frameworks for necessary new urban strategies and approaches.

Spatial planning in the face of crisis

Space, crisis, and planning systems

Since modernity, the role of space in economic and social life 'is less and less neutral, more and more active, both as instrument and as goal, as means and as end' (Lefebvre, 1992: p. 411). And more and more this deals with politics, since a 'politicized space destroys the political conditions that brought it about, because the management and appropriation of such a space run counter to the state' (ibid.: p. 416). This has become even more evident under the cultural conditions of postmodernity, insofar as space can be more 'flexibly' exploited for purposes of power (Harvey, 1989).

Indeed, no one should forget that the current global crisis originated from the US subprime mortgage crisis in 2008 and was triggered by a generalised financial speculation on the housing market under the lack of adequate regulations (Zandi, 2010; see also Chuliá, Guillen & Santolino, this volume). And, under the lack of adequate regulations and strategies, urban markets are worldwide the main 'space' through which the crisis is being slowly overcome through privatising gains and socialising losses (Forrest & Yip, 2011; Fujita, 2011). According to Piketty (2014), one effect of the current crisis is that in many countries the capital (i.e. wealth in the form of real estate property, financial assets, etc.) is growing now at a faster pace with respect to economy (more precisely, with a growth rate of 4–5 per cent vs 1–1.5 per cent per year). The income produced by capital tends to be concentrated in the hands of a small group of people, while labour income is dispersed through the entire population. Considering that wage growth is directly linked to the growth of the economy as a whole, economic inequality will worsen if the economy expands more slowly than income. And, as experienced over recent years especially in Europe, growing inequality can seriously undermine even the most solid democracies (Fukuyama, 2011).

Against this backdrop, and bearing in mind what has been discussed in the previous section, the role of spatial planning systems (i.e. the ensemble of devices addressed to the public control of space in given institutional contexts) should appear crucial. By virtue of constitutional powers, everywhere in the world the operation of planning systems – the action of their legal devices and of their administrative and technical cultures (Knieling & Othengrafen, 2009) – allows and conditions the transformation of space, with the resulting consequences for the life of cities and regions and, especially in times of crisis, for the social distribution of gains and losses that spatial development always implies.

Since spatial planning systems can operate in different ways, even within Europe (Davies et al., 1989; Newman & Thornley, 1996; CEC, 1997; ESPON, 2007; Janin Rivolin, 2008; Nadin & Stead, 2008; Muñoz Gielen & Tasan-Kok, 2010), one question is whether their diverse operational modes can help explain why the crisis hits certain parts of the world – such as Southern European countries – more strongly than others. This should in principle contribute to identifying those 'features' that should be changed in order to cope with the consequences of the crisis. However, since planning systems are rather complex 'institutional technologies' (Mazza, 2003; Janin Rivolin, 2012), to chase after 'an understanding of whether and how institutions themselves might be planned' (Bolan, 1991: p. 8) would probably be an unrealistic and naive exercise. More useful perhaps is to reflect on whether and under what conditions the crisis can become a driver of change in the more obsolete planning systems.

The 'conformative' model affecting Southern European countries

Although spatial ordering for the purposes of social and economic ordering is a human activity, which is lost in the mists of time, the institutionalisation of modern spatial planning put down roots in the phase of industrial and bourgeois revolution and the formation of modern states (Taylor, 1998; Hall, 2002). In the past century, particularly, the pressing needs of greater urbanisation, post-war reconstruction, and of Fordist development have supported the establishment of a model for the public control of space based on the ideals of hierarchy (top-down relations between planning tiers) and of dirigisme (state-led implementation of plans) almost everywhere in the world. While landowners and developers were especially concerned with the 'certainty' of property investments (i.e. based on rights previously assigned), an administrative and cultural context inspired by the welfare state paternalism has generally nourished the assumption that the state, as the keeper of collective interest, is expected to 'conform' projects of property development to its own strategy.

This traditional model of a spatial planning system, still largely prevailing in the world and applied especially in Southern European countries, can be labelled as the 'conformative' model, as it pursues a 'correspondence in form, manner, or character' or actions 'in accordance with some specified standard or authority' (Janin Rivolin, 2008: p. 168). It is pivoted on a 'preventive' binding zoning, which implies in general that: (a) a public spatial strategy is transposed in a binding plan, which assigns rights for land use and transformation; (b) based on this rights assignation, the delivery of permissions for development is subjected to a control of the proposed transformation projects in terms of conformity (whether they conform to the plan); (c) in cases (not infrequent) in which projects, albeit not conforming to the plan, are considered (for any reason) preferable to the existing assignation of rights, a new plan (or a substantive variation of the existing one) is needed in order to assign new rights for land use and transformation (ibid.: pp. 173–174).

Southern European countries, in particular, show structural path dependence on their 'urbanism tradition', characterised by 'a strong architectural flavour and concern with urban design, townscape and building control', and by regulations 'undertaken through rigid zoning and codes' (CEC, 1997: p. 37). But their allegiance to the traditional 'conformative' model of a spatial planning system has proven to be deleterious in terms of 'public-value capturing' over time (Muñoz Gielen & Tasan-Kok, 2010) because of the continuous creation of binding property rights (once the plan is approved, new land-use rights cannot be or can hardly ever be revoked) and of additional property income (new land-use rights imply higher property values). On the one hand, this tends to increase the rigidity and difficulty of public strategies, because any attempt to change or update implies new assignations of land-use rights, with the aforementioned consequences. On the other hand, while an incentive for spatial development for private interests is generally guaranteed, the public control of development projects is reduced, despite more or less genuine expectations, to a mere 'administrative burden', since a conformance control has little or no possibility of improving projects in the public interest apart from their formal coherence with the plan. Moreover, the difficulty of public strategies and the reduction of development control to an administrative burden are a reason for a general decrease of political and technical accountability in planning, with the possible creation of decision-making contexts open to corruptive practices (Janin Rivolin, 2008). And the circumstance that spatial strategies – at whatever scale – once agreed for local implementation are transfigured by what is illustrated above tends finally to trigger a vicious circle in the whole territorial governance process.

Ultimately, there are reasons to suspect that the operation of spatial planning systems in Southern European countries has not been indifferent to boosting the effects of the current crisis, especially as regards the social distribution of gains and losses. Because of the complex institutional nature of spatial planning systems (see 'Time of crisis, time for innovation?' subsection below), however, there are no signs of a consequent intensification of an increase in and conscious proposals for reform in planning systems in Southern Europe. Be that as it may, it seems clear that possible strategies and approaches for cities and regions in crisis, as proposed in the previous section, or concerning further bottom-up initiatives (particularly relevant in times of crisis), are strongly prevented by this traditional type of planning system, for which public spatial strategies are pursued by 'preventive' binding zoning.

Existing models for possible reform

As explained above, one major problem encountered in the application of conformative spatial planning systems is the 'flexibility' of public strategies, prevented in particular by the progressive creation of binding rights on land and of additional property incomes. Based on the juridical tradition of common law (Booth, 2007), the United Kingdom reacted early to this problem with the 1947 Town and Country Planning Act, which established that 'the development plan did not of itself imply that permission would be granted for particular developments simply because they appeared to be in conformity with the plan', rather 'in granting permission to develop, local authorities could impose "such conditions as they think fit"' (Cullingworth & Nadin, 2002: p. 93). The new system was completed by the 1968 Town and Country Planning Act, assigning to structure plans the provision of strategic tiers of development and to local plans the provision of (not binding) detailed guidance on land use.

This different type of spatial planning system, established in the UK (especially England) and in some Commonwealth countries since the post-war period (Booth, 2007), can be labelled as the 'performative' model by virtue of its address to 'the execution of an action' or 'the fulfilment of a claim, promise, or request' (Janin Rivolin, 2008: p. 168). It is based on indicative and non-binding zoning, which means that: (a) a public spatial strategy is transposed into a non-binding plan, i.e. not having juridical implications for the assignation of rights for land use and transformation; (b) for this reason, the delivery of permissions for development is subjected to control and negotiation of the proposed transformation projects in order to ensure their performance (i.e. their capacity to perform the public strategy); (c) new rights for land use and transformation are assigned contextually with the delivery of permissions for development.

More interestingly, despite their juridical regime of civil law (as opposed to the British common law), other countries have, over time, experienced the need to reform their planning systems according to similar features. The evidence of decision-making difficulties in growing societal complexity (Dahrendorf, 1968; Pressman & Wildavsky, 1973), on the one hand, and the Fordism crisis, the explosion of globalisation, and the consequent processes of spatial reorganisation (Harvey, 1989; Amin & Thrift, 1994), on the other, have indeed highlighted further the limits of the conformative model of a spatial planning system. The difficulty of plan implementation in the context of reconciling multilevel collective strategies to a growing plurality of local and individual projects of spatial development has been faced through substantial reforms, especially in North-western European countries (e.g. the Netherlands, Germany, Sweden, Denmark), and also by virtue of their 'comprehensive integrated approach' to the spatial planning system (CEC, 1997: pp. 36–37).

This third type of spatial planning system (Figure 4.1) can be labelled a 'reformed conformative' model insofar as it continues to be based on binding zoning, which is, however, approved as a 'final balance' after which transformation projects (the major ones, at least) have been negotiated, and thus controlled by the public authority, before that plan has assumed the force of law. Therefore, in this case: (a) a public spatial strategy is used as a basis for the collection of projects, their control and negotiation, which are finalised to share their final form and substance; (b) a binding plan assigns consequently the rights for land use and transformation; (c) permissions for development are delivered according to the plan (Muñoz Gielen & Tasan-Kok, 2010).

Therefore, despite the same juridical regime of Southern European countries, this model of a spatial planning system tends to reproduce the operational advantages of the performative model in terms of 'public-value capturing' (Muñoz Gielen & Tasan-Kok, 2010), insofar as it prevents a 'blind' pre-assignation of rights for land use and transformation through binding zoning, and postpones the latter after the public control of development projects. In general, it should be clear how a better control of spatial transformation and of property income (no development rights in land or higher values are previously guaranteed) and more flexibility and political autonomy in the design of public strategies (changes in public strategies do not imply the assignation of new land-use rights) can be crucial advantages in reducing the social costs of the current crisis. Moreover, the pivotal function assigned to the control of spatial development through technical evaluations (a performance control, aimed at improving projects with regard to the public strategy objectives) can guarantee a better accountability of political and of technical responsibilities (not simply in the strategy design, but especially in projects' approval). Overall, this means more

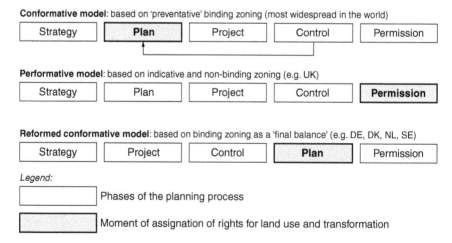

Figure 4.1 Three models of spatial planning systems (source: authors' visualisation).

transparency and an incentive for social responsibility and democracy, with the trigger of a virtuous circle in multi-scalar spatial strategies and in the whole territorial governance process.

Time of crisis, time for innovation?

Summing up, the Southern European countries, more seriously affected by the current crisis, are the ones that are ruled by a 'conformative' model of spatial planning that, despite long-running administrative habits and technical expectations, tends in general to weaken public control on the 'production of space'. On the one hand, this may help to explain why the crisis hits these countries more strongly; on the other, it may reduce the hope that possible new strategies and approaches for cities and regions in crisis, as proposed in the third section of the chapter, can be widely implemented. As described above, conformative planning systems indeed operate by the additional creation of land use rights (assigned by binding plans), which tends to favour private interests and to counteract or delay the opportunities for new public strategies and approaches. Considering the existence of other applicable models in Europe and their better performance with respect to these aspects (see 'Existing models for possible reform', above), specific features of possible reform in Southern European planning systems should therefore address one primary aim: to make sure that new land use rights (not only development permissions) are assigned not by more or less general plans, but following a transparent and unconstrained public control of specific development projects. Based on comparative analysis, this would help to reduce the unequal distribution of the effects of the crisis, and to increase the opportunities of social and economic innovation in urban and regional development.

In the light of this, the question is whether and to what extent theoretical arguments about crisis, change, and opportunities for innovation, as discussed in the second section of this chapter, can be applied to spatial planning systems. In order to answer this question it must be remembered that planning systems are very complex social constructs, triggered in the course of history by a social convention concerning the public assignation of land-use rights (Janin Rivolin, 2012). Since the institutionalisation of modern states, a spatial planning system should indeed be seen as an 'institutional technology of government', operating 'as a hinge between the government system ... and the spatial production and consumption system' (Mazza, 2003: p. 54, translated).

The concept of 'institutional technology' helps to explain the historical insurgence of spatial planning practices and cultures within the wider processes of institutionalisation and, in doing so, leads to the representation of the spatial planning systems as end-products of creative selection processes of trial and error based on:

   a) first, the *generation* of variety (in particular, a variety of practices and rules); b) second, *competition* and reduction of the variety (of rules) via selection; c) third, *propagation* and some persistence of the solution (the system of rules) selected.

(Moroni, 2010: p. 279)

Such a representation (Figure 4.2) may of course open various considerations on conditions and possible drivers of change as have been discussed previously, without forgetting that, in practice, 'the raw material on which institutional evolution acts is supplied by human trial and error, by intentional agents trying to deal with problems' (ibid.: p. 280).

In general, a spatial planning system seems potentially disposed, like any other technology, to renovate its 'capacities' in the face of crisis, particularly the 'command options' of the 'government system' on the 'spatial production and consumption system', which is led by individual profit and thus equally pressed by the search for innovation (Harvey, 1989; Lefebvre, 1992). Paraphrasing Schumpeter (1949), a planning system is continuously called upon to provide the public action with a 'creative response', because any 'adaptive response' is driven to leave the production of space the permanent hostage of prevailing individual interests. But 'in practice the process to adopt changes is rather slow and restrained by high transactions costs' (Fürst, 2009: p. 31), because of the complexity of institutional processes and the conditions imposed by political conflict and economic dynamics, against the background of innate social struggle for land use control (Plotkin, 1987).

Ultimately, the above question might be reduced to whether the social costs of the current crisis have eventually overcome the 'transactions costs' that have so far prevented a substantial reform of the 'conformative' planning systems that affect the development of Southern European countries. If the apparent disinterest of the EU and national governments in this matter, albeit in times of structural reforms, is a clue, it proves difficult to answer positively. In a way, if 'a

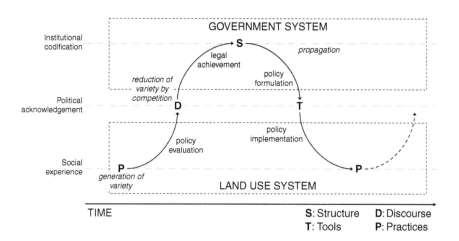

Figure 4.2 Simplified pattern of planning system evolution (source: authors' visualisation).

bridge exists from the technical knowledge that planners embrace to the institutional change that seems necessary for planning to be effective' (Beauregard, 2005: p. 206), this is made of an increased public awareness of the role of spatial planning for economic and social life.

Conclusion

The depth, reach, and structural implications of the recent economic and financial crisis brought about diverse challenges for European territories and societies. Furthermore, they added to the urgency to address these challenges by means of new forms of territorial governance and political binding. The crisis accelerated processes of structural change already in progress, set in motion new ones, and gave rise to debates on how innovative policies, strategies, and approaches could contribute to fostering the resilience of cities and regions. Since resilience results from the interrelation between short-term and long-term processes the crisis and the subsequent economic recession call both for the adjustment of urban policies to the scale of contemporary urban problems, i.e. the development of place-based approaches and solutions, and for the identification of long-term development pathways taking previous models into consideration.

Affecting individual places in different ways, the crisis has necessitated more responsibilities and rights for local and regional levels. More local power and governance capacity, increased resources, and reduced sectoral powers of central administration could enable the development of policies that are based on shared visions and strategies, and which mitigate problems and accept conflicts but do not avoid them. Only long-term strategic policies promoting shared future visions and the development of long-term views for systemic regional and metropolitan strategies can provide a way towards more integrated, flexible, and participative political and administrative models. In this context governance needs to be more inclusive, with stronger levels of participation at the very early stages of the processes.

However, political spaces are not (re)constructed as containers. Much time and effort are needed for socio-political systems to change and evolve, particularly when moving towards much more transversal, multilevel, and subsidiary approaches. The institutional and political territorial and environmental stances, most particularly in Southern Europe, with its more organic-driven governance dynamics (Seixas & Albet, 2012), have structural insufficiencies. Yet, and alongside the pressures for new state spaces in Western Europe, including some quite comprehensive European-wide proposals driven towards a new type of developmental policies (see, for instance, Barca's report, 2009), an increasingly active attitude from local and regional governments as well as from the citizenship itself could be recognised, particularly throughout the territories of Southern Europe. These are, for example, new forms of integrated green approaches with sound strategic and administrative capacitation. For most cities and metropolitan regions in Southern Europe, however, most of the changes occurring in established practices are still predominantly 'niche' situations that frame an initial stage for greater regime changes.

The effective adaptation and implementation of new strategies and approaches for cities and regions in crisis is related to the operation of the spatial planning systems in the countries concerned. Southern European countries, in particular, still show path dependence on their 'urbanism tradition' (CEC, 1997: p. 37). Their planning systems still follow a 'conformative' model, broadly based on 'preventive' binding zoning, which, albeit unintentionally, is the cause of the permanent multiplication of property rights and incomes and of the impairment of public strategies. This may have contributed to boost the effects of the current crisis in Southern European countries, especially when it comes to the uneven distribution of gains and losses. In the meantime, the traditional type of planning system casts some shadow on the possibilities for the application of new strategies and approaches in the cities and regions, especially those most seriously affected by the crisis.

Against this background, institutional change seems essential to increase the effectiveness of planning and to create favourable conditions for new bottom-up initiatives. In this context different models of planning systems already operate in other European countries and might constitute a reference for reform of planning systems in Southern European countries. The spatial planning systems in many North-west European countries, for instance, are aimed at preventing a 'blind' pre-assignation of rights for land use and transformation through zoning, which allows more flexibility and political autonomy in the design of public strategies and more effective public control of spatial transformation and of property income. Yet, the fact that the innovation of planning systems is slow and often restrained by high transaction costs, such as the complexity of institutional processes, political conflict, economic dynamics, and the social struggle for land use control should not be ignored. A provisional conclusion in light of this is that the crisis can become a driver of innovation in planning systems, insofar as it raises awareness of citizens and individual governments. Nevertheless, the very foundation of change in the existing system lies in the change of established practices and associated rules, which is also a key milestone for the establishment of new development paths.

Note

1 As expressed by the Green New Deal Group (2008: p. 2),

> the global economy is facing a 'triple crunch'. It is a combination of a credit-fuelled financial crisis, accelerating climate change and soaring energy prices underpinned by an encroaching peak in oil production. These three overlapping events threaten to develop into a perfect storm, the like of which has not been seen since the Great Depression.

References

Agamben, G. (2008) *Che Cos'è il Contemporaneo?* Rome, Nottetempo.
Amin, A. & Thrift, N. (eds) (1994) *Globalization, institutions and regional development in Europe*. Oxford, Oxford University Press.

Ascher, F. (1998) *La republique contre la ville: essaie sur l'avenir de la France urbaine.* Paris, Editions du l'Aube.

Bagnasco, A. & Le Galés, P. (eds) (2000) *Cities in contemporary Europe.* Cambridge, Cambridge University Press.

Barca, F. (2009) *An agenda for a reformed cohesion policy: a place-based approach to meeting European Union challenges and expectations.* Brussels, Economics and Econometrics Research Institute (EERI).

Beauregard, R. A. (ed.) (2005) Institutional transformations, special issue. *Planning Theory*, 4 (3), 203–310.

Bolan, R. S. (1991) Planning and institutional design. *Planning Theory*, 5/6, 7–34.

Booth, P. (2007) The control of discretion: Planning and the common-law tradition. *Planning Theory*, 6 (2), 127–145.

Bosher, L. & Coaffee, N. (2008) Editorial: International perspectives on urban resilience. *Urban Design and Planning*, 161 (4) Issue DP4, 145–145.

Brenner, N. & Elden, S. (2009) Henri Lefebvre on state, space, territory. *International Political Sociology*, 3 (4), 353–377.

Burkhalter, L. & Castells, M. (2009). Beyond the crisis: Towards a new urban paradigm. In: *The new urban question: Urbanism beyond neo-liberalism conference.* Fourth International Conference of the International Forum on Urbanism, Amsterdam/Delft, pp. 21–44.

CEC (Commission of the European Communities) (1997) *The EU compendium of spatial planning systems and policies.* Regional Development Studies, 28, European Communities, Luxembourg.

Chorianopoulos, I. (2002) Urban restructuring and governance: North–south differences in Europe and the EU urban initiatives. *Urban Studies*, 43, 2145–2162.

Clark, G. (2009) *Recession, recovery and reinvestment: The role of local economic leadership in a global crisis.* Local Economic and Employment Development (LEED) Programme, Organisation for Economic Co-operation and Development.

Cohen, M. P. (2011) *Cities in times of crisis: The response of local governments in light of the global economic crisis: The role of the formation of human capital, urban innovation and strategic planning.* Berkeley, Institute of Urban and Regional Development, University of California.

Cullingworth, B. & Nadin, V. (2002) *Town and country planning in the UK* (13th edn). London and New York, Routledge.

Dahrendorf, R. (1968) *Essays in the theory of society.* Stanford, CA, Stanford University Press.

Davies, H. W. E., Edwards, D., Hooper, A. J., & Punter, J. V. (1989) Comparative study. In: Davies, H. W. E. (ed.) *Planning control in Western Europe*, London, HMSO, pp. 409–442.

Edquist, C. (1997) Systems of innovation approaches: Their emergence and characteristics. In: Edquist, C. (ed.) *Systems of innovation: Technologies, institutions and organizations.* London and Washington, DC, Pinter, pp. 1–35.

ESPON (European Spatial Planning Observation Network) (2007) *Governance of territorial and urban policies from EU to local level.* ESPON Project 2.3.2, Final report, ESPON, Luxembourg.

ESPON (European Spatial Planning Observation Network) (2013) *ECR2 economic crisis: Resilience of regions.* Interim report. ESPON and Cardiff University. [Online] Available from: www.espon.eu/export/sites/default/Documents/Projects/AppliedResearch/ECR2/ECR2_Revised_Interim_Report.pdf [accessed 20 February 2015].

European Commission (2011) *Cities of tomorrow: Challenges, visions, ways forward.* [Online] Available from: http://ec.europa.eu/regional_policy/sources/docgener/studies/pdf/citiesoftomorrow/citiesoftomorrow_final.pdf [accessed 20 February 2015].

Forrest, R. & Yip, N. M. (2011) *Housing markets and the global financial crisis: The uneven impact on households.* Cheltenham and Northampton, MA, Edward Elgar.

Fujita, K. (ed.) (2011) The global financial crisis, state regime shifts, and urban theory, special issue. *Environment and Planning A*, 43 (2), 265–327.

Fukuyama, F. (2011) Dealing with inequality. *Journal of Democracy*, 22 (3), 79–89.

Fürst, D. (2009) Planning cultures en route to a better comprehension of 'planning process'. In: Knieling, J. & Othengrafen, F. (eds) *Planning cultures in Europe*, Farnham, Ashgate, pp. 23–48.

Geels, F. W. (2011) The multi-level perspective on sustainability transitions: Responses to seven criticisms. *Environmental Innovation and Societal Transitions*, 1 (1), 24–40.

Grabher, G. (1993) The weakness of strong ties: The lock-in of regional development in the Ruhr area. In: Grabher, G. (ed.) *The embedded firm: On the socio-economics of industrial networks.* London, Routledge, pp. 255–277.

Green New Deal Group (2011) *A green new deal: Joined-up policies to solve the triple crunch of the credit crisis, climate change and high oil prices.* London, New Economics Foundation, on behalf of the Green New Deal Group. [Online] Available from: www.new-economics.org/gen/z_sys_PublicationDetail.aspx?PID=258 [accessed on 25 March 2014].

Hall, P. (2002) *Urban and regional planning* (4th edn). London and New York, Routledge.

Harvey, D. (1989) *The condition of postmodernity.* Oxford, Blackwell.

Holling, C. S. (2001) Understanding the complexity of economic, ecological and social systems. *Ecosystems*, 4, 390–405.

Janin Rivolin, U. (2008) Conforming and performing planning systems in Europe: An unbearable cohabitation. *Planning Practice and Research*, 23 (2), 167–186.

Janin Rivolin, U. (2012) Planning systems as institutional technologies: A proposed conceptualization and the implications for comparison. *Planning Practice and Research*, 27 (1), 63–85.

Knieling, J. & Othengrafen, F. (eds) (2009) *Planning cultures in Europe: Decoding cultural phenomena in urban and regional planning.* Farnham, Ashgate.

Kooiman, J. (2003) *Governing as governance.* London, Sage.

Lang, T. (2010) Urban resilience and new institutional theory: A happy couple for urban and regional studies? In: Müller, B. (ed.) *German annual of spatial research and policy 2010, urban regional resilience: How do cities and regions deal with change?* Berlin/Heidelberg, Springer-Verlag, pp. 15–24.

Lang, T. (2012) How do cities and regions adapt to socio-economic crisis? Towards an institutionalist approach to urban and regional resilience. *Raumforschung und Raumordnung*, 70 (4), 285–291.

Lefebvre, H. (1992) *The production of space.* Oxford and Cambridge, MA, Blackwell.

Leigland, J. & Russell, H. (2009) *Another lost decade? Effects of the financial crisis on project finance for infrastructure.* Washington, DC, World Bank.

Martinez, J., Smoke, P., & Vaillancourt, F. (2009) The impact of the 2008–2009 global economic slowdown on local governments. In: United Cities and Local Governments (UCLG) (ed.) *The impacts of the global crisis on local governments.* Barcelona, United Cities and Local Governments, pp. 7–17.

Mazza, L. (2003) Appunti sul disegno di un sistema di pianificazione. *CRU – Critica della razionalità urbanistica*, 14 (1), 51–66.

Moroni, S. (2010) An evolutionary theory of institutions and a dynamic approach to reform. *Planning Theory*, 9 (4), 275–297.

Muñoz Gielen, D. & Tasan-Kok, T. (2010) Flexibility in planning and the consequences for public-value capturing in UK, Spain and the Netherlands. *European Planning Studies*, 18 (7), 1097–1131.

Nadin, V. & Stead, D. (2008) European spatial planning systems, social models and learning. *disP*, 172 (1), 35–47.

Newman, P. & Thornley, A. (1996) *Urban planning in Europe: International competition, national systems and planning projects.* London and New York, Routledge.

Olson, M. (1982) *The rise and decline of nations: Economic growth, stagflation and social rigidities.* New Haven, CT, Yale University Press.

Oosterlynck, S. & González, S. (2013) 'Don't waste a crisis': Opening up the city yet again for neoliberal experimentation. *International Journal of Urban and Regional Research*, 37 (3), 1075–1082.

Pelling, M. & Navarrete, D. M. (2011) From resilience to transformation: The adaptive cycle in two Mexican urban centers. *Ecology and Society* (16) 2. [Online] Available from: www.ecologyandsociety.org/vol.16/iss2/art11/ [accessed 20 February 2015].

Piketty, T. (2014) *Capital in the twenty-first century.* Harvard, MA, Harvard University Press.

Plotkin, S. (1987) *Keep out: The struggle for land use control.* Berkeley and Los Angeles, CA, and London, University of California Press.

Pressman, J. L. & Wildavsky, A. (1973) *Implementation.* Berkeley, CA, University of California Press.

Rhodes, R. (1997) *Understanding governance: Policy networks, governance, reflexibity and accountability.* Buckingham, Open University Press.

Romero, J., Jiménez, F., & Villoria, M. (2012) (Un)sustainable territories: Causes of the speculative bubble in Spain (1996–2010) and its territorial, environmental, and socio-political consequences. *Environment and Planning C: Government and Policy*, 30, 467–486.

Rotmans, J. & Loorbach, D. (2009) Complexity and transition management. *Journal of Industrial Ecology*, 13, 184–196.

Schumpeter, J. A. (1949) *The theory of economic development: An inquiry into profits, capital, credit, interest, and the business cycle.* Cambridge, MA, Harvard University Press.

Seixas, J. & Albet, A. (2012) *Urban governance in the south of Europe: Cultural identities and global dilemmas in urban governance in Southern Europe.* London, Ashgate.

Shiller, R. J. (2008) *The subprime solution: How today's global financial crisis happened, and what to do about it.* Princeton, NJ, and Oxford, Princeton University Press.

Smith, A., Voß, J., & Grin, J. (2010) Innovation studies and sustainability transitions: The allure of the multi-level perspective and its challenges. *Research Policy*, 39 (4), 435–448.

Taylor, N. (1998) *Urban planning theory since 1945.* London, Sage.

Van den Bergh, J. C. J. M., Trufferc, B., & Kallis, G. (2011) Environmental innovation and societal transitions: Introduction and overview. *Environmental Innovation and Societal Transitions*, 1 (1), 1–23.

Van Grunsven, L. & Smakman, F. (n.d.) *Industrial restructuring and early industry pathways in the Asian first generation NICs: The Singapore garment industry, Utrecht University.* [Online] Available from: http://econ.geo.uu.nl/peeg/peeg0507.pdf [accessed 20 February 2015].

Walker, B. & Salt, D. (2012) *Resilience practice: Building capacity to absorb disturbance and maintain function*. Washington, DC, Island Press/Center for Resource Economics.

Westley, F., Olsson, P., Folke, C., Homer-Dixon, T., Vredenburg, H., Loorbach, D., Thompson, J., Nilsson, M., Lambin, E., Sendzimir, J., Banerjee, B., Galaz, V., & Van der Leeuw, S. (2011) Tipping toward sustainability: Emerging pathways of transformation. *Ambio* 40 (7), 762–780. [Online] Available from: http://link.springer.com/article/10.1007%2Fs13280-011-0186-9 [accessed 20 February 2015].

Zandi, M. (2010) *Financial shock*. Upper Saddle River, NJ, FT Press.

Part II

Origins of the crisis and its socio-spatial impacts on Southern European cities

5 The neoliberal model of the city in Southern Europe

A comparative approach to Valencia and Madrid

Juan Romero, Carme Melo, and Dolores Brandis

Introduction

Since 2007 the Spanish economy has faced the worst financial and economic crisis of the past 50 years. The effects of such a deep recession are well known: growth in unemployment, intensification of public debts, an increase of poverty and inequality, the rise of socio-economic divides, loss of trust in institutions, and political discontent. These consequences become dramatically visible in cities.

The turmoil generated by the global financial system, limitless and unregulated since the 1980s, alongside the specific deficits of the Spanish institutional framework, such as its support of a growth model based on residential construction (Romero, Jiménez, & Villoria, 2012), ineffective accountability mechanisms, low-quality local and regional government institutions (Lapuente, 2009), flexible and discretionary land-use legislation (Iglesias, 2007), and a growing need for revenue at the local and regional levels of government (Fernández, 2008), have led to an unparalleled crisis. Following the trend in other parts of the world, such as Latin America and the United States, where financial markets had also been deregulated three decades earlier, Spain joined the group of countries that received a huge amount of financial capital injected into the home building industry in a scenario of abundant global liquidity.

The socialist government of Rodríguez Zapatero (2004–2011) was unable to pave the ground for a way out of the crisis, based on a different and distinctive model. When the situation seriously deteriorated, he was compelled to accept a series of social cuts following the neoliberal paradigm. This led to the worst electoral defeat of the socialist party in the democratic era, and to the absolute majority of the conservative party in the 2011 elections. National, regional, and local conservative governments have thereafter backed a series of measures responding to a clearly defined political strategy: a great reduction in social public spending, privatisation of the welfare state, and a major boost for political recentralisation processes.

In this chapter, the scope and the outcomes of these measures are analysed. Particular attention is paid to the effects they have had on the Spanish urban and metropolitan regions of Madrid and Valencia, where the conservative governments have been hegemonic for two decades at both the local and regional levels. Although there are other soft versions of the neoliberal city, namely Barcelona and Bilbao (Capel, 2003; Borja, 2010; Cucó, 2013b), there is consensus among academics that Madrid and Valencia represent paradigmatic examples of neoliberal thought applied to city administration (Rodríguez, García, & Muñoz, 2013).

The chapter proceeds as follows. First, the 'neoliberal turn' in Spanish city policy is explained, with a focus on its implications for urban development and the social divide in Spain and in both case studies, Madrid and Valencia. The application of the neoliberal model of urbanism is illustrated through an analysis of these two urban and Metropolitan Areas. The consequences that neoliberal strategies have had for these cities are assessed. Finally, recommendations that could be further developed into an agenda for both studied cases are summarised.

The neoliberal model of production and reproduction of the city

The 'neoliberal turn' in city policies took place in Spain in the second half of the twentieth century and has served the interests of the elite thereafter. Although there are specific local contexts, the basic characteristics of this model can be summarised along these lines: (a) consolidation of the real estate business as the driving force of economic activity, a process favoured by the adoption of the euro; (b) significant changes in both state and regional urban development legislation, resulting in intense and dispersed urbanisation and large residential developments; (c) mortgage law reform, which led to the financialisation of land and its inclusion in global capital circuits; (d) promotion of 'entrepreneurial urbanism' through solid coalitions between financial societies, land developers, and local and regional authorities; (e) public investment in mega events, great projects, and immense infrastructures (Díaz, 2013; Vives & Rullán, 2014).

The cases of Madrid and Valencia, among others, exemplify the implementation of the described model, which is at odds with the right to the city and good government of the territory claimed for metropolitan regions. Here urban development is not a vehicle for the improvement of the economic and demographic situation of the city, nor is it a means to channel the spatial effects of urbanisation (Pinson, 2011), rather, it is orientated towards unconditional growth and the privatisation of services and public space (Méndez, 2013).

In this approach, analysed among others by the scholars José Manuel Naredo and Fernando Gaja, territorial planning falls into the realm of the responsibilities of local governments. These, in turn, transfer the definition and implementation of urban development policies to the elite. Consequently, regulatory planning is rejected, metropolitan forms of governing the territory are absent, public–private partnerships are privileged, the role of the public sphere in the provision of public services is reduced, public space is gradually privatised, and participatory democratic processes are undermined. In addition, there is a tendency to favour singular urban projects and mega events. Planning is thus no longer conceived as a means for territorial coherence and protection of the general interest. It becomes, instead, a tool in the hands of partisan economic interests (Naredo, 2010; Gaja, 2013).

Conceptualising urbanism in the above way means providing the consolidated city with a series of urban transformations that seek to reproduce given spaces. This is achieved through strategic planning and executed by means of individual projects and author architectures, addressing the challenges of globalisation and international interurban competitiveness. In this sense, Madrid has attempted to attract investors with projects such as the 'Cuatro Torres Business Area', which has been built on the foundations of the former Real Madrid Sport City and is already a hallmark of the new city skyline, or the 'Operación Chamartín', located along rail land in the north of the city and paralysed by the real estate crisis. The case of Valencia has proved to be even more striking and unfortunate. Political leaders promoted great iconic urban projects and sport events such as 'The City of Arts and Sciences', 'The America's Cup', and 'Formula 1 Street Circuit'. The result has been enormous public sector investment in infrastructures of doubtful profitability and sometimes even failed projects.

As will be illustrated later in the chapter, proposals fostering urban growth in the city outskirts abound in the neoliberal urbanism model, with peripheral areas being valued as potential building land and subjugated to the logics of the real estate market. Territory is conceived as supporting infrastructure, encouraging any economic activity, while private agents obtain huge gains from land reclassification, urbanisation, and construction. The 1998 reform of the Urban Planning Legislation accomplished by the conservative government allowed the redefinition of the use of all the land that had previously been excluded from development. In fact, one of the basic tenets of neoliberal policy in Madrid and Valencia has been the liberalisation of land. Such a position is justified on the grounds that freedom of building will regulate the housing market. The truth is, however, that liberalisation aims at bringing the housing sector to the core of the economy, employment, and the municipal finances.

This process has been the result of a well-orchestrated strategy, embracing the financial system, urban developers, and political representatives, and applied in a deregulated and uncontrolled context that favoured a gigantic speculative real estate bubble. This created an optimal situation for new construction instead of rehabilitation, for housing conceived as investment and not as a product to be used, for market rate housing rather than social housing, for home-ownership to be prioritised over home-rental, and for surplus accumulation.

The reality of the speculative bubble proves that regional governments have promoted the reclassification of land that is not suitable for development. This has quickly made great amounts of land available in the market, and a variety of legislative and regulatory mechanisms approved by the Spanish parliament and the parliaments of the Autonomous Regions have been adopted to facilitate the management of new construction by private developers. Local administrations have benefitted greatly from this system, as wild urbanisation has become their main source of income.

This model, favoured due to growing cash flows in big cities and real estate investments, fuelled the Spanish speculative bubble, which was then inflated by the 2008 international economic and financial crisis. The crisis brought an end to the expansive phase of the Spanish economy and marked the beginning of a period of recession that is still ongoing. Needless to say, the real estate bubble and the subsequent economic crisis produced, partly, by its bursting, cannot be circumscribed to Spain and to the cities of Madrid and Valencia analysed in this contribution. Obvious differences in the time and magnitude of these two phenomena, the real estate boom, and the economic crisis, can be seen across the most economically developed parts of the world. In this respect, there is some evidence that the Spanish speculative bubble should not be compared with those of any other country in terms of the increase in housing prices, the number of affected units, and the growth of the real estate credit. Spain is among the nations that lead the world rankings in each of these different dimensions, and, if they are considered together, it is the most cited example of an unprecedented housing bubble in an economically advanced country (Campos, 2008).

Development abuses and the real estate bubble have had manifold impacts.[1] The stock of unsold new homes in Spain in June 2012 was 1.3 million, with Madrid, Barcelona, and Valencia accounting for 20.4 per cent of the total. There were unfinished developments, thousands of works brought to a halt due to a lack of funds, and scarce sales expectations. In the region of Valencia, for instance, these amounted to 8,467 hectares in 2012 (16 per cent of the residential land for development) (Burriel, 2014).

Two examples of the same process: housing developments in the residential outskirts of Madrid and government failure in the Metropolitan Area of Valencia

Housing developments in the residential outskirts of Madrid

The implementation of the neoliberal concept of urbanism described above and its consequences can be recognised, at different scales, in the production process that has taken place in several parts of the country. A focus will be placed here on the outskirts of Madrid. Reference to the production of residential outskirts is needed because the large amount of land for development brought into the market between 1991 and 1997 in the city of Madrid was used for housing. This played a key role in the quest for economic growth during the real estate boom, but it is now having a reverse effect since the first symptoms of the economic crisis became manifest in 2008 (Brandis & Río, 2007; Brandis, 2012a, 2012b). Today eroded land, empty plots, unfinished buildings, homes for sale, and an absence of infrastructure can be found in the periphery of Madrid.

The 1991 conservative local government undertook a revision of planning in order to establish a new urbanistic philosophy. As a result enough land was mobilised to guarantee a considerable number of houses. It was argued that land scarcity had generated a speculative spiral and thus expelled the citizens of

Madrid towards the metropolitan outskirts. In this way, the biggest unrivalled urban development programme aside of planning began (Brandis, 2014).

The process was backed by the regional conservative government. The 1996 *Regional Plan of Territorial Strategy* actively contributed to urbanisation by investing in infrastructure in the Metropolitan Area (Díaz, 2013). This complemented investments made by the central government, so new communication arteries were built and connected through ring roads to facilitate urbanisation. Most local governments in the Autonomous Region of Madrid approved urban planning measures to guarantee the expansion of land suitable for development and thus encouraged construction activity. This was crucial for increasing their revenues.

The Regional Plan was a gigantic project of residential extension and development grounded on big territorial reticulation intertwined with infrastructure, where productive activity became secondary. The regional *Land Law* (17 July 2001) openly approved the model of real estate hegemony, whose main pillars were logistics and housing, in other words, the control of trade flows and the construction of residential complexes, each one in its own place, according to their position in the social geography of conurbation and the status of their addresses (Roch, 2002).

The same growth-based patterns characterised the *Madrid Urban Development Plan* designed by the conservative government in 1997. The plan gave continuity to the expansive concept of urbanism initiated in 1991. Even greater amounts of land for development were brought into the market while the physical capacity of the city of Madrid was pushed towards its limits. The main reason given to justify this initiative was still price reduction, as high costs were said to be the main cause of housing scarcity. The reality revealed, however, that prices had increased notably since 1991. There was a substantial reclassification of undeveloped land that the former 1985 Plan had protected, mainly focused on the M-50 ring road, the expansion of radial motorways 2, 3, 5, and the M-45 ring road, all initiated from 1999 onwards. The aim was to build over 100,000 houses in 5,000 hectares (Brandis, 2014).

The above land development process, originated amidst the real estate boom, triggered excessive surface development, 2.5 times larger than that which had been established in the *Urban Development Plans* of 1991 and 1997, and almost doubled the number of houses. The housing needs of Madrid, which were around 5,000 homes annually, did not account for the number of planned new houses (Vinuesa & De la Riva, 2013). On top of it, over-supply did not result in a price drop because housing was seen as an enduring financial asset.

Negotiating practices were institutionalised to allow economic agents to participate safely. The aim was to facilitate the land development approved by the 1991 Urban Development Plans and the subsequent 1997 real estate developments. Buildability indices were defined and landowners were given considerable freedom to design partial plans. These measures were intended to accelerate arrangements and reduce the time frame between the elaboration of plans and the construction of houses, while restricting the participation of public administrations in the planning process.

Building contractors and real estate companies were the main urban development agents. They mobilised huge amounts of land to build new houses. Financial agencies provided abundant and cheap credit that fed the speculative bubble. Apartments and houses were sold 'off-plan', while construction was still in progress or even in those cases when it had not yet begun. Development projects were finalised, albeit individual units remained unsold. And prices did not stop rising.

It is important to note that the key features of these residential projects were oversimplification and a lack of complexity of urban forms. As a result, they have given rise to a stereotypical conglomerate that could be situated anywhere across the territory. Insularity is one of their central elements: they are located next to highways and arterial roads, and thus a connection with nearby urban areas is almost impossible. Other aspects of the finalised Urban Development Plans worth mentioning are zoning, the non-integration of uses, over-dimension of roads (a strong deterrent to pedestrian traffic), and the introversion of residential blocks with private facilities. When combined, these factors result in banal exercises of urban composition.

There are few squares and parks, and children playgrounds can be seen amidst shrubs, weeds, and an occasional dead tree (Brandis, 2013); nevertheless, the absence of public spaces as meeting places for neighbours is partly offset by private facilities, such as swimming pools, children's playgrounds, and benches. Buildings are surrounded by walls and railings so there is no place for the shops at street level that would revitalise neighbourhood life. Furthermore, the model of construction followed in Madrid has produced a new space of public use for Spanish cities: large malls. These are a central aspect of the neoliberal notion of the city as well as non-negotiable elements of planning.

The execution process of designed projects has been affected by the economic crisis. The level of completion of planned houses and the degree of occupancy provides evidence of the standstill of the sector in the middle of the economic crisis. Unfinished units and buildings not yet begun can be seen in those 7,000 hectares of periphery agreed for development from the 1990s, once designated to sustain over 200,000 dwellings. The current picture shows less than 80,000, that is 38 per cent of estimations. The profound real estate crisis and the economic difficulties faced by Spanish society point to a delayed and complicated execution of projects, especially those already behind schedule (Brandis, 2014).

The main problem concerning urbanisation in the outskirts of Madrid was not the lack of houses and land suitable for development, but, on the contrary, the excess of both land and building units, and the fact that these were underused. To this, the absence of political will by engaged actors to design coherent, balanced, and sustainable public policy should be added. The institutional framework was favourable for the housing industry, which became the national industry par excellence. The price to be paid for this was too high: unoccupied houses, unmet housing needs, thousands of mortgages throughout the country, and a vast amount of construction work, which had a negative impact on people's quality of life, the urban heritage, and the surrounding ecosystems.

Research by the Madrid Metropolitan Observatory (Rodríguez, García, & Muñoz, 2013) shows that the real estate cycle reached spectacular dimensions: 50,000 hectares were compromised for housing development between 1993 and 2003 in the Autonomous Region of Madrid. A total of 180,000 new houses were planned in emerging Madrid city neighbourhoods, while in the Autonomous Region of Madrid 800,000 dwellings were built between 1995 and 2008. These facts were shaped by a number of large urban planning operations, as mentioned earlier, and important sums of public investment in infrastructure (for example, kilometres of motorways and other high capacity roads doubled in the region).

Government failure in the urban and metropolitan region of Valencia

The case of Valencia has basic similarities with that of Madrid. Policies of identical orientation were implemented here as well; however, the Valencia model was not centred on intensive urbanisation of the Metropolitan Area. The local and regional governments focused instead on large real estate developments, mega-events, and investment in individualised big city projects through ad hoc *Partial Plans* and *Integrated Action Plans*. For more than 20 years conservative governments have enforced a model of city disguised as false modernity and based on the irresponsible abuse of public spending. Such a model rests upon well-defined elements: the construction industry as a key economic activity (which has brought debts to households and companies), big projects, and mega events (costly and ill-considered).

Recent work assesses public expenditure in big projects in the city of Valencia: 'The America's Cup' (€2,064 million), 'The City of Arts and Sciences' (€1,300 million approx.), and 'Formula 1 Street Circuit' (€235 million approx.) (Gaja, 2013). Despite the large sums of money invested in them, projects and events like these have been reduced in the aftermath to what Sánchez Ferlosio (1999) has termed 'empty boxes'. Such enterprises were sometimes prioritised over urban policies that would benefit the entire city. This has led to a risk of a split between the different areas that coexist within the city, insofar as there is general perception among the citizenry that there is one city to be visited and another, less glamorous, neglected city to live in. The failed attempt to consolidate a permanent 'Formula 1 Street Circuit' illustrates the ephemeral and ultramodern ideology inspiring the project of neoliberal Valencia over the last two decades (Ruiz & Santamarina, 2013).

The frustrated project of a 'spectacularised neoliberal city' has had consequences in the 'hidden city' which now become visible: the privatisation of urban space, an increase in regional and municipal public debt, material and symbolic relegation of some neighbourhoods, and unfinished, abandoned, or underused buildings and infrastructures (Hernández & Torres, 2013). The contrast between the two cities has been sharpened by two circumstances: the local government's decision to reduce the number of public services, and increasing fragmentation, inequality, and precariousness (Torres & García, 2013a).

The unsustainable model applied in Valencia in recent years has placed the city and the region in a very difficult situation. It could be argued that the Autonomous Region of Valencia is now a sort of *failed region* in which the capital, Valencia, faces a precarious economic situation and a high level of public debt (€968 million in 2013, according to data facilitated by the Bank of Spain in December 2013) that compromises the potential for good city government. This is the outcome of 15 years of the speculative housing bubble and erratic political management since the boom in 2007. According to Eugenio Burriel, there was a formidable residential and industrial land bubble, with rates over those of other Autonomous Regions, such as the Bask Country or Catalonia. Unlike Valencia, these regions 'implemented measures to set limits on land reclassification and low-density urbanization, and adopted a very rigorous supramunicipal territorial planning' (Burriel, 2014: p. 119).

The neoliberal model of city government has neglected to lead new forms of coordination at the metropolitan scale. In this sense, the metropolitan region of Valencia has a particular feature worth mentioning in this context. In addition to the 'real city', it has one of the five biggest *Huertas*[2] of the western Mediterranean area (Stanners & Bourdeau, 1995). Few European cities have such a privileged and valuable environment; however, nobody ensures its protection. Political actors in both the autonomous region and local government have proven unable to develop a meaningful policy for sustainable planning and management, and to devise coordination strategies at the metropolitan scale (Romero & Farinós, 2013). The periurban *Huerta* thus remains vulnerable to abuse.

The *Huerta* of Valencia was confronted with the same processes of dispersion of economic and residential activity faced by any Spanish large Metropolitan Area in recent years. Tremendous and chaotic development expansion, the disorganised localisation of industrial activities and services, land speculation, and environmental degradation are the effects of the lack of planning at the metropolitan scale and the passivity of the public administrations involved. Governments have not fulfilled their territorial planning responsibilities and failed to establish supra-local frameworks of planning and management. The neglect of farmers' needs must also be mentioned here. They should have been the key agents in the definition of a different system of production and consumption, one that is more sustainable and centred on localised agriculture (Romero & Francés, 2012).

No single democratic government has effectively attempted to overcome the lack of territorial management at the metropolitan level, to redress the rapid deterioration of one of the most amazing cultural landscapes of the Mediterranean basin, or to advance an agro-ecological model based on sustainable production, quality of life, and a conception of the agricultural space as a strategic reserve. The unfinished *Territorial Action Plan for the Protection of the Huerta of Valencia* (subjected to a public consultation process in 2010 and later abandoned by the regional government) is the last failure.

The neoliberal strategy of city government: austerity, public expenditure cuts, and privatisation policies

The *Stability Programme Update* sets the target of reducing public expenditure, from 45.2 per cent of GDP in 2010 to 39.7 per cent in 2017 (MINHAP, 2013). Such a decrease places Spain almost 25 per cent below the European average in the relative size of the public sector and, thus, in the welfare state's scope and provision. Table 5.1 shows the public expenditure breakdown.

Most cuts in social policy accepted by the Spanish government in the *Stability Programme*, vis-à-vis the EU, correspond to the Autonomous Regions and local governments. These are the levels of government responsible for most public social policy (education, health, and social services) (Romero, Collado, & Rodríguez, 2014). It is also important to highlight the existence of enormous asymmetries in the distribution of territorialised public spending in Spain, and the differences in funding per inhabitant to deal with public services, which fall under the competence of Autonomous Regions and materialise in cities. In this sense, the latest reports indicate that the Autonomous Region of Valencia is the most damaged, while the Region of Madrid has a better level of revenue due to being the country's capital and fiscal residence of large corporations (De la Fuente, Barberán, & Uriel, 2014).

Given that these policies take shape in cities, it is obvious that their impacts are also rendered more visible in cities. Several studies demonstrate the profound social consequences of these processes, for both the cases of Madrid (Canosa & García, 2014) and Valencia (Torres & García, 2013b; Cucó, 2013a).

Table 5.1 Expenditure breakdown: Stability Programme Spain, 2011–2016

Public expenditure	2011 (% of GDP)	2016 (% of GDP)	% variation of expenditure in the GDP
1 Public general services	5.7	6.1	7.2
2 Defence	1.1	0.8	−20.6
3 Public order and security	2.2	1.7	−22.4
4 Economic affairs	5.3	3.3	−38.0
5 Environmental protection	0.9	0.6	−30.6
6 Housing and community services	0.6	0.4	−42.4
7 Health	6.3	5.4	−15.6
8 Recreational activities, culture and religion	1.5	1.0	−36.1
9 Education	4.7	4.0	−15.7
10 Social production	16.9	16.6	−1.8
Total expenditure	45.2	39.7	−12.0

Source: authors' visualisation based on data from the Ministry of the Finance and Public Administrations, Stability Programme Update Spain 2013–2016, 26 April 2013.

Rise of poverty and social inequality

Available data is conclusive in pointing to the consequences of 'governing for the elite' (Oxfam Intermón, 2014). The recession has triggered a notable increase in poverty since 2008 in Spain, with alarming levels in some Autonomous Regions (Herrero, Soler, & Villar, 2012) and social segments. Analyses also reveal 'an increase in inequality slightly higher than average in the EU countries' (Ayala, Martínez, & Ruiz-Huerta, 2013: p. 52).[3] Experts agree on the most important trends: (a) the crisis has had a worst effect on employment in Spain than average in the EU territory; (b) inequality has risen more than ever, as revealed since information on annual household income was made available; (c) low-income households have reduced their income most considerably, whereas high-income family units have seen their resources decrease to a lesser extent; (d) Spain has shown limited capacity to tackle rising inequality through its tax and benefits system, while the processes of economic impoverishment and descendent social mobility are worsened by cuts in social protection; this affects income and equality of opportunities, and has a remarkable impact on vulnerable groups such as young people, migrants, women, and the long-term unemployed (Ayala, Martínez, & Ruiz-Huerta, 2013; Davia, 2013; Gradín & Del Río, 2013; FOESSA, 2014; Schraad-Tischler & Kroll, 2014).

These statements are supported by empirical evidence, which renders Spain a peculiar case:

a   The social divide has increased considerably between 2007 and 2013. In 2007, 16.3 per cent of the population faced 'severe and moderate exclusion', whereas in 2013 the percentage was over 25 per cent (FOESSA, 2014). The recent report 'Social justice in the EU' also states that:

> Developments in Italy and Spain suggest a similar trajectory for poverty as that seen in Greece. In both Italy and Spain, the crisis has facilitated a significant increase in the numbers of those at risk of poverty and social exclusion. In 2007, a total of 23.3 percent of Spain's population was already affected; by 2013, this rate had risen to 27.3 percent. In Italy, meanwhile, about 28.4 percent of people in 2013 were at risk of poverty and social exclusion. The rate of serious material deprivation increased there from 6.8 percent to 12.4 percent between 2007 and 2013.
>
> (Schraad-Tischler & Kroll, 2014: p. 24)

b   Exclusion from work is the most important dimension of social exclusion, evolving from 16.9 per cent in 2007 to 41.5 per cent in 2013. Although it is the most important, however, this is not the only type of exclusion. Young people to age 29 are the most vulnerable group. The exclusion process intensifies amongst migrants and youth affected by early school-leaving in the absence of compulsory studies. In fact, premature school dropouts are a negative element, a point to which we will return later. What is more, as indicated in the *Social Justice Index*, Spain is second-highest of all 28 EU member states in almost all categories analysed, namely unemployment, long-term unemployment, temporary jobs, and poor workers. Expert opinion is clear:

> Of course, the crisis-stricken countries of southern Europe in particular can only dream of having the investment flexibility to enable this degree of support for active labor market policies. The drastic austerity policies there have led to massive financial cuts in nearly all policy areas.
>
> (Schraad-Tischler & Kroll, 2014: p. 54)

c The recession has had a stronger impact on low-income households. Transition from medium to low income has risen, yet bottom-up progress (more frequent prior to the crisis) has decreased. A total of 10 per cent of higher income units have remained stable or even increased, whilst 10 per cent of lower income units are still falling (FOESSA, 2014).

d Inequity in wealth distribution has been largely produced by factors such as wage inequality, income instability, and the Spanish occupational structure, characterised by a high proportion of manual occupations (in 2007, the volume of employment in the construction sector was the highest in Europe). Spain has been dependent on productive sectors closely related to economic cycles, and, therefore, the crisis has destroyed many more jobs in Spain than elsewhere (FOESSA, 2014). Consequently:

> It is little surprise that Spain and Greece, each of which suffered considerably during the recent crisis years, fall clearly at the tail end of the rankings. Youth unemployment rates in both countries now stand well above 50 percent; given the lack of prospects for young people in these countries, this must be regarded as a lost generation.
>
> (Schraad-Tischler & Kroll, 2014: p. 42)

e Public policies have lost redistributive capacities since the beginning of the crisis. The amount of households receiving social aid was 29.9 per cent in 2007, 23.1 per cent in 2009, and 17.8 per cent in 2013. Nevertheless, 'mutual aid' and 'refamiliarisation' processes have become significant (43.4 per cent in 2007, 50.1 per cent in 2009, and 52.6 per cent in 2013) (FOESSA, 2014). This type of aid softens the negative impact of insufficient public policies and increased social exclusion.

Neoliberal city policies have deepened urban segregation, and recession has accentuated the housing problem; however, governments have not made enough effort to ameliorate the social emergency situation in Spain. The regional government of Madrid provides a good example: in 2003 it decided to sell state-subsidised houses to the Goldman-Sachs investment fund. This means that subsidised houses now belong to a private investor, a situation that is creating many tensions and conflicts with the occupants. Eviction processes have already started.

Differences at the regional level become significant in the Spanish case (Méndez, 2013). Regions where the urban development process generated a great deal of activity and employment in the building sector have been struck harder by the real estate crisis. Unemployment, urban poverty growth, and social exclusion are therefore higher in certain urban and metropolitan regions, like Madrid, and coastal areas such as Valencia.

The urban area of Valencia deserves special attention, as it is where unemployment indicators have worsened rapidly since 2008 (Pitarch, 2014; Salom & Albertos, 2014). These declining processes have had an impact on the central city and its historical centres, as well as on industrial metropolitan belts. For example, households in the Autonomous Region of Valencia are more exposed to vulnerabilities than the Spanish average, with 26 per cent of them facing social exclusion processes (69.8 per cent more than in 2007); one out of three people live in a state of social exclusion; child poverty is around 25 per cent; 49.5 per cent of citizens are suffering work-related exclusion; the unemployment amongst under-25-year-olds was 57.84 per cent in the second trimester of 2014; one out of three people are affected by residential exclusion; and 13 per cent of households are dealing with problems in securing a balanced diet (Lluch, Esteve, & Gimeno, 2014). A similar process of growing polarisation, deprivation, and social fragmentation characterised by a transition towards 'hourglass-shape' social structures is taking place in the city of Madrid (Rodríguez, García, & Muñoz, 2013).

Educational inequality and segregation: the great social divide

The real estate bubble and the economic crisis further aggravated the already delicate state of education and training in Spain, particularly among the thousands of youths who abandoned the education system too early. In recent studies, Spain features last of all 28 EU member states:

> 'Spain, with an early school-leaving rate of 23.6 percent, is currently the farthest from the overall low rates in Croatia and Slovenia, even though a reduction in early school-leaving figures has been observed here in recent years; in 2008, the early leaving rate of 18 to 24-year-olds was 31.7 percent. The SGI country experts describe a mixed picture in terms of developments and prospects in the Spanish educational system, in large part due to the current austerity policies' (Schraad-Tischler & Kroll, 2014: p. 42). As a result, today many people are trapped in the vicious circle of unemployment, precarious work, low income and lack of social mobility. The cutting of education expenditure will exacerbate this situation.
>
> (Fundación 1° de Mayo, 2013)

These facts all explain why the commitment with Brussels undertaken by the current government breeds rejection, a commitment to reduce 15.7 per cent of public spending in education by 2017, a decrease from 4.7 to 4.0 per cent of the GDP. A target like this was established by the *Stability Programme Update of*

Spain 2013–2016, mentioned earlier in the text, but the cuts are even higher when compared to levels in 2007. This is a dangerous reduction of public expenditure in education for a country that is far from the EU average.

The insufficient number of teachers, forced retirement, and the prohibition on replacing retired teachers, the frozen system of promotion, the rise in the number of students in a classroom, the increase of academic fees while cutting the number of scholarships, the lower budget for public schools and universities, and the attacks on the public system of scientific and technological research, are among the factors that will have negative and lasting consequences on Spanish society as a whole. There will be a reduction in spending of €200 million in comparison to the 2012–2013 academic year, and the recent announcement made by the government indicating that scholarships will be partially replaced by a loan system similar to the Anglo-North-American one, should not be underestimated. All these circumstances undermine society's capacity for innovation and adaptation to changes in the productive system.

Some of the consequences of these measures are already visible: brain drain, non-completion of higher education, difficulties in affording postgraduate studies for children in families with modest income, the suppression of teaching positions in the public education system, a decrease in the number of schools (especially in rural areas), overcrowded classrooms in urban centres, and a lack of teachers for students with special needs.

Madrid and Valencia were at the forefront of the 'conservative revolution' in Spain (Játiva, 2013). As well as cuts in public expenditure, the conservative regional and local governments in both Autonomous Regions implemented their own ideological agenda. Initiatives adopted, and described above, did not respond to recession, but aimed to undermine public education while funding private education institutions with public funds.

The right to health under attack

The Spanish government has assumed a 15.6 per cent reduction of public expenditure in health between 2011 and 2017, that is, from 6.3 to 5.4 per cent of the GDP (MINHAP, 2013). This implies a decrease of nearly €10,000, although cuts are more intense if the 2007–2017 period is considered (Table 5.1). At the same time, the conservative government has long been accomplishing a series of privatisations of the public health system in some Autonomous Regions (well before the recession started), for ideological reasons unrelated to efficient management. Privatisation started in the Autonomous Region of Valencia. This was the first region to introduce different mechanisms for the private management of public hospitals and the externalisation of services, starting at the Metropolitan Hospital of Alzira and later implemented in other public health centres.

The *2004–2007 Plan of Health Infrastructures* applied the model adopted in Valencia to the Autonomous Region of Madrid. Eight new hospitals were built with public money, although construction, maintenance, and operation were assigned to private companies for a period of up to 30 years and in exchange for tax. Similarly, the provision of certain basic services was privatised (Rodríguez, García, & Muñoz, 2013). Since the beginning of the recession, the Autonomous Region of Madrid has attempted to hand over several regional hospitals, virtually under an oligopoly regime, to investment groups made up of banks, service businesses, and national as well as international investment funds. Notwithstanding, this effort has partially failed due to the active mobilisation of social movements against privatisation. Another significant step backwards for the health system has been the violation of the rights of dependent people and their families. In suppressing these rights, the new 2012 legislation has destroyed a crucial sector of social services that served to complement and improve the health system (Observatorio de la Dependencia, 2013).

Cuts to the health budget affect staff, maintenance, investment, and pharmacy. Although there is not enough, or complete data yet, it is nonetheless possible to draw some conclusions about the impacts: (a) reduction of the number of health care centres and closure of the evening service (affecting, above all, citizens in rural areas); (b) long waiting lists (the number of patients on the waiting list as well as the waiting time reached record levels in 2013 and will presumably continue to grow); (c) congestion of emergency units; (d) a decrease in the number and scope of services offered and an obligation to pay for services provided free of charge in the past, such as non-urgent ambulance transportation and prosthesis; (e) the introduction of co-payment; (f) fewer professionals (compulsory retirement, vacancies unfilled, reduction of replacements); (g) prohibition to provide health care to undocumented migrant people; and (h) deterioration of health centres. These measures are undermining the Spanish health system, which was once among the world's top ten and is nonetheless still placed in a good position within the EU (Schraad-Tischler & Kroll, 2014). Citizens therefore distrust these reforms and claim a public health regime, as made evident by the 2012 *Health Barometer* (CIS & MSSSI, 2013).

Most social public policies in Spain, including both legislation development and funding, are competencies of the Autonomous Regions. Local governments also have some competencies, especially with regards to social services. For this reason, the evolution of social public spending in the city of Madrid, the only one for which there is available data, has been included (Table 5.2) in order to reflect on whether the evolution of social public expenditure has been paralleled by an increase in social needs triggered by the crisis. The table illustrates that the local government's approach, based on cuts in public spending, is coherent with the regional position.

Political disaffection and new social movements

Urban discontent has emerged out of the crisis. A variety of reasons can be put forward to explain such disappointment: an increase in material difficulties; reduction, deterioration, or suppression of public services; deprivation, insecurity, and uncertainty; low-quality democracy, corruption, discredit of politics and institutions, and political party endogamy.

Table 5.2 Evolution of social expenditure by Madrid City Council, Family and Social Services Area, 2008, 2010, 2011, and 2013 – final budgets on 31 December (in € millions)

	2008	2010	2011	2013*
Direction and management	9,207.287	9,820,186	9,011,183	9,309,221
Cooperation to development	20,480.05	15,965,651	1,652,432	–
Family, childhood, and voluntary service	25,702.30	27,314,476	28,430,053	33,601,315
Care for homeless people	14,100.56	16,813,589	13,257,397	–
Social emergency	5,878,024	7,297,339	5,920,473	25,623,031
Immigration	14,544.16	12,170,925	10,239,096	–
Social services	18,622,058	20,121,939	9,319,774	–
Equality, women, and conciliation	18,860,376	17,994000	12,590,912	34,271,678
Care for the elderly	31,167,802	39,556,914	34,015,753	76,214,098
Centres for elderly people	40,559,600	60,432,018	41,917,665	28,377,495
Education centres	31,081,270	42,693,546	36,125,335	–
Education services	7,335,215	7,231,654	5,060,328	5,650,904
Youth	3,770,062	2,820,277	1,665,734	2,138,235
Family and social services	701,663	740707	956,826	614,349
Total family and social services area	**242,010,421**	**280,969,221**	**210,162,961**	**198,725,061**

Source: authors' visualisation based on data from Madrid City Hall, Technical General Secretary, various years.

Note

* Criteria are different for 2013 since Madrid City Hall regrouped some of the former sections.

It could be argued that Spain is facing a gradual crisis of large traditional political parties and the emergence of new urban social movements, like the *Indignados* movement or the massive citizen protests in favour of public health and education (best known as 'citizen tides' and especially present in Madrid). These phenomena respond to a different conception of reality, politics, democracy, and civic engagement. They point to a break from the traditional politics that should not be read as a generational issue. Movements such as *Podemos* ('We can') have been able to channel some of the urban disappointment. The unexpected electoral result of *Podemos* in the recent European elections (1.2 million votes and five MEPs) highlights the existence of citizen concerns, which have been ignored so far. These movements have a political dimension (Castells, 2011). It is interesting to note that in Southern Europe general discontent is manifested through left-wing groupings, while in Eastern and Northern Europe citizens have turned to right-wing populism and new xenophobic political parties to express their disappointment, insecurity, and growing feelings of retreat.

Important political changes have taken place in the local and regional elections, held in May 2015. Some regions and cities, like those studied in this chapter, have been a privileged laboratory for testing neoliberal policies over more than two decades. Now these regions are facing a situation of institutional, political, social, and economic emergency. Today, 25 years later, Madrid and Valencia could also be a privileged laboratory for new political actors to develop an alternative agenda based on a new narrative.

Conclusion

The profound changes that have taken place in the last decades have struck at the foundations of the welfare state in Europe. Today's European society is more unequal and the so-called *Social Question* has re-entered the political agenda in Europe, especially in cities. Austerity measures have been tested before, and with negative results in many parts of the world (Oxfam Intermón, 2013), however, they are dominant in Europe. If these policies persist, an increase in poverty and instability can be expected.

Mediterranean countries joined the welfare state very late and they did so in a different context. Despite the progress achieved, the welfare state in Southern Europe should not be compared with the *Scandinavian*, *Anglo-Saxon* and *Continental* models. EU-27 public expenditure statistics comparing education, health, and social protection spending across countries prove this (Eurostat, 2013). In the case of Spain, we consider that this is the context in which the effects of the economic crisis of the late 2000s and the applied neoliberal policies must be placed.

Economic, cultural, and social transformation in a milieu of growing 'possessive individualism' (Moreno, 2013: p. 36) and the deregulation and mercantilisation of social policy have prompted instability, segmentation, insecurity, loss of cultural referents, and fear for the future. Polarisation and social tension are the outcome of these changes. The *old European periphery* (Ireland, Portugal, Greece, and Spain) is trapped between, on the one hand, structural deficit and welfare state underdevelopment and, on the other hand, new demands against a background of change. Moreover, Spain finds itself in a complex position within Europe. It cannot compete with countries in the *European Backbone*. Eastern Europe and the emergent economies are serious competitors, as these countries can offer cheaper and better-qualified workers.

The trend in the Organisation for Economic Co-operation and Development countries points at growing inequality if current public policy is maintained (OECD, 2008, 2011a, 2011b), as inequality can coexist with economic growth. It is thus imperative to reverse this trend and introduce policies targeting the social divide. This is paramount in urban and metropolitan cities and regions, above all in places like Valencia and Madrid where the neoliberal agenda has been implemented over a long period of time.

Cities and citizens should be better 'equipped'. In this sense, Jordi Borja's (2012, 2013) suggestive and comprehensive proposal, which considers four arenas, could be a good starting point. The first arena is the institutional terrain. There is a growing awareness of the importance of institutional deficits and the role 'extractive elites' play in hindering the progress of nations and the health of democratic systems (Acemoglu & Robinson, 2012).

The second area of action relates to fighting the 'social divide' to overcome poverty, inequality, fragmentation, and urban segregation. It is necessary to bring back the true meaning of the 'right to the city'. Research done on Valencia and Madrid (Cucó, 2013a; Observatorio Metropolitano de Madrid, 2013) shows that this may be the most difficult, yet the most pressing, challenge of today; that is addressing unemployment, fragmentation processes, reproduction of segregation, diversity, and target social groups at risk.

'Thinking together' as a metropolitan region is the third suggested field. It is a basic condition to better 'equip' metropolitan and urban regions, and enhance coordination and cooperation among political agents and among public and private actors. Nevertheless, failure in government experiences at the metropolitan level is one of the most notable features of the analysed case studies of Valencia and Madrid (Romero & Farinós, 2013). In contrast, there are many examples of good practices and imaginative forms of flexible collaboration (Pinson, 2011), as well as ambitious political proposals that seek to develop an agenda for the good government of the territory in metropolitan regions (Borja, 2013).

Finally, the 'political divide' between citizens and political parties must be reduced. Democratic innovations should be tested in cities and metropolitan regions. A new generation of initiatives based on information, participation, and public consultation, such as participatory budgeting, *e-democracy*, *e-transparency*, and *e-participation* abound in European and North American cities (Smith, 2009; Gutiérrez-Rubí, 2013). They represent a way to transcend traditional representative and electoral forms of democracy.

Notes

1 For a detailed discussion of these impacts, see Fernández (2008), Burriel (2008, 2014), Campos (2008), Naredo & Montiel (2011), Romero, Jiménez, & Villoria (2012), and Vinuesa (2013).
2 Arancha Muñoz (2009: p. 3) defines the *Huerta* of Valencia as:

> *a historical structure* consisting of a dense network of water channels, a system of rural roads, and traditional buildings like the 'alquerias' or 'barracas'. It is also *the agricultural activity* for the production of traditional crops … [and] *the land irrigated by the Tribunal de las Aguas*, the oldest active jury in Europe and the responsible of sorting out any dispute among the farmers concerning the distribution of water.

3 See also OECD (2014).

References

Acemoglu, D. & Robinson, J. A. (2012) *Why nations fail?* New York, Crown Business.
Ayala, L., Martínez, R., & Ruiz-Huerta, L. (2013) Desigualdad y redistribución en los países de la OCDE. In: Fundación Alternativas (ed.) *Primer Informe sobre la Desigualdad en España*. Madrid, Fundación Alternativas, pp. 26–72.
Borja, J. (2010) *Luces y sombras del modelo Barcelona*. Barcelona, UOC.
Borja, J. (2012) El fin de la anticiudad postmodernista y el derecho a la ciudad en las regiones metropolitanas. In: Belil, M., Borja, J., & Corti, M. (eds) *Ciudades, una ecuación imposible*. Barcelona, Icaria, pp. 279–320.
Borja, J. (2013) *Revolución urbana y derechos ciudadanos*. Madrid, Alianza Editorial.
Brandis, D. (2012a) Los grandes desarrollos residenciales de la periferia de Madrid: De la burbuja a la crisis inmobiliaria. In: Delgado, C., Juaristi, J., & Tomé, S. (eds) *Ciudades y paisajes en el siglo XXI*. Santander, Estudio, pp. 241–261.
Brandis, D. (2012b) El estancamiento de los últimos desarrollos urbanos de la periferia madrileña: Crisis inmobiliaria y estrategias de ordenación. In: Miramontes, A., Royé, D., & Villa, J. I. (eds) *Las ciudades y el sistema urbano: Reflexiones en tiempos de crisis*. Santiago de Compostela, Meubook, pp. 111–120.
Brandis, D. (2013) La crisis de los espacios públicos. In: Club de Debates Urbanos (ed.) *Madrid: Materia de debate* (Vol. III). Madrid, Club de Debates Urbanos, pp. 301–314.
Brandis, D. (2014) La producción inmobiliaria de la periferia madrileña (1991–2013). In: Michelini, J. J. (ed.) *Desafíos metropolitanos*. Madrid, La Catarata, pp. 169–189.
Brandis, D. & Río, I. (2007) Los últimos desarrollos urbanos en la periferia de la ciudad de Madrid. In: Artigues, A., Bauzá, A., Blázquez, M., González, J. M., Murray, I., & Rullán, O. (eds) *Los procesos urbanos postfordistas*. Actas del VIII Coloquio y Jornadas de Campo de Geografía Urbana, Palma, AGE/Universitat de les Illes Balears, pp. 71–87.
Burriel, E. (2008) La década prodigiosa del urbanismo español. *Scripta Nova*, XII (270). [Online] Available from: www.ub.edu/geocrit/sn/sn-270/sn-270-64.htm [accessed 7 December 2014].
Burriel, E. (2014) El estallido de la burbuja inmobiliaria y sus efectos en el territorio. In: Albertos, J. M. & Sánchez, J. L. (eds) *Geografía de la crisis económica en España*. Valencia, PUV, pp. 101–140.
Campos, J. L. (2008) *La burbuja inmobiliaria*. Madrid, Marcial Pons.
Canosa, E. & García, A. (2014) Segregación y fragmentación social en la región urbana madrileña: Los modelos residenciales de las clases altas en la ciudad. In: Michelini, J. J. (ed.) *Desafíos metropolitanos*. Madrid, La Catarata, pp. 124–145.

Capel, H. (2003) A modo de introducción: Los problemas de las ciudades: Urbs, civitas y polis. In: Capel, H. (ed.). *Ciudades, arquitectura y espacio urbano.* Almería, Caja Rural Intermediterránea, pp. 9–22.

Castells, M. (2011) Situarse fuera del sistema político para obligarlo a cambiar. *La Vanguardia*, 22 October.

CIS (Centro de Investigaciones Sociológicas) & MSSSI (Ministry of Health, Social Services and Equality) (2013) *Barómetro Sanitario, 2012.* [Online] Available from: www.msssi.gob.es/estadEstudios/estadisticas/sisInfSanSNS/informeAnual2012.htm [accessed 18 December 2014].

Cucó, J. (ed.) (2013a) *La ciudad pervertida: Una mirada sobre la Valencia global.* Madrid, Anthropos.

Cucó, J. (2013b) Éxitos y perversiones en las fórmulas neoliberals: Los contrastes entre Barcelona, Bilbao y Valencia. In: Cucó, J. (ed.) *La ciudad pervertida: Una mirada sobre la Valencia global.* Madrid, Anthropos, pp. 213–244.

Davia, M. A. (2013) Mercado de trabajo y desigualdad. In: Funfación Alternativas (ed.) *Primer informe sobre la desigualad en España.* Madrid, Fundación Alternativas, pp. 75–133.

De la Fuente, A., Barberán, R., & Uriel, E. (2014) Un sistema de cuentas públicas territorializadas para España: Metodología y resultados para 2011. *Fedea, Estudios sobre Economía Española*, 2014/03, 1–59.

Díaz, F. (2013) Sociedad, espacio y crisis de la ciudad neoliberal. In: Cucó, J. (ed.) *Metamorfosis urbanas: Ciudades españolas en la dinámica global.* Barcelona, Icaria, pp. 81–107.

Fernández, R. (2008) El Tsunami urbanizador español y mundial. *Boletín CF+S*. 38/39. [Online] Available from: http://habitat.aq.upm.es/boletin/n38/arfer.html [accessed 7 September 2014].

FOESSA Foundation (2014) *VII report on exclusion and social development in Spain.* Madrid, FOESSA.

Eurostat (2013) *European social statistics* (2013 edn). European Union.

Fundación 1º de Mayo (2013) *Educación de calidad para empleo de calidad.* Madrid, Fundación 1º de Mayo.

Gaja, F. (2013) Tras el tsunami inmobiliario: Salir del atolladero. In: Observatorio Metropolitano (ed.) *Paisajes devastados después del ciclo inmobiliario: Impactos regionales y urbanos de la crisis.* Madrid, Traficantes de Sueños, pp. 313–353.

Gradín, C. & Del Río, C. (2013) El desempleo de inmigrantes, mujeres y jóvenes. In: Fundación Alternativas (ed.) *Primer informe sobre la desigualad en España.* Madrid, Fundación Alternativas, pp. 136–191.

Gutiérrez-Rubí, A. (2013) Queremos legislar. *El País*, 24 March 2013.

Hernández, G. M. & Torres, F. (2013) El impacto de la Valencia glocalizada en el Centro Histórico popular. In: Cucó, J. (ed.) *La ciudad pervertida: Una mirada sobre la Valencia global.* Madrid, Anthropos, pp. 19–40.

Herrero, C., Soler, A., & Villar, A. (2012) *La pobreza en España y sus Comunidades Autónomas.* Valencia, IVIE.

Iglesias, F. (ed.) (2007) *Urbanismo y democracia: Alternativas para evitar la corrupción.* Madrid, Fundación Alternativas.

Játiva, J. M. (2013) Catalá impulsa una revolución conservadora con las privatizaciones. *El País*, 2 September 2013.

Lapuente, V. (2009) Problemas institucionales y corrupción. In: Estefanía, J. (ed.) *Informe sobre la democracia en España.* Madrid, Fundación Alternativas, pp. 191–224.

Lluch, E., Esteve, E., & Gimeno, B. (2014) *Crisis y derechos sociales: Análisis y perspectivas Comunitat Valenciana 2014*. Valencia, Observatorio de Investigación sobre Pobreza y Exclusión en la Comunidad Valenciana.

Méndez, R. (2013) *Las escalas de la crisis: Ciudades y desempleo en España*. Madrid, Fundación Primero de Mayo.

MINHAP (Ministry of the Finance and Public Administration) (2013) *Actualización del programa de estabilidad del reino de España 2013–2016*. [Online] Available from: http://ec.europa.eu/europe2020/pdf/nd/sp2013_spain_es.pdf [accessed 18 December 2014].

Moreno, L. (2013) *La Europa asocial*. Madrid, Península.

Muñoz, A. (2009) The protection plan for the Valencian huerta. Paper presented at the conference *Metropolitan Landscapes*, 10–11 November 2009.

Naredo, J. M. (2010) El modelo inmobiliario español y sus consecuencias. *Boletín CF+S*, 44, 13–27.

Naredo, J. M. & Montiel, A. (2011) *El modelo inmobiliario español y su culminación en el caso valenciano*. Barcelona, Icaria.

Observatorio de la Dependencia (2013) *X dictamen del observatorio de la dependencia*. Madrid, Observatorio de la Dependencia.

Observatorio Metropolitano de Madrid (eds) (2013) *Paisajes devastados*. Madrid, Traficantes de Sueños.

OECD (2008) *Growing unequal? Income distribution and poverty in OECD countries*. Paris, OECD.

OECD (2011a) *An overview of growing income: Inequalities in OECD countries: Main findings*. Paris, OECD.

OECD (2011b) *Divided we stand: Why inequality keeps rising?* Paris, OECD.

OECD (2014) *Income inequality update: Rising inequality: Youth and poor fall further behind*. Paris, OECD.

Oxfam Intermón (2013) *La trampa de la austeridad: El verdadero coste de la desigualdad en Europa*. Madrid, Oxfam Intermón.

Oxfam Intermón (2014) *Gobernar para las élites: Secuestro democrático y desigualdad económica*. Madrid, Oxfam Intermón.

Pinson, G. (2011) *Urbanismo y gobernanza de las ciudades europeas: Gobernar la ciudad por proyecto*. Valencia, Universitat de Valencia.

Pitarch, M. D. (2014) Desigualdades regionales, pobreza y vulnerabilidad social en España durante la crisis (2007–2013). In: Albertos, J. M. & Sánchez, J. L. (eds) *Geografía de la crisis económica en España*. Valencia, PUV, pp. 201–229.

Roch, F. (2002) Agentes sociales y tendencias urbanísticas: Hegemonía inmobiliaria y pérdida de urbanidad. *Boletín CF+S*. 29/30. [Online] Available from: http://habitat.aq.upm.es/boletin/n29/afroc1.html [accessed 7 September 2014].

Rodríguez, E., García, B., & Muñoz, O. (2013) Del Madrid global a la crisis urbana. In: Observatorio Metropolitano (ed.) *Paisajes devastados después del ciclo inmobiliario: Impactos regionales y urbanos de la crisis*. Madrid, Traficantes de Sueños, pp. 123–177.

Romero, J. & Farinós, J. (2013) Cities and urban and metropolitan regions in Spain: A new agenda in a global context. In: Seixas, J. & Albet, A. (eds) *Urban governance in Southern Europe*. Farnham, Ashgate, pp. 123–148.

Romero, J. & Francés, M. (eds) (2012) *La huerta de Valencia: Un paisaje cultural con futuro incierto*. Valencia, Publicaciones de la Universidad de Valencia.

Romero, J., Collado, J. C., & Rodríguez, M. T. (2014) La economía política de la desigualdad: Los recortes en el sector público y sus repercusiones para el Estado de

Bienestar en España. In: Albertos, J. M. & Sánchez, J. L. (eds) *Geografía de la crisis económica en España*. Valencia, PUV, pp. 329–376.

Romero, J., Jiménez, F., & Villoria, M. (2012) (Un)sustainable territories: Causes of the speculative bubble in Spain (1996–2010) and its territorial, environmental, and socio-political consequences. *Environment and Planning C: Government and Policy*, 30, 467–486.

Ruiz, M. A. & Santamarina, B. (2013) La Valencia bipolar y trepidante: Discursos y representaciones sobre transformación urbana. In: Cucó, J. (ed.) *La ciudad pervertida: Una mirada sobre la Valencia global*. Madrid, Anthropos, pp. 117–140.

Salom, J. & Albertos, J. M. (2014) La crisis económica en los distritos industriales valencianos. In: Albertos, J. M. & Sánchez, J. L. (eds) *Geografía de la crisis económica en España*. Valencia, PUV, pp. 467–495.

Sánchez Ferlosio, R. (1999) *El alma y la vergüenza*. Barcelona, Destino.

Schraad-Tischler, D. & Kroll, C. (2014) *Social justice in the EU: A cross-national comparison: Social Inclusion Monitor Europe (SIM)-index report*. Bertelsmann Stiftung. [Online] Available from: www.bertelsmann-stiftung.de/en/publications/publications/publication/did/social-justice-in-the-eu-a-cross-national-comparison/ [accessed 7 September 2014].

Smith, G. (2009) *Democratic innovations*. Cambridge, Cambridge University Press.

Stanners, D. & Bourdeau, P. (eds) (1995) *Europe's environment: The Dobris assessment*. Copenhagen, European Environmental Agency.

Torres, F. & García, P. (2013a) La ciudad ocultada: Desigualdad y precarización en la Valencia global. In: Cucó, J. (ed.) *La ciudad pervertida: Una mirada sobre la Valencia global*. Madrid, Anthropos, pp. 163–188.

Torres, F. & García, P. (2013b) La ciudad fragmentada: Análisis comparativo de cuatro barrios emblemáticos. In: Cucó, J. (ed.) *La ciudad pervertida: Una mirada sobre la Valencia global*. Madrid, Anthropos, pp. 191–211.

Vinuesa, J. (2013) *El festín de la vivienda: Auge y caída del negocio inmobiliario en España*. Madrid, Díaz & Pons.

Vinuesa, J. & De la Riva, J. M. (2013) Los grandes desarrollos del PG97, un grave error de planteamiento y una amenaza para el futuro urbanístico de Madrid. In: Vinuesa, J., Porras, D., & De la Riva, J. M. (eds) *Reflexiones a propósito de la Revisión del Plan General de Madrid*. Madrid, Grupo TRYS, pp. 493–512.

Vives, S. & Rullán, O. (2014) La apropiación de las rentas del suelo en la ciudad neoliberal española. *Boletín de la Asociación de Geógrafos Españoles*, 65, 387–408.

6 Governance and local government in the Lisbon Metropolitan Area

The effects of the crisis on the reorganisation of municipal services and support for people

José Luís Crespo, Maria Manuela Mendes, and Jorge Nicolau

Introduction

Portugal is one of the countries in the European Union with the highest levels of inequality in income distribution. According to Rodrigues and Andrade (2013) the financial crisis and the austerity policies applied in 2010 have led to a fall in the efficiency of all redistributive instruments, less efficacy of social transfers, and a reversal in the previous trends of inequality and poverty reduction, and the policy measures implemented in 2012–2013 have accentuated these effects.

In this national context the financial crisis also affected the administration abilities of the organisation and provision of municipal (local) public services. The aim of this text is not to discuss the overall effects of the crisis, but to debate some that were obvious at the local level, mainly the effects on local government. The analysis presented here will focus on the Lisbon Metropolitan Area (LMA), which encompasses about 26 per cent of the Portuguese population and comprises 18 municipalities[1] with different dimensions and different realities in population, territorial, and economic terms.

Urban systems are characterised by relational webs and complex patterns of interdependence that involve actors, institutions, and functions. The manner in which cities and local government structures are organised and managed is determined by and reflects changes in the social, economic, and spatial structure of urban areas. According to a report from the World Bank (1997), the existing differences in the performance of municipalities and states can be explained, in part, by differences in governance.

To assess the level of inclusion of governance practices in urban and territorial contexts, different empirical analyses are used with the aim to ascertain whether, in the context of governance, this has eclipsed the government. Although there are 'new' political instruments, the change from government to governance can be differentiated in political jurisdictions and even in the type of instruments used.

The 'new' instruments were also adopted in the provision of public services, and are still mutating at the beginning of the century. There has been an increasing interest in innovations in the public sector. These are more responsive to the needs and aspirations of the citizens and the users of the services (Altschuler & Behn, 1997; Borins, 1998; Hartley, 2005; Moore, 2005; Mulgan & Albury, 2003; Albury, 2005; Moore & Hartley, 2008). From this perspective it is important to discuss what constitutes public sector innovation, what kind of changes in governance count as important innovations, whether they are sufficient for a rapidly changing society, and what structures and processes promote or slow down innovations (Hartley, 2006; Osborne & Brown, 2005; Moore, 2005).

Today, changes in the production systems of the public administration are evident, where the governments try to find, beyond their borders, additional resources to obtain greater operational capacity and legitimacy to achieve their goals. Some innovations involve organisational changes of governance and of the municipal services. In other cases, innovations unite elements from different organisations to create more effective ways of solving existing problems through new approaches and instruments (Skelcher, 2005). The focus of administrative practice is moving from a hierarchical government to a practice marked by greater reliance on horizontal relationships and associative forms of governance (Hill & Lynn, 2004). These changes, in line with other changes associated with networked governance, have implications for management, both in terms of organisational and interorganisational processes.

The appearance of new forms of governance is also related to the weakening of the capabilities of the administration, particularly of its financial resources. The first major driver of the economic crisis was the increase in government expenditure. The expenditures, allocated to many services, was more or less automatically affected by inflation. The states undertook the slow and gradual process of restructuring of their governmental expenditure. This has been costly for the state and has found its expression in different programmes, financed with borrowed money, which quickly led to a high budget *deficit* (Kettl, 2002).

Against the background of the above considerations, the current chapter will be structured as follows. First, the key concept of governance will be reviewed. Based on the insights gained the casual factors that equate the capacities of state administration will be discussed. Particular attention will be paid to the interplay between the financial crisis and its effects on the capacities of local government in providing public services to the communities. The chapter continues with a discussion on the recomposition of the state administration in Portugal, especially at the local level and in the municipalities' organisation models of LMA. It ends with concluding notes.

Governance – the concept of a variable geometry: between the consensus and its delimitation

In order to make governance an operational concept, it is necessary to distinguish between governability, government, and governance. Governance is understood as 'the ability to produce consistent decisions, develop effective policies or create programs' (Dente, Bobbio, & Spada, 2005: p. 47); in this chapter the term 'govern' is used to represent the activity, and the term 'government' is used as a synonym for institutional structure. It is much more efficient to govern if predetermined goals are achieved or the results are considered positive. 'Governance' is seen as a set of actions, practices, and processes that relate to government practice, while 'the government' refers to the field of political institutions and 'organisational' structures (Dente, Bobbio, & Spada, 2005).

Governance indicates a broader phenomenon in relation to the unique structure of government. From the point of view of the actors involved, the government is in fact linked to activities, which are the business of a formal authority, while governance relates to activities that follow a common purpose. The use of governance can describe the government practice if it includes not only formal governmental organisations, but also the mechanisms of informal participation of a multiplicity of actors, in order to make decisions and acts based on policy (Rhodes, 1997).

From a theoretical point of view, the term 'governance' seeks to include a diversity of forms of 'social' coordination (of actions and actors). In this context, coordination refers to the way various, but interdependent, actions are organised together to achieve specific objectives in the economic, political, etc. field. It should also be mentioned that, in models of governance, the main institutional spheres are not regarded as different areas in which the roles and functions of the system are established and repeated over time: on the contrary, in the interior, attention is given to the specific systems of action of a multiplicity of actors and interaction mechanisms, diversely institutionalised and formalised, in the relationship between them (Jessop, 1995; Jordan, Wurzel, & Zito, 2005; Dente, Bobbio, & Spada, 2005).

The consolidation of a targeted focus on specific interventions of actors in decision-making processes and government mechanisms, which are characteristics of the study of governance, highlights the multiplicity of forms and principles of action in various areas, the fragmentation of power between several levels that make up the political-administrative systems, and the plurality of internal relationships (Rhodes, 1997). In this regard, it could be argued that a relevant change occurred in the form of organisation of the state, with the overcoming of the state pyramid towards an organisational model contained in the formula of state-network.

The central feature that defines a model built on governance is, therefore, the recognition of the limits of classical separation between state, market, and civil society. The various non-institutional actors have the potential to play an active role in the definition of options and actions of common interest. In a given policy area, all actors are interdependent, because 'no one has knowledge or resources to perform a policy on their own' (Rhodes, 1997: p. 50). The outcome of the policies is not a product of the actions of a single actor or a result imposed 'from above', but derives from the interaction and negotiation between a multiplicity of actors. The relationships between the various actors also have more varied settings that combine variable characteristics and complex sets of competitive, cooperative, and confrontational interactions. From this perspective, governance is seen as a mode of action aimed at the construction of agreement frames that, instead of the predefined hierarchy of powers, include the construction of the interests at stake and the expectations of different actors (Rhodes, 1997). In short, the general framework of governance relates to problem-solving for politics (in the sense that these are associated with the achievement of collective goals or purposes) in the interior and to the specific settings of institutions, organisations, and (hierarchical) governmental and (non-hierarchical) extra-governmental practices (Jessop, 1995).

Despite the differences in the definition and characteristics of governance, there is consensus on its axial dimensions. (i) Governance refers to the emergence of 'styles' of government, in which the boundaries between the public and private sector are blurred. In this way, the state is losing its capacity as 'director' and the control is shifted to international and regional organisations, such as the EU, autonomous regions, and municipalities, or to international corporations, non-governmental organisations, and other private or semi-private agents (Dente, Bobbio, & Spada, 2005). (ii) Governance highlights the growing importance of multilevel government structures such as the EU, for the dissemination of 'new' forms of governance. This issue received encouragement by the publication of the European Commission's White Paper on European Governance (CE, 2001); however, it focuses mainly on the EU level, without giving enough attention to the way the 'new' forms of governance are (or could be) implemented in member states and at local levels of power. (iii) Governance and government are often, and especially in the more traditional political science literature, regarded as two poles on a *continuum* of different types of governing (Borlini, 2004). If the extreme form of government was the 'strong state' in the era of 'big government', then the extreme form of equality governance is essentially the self-organisation and coordination of the network of social actors. (iv) Governance is characterised by an increasing use of non-regulatory political instruments. These are proposed, designed, and executed by non-state actors, often working in partnership with state agents, but sometimes independently. However, political scholars defend the opinion that often the very essence of governance focuses on mechanisms and not on the recourse to authority and government sanctions. Thus, under an approach of 'government', society is directed by the central government, while in the model of 'governance', society is more autonomous in its decisions and does not depend only on the orientation of the government (Kooiman, 2003).

The characteristics of governance as known today are the result of evolution and are interconnected with a set of reasons for their emergence and development. In the next section an attempt will be made to identify and analyse some of these reasons.

Causal factors that equate the capacities of the state and the administration

During the 1950s and 1960s, many governments diversified their revenue system through the introduction of excise duties (for example, the value added tax); however, even these strategies could not hide the fact that the overall level of taxation had reached its maximum efficiency. Surpassing that level would probably be counterproductive since it would encourage the capital flight and tax evasion of citizens. In the 1970s, taxes in several countries had reached the maximum level.

The management of the recent financial crisis is associated with a change in the structure of revenue and expenditure. Another aspect of this issue is the reduced political support and the reluctance of the population for further tax increases, which is only surpassed by the resistance to cuts in public spending. From a governance perspective, governments are unable to transform the economy, when the expenditure patterns are politically sensitive and administratively 'blocked', and where taxes and other revenues need to be handled with some political caution. Governments have not been totally inert, because they verified that the excise duty causes less resistance than income tax and have realised that the fees and taxes related to specific expenses are more acceptable to the public (Pierre & Peters, 2000).

In this context, the economic and financial crisis has encouraged the development of new instruments of governance and governance has become an attractive philosophy and political strategy. There are three main reasons for its growing popularity: (i) involvement of private actors and organised interests in the activities of provision of public services; (ii) incorporation of the managerial type of 'thinking' from the private sector to the public sector; (iii) diversifications of the provision of public services has emerged as an attractive strategy.

The economic crisis has forced the state to become more likely to operate through networks and other forms of public–private partnerships. Since it is no longer possible to have the financial and organisational resources needed to maintain the previous level of public services, the state now 'intends' to play a coordinating role, bringing together public and private resources with few direct costs to the public budget (ibid.). The crisis has also had a profound effect on the design of the public services, today a greater emphasis on consumer choice and diversification can be seen.

The differences in the way various ideological orientations understand the performance of the state indicate that success or failure depends, to a certain extent, on the ideological framework of the observer (ibid.); however, the performance of the state should be analysed in addition to the different ideological or partisan positions. Most Western democracies seem to share a common dilemma: how to manage the expectations of voters, elected officials, and civil servants as a vehicle for the transformation of society, on the one hand, and the limited capacity of the state, on the other.

The state's fiscal crisis and the growing popular frustration with the government have constrained that perspective. The state has come to be seen as overly big and costly, unable to provide adequate services.

At the conceptual level, governance arose from the shared conviction that in a variable geometry 'the traditional structures of authority ... have failed' (Kooiman, 1993: p. 251) and that the modern state is now obliged to incorporate a cycle of (re)legitimation. 'The traditional conceptualisations' of the government, which recognises the state as the most prominent actor in public policy, are considered an outdated approach (Kooiman, 2003). Instead, the governance seeks to add 'the totality of theoretical conceptions on governing' (ibid.: p. 4) and is considered an effective 'orientation process to society' (Peters, 2002: p. 2).

The changes in principles, methodologies, and forms of collective action in the urban and territorial field, appear to be strictly linked to the transition to a new regime of capitalist accumulation (Harvey, 1989) and the crisis of the Fordism model (considered not only a model of production organisation, but also a model of economic and social regulation). Governance is convened as an adjusting model of local economies, able to be framed in the post-Fordism regime of accumulation, and specifically associated with new forms of institutions and economic and social adjustment. According to Healey (2004), the main changes seem to be related to the following two factors. The first is the partial removing of the powers and functions of the state policies, with the change in the organisational structure, which goes from the so-called 'pyramid state' to a new model of organisation of the state 'network'. The second is the presence of a new 'growth model', characterised by greater flexibility, mobility of capital, product specialisation, short production run, and less stable uses of work.

Two main changes to the current use of governance can be identified. The first relates to the involvement of an increasing number of public, private, and semi-public stakeholders in local policy action, with the redefinition of the role of local authorities. The second change relates to the growing importance assumed by policies that aim to promote local development and proactive action strategies to define cities and territories with a competitive profile.

In conclusion, as a consequence of the process of decentralisation of duties and responsibilities carried out by the state, local and regional authorities (mainly municipalities) in Portugal are responsible for the provision of a significant number of public services. To provide these services as near to the citizen as possible, a redistribution of roles is necessary so that these are provided by the most appropriate organisational structure. According to Figueiredo (2009), Portugal experiences a twin crisis: the international crisis and a crisis determined by the long and painful process of structural change of the Portuguese economy which occurred concomitantly but with demonstrations at various levels of development.

Portugal: the (re)composition of the state and the decentralisation process

The (re)composition and (re)configuration of the territories and of the public action directed to their management, in particular in urban areas, are based on factors and components with different dimensions. One is based on the reforms of the organisational, administrative, and cultural structures of the public sector, with a view to better adjust them to the contemporary needs and requirements. The logical differences and administrative reform processes, although based on relatively similar premises, have assumed different and varied shapes, built on two main logics: (i) a new public administration, and (ii) a new public management (Seixas, Branco, & Garson, 2012). The first logic is based on organisational reforms of the Weberian administration models, which maintains the perspective of the direct conduct of public services, such as the (re)structuring towards flexibility of processes; the decentralisation of the administrations of the centralised public services; and, also, towards a closer relationship between the administration and the citizens. The second logic incorporates the perspectives of management efficiency, and it is related to decisions of delegation and devolution of competences to more efficient actors; it involves shared management procedures of public services by different actors, the recourse to outsourcing, privatisation with generalist regulation of certain areas of collective management, and includes as well the alienation of other municipal positions for private urban production.

The emergence of additional structures of municipal administration in Portugal could have taken place only after the April Revolution of 1974 and the 1976 Constitution, with the formalisation of political power with the status of autonomous administration. Since then, the municipalities have taken on a growing role in the processes of development of their territories, materialised in a gradual increase of their competence in various areas (see Table 6.1).

The process of decentralisation of powers from the central administration to the local in Portugal started in the late 1980s, and together with its subsequent developments led to a significant change in the legal framework for municipal management, adjusting this to the requirements of an effective and efficient intervention of authority in the promotion of municipal development. It can be confirmed that the Act of 1984 was inadequate for the reality of the municipal administration. The consolidation of local autonomy in this period, which resulted in the decentralisation of competences in various sectors to the local authorities, assumed that the organisation of the communal services was made in such a way that would allow the local authorities to find answers to requests arising from their new duties and responsibilities (Crespo, 2013).

As Table 6.1[2] illustrates, these competences have increased the various legislative frameworks over time.

All over Europe and in Portugal, especially in the last two decades, the municipal companies as initiatives and local government have been consolidated and extensively used. This strategy seeks to explore the advantages associated with the public sector, which result from (or result in) business and organisational forms for the development of missions of public accountability. The figure of the company has also asserted itself as an organisational model for promoting a *municipal economic initiative*, and, in this context, as a response to the financial difficulties of local authorities. In a different concept, the institution of companies has also emerged as a way of developing partnerships, involving municipal entities and private partners or other public partners (Crespo, 2013).

In recent years, municipal and inter-municipal companies and institutions, with responsibilities for the management of services and areas of the local administration jurisdiction, have emerged in Portugal. These aimed to promote

Table 6.1 Evolution of the duties of the municipalities

Law No. 79/77	Decree Law No. 100/84	Law No. 159/99
Local authorities are responsible for all matters related to the corresponding interests and in particular: • to administration of own property and under their jurisdiction; • to promotion; • to public supply; • to culture and assistance; • to public health.	Local authorities are responsible for all matters related to the common and specific interests of the population and in particular: • to administration of own property and under their jurisdiction; • to development; • to public supply; • to public health and basic sanitation; • to health; • to education and teaching; • to culture, hobbies, and sports; • to environmental protection and defence and protection of the quality of life of the corresponding population; • to civil protection.	Municipalities are responsible for the following areas: • rural and urban equipment; • energy; • transport and communications; • education; • heritage, culture, and science; • hobbies and sports; • health; • social security; • housing; • civil protection; • environment and basic sanitation; • consumer protection; • promotion of development; • spatial planning and land use; • municipal policy; • external cooperation.

Source: authors' elaboration based on Conceição (2004: p. 364).

conditions of flexibility, in particular in terms of contract, and institutional articulation for greater profitability in the provision of communities services.

In this context, local authorities sought to find new forms of management of property and public interest through the transition from direct management to a business scheme, seeking partnerships with other municipalities or other public and private entities. Relationships between municipalities have been marked by the expansion of cooperation and trade systems and by increased competition (Crespo & Cabral, 2010, 2012; Crespo, 2013).

The development of inter-municipal cooperation agglomerations and municipalities poses a number of problems, related to the definition of relevant management scales. One can admit that, even though it is increasingly necessary to take into account a more diverse and broader context of spatial relations, in a supra-municipal scale, the reorganisation of administrative boundaries can allow greater efficiency in public intervention. This argument is often associated with looking for a scale that allows a better organisation of public services and a greater capacity of local government. The issue of scale has been the subject of several studies (Marshall, 1982; Porter, 1998), whose conclusions do not confirm the advantage of the agglomeration, at least in more urbanised contexts. The results of the studies do not corroborate the existence of a relationship between the local scale of the municipalities and the effectiveness of public services and claim that the latter depends on factors related to the methodology of analysis, the spatial context, the type of considered functions, and the organisational solutions adopted in its provision. Scepticism results essentially from the perception that more fragmented structures and a closer relationship to citizens can increase the accountability of services (Conceição, 2004).

Organisational models of the local administration in Portugal

The local administration represents a subdivision of the state or public administration and covers all administrative bodies, whose power refers to the interests of the population of a certain part of the national territory. It is stipulated in the Constitution of the Portuguese Republic that local authorities are part of the organisation of the state, such us municipalities, parishes, and the administrative regions (to be set up). The latest figures indicate that in Portugal there are 308 municipalities, 278 of which are on the mainland and 30 in the Autonomous Regions of the Azores and Madeira; 3,091 parishes,[3] 2,881 in the continental territory, and 210 in the islands (ANMP, 2014). Additionally, there exists a framework for the establishment of other forms of municipal organisations such as inter-municipal communities of general purpose, associations of municipalities of specific purpose, associations of parishes, large Metropolitan Areas, urban communities, and municipal and inter-municipal companies.

Local authorities have their own personnel, heritage, and finance and their management is the responsibility of the respective departments. For this reason, the guardianship of the state over the financial and heritage management of municipalities and parishes is only for inspection purposes and can only be exercised in accordance with the provisions of the law. Democracy and local autonomy are therefore safeguarded (Crespo, 2013).

In this context, to achieve efficiency, equity, and the well-being of citizens, local authorities have several management modalities for local public services. Some of these modalities will be analysed in the Portuguese case in a context of austerity, particularly the municipalities of the Lisbon Metropolitan Area.

In the 1980s legislative initiatives aimed, in an initial phase, to adapt the organisational structure of the municipalities to the new reality of urban management that began to seek principles of rationality and efficiency. Indeed, according to the principles of management and organisation listed by the regulatory decree,[4] local authorities had the ability to reset their organic structure and staff resources in order to adjust them to their needs of action in the various fields of competence, favouring the objectives and policies that they had established and using the best combination of their human, technical, and financial resources.

The recent legislation[5] revision aimed to create conditions for the local authorities to comply with their wide range of duties. These duties are related to the pursuit of either local interests or of general interests that could be pursued more effectively by the municipal administration by virtue of the close relationship with the people, within the principle of subsidiary framework. By decreasing the number of structures and decision-making levels, there was an attempt to contain the spread of functions or competences through small organic units and the use of flexible models of functioning, taking into account the staff[6] and the available technologies. Other objectives were related to the simplification, rationalisation, and the (re)engineering of administrative procedures that seek to provide efficiency, effectiveness, quality, and agility in the performance of their duties, in a logic of rationalisation of services and the establishment of transversal work methodologies through the aggregation and sharing of services (Crespo, 2013).

With this new legislation the objective was to give greater rationality and operability to local services, ensuring that a greater decision-making autonomy and a more direct accountability of the members of local government. This Decree Law also stated that the city halls and parish councils should promote review of their services until 31 December 2010.

When comparing the two periods (1984 and 2009), distinguishing features can be identified (see Table 6.2). First, in this period the scope of changes in some competences was extended and the competences of the municipal level were transferred to the parish scale. Second, the organisation model gradually changed from vertical structures to a more flexible nature and a diversity of models of organisation of services. In addition, simplifications were introduced by the creation and modification of the structures of the organisation of services. Competences and the decision (making power) moved from the centralised Municipal Assembly to various municipal organs, based on sharing and interdependency in the various organisational structures of service delivery.

Table 6.2 Distinguishing features of the organisational regimes of the municipal services

	Decree Law No. 116/84 of 6 April	*Decree Law No. 305/2009 of 23 October*
Scope	• Municipal services	• Municipalities and parishes
Organisational model	• Based on permanent vertical structures	• Diversity of organisational models
Structure	• Exceptional nature of the management of projects • Management of organic units	• Simplification of the formalities of creation and modification of structures • Management and coordination of organic units
Organisation and competences	• Centralisation of powers in the Municipal Assembly	• Sharing and interdependence of competences in various organs

Source: Crespo (2013).

The structuring principles of the organisation and functioning of the services, as referred to in the legislative framework, should be based on:

- *efficiency* and *allocation of resources*, in order to meet the public needs, assuming the best combination of available resources and minimising the cost of utilisation thereof;
- *unit* and *efficiency of action*, so that an institution is unique and effective in the pursuit of its mission to achieve its objectives, by applying the proper rules and techniques: with the unit one seeks to avoid conflict, duplication, interference, and overlap, and with efficiency one tries to achieve a greater economy, efficacy, simplification, and promptness;
- *rationalisation*, adopting measures that ensure a greater profitability and a better organisation of services and a cost–benefit balance;
- *simplification*, at internal level, through the organisation and simplification of internal circuits, and at external level, through an organisation and operation based on relationship with the citizens;
- *legality* promoting the ideal that the departments of the public administration should act in accordance with the law, within the limits of the powers conferred upon them and according to the purposes of these powers (Crespo, 2013).

In this context, there was a division of powers between the Municipal Assembly (adoption of the organisational model and acceptance of the nuclear structure), the City Hall (acceptance of the flexible structure and creation of multidisciplinary teams), and the Mayor (creation of organic subunits). This was the first period of (re)organisation and (re)adaptation of local services to a new legal framework, in which the duties and competencies resulting from the legislative framework of 1999[7] were associated.

A new act in 2012 (Status of the Ruling Personnel of Services and Bodies of the Central, Regional, and Local Administration of the State) obliged the municipalities to approve the adequacy of their organic structures to established rules and criteria by 31 December 2012. This legislation introduced new rules of admissibility for the appointment of ruling positions, which depended on the following factors: population, including the resident population, according to the last census; tourist accommodation, according to the last census; and the percentage share of participation in the total amount of the funds referred to in Article 19(1) of the Law of Local Finances (LLF) (Crespo, 2013).

The internal structure of services involves four levels: organic units, organic subunits, multidisciplinary teams, and project teams. The organisational models adopted can be of three types: hierarchical structure model, matrix structure model, and mixed structure model (Crespo, 2013).

The hierarchical structure model has a single line of responsibility and is composed of departments with managerial functions and operational and supporting services (Figure 6.1). It thus encompasses nuclear units and flexible

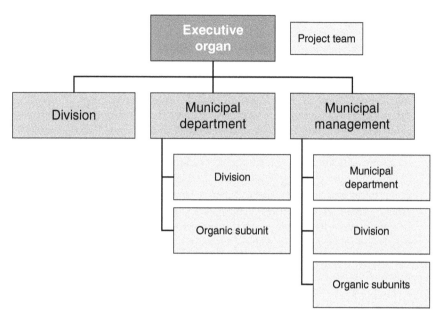

Figure 6.1 Hierarchical structure of the organisation of municipal services (source: Crespo, 2013).

units. In the nuclear structure it is possible to find municipal administration and municipal departments, a fixed departmentalisation. The flexible structure is characterised by divisions, organic units, and organic subunits, with the idea of a permanent adaptation of the services to the needs of operation and optimisation of resources. The temporary structures are linked to project teams; these are justified in their creation by a temporary project whose pursuit should be ensured by a separate team, bearing in mind the increase of flexibility and efficiency of the management. These teams are limited in time, however, and must have goals to be achieved, with targets and indicators (Crespo, 2013).

The matrix structure model has, as assumption of its adoption, operational areas which may be developed primarily for projects and should be grouped by competences or products and established on the basis of functional mobility.

The organisation of the matrix structure seeks to maximise the virtues (specialisations) and minimise the weaknesses (rigidity) of the hierarchical structure. It also tries to combine the advantages of a hierarchical (vertical) structure with the advantages of a transversal structure (Figure 6.2).

The mixed structure model combines features of a hierarchical structure with those of a matrix structure. Normally, in its organisation, it has a greater preponderance of characteristics of a hierarchical structure through nuclear and flexible units and subunits, compared to the weight of the multidisciplinary teams in the structure of a mixed organisation (Crespo, 2013).

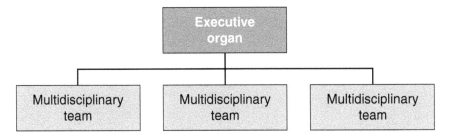

Figure 6.2 Matrix structure of the organisation of municipal services (source: Crespo, 2013).

The crisis and economic restructuring led to the recognition of municipal intervention as an actor and partner in the investment processes and territorialisation of public policies with a larger scope for intervention. In addition, the supra-municipal level gained ground with regard to the rationalisation and efficiency of public investment (Figueiredo, 2009).

The influence of the crisis on the organisation of municipal services in LMA

Within the legislative frameworks of 2009 and 2012, which made different organisational models of the municipal services, this analysis will focus on the nuclear structure of the different municipalities of the LMA, considering the jurisdiction and competence within municipalities resulting from the 1999 legislation.

The administrative modernisation of public administration in Portugal started in the late 1990s and the recent legislative changes, namely in the areas of urban licensing, performance evaluation, as well as in the status of managers, imposed a deepening of the (re)engineering and (de)materialisation reforms of administrative processes, as well as the adoption of more flexible organisational models, suitable for the provision of prompt and more qualified responses to the community.

The organisational structure of services arises essentially marked by the need of compliance in relation to the filling of the maximum executive positions, which result from Law No. 49/2012, of 29 August. This is the main thread of most of the solutions adopted in the services organisation, which intend relaying an optimisation of human and material resources, as well as efficiency in the exercise of their public service legally entrusted to the municipality.

As shown in Figure 6.3 there is a direct relationship between external interventions in Portugal (in the three mentioned periods) and the emergence of legislation that influences the local administration. In 1977/1978, 1983/1984, and 2011/2014 there was an increase in legislative output in order to define, delimit, and reorganise local government services.

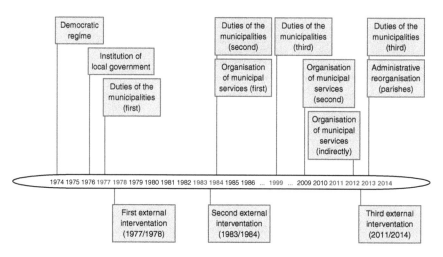

Figure 6.3 Legislative developments in local government and external interventions in Portugal (source: Crespo, 2013).

The organic restructuring established an opportunity to deepen internal reflection of the organisational effectiveness of city hall services and to introduce improvements into the organic structure. The organisational proposals regarding the municipal services therefore built and highlighted the organic coalescence principle which presided over the development of the organisational regulations of the municipal services, aiming to optimise the available resources and the development of local authorities as well as to achieve the organisational effectiveness of citizens. In addition, by reducing and simplifying the organisation of municipal services, the new structures intended to promote efficiencies related to the building of the internal articulation and to highlight the importance of the organisational management by seeking continuous improvement (Crespo, 2013).

The publication of Law No. 49/2012 of 29 August 2010 established that the municipalities should, compulsorily, adapt organic structures according to the criteria set out before 31 December of 2012. This legal determination aimed to reduce the number of managerial staff in local administration and, naturally, in LMA municipalities through the implementation of quantitative criteria, exclusively. In fact, the adopted criteria did not consider the nature of the organisations or the dynamics of the territory, its characteristics or needs. In the framework of local government autonomy, the governing bodies of the municipalities were exclusively empowered with the creation of organic structures more adequate to the reality within their territories, taking into consideration their specificities, in an attempt to intervene and respond in an appropriate manner to their population.

The above mentioned law, as well as Law No. 8/2012 of 21 December 2012,[8] directly influenced the intervention of municipalities in providing municipal services, promoting the corporatisation and privatisation of a set of services provided by the municipalities, such as water distribution, urban solid waste collection, and education. A potential result of this legislative framework was a reduction of municipal services, with direct implications for the provision of public services. It was the municipalities, which were more affected, that favoured direct management of the municipal services and that directly exercised their powers, not having opted for outsourcing. These were the municipalities from the south part of the LMA, which were ideologically closer to the political left. This potential weakening of municipal action through organisational norms may have contributed to the weakening of the public services provided to the population by the municipal action.

The municipalities of the LMA promoted revision of their services and implemented the described principles and philosophy of organisation. Despite the flexibility and diversity of the organisational model, most LMA municipalities have adopted a hierarchical structure through a line of responsibility, set by bodies with management tasks and services of an operational and support nature (Crespo, 2013).

While analysing the organisational models of the municipal services of the LMA, in light of the transformations resulting from the 2009 and 2012 legislation, it is possible to draw a set of conclusions. Most municipalities of the LMA adopted an internal organisation regarding the municipal services in the framework of the hierarchical structure model. The exceptions were the municipalities of Alcochete and Loures, which have a mixed structure model. The municipalities of Barreiro, Moita, Palmela, and Vila Franca de Xira adopted, with the legal framework of 2009, a mixed model; now with the new act (2012) they have changed their organisation to a hierarchical model of municipal services.

All LMA municipalities that updated their organisation (from 2009 to 2012) reduced and/or merged the units with their competences, regarding the provision of services to the population. Figures 6.4a and 6.4b show the reduction in the number of nuclear structures in the organisation and provision of services in the municipality of Alcochete. This has led municipalities to choose one type of service over others that have then disappeared from the nuclear structure of the organisation or in some cases, been integrated in the same line structure.

Table 6.3 also demonstrates a reduction in terms of staff numbers in almost every local authority of the LMA for the period 2009 to 2012. In overall terms, the reduction in Portugal amounted to 6.4 per cent, while in the LMA municipalities the reduction was residual (0.8 per cent). The total reduction of the number of employees of municipal services was partially misrepresented by the municipalities of Odivelas and Sintra, which showed an increase in the number of employees of 39.6 and 52.8 per cent respectively between 2009 and 2010 (years of local elections).

In accordance with the memorandum signed by the parties in power with Troika in 2011, a reduction of 6 per cent by 2014 in the city halls and regional government staff is anticipated. Consequently, the central administration only has to implement a reduction of 3 per cent. In future investigations it will be necessary to clarify whether the staff reduction is affecting the quality, quantity, and scope of the public services provided to the community in a negative way. This reduction has meant that more people were left out of the services provided by the municipalities and their quality was affected.

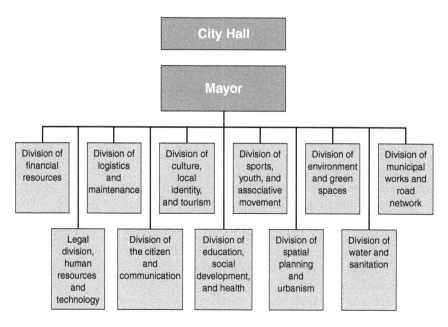

Figure 6.4a Organisation of the nuclear structure of municipal services, Alcochete, 2010 (source: Crespo, 2013).

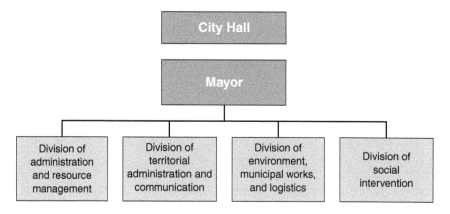

Figure 6.4b Organisation of the nuclear structure of municipal services, Alcochete, 2012 (source: Crespo, 2013).

Table 6.3 Evolution of the number of employees in municipal services, 2009–2012

Municipalities	2009	2010	2011	2012	Variation 2009–2010 (%)	Variation 2009–2012 (%)
Alcochete	410	416	399	378	1.0	−8.3
Almada	1,492	1,512	1,502	1,485	1.3	−0.5
Amadora	1,709	1,677	1,710	1,657	−1.9	−3.0
Barreiro	846	819	846	817	−3.2	−3.4
Cascais	1,479	1,537	1,513	1,474	3.9	−0.3
Lisboa	10,106	9,983	9,727	9,249	−1.2	−8.5
Loures	2,230	2,206	2,157	2,148	−1.1	−3.7
Mafra	942	1,013	1,016	971	7.5	3.1
Moita	814	822	797	780	1.0	−4.2
Montijo	941	878	859	815	−6.7	−13.4
Odivelas	889	1,213	1,308	1,241	36.4	39.6
Oeiras	1,765	1,817	1,848	1,805	2.9	2.3
Palmela	1,023	1,001	985	944	−7.7	−2.2
Seixal	1,629	1,694	1,726	1,652	4.0	1.4
Sesimera	1,005	1,016	970	931	1.1	−7.4
Setúbal	1,440	1,419	1,422	1,367	−1.5	−5.1
Sintra	1,721	2,796	2,760	2,629	62.5	52.8
Vila Franca De Xira	939	895	845	801	−4.7	−14.7
Total – Lisboa Metropolitan Area	31,382	32,714	32,390	31,144	4.2	−0.8
Total – Portugal	134,430	135,527	131,522	125,889	0.8	−6.4

Source: authors' elaboration based on data from Social Balance – SIIAL (Integrated Information System for Local Authorities), 2013.

Concluding remarks

The recent financial and economic crisis, which mainly affected the countries of the Western world, has influenced the ability of central and local administrations to perform their administrative and social functions. In Portugal, the crisis became more obvious and the country had to ask for external help, and rely on it for a period of three years. In this context and in a direct way, the central government made changes in legislative terms, varied in nature, as a response to the commitments it entered. As illustrated in this chapter, these legislative changes have affected the performance of the local government on two levels. On the one hand is the organisation of services provided to the population by reducing organisational structures, although local authorities have more competencies resulting from the administrative decentralisation processes; on the other hand, reducing the number of municipal employees potentially influences the services provided to the population negatively.

The study conducted shows that despite the financial crisis and the current trend of changes in the system and in the political-administrative structure, the state and/or the local governments, through the municipalities, are still key actors in the implementation of public policies, land use planning, and also in providing services to the population. In these lines it should also be added that the legislative framework has limited the options available in terms of public service organisation, associated with a prevailing technical culture based on a traditional view of service provision, as well as with a strong ideological component of local power.

It is also possible to conclude that the state and the local governments still remain the key drivers for the prosecution of the collective interest, namely in terms of guidance for planning and the provision of public services to the population. The governance does not mean the end or the reduction of the administration, but its transformation and adaptation to the present society. In particular, the state and the local authorities still remain crucial to the goal definition, as well as being its delivery agent. At the same time, different forms of governance are incorporated into several institutional levels.

From the considerations and analyses of the theories and policies, it is possible to systematise types of interventions in the governance structures seen from a governance perspective. The policies of the central government can guide the coordination and collective action processes beyond the scope of the public, private, and voluntary sector, but the state should not impose such policies, instead negotiating not only the decision-making policy, but also its implementation with its partners. At a local level, the local government has an important role to play in the promotion of new forms of governance, since it is positioned between the traditional vertical axis of the power and the public administration and the new horizontal axis of the partnership between government, private sector, and social society.

The state is responsible for encouraging communities to be the key players of its own development processes, building an environment of trust, cooperation, and articulation between the different stakeholders. The new role of the central administration sets several challenges to its organisation and to the way it relates to the stakeholders involved. The challenges are related to its (re)structuring and to the establishment of cooperation, the promotion of an organisational culture of consultation and dialogue, and the release of the bureaucratic instruments of internal communication and control.

The April Revolution of 1974 and the 1976 Constitution established local autonomy, in which the municipalities assumed the figure of politic power structures with autonomous administration status. Since then, the municipalities have assumed an increasingly prominent role in the development processes of their territories, as evidenced by a gradual increase in their competences in a wide variety of areas. It is undisputable that the Portuguese municipalities and the local and regional governments throughout Europe must face new expectations of and demands for better services from citizens, taking into account the need to rationalise the use of the (scarce) public resources in a context in which the global tendency for new public management practices is clear.

In this respect, the local governments intend to find new ways to manage public property and public interests, which so far have been focused on the transition of a direct management into a business scheme, trying to establish partnerships with other municipalities, or other private and public entities. There is a clear change in the role of the local power, from an interventional government that does everything by itself, to a more strategic government.

Notes

1 The municipalities of Alcochete, Almada, Barreiro, Moita, Montijo, Palmela, Sesimbra, Setúbal, and Seixal on the south bank of the River Tejo; and the municipalities of Amadora, Cascais, Lisboa, Loures, Mafra, Odivelas, Oeiras, Sintra, and Vila Franca de Xira, on the north bank of the River Tejo.
2 Law No. 75/2013 of 12 September gives the ability for parishes to take on more duties after an understanding with the municipalities in which they are located.
3 Law No. 11-A/2013 of 28 January approved the administrative reorganisation of the parish territory, as referred to in the memorandum of understanding that the Portuguese government signed with the Troika.
4 Decree-Law No. 116/84 of 6 April, later supplemented by Law No. 44/85 of 13 September.
5 Decree-Law No. 305/2009 of 29 October.
6 Law No. 49/2012 of 29 August, adapts Law No. 2/2004 of 15 January to local administration, as amended by Laws No. 51/2005 of 30 August, 64-A/2008 of 31 December, 3-B/2010 of 28 April, and 64/2011, of 22 December, which approves the personnel statute of governing services and bodies of the central, regional, and local administration of the state. This legislation will influence and change some organisations and structures of the departments of city halls, because it establishes a set of quantitative criteria for the appointment of governing positions.
7 Law No. 159/99 of 14 September.
8 Known as commitment laws.

References

Albury, D. (2005) Fostering innovation in public services. *Public Money and Management*, 25, 51–56.

Altschuler, A. & Behn, R. (1997) *Innovations in American government*. Washington, DC, Brookings Institution.

ANMP (Associação Nacional de Municípios Portugueses) (2014) *Contratos dos municípios*. [Online] Available from: www.anmp.pt/munp/mun/mun10111.php?cod=20140110 [accessed 9 August 2014].

Borins, S. (1998) *Innovating with integrity*. Washington, DC, Georgetown University Press.

Borlini, B. (2004) *Governance e governance urbana: Analisi e definizione del concetto*. [Online] Available from: www.sociologia.unical.it/ais2004/papers/borlini%20paper.pdf [accessed 10 January 2014].

CE (Commission Européenne) (2001) *Gouvernance Européenne: Un livre blanc*. COM 428 final. Brussels, Commission of the European Communities.

Conceição, P. (2004) A governância dos territórios e as novas políticas urbanas: Tópicos para um debate alargado. *A obra nasce: Revista de Arquitectura da Universidade Fernando Pessoa*, 2, 86–99.

Crespo, J. (2013) *Governança e território: Instrumentos, métodos e técnicas de gestão na Área Metropolitana de Lisboa*. PhD Thesis, Faculty of Architecture, Technical University of Lisbon.

Crespo, J. & Cabral, J. (2010) The institutional dimension of governance in the Lisbon metropolitan area. *Análise Social*, 197, 639–662.

Crespo, J. & Cabral, J. (2012) The institutional dimension of governance in the Lisbon metropolitan area. In: Seixas, J. & Albet, A. (eds) *Urban governance in Southern Europe*. Burlington, VT, Ashgate, pp. 27–50.

Dente, B., Bobbio, L., & Spada, A. (2005) Government or governance of urban innovation? *DISP*, 162, 41–52.

Figueiredo, A. (2009) *Sociedade da informação: Desafios e possibilidades para o poder local*. Association for the promotion and development of the information society. 30 October 2009. Auditorium of the Portuguese Communications Foundation.

Hartley, J. (2005) Innovation in governance and public services: Past and present. *Public Money and Management*, 25, 27–34.

Hartley, J. (2006) *Innovation and its contribution to improvement: A literature review for policy-makers, policy advisors, managers and academics*. London, Department of Communities and Local Government.

Harvey, D. (1989) *The urban experience*. Baltimore, MD, Johns Hopkins University Press.

Healey, P. (2004) Creativity and urban governance. *Policy Studies*, 25 (2), 11–20.

Hill, C. & Lynn, L. (2004) Governance and public management, an introduction. *Journal of Policy Analysis and Management*, 23 (1), 3–11.

Jessop, B. (1995) The regulation approach, governance and post-Fordism: Alternative perspectives on economic and political change? *Economy and Society*, 24 (3), 307–333.

Jordan, A., Wurzel, R., & Zito, A. (2005) The rise of new policy instruments in comparative perspective: Has governance eclipsed government? *Political Studies*, 53, 477–496.

Jouve, B. (2003) *La gouvernance urbaine en questions*. Paris, Elsevier.

Kettl, D. (2002) *The transformation of governance: Public administration for the twenty-first century*. Baltimore, MD, Johns Hopkins University Press.

Kooiman, J. (1993) *Modern governance: New government–society interactions*. London, Sage.

Kooiman, J. (2003) *Governing as governance*. London, Sage.

Marshall, A. (1982) *Princípios de economia: Tratado introdutório*. São Paulo, Editora Abril.

Moore, M. (2005) Break-through innovations and continuous improvement: Two different models of innovative processes in the public sector. *Public Money and Management*, 25, 43–50.

Moore, M. & Hartley, J. (2008) Innovations in governance. *Public Management Review*, 10 (1), 3–20.

Mulgan, G. & Albury, D. (2003) *Innovations in the public sector*. London, Cabinet Office.

Osborne, S. & Brown, K. (2005) *Managing change and innovation in public service organizations*. London, Routledge.

Peters, B. (2002) Governance: A garbage can perspective. *Political Science Series*, Institute for Advanced Studies, Vienna, [S.I], 1–23.

Pierre, J. & Peters, B. (2000) *Governance, politics and the state*. Basingstoke, Macmillan.

Porter, M. (1998) Clusters and the new economics of competition. *Harvard Business Review*, [S.I], November–December, 77–90.

Rhodes, R. (1997) *Understanding governance: Policy network, governance, reflexivity and accountability*. London, Open University Press.

Rodrigues, C. & Andrade, I. (2013) Robin Hood versus piggy bank: Income redistribution in Portugal 2006–10. *Working Papers*, Lisbon, ISEG.

Seixas, J., Branco, R., & Garson, S. (2012) *A governação metropolitana na Europa*. Rio de Janeiro, Observatório das Metrópoles. [Online] Available from www.observatorio-dasmetropoles.net/download/governanca_europa.pdf [accessed 10 September 2013].

Skelcher, C. (2005) Jurisdictional integrity, polycentrism, and the design of democratic governance. *Governance: An International Journal of Policy, Administration, and Institutions*, 18 (1), 89–110.

World Bank (1997) *World development report 1997: The state in a changing world*. New York: Oxford University Press. [Online] Available from: https://openknowledge.worldbank.org/handle/10986/5980 [accessed 10 October 2013].

7   Athens, a capital in crisis

Tracing the socio-spatial impacts

Konstantinos Serraos, Thomas Greve,
Evangelos Asprogerakas, Dimitrios Balampanidis,
and Anastasia Chani

Introduction

The 2007 economic and financial crisis spread as a phenomenon with global dimensions but, at the same time, it had important local particularities. In Greece, the problem emerged primarily as a massive budget deficit. However, in conjunction with the austerity measures implemented thereafter and the delay in the implementation of necessary institutional and structural changes, it finally culminated in a prolonged recession with devastating consequences for a wide range of social groups. Today, after five years of economic recession, we still cannot refer to a post-crisis era, since the country still depends on the International Monetary Fund (IMF) and the European Central Bank's (ECB) financial assistance, and the long-awaited development is not yet evident.

The current and ongoing economic crisis is the first phenomenon of its kind and scale in the post-Second World War period in Greece. As such, it is of unprecedented importance for the vast majority of the Greek population and also for the state as a body. The impacts caused by the crisis in a country with Greece's particularities are quite unknown and it is not easy to estimate them accurately since we have no reliable experience on which to call. Therefore, the questions concerning the understanding and interpretation of this phenomenon, the assessment of its impacts, and the formulation and implementation of appropriate relative policies and actions constitute a wide field for research and experience exchange of particular interest in Greece and abroad.

The present chapter considers the demographic and spatial development of the city of Athens, studying the findings of research and analysis so far on the evolution of the crisis. Through a space analysis approach, combining issues of urbanism, land planning, and social geography, it attempts to provide a comprehensive understanding of the socio-spatial implications of the crisis, an overview of its causes, and its visible aspects and trends regarding real estate economy, access to housing, commercial activities, investments, urban development and policies, use and condition of public space, infrastructure and transport, and environmental changes.

A particular emphasis is given to the city of Athens, which, as the capital of a centralised state, comprises a large proportion of the country's total population, political power, administration, services, and economic activities. In fact, during the 2000s and before the outbreak of the crisis, the metropolitan region of Athens accounted for about 40 per cent of the country's economic performance, 50 per cent of its income and savings, 60 per cent of income taxes, and 70 per cent of the turnover in the construction and production sector (ELSTAT, 2013c). According to available data and research findings, a comparative analysis is feasible only for the country as a whole and, for the time being, not for other cities or urban agglomerations.

Apart from the socio-spatial impacts of the crisis, the chapter takes into account the current policies applied in the institutional and organisational field and at the level of spatial interventions. In doing so it aims at investigating and systematically estimating the impacts of the economic crisis and the above-mentioned policy agenda in terms of both spatial and social dimensions.

In the following sections, the chapter refers to the particular socio-spatial context of modern Athens, outlines the local causes of and conditions underpinning the outbreak of the crisis in the country, and analyses socio-spatial impacts of the crisis in Athens according to available relevant data. Lastly, it investigates the spatial planning implemented during the crisis, focusing on general regulations and policies, strategic local spatial development plans, major urban interventions, and the need for relief actions and initiatives, before drawing some conclusions and raising a number of questions.

Athens: socio-spatial context, demographics, and urban growth

The modern city of Athens is a relatively newly constructed city. Only since the 1800s has it experienced an impressive transformation from a small village around the Acropolis to a metropolis with an increasing population and sprawling spatial development across Attica. After becoming capital of the Greek state in 1834, Athens was developed according to the First Plan, edited by Kleanthis, Schaubert, and Leo von Klenze, which proposed the characteristic current urban structure of the city in the form of a triangle around the historic residential web (Plaka) (Figure 7.1). The development of the modern Greek state, the choice of Athens as its capital, and the comparatively extensive urban planning scheme, happened as a result of the strong influence of European philhellenism, which in the case of Athens was represented by the under-age King Otto von Wittelsbach and his Bavarian troika.

For about a century after the foundation of the capital, its population and area did not increase significantly. The first signs of such a development were noticed after the Greek–Turkish War in 1922, when Athens absorbed more than a million refugees from Asia Minor, who mostly settled in self-made settlements, arbitrarily installed in the suburban area. However, the biggest population and housing boom occurred after the end of the Civil War in 1949, when a huge wave of rural migrants was attracted by the economic growth and prosperity, which, in comparison with the countryside, were gradually established in Athens.

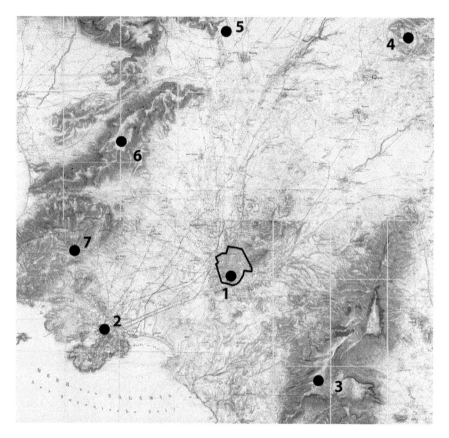

Figure 7.1   Athens, populated area in 1894 (black line); (1) Acropolis Hill, (2) Piraeus Port City, (3) Mount Hymettus, (4) Mount Pentelikon, (5) Mount Parnes, (6) Mount Poikilo, (7) Mount Aigaleo (source: Curtius & Kaupert, 1881, edited by the authors).

Many people were also driven to dwell in private small-scale developments on the outskirts of the city, an event facilitated by the tolerance of the government and the absence of a structured urban and housing policy (Maloutas et al., 2012).

From 1950 to 1970, the main housing development policy of the city was based on the system of 'Antiparohi', which emerged as the dominant model of urban development. It was based on the partnership between landowner and contractor for the construction of a residential building, on the basis of generous tax breaks, along with favourable planning regulations (ibid.). 'Antiparohi' led to massive construction of the characteristic Athenian blocks and had two opposing effects on the urban territory. On the one hand, it caused very high density, extensive urban sprawl, a general lack of public spaces and green areas, and serious traffic problems. On the other hand, it favoured the achievement of a high level of social cohesion, allowing a wide range of social classes to have access to affordable housing, and eased the establishment of a beneficial mix of land uses thanks to minimal restrictions. In the 1980s the 'Antiparohi' system spread all over Attica. Although the housing density in the periphery decreased, new uses emerged, such as office blocks along the avenues and shopping centres linked with residential areas, and the result was a more or less spontaneous network of local urban centres all over Attica.

After 1990, Greece turned into a major destination for economic immigrants and refugees, mainly from the Balkans and Eastern Europe but later from the Middle East, Asia, and Africa. These immigrants and refugees settled primarily in deprived and cheap central neighbourhoods, but moved also to other municipalities in the Athens Basin, as well as outside Attica, in search of work.

Nowadays, the population in the metropolitan region of Athens stands at 3.8 million. It started with 4,000 inhabitants in 1831 (ELSTAT, 2011; Mpiris, 1966; Travlos, 1960). The densely populated area spreads out across the Athens Basin. To the north and east it is surrounded by mountains (Hymettus, Pentelikon, Parnes, Poikilo, and Aigaleo) and to the south-west it is defined by the seafront (Figure 7.2). Despite a historically entrenched social division between the neighbourhoods of the working class in the west and those of the upper-middle class in the east, the city managed over the years to create conditions for harmonic and complementary social coexistence. Refugees from Asia Minor in the 1920s, rural

Figure 7.2 Athens, densely populated in 2014 (source: OpenStreetMap (www.openstreet-map.org), edited by the authors).

migrants in the 1960s, and immigrants in the 1990s developed a diverse and cohesive urban society based on a small-scale family-oriented economic structure with widespread real estate ownership.

Heading towards crisis

The causes of the current economic crisis in Greece can be traced back in time. In the following, some of the most crucial factors that have paved the way for the outbreak of the crisis are analysed. First, in 1981, the country's EU membership marked the beginning of a period of economic growth and development. However, the EU financing was also accompanied by disproportionate external borrowing, which led to the widening of a costly and wasteful state. After the entry of Greece into the Eurozone in 2001, new financing possibilities for both the public and the private sector emerged through further access to favourable bank loans with low interest rates. Thus, although a significant territorial upgrade should be noted (e.g. local facilities all over the region, metropolitan infrastructures such as airport, metro, urban motorways, wastewater treatment plant, gas network, widening of housing opportunities related to residential extensions) the economic growth and prosperity of the last decades have been heavily dependent on external finance focusing at the same time mainly on local consumption (Bank of Greece, 2010, 2011; Tsakalotos, 2014). This inevitably resulted in a major imbalance between state expenses and financial ability as well as between borrowing and repayment ability.

Despite the heavy dependence of the Greek economy on external financing, the state decided to undertake the organisation of the Olympic Games in 2004. During the preparation period Athens experienced a heavy boost in the construction of metropolitan public infrastructures as well as of large urban and technical Olympic projects. The initial budget was doubled and the expenditure was disproportionately high for a public investment; it finally proved not to be economically, socially, or spatially profitable (Kalantzopoulou & Belavilas, 2014; Stathakis & Nikolakakis, 2014). During these years of spurious prosperity, the real estate and construction sectors were once again significantly reinforced. For decades the construction industry was one of the main levers contributing to the growth of the Greek economy (Vaiou, Mantouvalou & Mavridou, 2000), but this time it led to a real estate boom connected with an extended urban sprawl phenomenon mainly along the northern and eastern areas of the metropolitan region.

The fact that a wide range of social groups were attracted by bank lending with low interest rates offered people significant purchasing power and gave rise both to the demand for and to the offer of houses. Housing loans in Greece increased from €11 billion in 2000 to €80 billion in 2008, newly constructed residences almost doubled in five years, and real estate prices more than doubled in a decade (Kandyla & Triantafyllopoulos, 2009), which constituted significant relative growth rates in comparison with the past. The economic growth and prosperity described above reached their limits in 2007. The construction sector and the real estate market started to decline (Figures 7.3, 7.4, 7.5). As a result,

despite a continuous fall in prices (Figure 7.3), a large number of newly constructed residences, estimated at over 150,000 (Vlamis, 2014), remained unsold
whereas the Olympic public infrastructure was barely used and not maintained.

However, the crisis in Greece did not break out as a bubble of the construction sector and subprime mortgages. It emerged as a massive budget deficit
(which rose to 15.4 per cent of GDP in 2009, much higher than the EU's 3 per
cent limit) (OECD, 2011) with a simultaneous inability to attract further external
finance. To repay the huge sovereign debt, the Greek government agreed with
the Troika (European Commission, IMF, ECB) on a bailout, which envisioned

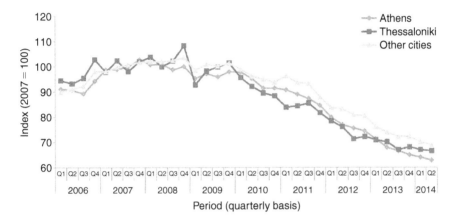

Figure 7.3 Index of new (up to five years old) apartment prices by geographical area
(source: authors' elaboration based on data from Bank of Greece, 2014).

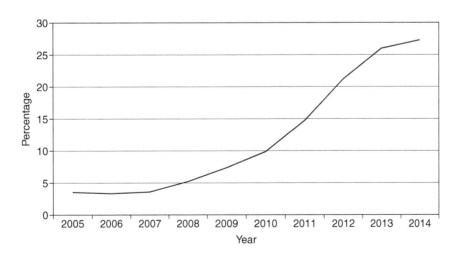

Figure 7.4 Percentage of housing loans in delay (source: authors' elaboration based on
data from Bank of Greece, 2014).

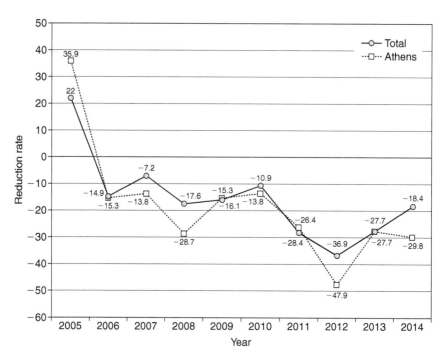

Figure 7.5 Construction permits' reduction rate (source: authors' elaboration based on data from Bank of Greece, 2014).

large budget cuts, thousands of dismissals in the public sector, an extensive privatisation programme of public property, and the over-taxation of income and property while the already weak welfare state was dramatically shrinking.

As a result, the crisis turned to be a multi-faceted phenomenon affecting the whole country, with various effects on the territory and on people's everyday lives. The following analysis focuses on the socio-spatial impacts of the crisis on Greece in general and on the city of Athens in particular.

The socio-spatial impacts of the crisis on Greece and on the city of Athens

Access to housing, cost of living, taxation of property, and real estate trends

Since the emergence of the crisis some of its most considerable socio-spatial effects have been identified in the housing sector and concern an ever wider range of social groups. Among the most crucial developments over the last few years is the decrease in household income and purchasing power along with the increase in fixed operating expenses, mortgage over-indebtedness, new legislation for the taxation of residential property, and the new regulatory framework for the real estate market (Balampanidis, Patatouka & Siatitsa, 2013b).

During the year 2012 there was a drastic reduction in private sector wages of 22.2 per cent on average, significant delays in the payment of salaries, and increase in flexible forms of employment (SEPE, 2012) as well as a greater reduction in public sector wages and pensions by 8 per cent of GNP during the period 2010–2011 (INE/GSEE-ADEDY, 2012). At the same time, unemployment reached historic levels in the first quarter of 2013, standing at 27.4 per cent, which corresponds to almost 1,400,000 unemployed people (ELSTAT, 2013a). The drastic reduction in incomes and consumers' purchasing power was accompanied by a significant increase in households' fixed operating costs. The successive rises in the price of electricity, heating oil, and gas have taken many households into so-called 'energy poverty' (Panas, 2012).

Especially as regards homeowners, expenses have been complemented by new taxes on real estate property. In 2012, the Greek government imposed a one-year emergency property tax (known as 'haratsi') to be levied through electricity bills, with no tax-free threshold.[1] However, this emergency tax continued to be levied in 2013 and the first semester of 2014.[2] By the second semester of 2014, this 'temporary' measure was supposed to be replaced by a permanent and single property tax, which was expected to widen the taxable base and involve a primary tax with no tax-free threshold even for citizens' main residence.[3]

Along with the increase in household fixed operating costs and the imposition of new tax charges, one should also consider mortgage over-indebtedness. For the period 2000–2008, it was estimated that the total outstanding amount of housing loans increased sevenfold (Kandyla & Triantafyllopoulos, 2010). Today, a large number of housing loans are non-performing. For over-indebted households, recent legislation provides for minimum protection of debtors through the right to negotiate with the bank,[4] and auctions have been suspended for the sixth consecutive year under certain conditions and only for main residences.[5]

Because of the dramatic developments presented above, a worryingly large number of households can no longer afford adequate housing and decent living conditions; this is especially true for the most vulnerable social groups, such as immigrants, women, elderly people, and the unemployed. According to press reports, low living standards persist, since young people return to their parental home or several families have to share one apartment. At the same time, an increasing number of owners cannot find a tenant and rent out their apartments simply for the payment of property bills and taxes or allocate to the state the rents, which remain outstanding for months (Kanellis, 2012).

Lastly, a large number of tenants or owners are threatened with eviction, foreclosure, or auction. In fact, the most extreme impact of the crisis on access to housing is reflected in the increasing number of homeless people. Although there is no official data-collection strategy on homelessness in Greece and despite the methodological constraints of various reports, it was estimated that the number of homeless people in 2011 reached 20,000. It is also believed that homelessness is concentrated particularly in the region of Attica, which includes Athens, where the number of homeless people has reached 15,000 (FEANTSA, 2012). The statistics show that more than half of them have lived on the street for under two years, namely after the outburst of the crisis and having recently lost their job (Klimaka, 2012).

Under the conditions of increasing housing insecurity described above, and while the number of the homeless is dramatically rising, the state not only avoids guaranteeing a minimum level of social protection, but has even abolished sparse housing provision like the Social Housing Organisation.[6] Instead of forming a stronger social housing policy, the new measures announced by the Greek government aim exclusively at relaunching the land and housing market, facilitating private investment and concentrating the real estate property in the hands of only a few major owners. The new legislation for the operation mode of the famous Real Estate Investment Companies (REICs) is an illustrative example. From now on, REICs will also have the right to invest in primary and secondary (holiday) residences, public land, and real estate property, while they will enjoy an ever more favourable tax regime. The higher tax rate amounts to only 0.125 per cent of their annual assets, and they are exempted from taxes on property transfer, income, and capital gains.[7] Given the prospect of the loss of property of many households and the speculative investment by large private investors, it is expected that land and real estate property will be concentrated in the hands of a few owners and residential segregation will increase.

Nevertheless, this trend of massive investment in housing is not yet reflected strongly in the real estate market in Athens, as the market values have continued to fall steadily since 2008 (10 per cent average annual reduction in apartment prices) (Figure 7.6).

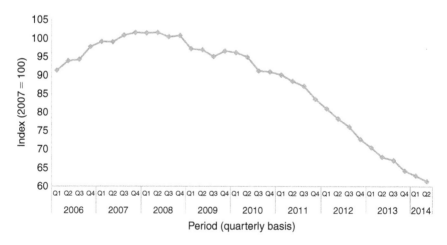

Figure 7.6 Index of apartment prices in Athens (source: authors' elaboration based on data from Bank of Greece, 2014).

It should be underlined that this reduction is not equally distributed geographically in Athens and it depends on the characteristics of the neighbourhood and of course the specific features of each property (age, level, view, etc.). It depends also on the prices prevailing in each area before the crisis; this explains why reduction is greater in the northern and southern suburbs of Athens, where the 'expensive' neighbourhoods are traditionally located. Owners and tenants tend to move to other neighbourhoods in search of lower housing prices (ELIE, 2013).

On the other hand, according to many real estate agencies, there is a variety of old but well maintained apartments which are available at a market value lower than €1,000/m^2 in dense and overpopulated central areas of Athens (for example, Kipseli, Patisia, and Gkizi). Empirical observation suggests there is an increase in renovations in these areas, indicating a trend of residents returning to central neighbourhoods of Athens, albeit firm conclusions cannot as yet be drawn.

Commercial activities

In the commercial sector, which has also been deeply affected by the economic crisis of the last few years, an escalating recession can be observed. The two essential characteristics of this recession are the dramatic increase of closed stores and the consistent fall in open businesses' turnover. According to ongoing research, the phenomenon of store closures is observable in all the major cities of Greece, especially in the capital (INEMY/ESEE, 2011b).

In the centre of Athens the percentage of closed stores along the most important commercial avenues reached 31 per cent in 2012 compared with 18 per cent in 2010 (Figure 7.7). Commercial stores along central avenues are paradoxically more affected by the crisis, but those along less important roads have suffered too (Figure 7.8). In total, the percentage of closed stores varied from 22 to 42 per cent in 2012 versus 15 to 25 per cent in 2010 (INEMY/ESEE, 2012). As regards open commercial businesses, their turnover decreased by 14.4 per cent in 2013 compared with 2012 (ELSTAT, 2013b). In Piraeus, the port of Athens, closed stores reached 440 in 2011 versus 104 in 2009, and open businesses' turnover decreased by more than 40 per cent during the discount period in 2011 versus 20 to 40 per cent in 2009 (ESP, 2007, 2011).

It is estimated that the main reasons for the increasing number of closed stores in Athens' city centre are (in order of importance) high rents, the decrease of consumers' purchasing power, and the shrinkage of the middle class as well as the suburbanisation of large enterprises and hypermarkets (INEMY/ESEE, 2012). As regards Piraeus, in the opinion of traders, the main reasons for the decrease in their businesses' turnover are (in order of importance) the hypermarkets, the informal trade, and the current economic difficulties of consumers (ESP, 2007, 2011).

In other central neighbourhoods of Athens (like Kypseli, Metaxourgio, and Exarcheia) and in Piraeus' city centre, the percentage of closed shops is similar,

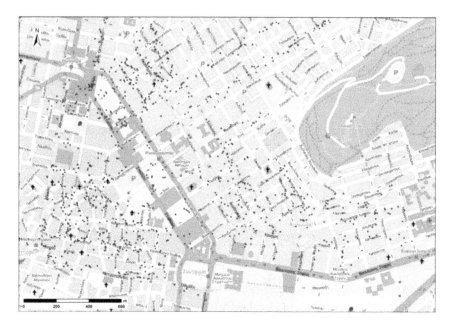

Figure 7.7 Map of closed businesses in the centre of Athens (source: INEMY/ESEE, 2012).

varying from 18 to 43 per cent (Balampanidis et al., 2013a). However, not all types of commercial activities are affected in the same way. To give a characteristic example, expensive clothing stores are often replaced by fast food restaurants and bakeries or wholesale shops. At the same time, there are certain businesses that resist crisis better, mostly traditional small stores, specialist markets, or new forms of entrepreneurship. Lastly, commercial businesses react better to the crisis in some distant neighbourhoods of Athens, where the number of closed shops varied from 17 to 22 per cent in 2011 (INEMY/ESEE, 2011a).

Consequently, the commercial real estate in Athens is facing a great recession and the rental values of both retail shops and offices are in continuous decline because of the reduced demand for commercial property and the frequent

Figure 7.8 Closed businesses in the centre of Athens, 2014 (source: authors' visualisation).

renegotiation of lease agreement terms (Vlamis, 2014). This situation affects the whole of Athens' city centre; even in high-class neighbourhoods, such as Kolonaki, the rental values of offices without parking space decreased by 4.6 per cent in the third quarter of 2014 in comparison with the third quarter of 2013 and in Syntagma Square by 5 per cent (Geoaxis, 2014).

The aforementioned facts contribute to the creation of a hostile ground for further establishment of businesses along with the fragile Greek economy and the rapidly changing tax regime. On the other hand, because of the availability of cheap commercial spaces, there may be room for the establishment of young entrepreneurs, especially regarding the creative industry, but there is not still enough data to confirm this. Finally, the situation has had various repercussions on public space, as described in the next subsection.

Public space

Public space is the field where the immense changes in economic, political, and social conditions are most visible. As far as the public space of Athens is concerned, the effects of the crisis are multiple and contradictory. On the one hand, public space has become more valuable and competitive during the crisis thanks to one of its key features, free access. Indeed, as an open and freely accessible space, it is now better visited and hosts various collective activities and free open-air events, leading to functional and cultural regeneration. On the other hand, under the pretext of the crisis, the quality of public space and its free use are often compromised. In addition, privatisation projects and the rapid changes in building coefficients and land uses without further consultation (Papaioannou, 2014) present real risks to the future of the city. This situation is further aggravated because of the cancellation of small regeneration projects in deprived neighbourhoods of Athens and the already inadequate funding is directed to more iconic redevelopment projects (see the fifth section of the chapter). Last but not least, many public spaces in the city's neighbourhoods are deprived of public infrastructure of high quality and remain unmaintained because of the lack of public funding.

Moreover, it is possible that the abandoned commercial buildings are aggravating the desolation of these districts resulting in the phenomenon of intense degradation. At the same time, touristic and attractive areas are being upgraded, or neighbourhoods are facing gentrification, with doubtful results because of the continuous economic crisis (Triantafyllopoulou & Sayas, 2012).

Furthermore, public space is where the brutal consequences of the crisis have become visible: drug use and trade, sex trafficking, increase of unemployed and homeless people (both Greeks and immigrants), and sheltering in public squares such as Omonia Square at the heart of the city centre. This in turn raises the question of a humanitarian crisis.

The physical decay of public space along with social degradation has increased feelings of fear and insecurity and prepared fertile ground for social anger. Such phenomena are predominantly located in the underprivileged central

Figure 7.9 Concentrations of homeless people in Athens, (1) Omonia Square, (2) Syntagma Square, (3) Acropolis Hill, (4) Lycabettus Hill (source: authors' elaboration based on Klimaka, 2012).

neighbourhoods of Athens (Kipseli, Agios Panteleimonas), but have also dramatically spread across the centre of the city (starting in the areas around Omonia Square and Lavriou Square). Financial insecurity and the inability to cover basic needs are worsened by everyday violence in several neighbourhoods of Athens. Public space has been claimed for actions of hate and racist practices, such as free meals only for Greek people, organised by extremist far-right groups, and also the phenomenon of racist violence. This situation creates a generalised sense of fear and even affects the everyday life of people living in 'calm' areas, such as Sepolia, near the disaffected ones (Vaiou, 2014).

The last and very important spatial impact of the crisis is the fact that public space has been transformed into a receptor for social indignation and a field of expression for social rage with massive demonstrations, protests, solidarity initiatives, and public assemblies: e.g. the movement of *Indignados* at Syntagma Square in 2011, which lasted more than two months.

Transport and environment

The effects of the crisis on the transport field are also multiple and contrasting. The most important among them is the reduction of the traffic volume in central roads of Attica. Overall, since 2009 traffic volume along the major roads of Athens has decreased by up to 16 per cent (Region of Attica, 2013). These percentages are strongly related to the increase in fuel prices, tolls, and vehicle taxes, together with a parallel reduction in people's income. In addition, new registrations of private cars fell by 29.8 per cent in 2011 and 41.7 per cent in 2012 (Alpha Bank, 2013), and reduction in the use of taxis has been dramatic since 2010 (Kathimerini, 2010). This has resulted in significant reduction of air and noise pollution, fewer accidents, and a notable increase in the use of alternative mobility means (i.e. walking, cycling, and public transport).

However, instead of an increase in the revenues from public transport, there has been a noticeable reduction, which means that passengers cannot afford to pay for tickets. Indeed, Athens Urban Transport Organisation (OASA) has recorded a decline in passenger traffic up to 20 per cent since 2009 (Eleftherotypia, 2013). There are many reasons for this phenomenon, including the consequences of the economic crisis for citizens' income and unemployment rates as well as the reduction of services and increase in fees because of a lack of public funding.

Regarding the environmental impacts, the available data indicates that since 2008 there has been a strong correlation between the reduction of pollutants measured over large areas of Greece and several financial indicators. More specifically, in Athens, a noticeable decrease in several pollutants such as SO_2 and NO_x is associated with the economic crisis mainly because the crisis has caused the reduction of industrial activities in urban and suburban areas, the reduction of traffic volume, and the increase of natural gas consumption instead of oil consumption (Vrekoussis et al., 2013).

However, there have also been dramatic environmental consequences. Since people's income has decreased, there has been a significant increase/trend in illegal logging both in green spaces in the city and in forest areas on the outskirts because of the search for alternative heating fuel. Hence, increased biomass burning in the winter seasons of 2012 and 2013 caused smog and high particle concentration in the atmosphere of major Greek cities (Saffari et al., 2013), including of course Athens, where the phenomenon was very marked. This forced the Ministry of Environment, Energy, and Climate Change (YPEKA) to issue directives to address the trend in the interests of public health (YPEKA, 2013).

It is now obvious that the current crisis in Greece is a multifaceted phenomenon with socio-spatial impacts on people's everyday lives and not only at a macro-economic level. Additionally, it is an ongoing phenomenon which is gradually deepening and therefore it must urgently be addressed through the implementation of appropriate policies. In this complex and difficult context, many spatial policies are under way. These policies, some of which are controversial regarding their efficiency and target, are analysed in the following section, including official general regulations, strategic spatial and development plans for Athens, as well as major urban interventions.

Spatial policies and initiatives in the crisis era

General regulations and policies

Spatial planning aims at providing a framework for urban development through which the socio-spatial impacts of the crisis can be addressed. Conversely, spatial planning in Greece seems to be weakened as a result of current policies.

The main urban and regional planning laws have recently been revised in order to reduce the levels of the planning system and to make it more flexible and responsive as spatial planning is considered to create obstacles concerning private investment. This new institutional framework[8] stems from a state of emergency thus questioning its ability to address the existing problems and shortcomings of the spatial planning system such as the absence of consistent, long-term policies and the frequent departures from approved plans (ITA, 2006; Wassenhoven et al., 2005; Wassenhoven, 2013) and to ensure effective matching of spatial and development policies (Asprogerakas & Zachari, 2012). The attempt also incorporates previous regulations such as provisions to facilitate private investments of strategic importance deviating from the mainstream spatial and planning legislation.[9] The treatment of space as an economic object and its use as a tool of crisis management without necessarily including social participation or measures to ensure protection of the environment have created concerns (Klampatsea, 2012).

Other major policies with spatial implications that have been applied in Greece during the period of the crisis focus mainly on revenue collection. These include the imposition of a fee for the 'regularisation' of illegal or semi-illegal constructions (called 'afthereta'). Law 4014/2011[10] on the 'regularisation' of illegal buildings was declared unconstitutional[11] by the Council of the State, the Supreme Court of Cassation, with special reference to its non-environmentally friendly nature. The Council of State, interpreting Article 24 of the Constitution, notes that urban development should be based on spatial planning to ensure the functionality of settlements and better living conditions for residents. Furthermore, reference is made to the drastic reduction in resources and capabilities of the Green Fund, an organisation mainly funded by the regularisation procedure in order to apply environmentally friendly urban programmes such as the development of parks and green spaces. This has led to deviation from the initial target of the organisation and a weakening of its role at a time when the need for effective public funding of urban policies is crucial (Serraos & Asprogerakas, 2012). In response, the Ministry of the Environment and Climate Change (YPEKA) introduced a new law[12] in 2013, arguing that it considers the legal weaknesses of the previous one. The new law is to be judged by the Council of the State.

Spatial and development plans in the Athens area

In relation to the spatial planning specifically in the Athens area a new city master plan known as the Regulatory Plan of Athens (RSA) was recently approved by the parliament. It is the last in a series of attempts to update the previous Master Plan dating from 1985. The new revision adopted three main strategic objectives: (1) balanced economic development and the strengthened international role of Athens; (2) sustainable spatial development, effective protection of the environment and cultural heritage, and adaptation to climate change; (3) improvement of the quality of life by balancing the distribution of resources and the benefits of development.[13] The plan strongly emphasises the concept of the compact city. Although a first draft of the RSA was completed in 2011, further elaboration was necessary as the plan faced substantial changes after extensive consultation with various social actors and stakeholders including the municipalities involved (Skayannis, 2013).

We must mention the recent merger of the Organisation for the Planning and Environmental Protection of Athens (ORSA), which has been mainly responsible for the RSA since 1985, with the Ministry of Environment as part of a public administration cost reduction programme. The recentralisation of metropolitan spatial planning governance undermines the effective implementation of the RSA.

An important planning initiative is the pilot of the 'Plan of Integrated Urban Intervention' (SOAP) which aspires to address the spatial implications of the crisis primarily in the centre of Athens. It was prepared by the Municipality of Athens and the ORSA through the promotion of integrated strategies such as urban planning, social cohesion, economic revitalisation, and environmental sustainability. The main objectives of the Athens SOAP are support of the economic base, recovery of social and cultural cohesion and re-habitation of the area, restoration of security, public space improvement, strengthening of the identity and the image of the city, as well as governance arrangements and public participation during the formation procedure.[14] The suggested actions are organised as horizontal, geographical actions (which focus on specific areas) and integrated actions (multidisciplinary actions). SOAP constitutes an integrated approach with a long-term scope (2020), designed to revitalise the city's downtown area with a comprehensive set of interventions. The implementation of the actions envisioned by the plan is a great challenge as it requires the collaboration of several public bodies from central government and local authorities.

Major urban interventions

The shortfall in funding resulted in annulment of public urban investment, which could have been used as a trigger to revitalise the urban environment. The two major urban interventions that are currently under way in Athens are initiatives of the private sector. These projects did not emerge as responses to the crisis but they have attracted great publicity and, in the short term, will secure job positions and have a positive impact on public psychology.

The first one is the construction of the new National Library and Greek National Opera (SNFCC) sponsored by the Stavros Niarchos Foundation, a concept dating back to 1998 which was finally announced in 2006 (Figure 7.10). The project will be developed at the site of the old racetrack in Athens, which is

Figure 7.10 Greek national opera construction site, 2014 (source: authors' visualisation).

located 4.5 km south of the centre, on the edge of Faliro Bay. Objections to the intervention are limited and mainly concern the capacity of the state to maintain the centre when complete.

The second project is the pedestrianisation of a major avenue in the centre of the city (Panepistimiou Avenue). The general proposal includes transportation projects (extension of the tram line) and the formation of the street as an open public space, a linear square for pedestrians, cyclists, and public transport. The Alexander S. Onassis Public Benefit Foundation, in collaboration with the YPEKA, has designed the project, which will be implemented through public funding (with a budget of €92 million). However, there are reservations concerning the intervention. These relate to the lack of feasibility and the expected social impact as well as the effectiveness of funding (Skayannis, 2014).

In the past, major projects have often been implemented with funds provided by 'benefactors'. However, a point of concern is that large-scale interventions with the involvement of the private sector set a trend of government withdrawal from public space and limit the opportunity for dialogue with the civil society. What is also questionable is the ability of the public to mobilise available resources in order to address the crisis effects and spatial development in general by maintaining a strategic role and meeting environmental and social cohesion goals. An illustrative example in this regard is the case of the former 'Hellinikon' airport which, despite a number of studies and an international architectural tender for its development, was finally included in the privatisation programme together with other public real estate assets and companies, and it is going to be developed as a private investment project.

Conclusions and open questions

The financial crisis that broke out in Greece in 2009 turned out to be an unprecedented phenomenon of the post-war period, which found both the state and its citizens unprepared to manage it independently. This happened despite the fact that the recent Greek economic and socio-political growth model provided clear indications which should have forewarned the state about what was about to follow.

Accordingly, the state reacted, in agreement with lenders and financiers, in a markedly rushed manner, adopting easy financial measures starting with cuts in government spending. In this sense, salaries and pensions were fixed, and every kind of taxation was increased, with particular emphasis on the over-taxation of real estate. At the same time the need to promote the most difficult measures to restructure the economic and productive structure of the country was apparently seen as a secondary priority, which first would not have quick direct effects and second would affect more deeply the known economic and political mechanisms of Greek society. The direct results of the above-mentioned measures were rapidly declining incomes and dramatic increase in the cost of living owed, *inter alia*, to increased taxation.

In terms of urban economy with significant spatial effects, the developments which need to be highlighted are associated with the collapse of the housing market and all sectors related to construction, maintenance, and property management, as well as the plummeting of commercial and business activities. This is easily noticeable in the town centre environment with the massive closure of businesses and consequently the desolation of traditional shopping streets, and also the general deterioration of the functional richness, vitality, and image of the city centre. An important consequence of the above development with essential social effects is the unemployment increase of more than 25 per cent in 2014, which is unprecedented for Europe and Greece.

In addition, contrasting effects could be identified on both public space and the environment. A gradual degradation of public space can be observed because of reduced maintenance, while at the same time an increase in its use has been recorded. This could be explained by the improved attractiveness of open space activities in comparison with other leisure events of higher cost. In the environmental field, a reduction in vehicular traffic can be observed, which is probably a result of the increased fuel cost. On the other hand, the authorities recorded an increase in air pollution in urban areas during the winter 2013, because of the increased use of fireplaces in combination with unsuitable forms of biomass. This is directly connected with another phenomenon, hitherto unfamiliar to the Greek reality, which is widespread illegal logging. Despite the increased guarding and monitoring of forest areas by the relevant government agencies, the results are not satisfactory.

As a consequence of the reduction of public expenditure the welfare state is shrinking rapidly. This has an immediate impact on the increasing homelessness and generally on the degradation of everyday life in urban areas. Moreover, a confusing approach on the part of the state agencies has been observed concerning the methods and strategies needed to address the spatial and social effects of the economic crisis. A substantial weakness is evident in the programming of broader spatial planning policies, and particularly in the design and promotion of effective long-term urban development policies. In contrast, the emphasis presently lies mainly on policies which aim at ensuring the growth of government revenues. As an illustrative example, it is worth mentioning the legalisation of almost every kind of illegal building, unfortunately without any substantial provision for countervailing measures to ensure the necessary 'environmental balance' (Serraos, 2012; Ploumidi & Serraos, 2012). At the same time, the necessary pursuit of private investments is directly connected with the exploitation and use of the land and natural resources of the country, and therefore essentially intervenes in broader spatial and urban planning, significantly degrading this process (Avgerinou, Wassenhoven, & Serraos, 2007). This creates a risk of imposing irreversible degrading impacts on the natural environment and the landscape as well as on the functional, economic, and social structure of the visible space.

The above remarks relate to the known pathogenesis of the Greek administrative system as well as the spatial planning and implementation system. In times of crisis, existing issues emerge more intensively. They concern, *inter alia*, non-effective and non-profitable management of consultation processes, the lack of horizontal and vertical coordination of policies, plans, and actions for urban space, and difficulty in forming and continuously adapting spatial policies (Serraos, Gianniris, & Zifou, 2005; Serraos, Asprogerakas, & Ioannou, 2009).

Apart from the difficulty of forming a balanced long-term planning procedure, the state seems to be unable to respond effectively to relief needs. Although some relevant actions have been implemented by state agencies as well as by social collective bodies to meet the daily needs of citizens (for example, homeless hostels, a social grocery, and a pharmacy provided by Athens Homeless Shelter), the lack of large-scale, immediate, and effective measures is obvious.

Many questions for further research arise from this preliminary work on the socio-spatial impacts of the economic crisis on the Athenian area. Among them, a special focus could be placed on the clarification of the role and capabilities of the urban planners in the midst of crisis as well as on the formulation of core parameters and priorities for a new, modern, flexible, and balanced development model covering the countryside, the cities, and spatial planning after the crisis. More specific questions concern the development of targeted urban policies for balanced economic, environmental, and socio-spatial development. The formulation of a clear new strategy for the management of Athens as an important European capital, on the assumption that the current crisis expresses the collapse of the post-war development model, constitutes a much wider and challenging task.

Notes

1 Law 4021/2011, Art. 53, GG A218/03.10.2011, Emergency Special Tax on Electrified Buildings (in Greek).
2 Law 4152/2013, GG A107/09.05.2013, Emergency measures for the implementation of the Laws 4046/2012, 4093/2012, and 4127/2013, Art. 1, Emergency Special Tax on Immovable Property (in Greek).
3 Law 4223/2013, GG A287/31.12.2013, Single property tax and other provisions (in Greek).
4 Law 3869/2010, GG A130/03.08.2010, Debt restructuring for over-indebted persons and other provisions (in Greek).

5 Law 4224/2013, GG A288/31.12.2013, Governing Council of private debt management, Hellenic Republic Asset Development Fund, and other emergency provision, Art. 2, Suspension of auctions (in Greek).
6 Law 4046/2012, GG A28/14.02.2012, Annex V1 E, Structural reforms (in Greek).
7 Law 4141/2013, GG A81/05.04.2013, Developing investment tools, credit supply and other provisions, Art. 19, Amendments to the Law 2778/2999, Real Estate Investment Companies (in Greek).
8 Law 4269/2014, GG 142/A/2014, Regional and urban planning reform – sustainable development (in Greek).
9 Law 3775, GG 122/2009, Transfer pricing documentation rules, business rules underfunding, accelerated licensing and other provisions, and Law 3986, GG 152/2011, Urgent measures for the implementation of the medium term financial strategy 2012–2015 (in Greek).
10 Law 4014, GG 209/A/2011, Environmental licensing of projects and activities, arbitrary regulation creating environmental balance and other Ministry of Environment competence provisions, (in Greek).
11 Council of the State decision No. 3341/2013.
12 Law 4178, GG 174/A/2013, Arbitrary building confrontation – environmental Balance and other provisions (in Greek).
13 Law 4277, GG 156/A/2014, New structural plan of Athens – Attica and other provisions (in Greek).
14 Joint Ministerial Decision Draft, Plan of integrated urban intervention for the centre of Athens (in Greek).

References

Alpha Bank (2013) *Weekly economic report 24.10.2013* (in Greek). [Online] Available from: www.alpha.gr/page/default.asp?id=2450& [accessed 6 January 2015].
Asprogerakas, E. & Zachari, V. (2012) Territorial cohesion and spatial planning: The need for policy coordination in Greece. In: *The future of development and spatial planning of Greece*. Conference Proceedings, Hellenic Association of Regional Planners, University of Central Greece, NTUA. 25 February 2012. Delphi, Greece (in Greek).
Avgerinou, S., Wassenhoven, L., & Serraos, K. (2007) *Integrating and updating the research project entitled: Development of the Ellinikon airport area of Greece*. Research programme, Department of Town and Regional Planning, NTUA (in Greek).
Balampanidis, D., Belavilas, N., Gleni, V., Polyzou, I., & Prentou, P. (2013a) The effects of crisis on the commercial activities in central neighborhoods of Athens and Piraeus: Resistance and dynamics. In: *Changes and redefinitions of space in Greek crisis*. Conference Proceedings. 1–3 November 2013. Volos, Greece, University Press of Thessaly, Vols 102–110.
Balampanidis, D., Patatouka, E., & Siatitsa, D. (2013b) The right to housing during the period of crisis in Greece. *Geographies*, 22, 31–43 (in Greek).
Bank of Greece (2010) *Report of the governor of the Bank of Greece for the year 2009* (in Greek). [Online] Available from: www.bankofgreece.gr/BogEkdoseis/ekthd-kth2010.pdf [accessed 10 November 2014].
Bank of Greece (2011) *Report of the governor of the Bank of Greece for the year 2010* (in Greek). [Online] Available from: www.bankofgreece.gr/BogEkdoseis/ekthd-kth2010.pdf [accessed 10 November 2014].
Bank of Greece (2014) *Summary of short-term indices key available for real estate market*. [Online] Available from: www.bankofgreece.gr/Pages/el/Statistics/realestate/indices.aspx [accessed 3 November 2014].

Curtius, E. & Kaupert, J. A. (1881) *Karten Von Attika*. Berlin, Dietrich Reimer.

Eleftherotypia (2013) *Crisis 'kicked out' 20% of passengers from OASA*. 3 March 2013. [Online] Available from: www.enet.gr/?i=news.el.article&id=347738 [accessed 3 March 2014].

ELIE (Hellenic Valuation Institute) (2013) 'Rents' reduction: A large research by Chrisi Eukairia. 17 April 2013. [Online] Available from: www.elie.gr/index.php/el/news-publications/75-pub0170413 [accessed 10 November 2014].

ELSTAT (Hellenic Statistical Authority) (2011) *Table: The De Jure (registered) population 2011*. ELSTAT, Athens. [Online] Available from: www.statistics.gr/portal/page/portal/ESYE/PAGE-census2011 [accessed 27 October 2014].

ELSTAT (Hellenic Statistical Authority) (2013a) *Labour force survey: 1st quarter of 2013*. [Press release] ELSTAT, Athens, 1 (in Greek). [Online] Available from: www.statistics.gr/portal/page/portal/ESYE/BUCKET/A0101/PressReleases/A0101_SJO01_DT_QQ_01_2013_01_F_GR.pdf [accessed 12 November 2014].

ELSTAT (Hellenic Statistical Authority) (2013b) *Turnover index for retail trade*. July 2013. ELSTAT, Athens (in Greek). [Online] Available from: www.statistics.gr/portal/page/portal/ESYE/PAGE-themes?p_param=A0508 [accessed 12 November 2014].

ELSTAT (Hellenic Statistical Authority) (2013c) *National and regional accounts 2000–2008*. ELSTAT, Athens. [Online] Available from: www.statistics.gr/portal/page/portal/ESYE/PAGE-themes?p_param=A0702 [accessed 12 November 2014].

ESP (Piraeus Traders Association) (2007, 2011) *Annual researches of Piraeus Traders Association*. ESP, Athens (in Greek).

FEANTSA (European Federation of National Organisations working with the Homeless) (2012) *Greece: FEANTSA country fiche*. FEANTSA, Brussels. [Online] Available from: www.feantsa.org/spip.php?article853&lang=en [accessed 27 October 2014].

Geoaxis (2014) *Geoaxis value observatory: Office spaces*. [Online] Available from: www.geoaxis.gr/images/parathrhthrio/paratiritirio%20axiwn%20geoaxis_q3_2014.pdf [accessed 3 November 2014].

INE/GSEE-ADEDY (Labour Institute of the Greek General Confederation of Greece) (2012) *Greek economy and employment: 2012 Annual report*. INE/GSEE-ADEDY, Athens, 17, 264–266, 334–337. [Online] Available from: www.inegsee.gr/sitefiles/files/EKTHESH%2014.pdf [accessed 27 October 2014] (in Greek).

INEMY/ESEE (Institute of Commerce and Services of National Confederation of Hellenic Commerce) (2011a) *Results of a new research on closed businesses along central commercial roads of Attica*. INEMY/ESEE, Athens (in Greek).

INEMY/ESEE (Institute of Commerce and Services of National Confederation of Hellenic Commerce) (2011b) *Closed businesses in Greece*. INEMY/ESEE, Athens (in Greek).

INEMY/ESEE (Institute of Commerce and Services of National Confederation of Hellenic Commerce) (2012) *Closed businesses in the city center of Athens*. Geobasis. INEMY/ESEE, Athens, 18–21, 25 (in Greek).

ITA (2006) *Urban planning, implementation problems and proposals for reform*. Report of Scientific Committee, Institute of Local Government, Athens (in Greek).

Kalantzopoulou, M. & Belavilas, N. (2014) From the Olympic Games to the memorandum: The establishment of emergency measures in spatial planning and development. *Geographies*, 23, 3–6 (in Greek).

Kandyla, T. & Triantafyllopoulos, N. (2009) Psychological factors in the housing market in Greece during the period 2004–2007. *Research Papers Series*, 15(13), 243–246 (in Greek).

Kandyla, T. & Triantafyllopoulos, N. (2010) House buyers' behaviour in Greece during 2004–2007. *Aeihoros*, 13, 94–117 (in Greek).

Kanellis, V. (2012) Allocating the outstanding rents to the Tax Office. *Imerisia*, 8 December 2012 (in Greek).

Kathimerini (2010) *Taxi without passengers*. 19 June 2010. [Online] Available from: http://news.kathimerini.gr/4dcgi/_w_articles_ell_100013_19/06/2010_405194 [accessed 3 March 2014].

Klampatsea, E. (2012) The design of the space as a means of crisis management in Greece. In: *Conference Proceedings of third National Conference of Planning and Regional Development*. 27–30 September 2012. Volos, Greece, University of Thessaly, pp. 163–169 (in Greek).

Klimaka NGO (2012) *Homelessness in Greece in 2012*. NGO Klimaka, Athens. [Online] Available from: www.klimaka.org.gr/newsite/downloads/Research%202012_Homeless ness.pdf [accessed 27 October 2014] (in Greek).

Maloutas, T., Arapoglou, V., Kandylis, G., & Sayas, J. (2012) Social polarization and de-segregation in Athens. In: Maloutas, T. & Fujita, K. (eds) *Residential segregation in comparative perspective: Making sense of contextual diversity*. Burlington, Ashgate, pp. 257–283.

Mpiris, K. (1966) *Athens: From 19th to 20th century*, Athens, Kostas H. Mpiris (in Greek).

OECD (2011) Country notes. *OECD Journal on Budgeting*, 11 (2). [Online] Available from: http://dx.doi.org/10.1787/budget-11-5kg869h4t8lx [accessed 27 October 2014].

Panas, E. (2012) *Research on energy poverty in Greece*. Athens University of Economics and Business, Department of Statistics, 4–7. [Online] Available from: http://library.tee.gr/digital/m2600/m2600_panas.pdf [accessed 27 October 2014] (in Greek).

Papaioannou, T. (2014) *Asteras vouliagmenis*. 27 January 2014. iekemtee.gr. [Online] Available from: http://goo.gl/K9i9Fa [accessed 3 March 2014].

Ploumidi, E. & Serraos, K. (2012) Upgrade of densely built urban areas by creating a network of small scale outdoor green spaces: The idea of 'pocket parks'. In: *Conference Proceedings of 3rd National Conference of Planning and Regional Development*. 27–30 September 2012. Volos, University of Thessaly, pp. 512–517.

Region of Attica (2013) *Changes in data traffic on main roads in Athens Traffic Management Centre* (in Greek). [Online] Available from: www.patt.gov.gr/main/attachments2/6500_13_02_13_dimosieusi_kdk. [accessed 3 May 2014].

Saffari, A., Daher, N., Samara, C., Voutsa, D., Kouras, A., Manoli, E., Karagkiozidou, O., Vlachokostas, C., Moussiopoulos, N., Shafer, M. M., Schauer, J. J., & Sioutas, C. (2013) Increased biomass burning due to the economic crisis in Greece and its adverse impact on winter-time air quality in Thessaloniki. *Environmental Science and Technology*, 47 (23), 13313–13320.

SEPE (Hellenic Labour Inspectorate) (2012) *Activity report of SEPE for the year 2012*. Ministry of Labour, Social Security and Welfare, Athens, 36(41) 50–59. [Online] Available from: www.ypakp.gr/uploads/docs/6810.pdf [accessed 27 October 2014].

Serraos, K. (2012) The tackling of the 'urban arbitrariness' and the idea of the 'environmental balance'. In: *Conference Proceedings of third National Conference of Planning and Regional Development*. 27–30 September 2012. Volos, Greece, University of Thessaly, pp. 389–398.

Serraos, K. & Asprogerakas, E. (2012) Planning and place branding: Effective tools for urban development in Greece during the economic crisis. In: Defner, A. & Karachaliou, N. (eds) *Marketing and place branding: The international experience and the situation in Greece*. Volos, University of Thessaly, pp. 57–81 (in Greek).

Serraos, K., Asprogerakas, E., & Ioannou, B. (2009) Planning culture and the interference of major events: The recent experience of Athens. In: Knieling, J. & Othengrafen, F. (eds) *Planning cultures in Europe: Decoding cultural phenomena in urban and regional planning.* Farnham, Ashgate, Urban and Regional Planning and Development Series, pp. 205–220.

Serraos, K., Gianniris, H., & Zifou, M. (2005) The Greek spatial and urban planning system in the European context. In: Gabriella, P. & Cesare, B. (eds) *Complessitá e Sostenibilitá, Prospettive per i territori europei: Strategie di pianificazione in dieci Paesi.* Milano, Poli.design.

Skayannis, P. (ed.) (2014) RETHINK Panepistimiou str: The riposte. *Aeichoros*, 18, 158–205 (in Greek).

Skayannis, P. (2013) The (master) plans of Athens and the challenges of its re-planning in the context of crisis. *International Journal of Architectural Research*, 7 (2), 192–205.

Stathakis, G. & Nikolakakis, M. (2014) The political economy of 'Foivos' and Athina'. *Geographies*, 23, 7–9 (in Greek).

Travlos, I. (1960) *The urban development of Athens.* Athens, Travlos (in Greek).

Triantafyllopoulou, E. & Sayas, J. (2012) *Neighborhoods fighting crisis.* [Online] Available from: www.assoeconomiepolitique.org/political-economy-outlook-for-capitalism/?p=503 &aid=504&sa=0 [accessed 15 March 2013].

Tsakalotos, E. (2014) Contesting Greek exceptionalism within the European crisis. In: Featherstone, K. (ed.), *Europe in modern Greek history.* London, Hurst & Company, pp. 95–117.

Vaiou, D. (2014) Tracing aspects of the Greek crisis in Athens: Putting women in the picture. *European Urban and Regional Studies*, doi: 10.1177/0969776414523802.

Vaiou, D., Mantouvalou, M., & Mavridou, M. (2000) Post war urban planning in Greece between theory and conjuncture. In: *Proceedings of the second Conference of History of City and Urban Planning Society 'Urban Planning in Greece 1949–1974'*, Volos, Greece, University of Thessaly, pp. 25–37 (in Greek).

Vlamis, P. (2014) Greek fiscal crisis and repercussions for the property market. *Journal of Property Investment & Finance*, 32 (1), 21–34.

Vrekoussis, M., Richter, A., Hilboll, A., Burrows, J. P., Gerasopoulos, E., Lelieveld, J., Barrie, L., Zerefos, C., & Mihalopoulos, N. (2013) Economic crisis detected from space: Air quality observations over Athens/Greece. *Geophysical Research Letters*, 40, 1–6.

Wassenhoven, L. (2013) Planning policy and law in hard times: The case of Greece under the current crisis. [Keynote speech] *Conference – Rethinking Planning Law in the Crisis Era: New Scope, New Tools, New Challenges.* Platform of Experts in Planning Law, Athens, 17–18 October.

Wassenhoven, L., Asprogerakas, E., Gianniris, E., Pagonis, T., Petropoulou, C., & Sapountzaki, P. (2005) *National overview: Greece.* School of Architecture, National Technical University of Athens. Report for the Research Program 'Governance of Territorial and Urban Policies from EU to Local Level'.

YPEKA (2013) Clarifications on the provision of measures to address exceptional episodes of airborne particles. [Press release] 6 November 2013. [Online] Available from: www. ypeka.gr/Default.aspx?tabid=389&sni[524]=2743&language=el-GR [accessed 15 March 2014].

8 A new landscape of urban social movements

Reflections on urban unrest in Southern European cities

Frank Othengrafen, Luís del Romero Renau, and Ifigeneia Kokkali

Introduction

From 2008 onwards, a rapidly unfolding economic recession with global dimensions has been provoking popular protest and unrest in many parts of the urban world. Arising from apparently different claims, that sometimes seem to be very local in nature, these protests appear to be desperately seeking to bring back to the political agenda the unsustainability and destructiveness of neoliberal forms of economic – including urban – growth, and of urbanisation as well. Cities across Europe, including London, Stockholm, Paris, and Madrid, Barcelona, Rome, Athens, Istanbul and Kiev, have erupted in massive demonstrations, strikes and protests, often accompanied by violence (Brenner, Marcuse, & Mayer, 2009: p. 176). These movements were soon joined by the 'Occupy Wall Street' movement in New York City's Zuccotti Park (September 2011), which was quickly followed by a wave of occupations in cities throughout the US and the world (Juris & Maple, 2012).

Studying the chronology and the geography of the spread of these protests, which have mainly taken the form of collective sit-ins in public urban spaces – in particular, piazzas and parks – sheds light on the catalytic role played by the 'blow-up' in the Arab world some months earlier (December 2010). Protests spread indeed from North Africa to Southern Europe, then to the rest of Europe, the US, and the rest of the world. This, then, means that, despite the local micro-reasons which fuel people's expression of discontent, there should also be some global reasons that lead local reaction and protest. Nonetheless, protests worldwide were overwhelmingly urban, thus bringing to the fore the injurious effects (and side effects) of contemporary urban growth for humans and the environment.

According to Harvey (2012), the current socio-economic crisis is an urbanisation crisis, growing out of speculative investments relating to the built environment and to the massive redistribution of real income that is embedded in the operations of the capitalist city. This might help to explain why, for example, many middle-sized towns in Spain, Italy, or Portugal doubled the proportion of built land but not their population in less than a decade.

Speculative investments are also behind the fact that 911,568 new housing units were planned to be built in Spain in 2006, enough to accommodate more than 3.5 million new inhabitants (INE, 2012), which is far above the expected population growth. Urbanisation thus plays a major role as it is, on the one hand, the driver for economic development but, on the other hand, has been accomplished, to a large extent, through loans and debts which have contributed to the speculative bubble of the real estate markets and the eruption of the crisis, first in the US, then in Southern European cities. The crisis particularly affected the construction sector as one of the backbones of national economies in most Southern European countries, resulting in unemployment and a decrease in real income per capita.

The crisis has strong impacts on Southern European countries and cities. In the case of Spain, for example, the unemployment tax rose from 8.8 to 25 per cent in only four years from 2008 to 2012; additionally, only in 2012, over 400,000 businesses had to close down in the country (Segovia, 2013). Similarly, in Greece, the unemployment rate reached 27.4 per cent in the first quarter of 2013 (ELSTAT, 2013). Additionally, the average declared income has decreased in most Southern European countries and cities since the beginning of the socio-economic crisis. In Athens, for example, it fell from €20,060 in 2008 to €18,750 in 2012, recording a decline of 6.5 per cent. All these developments led to a decline in the construction sector, which has been a cornerstone of Southern European national economies for decades, resulting in a further decrease in GDP and thus intensifying the impact of the crisis.

The combined effects of the crisis on (urban) growth and austerity policies have dramatically emphasised social fragmentation, polarisation, and instability. These consequences represent an 'economic policy of insecurity', with increased poverty and inequality, lack of job stability and endemic insecurity, transfer of the sense of risk to the individual, increasing social fractures, and, finally, a rupture of the 'social contract' of the previous decades, namely the link between capitalism, the welfare state, and democracy, all of which has led to increased disaffection and social polarisation (Beck, 2012). The worsening of working conditions, higher unemployment, and lower earnings for young people has been a constant feature of European social reality since the 1980s and 1990s, with young employees having a stronger presence in sectors with high employee turnover, temporary positions, and part-time jobs (Sotiris, 2010). Additionally, in countries such as Greece or Spain, many students have noted that better qualifications do not necessarily lead to better employment prospects (ibid.: p. 204). In this context, many people, particularly in Southern European cities, have expressed their opposition to these neoliberalisation trends, including the efforts to manage the crisis through more austerity policies – a choice that has been largely presented as being without alternative.

It can be argued that a new landscape of protest movements occurred as one response to the crisis. It is thus the aim of this chapter to reflect on these public protests and social movements in Southern European cities. How did they occur? Which actors are involved in or are part of the social movements? What is the focus of action? Do these protests address global or local issues? How are these protests organised? How do they differ from previous (urban) social movements? To address these questions, the evolution of urban social movements in the recent past will first be presented. On this basis, a 'typology' of (urban) social movements or protests is introduced and then used to analyse current conflicts and protests in Southern European cities, particularly focusing on the two case studies of Madrid and Valencia. Finally, conclusions with regard to the new landscape of protest movements are drawn.

The history of urban movements and protests

The deep transformations of the late 1960s – from the American civil rights and anti-Vietnam movements in May 1968 in France, and the students' and workers' protests in Italy, Germany, and Mexico, or even the anti-regime protests in Franco's Spain (and later on against the military junta of Greece) – flag the beginning of an era of mobilisations that seemed to eventually pave the way for 'a movement society' (Meyer & Tarrow, 1998). To catch up with the new developments, the study of social movements started growing during this same period to reach – at the end of the 1980s – an 'explosion' of theoretical and empirical work in the field (see Della Porta & Diani, 2006). As Pickvance (2003: p. 104) points out, there is, however, a separation of social movement theorising from writing on urban movements. The latter are cut off from the former, despite the fact that they represent a dimension of social movements. The reasons why this has occurred are beyond our scope here. Still, it is no surprise that the theorisation of urban movements is rooted in the same turbulent events of the late 1960s and early 1970s, the time at which the term 'urban social movements' (USM) also saw the light of day in the writings of Manuel Castells. This concept, which has been associated with Castells ever since, contains ambiguity even in the writings of the author himself, assuming slightly different expressions and being represented by different exemplary paradigms (for instance, in *The Urban Question*, 1977, and in *The City and the Grassroots*, 1983). Pickvance (2003) stresses indeed that the usage of the concept becomes more generic over the course of time. In a restrictive usage, 'urban social movements' can only be characterised as those citizen actions with the highest urban and political effect (in a scale including also the intermediate level of 'protest' and the lower level of 'participation'); whereas the more generic usage refers to citizen action irrespective of its actual and potential effects (ibid.: p. 103). He further points out that the adoption of the generic usage of the concept resulted in circumventing 'a careful assessment of the actual (and highly diverse) effects of urban movements'. This led authors, he continues, to 'automatically interpret opposition changes in the built environment as anti-capitalist rather than ... NIMBY' (ibid.).

From a slightly different perspective (and probably in an attempt to be less normative), Mayer (2009: p. 364) prefers to refer to a second phase of 'urban social movements' induced by the austerity politics of the 1980s, the first phase being the turmoil of the late 1960s and 1970s. In stressing the transformation of the relations between movements and local states from oppositional to cooperative, Mayer underlines that 'movements shifted their strategies from protest to program', and turned from 'confrontational groups that used to organize strikes and public hearings' to professionalised and institutionalised organisations that acquired the role of 'delivering ... services' (ibid.: p. 364). This change led to these organisations distancing themselves from newly mobilising groups which were not part of this cooperation with the local state; additionally, a radicalisation of some groups whose claims were not addressed by the above arrangements could be observed. In addition to these developments, Mayer stresses the complexity of the movement terrain in the 1980s, with the introduction of a variety of middle-class movements with concerns ranging from NIMBY to environmental, defensive, and so forth. Summing up the situation of the urban movement terrain during the 1980s, Mayer estimates that cities experienced very fragmented forms of urban protest compared to the situation in the late 1960s and 1970s. The author stresses that the forms of urban protest of the 1980s did not include any 'overarching battle cries or convergence in joint action' (ibid.: p. 364). This fragmentation has developed further since the 1990s when several defensive movements came into being, ranging from anti-gentrification (with slogans such as 'Die, yuppie scum!') to anti-globalisation movements (such as 'Reclaim the Streets') (ibid.).

At the dawn of the twenty-first century, however, the calls for urban and social equality that generated the urban social movements in the late 1960s seem to be back. As Harvey (2008) highlights, the new financial mechanisms and the new financial markets fostered urbanisation processes in many countries and cities, being a driver for the expansion of the capitalistic system. Under these conditions, growth has been maintained in Europe and North America, but, as Mayer (2009: p. 365) points out, it has been jobless. Moreover, it has been accompanied by increasingly sharp socio-spatial polarisation and divides which finally led to massive public protests. There has indeed been an undoubted rise in (income) inequalities in Europe, as different EU and OECD reports demonstrate. In the last 20 years, the richest 10 per cent has become even richer, with inequality increasing almost everywhere.[1] In this context, it is not surprising that the Occupy movement has expanded so quickly and so massively around the world, providing a powerful slogan: they – those at the top of the wealth and income scale – are the 1 per cent, while the rest of us are the remaining 99 per cent (Juris & Maple, 2012). The different Occupy movements seem to be positioned between the local and the global scale: while they often have a local focus (that is, very specific localised claims), they appeal nonetheless to the more global claim for equality. It can, then, be suggested that current urban social movements range rather from 'local' movements that contest corporate urban development, surveillance, policing, and commercialisation of public space to transnational, anti-globalisation movements, including global justice movements (Mayer 2009: p. 366).

Urban social movements and protests as escalation of asymmetrically conflictual situations

But how do current urban social movements differ from those in the past? What is specific about current public protests? Why do they occur? In the first instance, the recent (urban) social movements across the globe seem to address trans-national issues, and the protests that erupted in Southern Europe are no excep-tion. Yet, as mentioned earlier, the current protests may also have a more (or apparently more) local character. What these protests or social movements, whether globally or locally oriented, have in common is that they occur as a con-sequence of a serious incompatibility between two or more opinions, principles, or interests that can be attributed either to structures (object sphere) or personal settings (subject sphere) (Glasl, 2004; Reuber, 2012). These competing interests do not necessarily result in protests – as societal change comes about through the struggle between conflicting interests they have to be regarded as a driving force behind social, economic, or technological innovation in the first place. However, as societies are dynamic entities constantly undergoing change as a result of competition over scarce resources, conflicts among the competing interests or principles can nevertheless escalate (Glasl, 2004; Jehn & Bendersky, 2003). This becomes apparent, for example, in the *Indignados* movement or the MM15 initi-ative in Spain or the protests in Athens or the current 'Right to the City' initi-atives in various cities. These protests often occur in situations with asymmetric (power) constellations and decision-making powers, which may be of a legal, structural, institutional, or moral nature allowing one actor or group, for example a government or a private investor, to play a dominant role (Bonacker & Imbusch, 2010: p. 72; Othengrafen & Sondermann, 2015).

Following Sears and Cairns (2010), the current financial or socio-economic crisis can then be understood as structural conflict, that is, the inevitable outcome of the inequalities and instabilities in Western societies. Here, massive demon-strations, strikes, and protests emerged as a reaction to the present structure of the global economic system enabling the largest banks and institutions to avoid government regulation and take huge risks that only reward a select few. A structural conflict becomes apparent (e.g. Reuter, 2000; Siebel, 2009): the funda-mental social protests reflect the loss of confidence in economic or political actors and, amongst other things, demand the participation of the majority of the population in economic and social progress. These protests are based on struc-tural or social imbalances and are not necessarily bound to a specific place as shown by the (urban) social movements of the 1970s or the current Occupy pro-tests in many cities (see also Othengrafen & Sondermann, 2015). In most Southern European countries the protests also address the welfare state and its scope, achievements, or outputs as the various governments, even during the decades of economic and urban growth based on Keynesian-style state policies, scarcely contributed to developing a welfare state with various and compre-hensive achievements for all individuals. In the case of Spain, for example, citizens have experienced during the last few years the dramatic reduction or even suppression of basic public policies, such as public housing, free access to the education, health, or judicial system, or social wages for handicapped people. Maybe one of the most striking examples is the sale of a stock of around 3,000 public housing units in Madrid to the international investment fund Goldman Sachs for less than half of its estimated price (Noriega, 2014), leaving the most important urban area of the country without public policies for housing and making way for urban social movements.

Urban social movements in Southern European cities also occur as a consequence of institutional inadequacies such as the lack of adequate (local) budgets or the lack of socially redistributive urban planning policies that are typical of welfare state policies in many Northern European countries. It is also in this context, that many protests – also in many Northern European states – are addressing the lack of transparency in formal procedures and decision-making processes, including the question of to what extent planning considerations and political decisions are coherent (e.g. Brettschneider, 2013; Renn, 2013). Furthermore, corruption is a major challenge for urban politics, particularly in Southern European countries. According to Harvey (2012: p. 79), much of this relates to how public investments are allocated to produce something that appears to be for the common good but which promotes private asset values for privileged property owners. Corruption cases have indeed affected many local, regional, and even national administrations in different European countries, and represent perhaps the biggest hindrance for urban governance. In the Spanish region of Murcia, for example, local representatives in 57.8 per cent of the municipalities in the region have been found guilty in corruption cases (Jerez, Martín, & Pérez, 2012). Apart from the economic cost, corruption cases are one of the reasons for the crisis of confidence towards traditional institutional forms of representation at different local and regional levels, which has undoubtedly led to the emergence of fervent protests and, in turn, of new social movements such as the *Indignados* movement in Spain.

Additionally, significant cost increases caused by urban mega-projects may also be a reason for protests (Leontidou, 2012; Renn, 2013). These kinds of projects can be seen as an expression of the change from universalistic to spatially targeted and place-focused approaches triggering socio-spatial inequalities between urban areas that benefit from various urban projects and investments and other areas left without any intervention. The emphasis on different sports or cultural mega-events is a good example of this shift in planning in Southern European cities: the Olympic Games (Barcelona 1992; Athens 2004; Torino 2010); International World Exhibitions (Seville 1992; Lisbon 1998; Zaragoza 2008; Milan 2015), or Cultural European Capitals (Thessaloniki 1997; Porto 2001; Salamanca 2002; Patras 2006, etc.). As Alexandri (2014) points out, for Athens, the Olympic Games in 2004 favoured projects that contributed to the success of the Olympic Games, presenting Athens as a vivid, attractive area. However, these projects, including the construction of new prestigious buildings and innercity metro stations, the development of promenades and pedestrian areas, together with the 'beautifications of public spaces' (ibid.: p. 4), changed the land use values in the city centre considerably by contributing to a sharp rise in property prices resulting in the displacement of former land uses and residents (Vaiou 2002; cited in ibid.: p. 4). Obviously, the public expenditures for the Olympic Games contributed to the increase in the public debt, restricting the room for manoeuvre of local authorities; this became even more important at times such as during the current socio-economic crisis. In this context, the recent public protests can also be viewed as an attempt to overcome the asymmetric (power) constellations and decision-making powers.

Public protests and urban social movements: Valencia and Madrid

Madrid and Valencia have experienced a similar economic and social crisis, as a result of – amongst other things – two decades of neoliberal urban policies and management. In both cases the council has been ruled continuously by a conservative absolute majority since 1991, resulting in an 'entrepreneurial urbanism', that is, a model of neoliberal urban management that is based on three policies, based on the aforementioned factors: privatisation, festivalisation, and urban growth, which together have given rise to the emergence of urban protests and movements.

First, the privatisation of public enterprises and sectors has been one of the main axes of the urban policies. Madrid was consolidated during the 1990s as the economic capital of the country when the city became the headquarters of major multinational companies, many of which were former public enterprises that were privatised during this decade, particularly in the energy sector. In this context, Madrid and Valencia have also developed their own ideological agenda that has the strategic objective of gradually reducing the weight of public education for public–private partnerships and private education and that has nothing to do with the recession. An example summarises the deeper meaning of this strategy: while investment budgets and jobs for teachers in the public system are reduced, the budget for educational public–private partnerships increases, even at secondary school level, and some local governments provide free land to build private schools whereas for years they have refused to extend the network of public schools. Public protests arose, amongst others, in defence of the public educational system, especially in Madrid, where in 2011 approximately 3,000 teachers were dismissed, whereas the rest of the teachers in the region had to add two more hours of classes (González, 2011).

Second, the festivalisation of the urban space is another axis that has marked the urban management of both cities. The model of 'show urbanism' pivots on a number of bulky and expensive architectural projects that have spread over both cities. 'Show urbanism' is associated with economic development and combined with sports and cultural mega-events (Cucó, 2013: p. 161) such as the new Mestalla stadium, the City of Arts and Sciences designed by the star architect Santiago Calatrava, and the new design of the port for the America's Cup and Formula 1 in Valencia as well as the complex of the skyscrapers *de la Castellana* or the dozens of sports facilities built for the Madrid Olympic bid in 2012, 2016, and 2020. This model of urban spectacle is also another form of privatisation, since many urban projects that have emerged from public funds, ended up bene-fitting private real estate projects for the upper social classes (Gaja, 2013). However, as festivalisation strategies only favour a few and discriminate against broader swathes of the population, civic initiatives appear, such as Madrid's 'Anti Eurovegas Comitteee', which protested against a large gambling resort project of six casinos and 12 skyscraper hotels proposed in 2012 by Las Vegas Sand Corporation to be built in the west of Madrid. In this case, the protests were successful: the project was finally rejected.

Third, the other major component of this city management model has been the spectacular urban growth in both cities. Madrid is the best example of this neoliberal model with disproportionate residential operations (officially called Urban Action Programmes) in the 1990s, leading to the liberalisation of 8,000 hectares of land, developing virtually all the available urban land of the muni-cipality of Madrid, whose viability is currently complicated, due to the crisis. The case of Valencia and its Metropolitan Area is even blunter: failure of forms of metropolitan governance, progressive destruction of one of the most important cultural landscapes of the Mediterranean basin, the *Huerta de Valencia*, due to residential and industrial uses, and the construction of new infrastructures. However, the vast majority of these new developed areas remain empty today.

As a consequence and reaction to this city management model, dozens of urban social movements arise, in line with the high social, environmental, or economic costs. According to the Ministry of Finance and Public Administra-tions (2014), Spanish municipalities had an overall debt of more than €35 billion at the end of 2013, and the two biggest municipalities in the country, Madrid and Barcelona, had a debt of around €8.2 billion. The fiscal crisis that many local administrations face due to austerity politics is a consequence of previous pol-icies and challenges municipalities not only to guarantee accessibility to basic facilities such as social services, schools, or hospitals, but also to promote new economic activities to fight unemployment in these cities. As a consequence, urban protests occurred to express disagreement with the situation and to call for new solutions and political responses. However, the origin of some of these pro-tests dates back to the 1990s, when Spain entered a period of economic boom based on real estate and tourism that was fostered by generous public investment in infrastructures (motorways, ports, airports, and high speed trains). Here, social movements not linked to political parties or traditional social movements emerged to fight for the protection of the environment, cultural or natural her-itage, public housing, or the quality of life.

Some of these movements are purely NIMBY, reacting against an urban plan or project for their impact on the immediate surroundings of the protesters' homes but most of them, similar to developments in other countries, argue for a broader change in the urban policy model and a turning away from festivalisa-tion, privatisation, and neoliberal planning strategies. These urban social move-ments are characterised by a horizontal structure, a social heterogeneity of the actors (they cannot be considered class movements), and most of them emerge on an ad hoc basis (they exist as long as the contested urban plan or project is discussed). A good example is the array of protests organised as a reaction to redevelopment plans in symbolic areas such as the *Puerta del Sol* square in Madrid or the port of Valencia. The *Puerta del Sol* square in Madrid is a traditional place for public protests and was restored for the last time in 2009. Nevertheless, in 2012, the town council approved a new redevelopment project for the square that included the installation of different kiosks. This raised public protests as the redevelopment plan was interpreted as an attempt to reduce the area for demonstrations (Martiarena, 2012). In the case of Valencia, the port has been the object of different redevelopment projects to host mega-events such as Formula 1 or the America's Cup. In this case, many inhabitants protested against the privatisation of this former public space and the degradation of industrial heritage linked to the port. Again, a committee of citizens was established to coordinate and somehow 'formalise' the protests against these mega-events.

In summary, the last decade has been characterised by a vivid landscape of urban conflicts in both cities, linked to both the economic boom of the country (before 2008) and the current socio-economic crisis (since 2008). Even since the Iraq war in 2003 both cities had been 'places' for protests and demonstrations, including the recent 'tide protest movements' (*mareas*) against the privatisation of education (green tide), land for mining and fracking (blue tide), and health (white tide), especially in Madrid. On 15 May 2011, for example, hundreds of citizens occupied the town hall square of Madrid and Valencia, an occupation that lasted for months. Although this movement appeared in dozens of cities in Spain, the movement in Madrid and Valencia was more durable and supported than in any other Spanish city. At present, both cities are experiencing a renaissance of new and highly active social movements, especially using the internet, digital media, and social networks (Anduiza, Cristancho, & Sabucedo, 2013). However, these citizens' movements have been severely repressed by the government and few citizens' demands have been met. In total, only 12 per cent of urban conflicts that emerged in Madrid and Valencia between 2002 and 2013 reached an agreement with politicians or planners; in a minority of cases (19 per cent) the plan or project that unleashed protests, was finally withdrawn (Del Romero, 2014). Against this background of great relevance is the new citizenship law. This controversial security law, pushed through Congress by the ruling party, imposes heavy fines for street protestors who carry signs 'harmful to Spain or the regions', and grants private security guards the right to help the police break up demonstrations. Protesting in front of Congress, the Senate, or regional assemblies has been considered a serious offence since 12 December 2014.

A new landscape in protest movements in Southern European cities

One of the main consequences of the crisis in Southern European cities is the emergence of a renewed landscape of protest movements. As explained in the previous section, new social movements, such as the *Indignados* movement in Spain or the protests in Athens, came on the scene between 2010 and 2011.

However, these social movements did not appear all of a sudden in 2011, 'but have been incubated over long periods of time in their respective weak civil societies' (Leontidou, 2010). According to Leontidou (2012: p. 305), the Greek protests, for example, were mainly 'incubated between frequent rallies after the 2004 Olympics … and cosmopolitan networks protesting against neoliberal globalization'. This already indicates that Mediterranean social movements have some features in common: they propose new models of representation on a communitarian base (Negri, 2012: p. 199) seeking direct democracy (Leontidou, 2012), are more proactive than the traditional NIMBY social movements, used to be organised in digital networks, and had a key role in some land-use conflicts.

According to Negri (2012), these movements are key actors in some of the urban conflicts in the last few years in Southern European cities, particularly with regard to the construction of infrastructures, promotion of redevelopment plans, or celebration of sports mega-events. Additionally, the 'new' social movements seem to have a different focus of action which goes beyond the protest against a definite facility, urban plan, or political decision; they address structural conflicts in particular and, to a lesser extent, process conflicts (visible in the protests demanding forms of direct democracy) and conflicting objectives or policy priorities (e.g. claims for the 'Right to the City').

One example where these developments become obvious is the MM15 conflict in Spanish cities like Valencia, Madrid, or Barcelona, which occurred with the peaceful occupation of central public squares and places. After the long occupation of public squares (from May to August in both cases) and the violent eviction by police intervention, the MM15 assembly decided to continue their action 'in the neighbourhoods'. The focus of public protest moved from the city centre to different neighbourhoods, thus reactivating old conflicts especially in working-class neighbourhoods. One example is the suburb of Russafa in Valencia, a traditional working-class and multi-ethnic suburb that is being gentrified. Some 'old' protests, such as those concerning the construction of a public school, the modernisation of the secondary school, and the rejection of a private parking project in the only existing green area of the suburb, were boosted by the action of residents of the suburb who, however, had never been involved in public protests until the MM15 demonstrations.

Looking closer at these new social movements in Spain, Greece, or Portugal, the heterogeneous composition of protesters is conspicuous: social movements such as the *Indignados* in Spain or the Greek Squares movement (including Syntagma Square in Athens) belong neither to the classical workers' or student movements, nor to an explosion of disenfranchised socially excluded citizens such as in 2005 in the French *banlieues* or the 2011 London riots. They emerged rather as a series of informal networks of citizens, including students, senior citizens, workers, immigrants, and so on, after some years of austerity (Sotiris, 2010: p. 207). The deterioration of employment prospects, the restructuring of the educational and the health system, the overall rise of inequalities and the net degradation of living conditions for the majority, the increasingly securitarian policies threatening basic individual rights, as well as the aggressive reaction of police to the first demonstrations, the overall democratic deficit (e.g. authoritarian and corporate-interest laws coming into effect overnight), and several corruption cases that become public in recent years, provided the material basis for this unity. One of the main novelties of these movements was their horizontal and digitally networked organisation with a total exclusion of trade unions and political parties (including all the left-wing parties at least in Spain). These movements seek new notions of citizenship that expand the decision-making control of citizens incorporating new demands such as, for example, the above-mentioned right to the city or just the right to participate actively in urban policy (Purcell, 2003), so they protest not against a definite urban plan, project, or political decision, but against the foundations of representative democracies proposing more active forms of democracy.

This is one of the novelties in the landscape of social movements in Southern European cities: the adoption of proactive attitudes beyond NIMBY or purely reactive forms of protesting. The MM15, the most important movement of the *Indignados* movement in Spain, for example, can be defined as an umbrella of informal networks of citizens that, apart from protesting against neoliberal policies through the occupation of public spaces, developed hundreds of ideas to promote structural changes for improving the quality of democracy, such as new tools for transparency in political parties, nationalisation of strategic economic sectors, such as banking, mass media, or energy, self-management projects (for example, creating urban farmlands), a universal basic income for all citizens, tools for participative planning, and different protest movements against the privatisation of the health system, public TV channels, universities, and so on. Finally, this array of social movements entered the institutional political arena in 2014 with the creation of new political parties like *Podemos* (We Can), *Guanyem Barcelona* (Let's Win Barcelona), or *Partido X*. Similarly, through this array, the existing Greek left-wing party Syriza has clearly enlarged its electoral base from 5 per cent in the national elections of 1996 to 27 per cent in June 2012 and 36 per cent in 2015, now representing the strongest political power in Greece. The key question to be addressed in the near future covers the role that the representatives of these new parties and social movements will play, once they become part of the local, national, or European administrations they have been criticising.

Public squares and places are central for social movements, as the examples of Madrid and Valencia also indicate. First of all, 'certain piazzas and urban public places have come to be the recurrent locations of mobilisations through time' (Leontidou, 2012: p. 302). The 'historical role' of public spaces for social movements is highlighted by Leontidou (2012) and Dalakoglou (2012) when comparing the public protests and unrest in the Syntagma piazza in Athens in 1944 and 2008, the latter representing the 'beginning of massive movements for direct democracy, politicizing grassroots protest against accumulation by dispossession ... as the debt crisis has been deepening' (Leontidou, 2012: p. 303).

Besides, many urban social movements emerge as public spaces are increasingly privatised and commercialised, both legally and physically, showing the high priority that public spaces have for political and administrative actors who use them as an important component for strategic urban development. This might result in diverging interests between civic and political–administrative actors concerning the concrete uses of these places, their accessibility, or their design, so that the use and composition of public spaces may then become a source of conflict providing ground for protests (Madanipour, 2010; Othengrafen, Reimer, & Sondermann, 2015; Siebel, 2007).

Moreover, public spaces can also be seen as material spaces that actors adopt and produce according to their values and their actions (Helbrecht & Dirksmeier, 2012: p. 14). Following Siebel (2007: p. 80), public spaces then present the scenery for a play written by the economic system, orchestrated by the political system, and performed by the citizens. Using the examples of Madrid and Valencia, the function of public spaces as scenery for protests can be illustrated: by appropriating and symbolically recapturing public spaces, the citizens want to draw attention to the deficits of social, political, and economic participation and to argue for new ways of participative democracy such as *Democrácia Real YA* (Youkhana & Jüssen, 2015). The economic crisis had strong mobilising and connecting powers for the majority of the population. This became particularly evident from the protests under the slogan 'take the road' (*toma la calle*) which took place over several weeks and highlighted the crucial importance of public spaces as arenas for (public) discussions and as scenery for protests. If we recall, besides, that similar slogans have been used during the past decades for similar claims (such as the anti-globalisation 'Reclaim the Streets' movements of the 1990s), the centrality of public space, and in particular of squares, becomes obvious in citizen mobilisation and public protest.

Conclusions

In the light of a growing number of urban protests in Mediterranean cities, including Southern European cities, and, in turn, of the generation of several new urban social movements that address various issues, this chapter not only contributes to the ongoing reflection of scholars on the reasons that gave birth to these movements and the ways in which they have been organised and expressed, but also considers their potential impact on the current socio-economic crisis of Southern European countries. Following Crouch (2004), post-democratic institutions, such as the European Parliament, the European Central Bank, and even some national and regional parliaments dominated by a neoliberal agenda, face important urban unrest, particularly in Southern Europe. Studying the specific cases of Madrid and Valencia sheds lights on the way in which neoliberal agendas in Southern European cities have led to massive demonstrations, protests, and urban social movements. It becomes obvious that conflicts and protest movements are directly addressing the institutional crisis and democratic deficits in the two cities, but also on a national or European level.

Our analysis has further demonstrated that public protests and urban social movements are positioned between the local and the global scale. While they often have a local focus (that is, very specific localised claims), they appeal nonetheless to the more global claims for equality. It can, then, be suggested that current urban social movements in Southern Europe range from rather 'local' movements that contest corporate urban development, surveillance, policing, and commercialisation of public space to transnational anti-globalisation movements, including global justice movements. In this sense, localised NIMBY protests can assume greater dimensions and evolve into urban social movements potentially addressing global issues. Yet, they may also address structural conflicts (e.g. defying neoliberal agendas, fighting against the growing social divide in societies, fighting against corruption, calling for 'right to the city') and, to a lesser extent, process conflicts (visible in the protests demanding forms of direct democracy and/or calling for changes in the electoral law or legal system).

Currently, after seven years of crisis, street protests are beginning to enter the political and electoral arena, which could result in significant political changes in the short term, both for the management of the city and the economic and political model of the European Union. Both in Madrid and Valencia, the conservative absolute majority could lose local and regional elections and all electoral surveys show an electoral defeat of the traditional political formations (as has happened in many European countries), in the face of victory for new and old political groups that propose a revision of the Constitution, relations with the EU, banks, and the economic model. Greek's Syriza took power at the beginning of 2015 with a political agenda opposed to the EU austerity policy and public debt.

However, there is the danger that urban politics at both the national and the local level become extremely polarising between conflicting parties. This also includes the threat that protests between different social groups or between urban social movements and the government become manifest and violent over time. The key issue for future research, then, is to analyse and understand the various motives and rationales behind the protests, the public reactions on protests, or the demands of urban social movements and public strategies to contribute to social cohesion over the long run as well the role of urban planning in these processes.

Note

1 See http://inequalitywatch.eu/spip.php?article58.

References

Alexandri, G. (2014) Reading between the lines: Gentrification tendencies and issues of urban fear in the midst of Athens' crisis. *Urban Studies*, doi: 10.1177/0042 098014538680.

Anduiza, E., Cristancho, C., & Sabucedo, J. M. (2013) Mobilization through online social networks: The political protest of the indignados in Spain. *Information, Communication and Society*, 17, 750–764.

Beck, U. (2012) La política económica de la inseguridad. *El País*, 27 May 2012.

Bonacker, T. & Imbusch, P. (2010) Zentrale Begriffe der Friedens- und Konfliktforschung: Konflikt, Gewalt, Krieg, Frieden. In: Imbusch, P. & Zoll, R. (eds) *Friedens- und Konfliktforschung: Eine Einführung*. Wiesbaden, Verlag für Sozialwissenschaften, pp. 67–142.

Brenner, N., Marcuse, P., & Mayer, M. (2009) Cities for people, not for profit. *City: Analysis of Urban Trends, Culture, Theory, Policy, Action*, 13, 176–184.

Brenner, N., Marcuse, P., & Mayer, M. (2011) *Cities for people and not for profit: Critical urban theory and the right to the city*. London, Routledge.

Brettschneider, F. (2013) Großprojekte zwischen Protest und Akzeptanz: Legitimation durch Kommunikation. In: Brettschneider, F. & Schuster, W. (eds) *Stuttgart 21: Ein Großprojekt zwischen Protest und Akzeptanz*. Wiesbaden, Verlag für Sozialwissenschaften, pp. 319–328.

Castells, M. (1977) *The urban question: A Marxist approach* (Alan Sheridan, translator). London, Edward Arnold (original publication in French, 1972).

Castells, M. (1983) *The city and the grassroots: A cross-cultural theory of urban social movements*. London, Edward Arnold.

Crouch, C. (2004) *Post-democracy*. Cambridge, Polity Press.

Cucó, J. (2013) *Metamorfosis urbanas*. Barcelona, Icaria.

Dalakoglou, D. (2012) Beyond spontaneity. *City: Analysis of Urban Trends, Culture, Theory, Policy, Action*, 16, 535–545.

Del Romero, L. (2014) Urban unrest and new social movements: Lessons from Spain. In: *Conflicts in the City: Reflections on Urban Unrest*. Valencia, University of Valencia, 3–4 April 2014.

Della Porta, D. & Diani, M. (2006) *Social movements: An introduction* (2nd edn). Oxford: Blackwell Publishing.

ELSTAT (Hellenic Statistical Authority) (2013) *Labour force survey: 1st quarter of 2013*. [Press release] (in Greek). [Online] Available from: www.statistics.gr/portal/page/portal/ESYE/BUCKET/A0101/PressReleases/A0101_SJO01_DT_QQ_01_2013_01_F_GR.pdf [accessed 12 November 2014].

Gaja, F. (2013) Tras el tsunami inmobiliario: Salir del atolladero. In: Observatorio Metropolitano (ed.) *Paisajes devastados: Después del ciclo inmobiliario: impactos regionales y urbanos de la crisis*. Madrid, Traficantes de Sueños, pp. 313–352.

Glasl, F. (2004) *Konfliktmanagement: Ein Handbuch für Führungskräfte, Beraterinnen und Berater* (8th edn). Stuttgart, Haupt.

González, C. (2011) Preguntas y respuestas del conflicto de la educación en Madrid. In: *El Mundo*, 07. September 2011. [Online] Available from: www.elmundo.es/elmundo/2011/09/07/madrid/1315380605.html [accessed 9 February 2015].

Harvey, D. (2012) *Rebel cities: From the right to the city to the urban revolution*. London, Verso.

Harvey, D. (2008) The right to the city. *New Left Review*, 53, 23–40.

Helbrecht, I. & Dirksmeier, P. (2012) Auf dem Weg zu einer Neuen Geographie der Architektur: Die Stadt als Bühne performativer Urbanität. *Geographische Revue*, 14, 11–26.

INE (2012) *Estadísticas de la construcción, 2012*. [Online] Available from: www.ine.es/jaxi/menu.do?type=pcaxis&path=/t07/a081/a1998/&file=pcaxis [5 February 2015].

Jehn, K. A. & Bendersky, C. (2003) Intragroup conflict in organizations: A contingency perspective on the conflict-outcome relationship. *Research in Organizational Behaviour*, 25, 187–242.

Jerez, J. M., Martín, V. O., & Pérez, R. (2012) Aproximación a una geografía de la corrupción urbanística en España. *Eria*, 87, 5–18.

Juris, J. & Maple, R. (2012) Occupy, anthropology, and the 2011 global uprisings: Fieldsights – hot spots. *Cultural Anthropology Online*. [Online] Available from: http://culanth.org/fieldsights/63-occupy-anthropology-and-the-2011-global-uprisings [10 November 2014].

Leontidou, L. (2010) Urban social movements in 'weak' civil societies: The right to the city and cosmopolitan activism in Southern Europe. *Urban Studies*, 47, 1179–1203.

Leontidou, L. (2012) Athens in the Mediterranean 'movement of the piazzas': Spontaneity in material and virtual public spaces. *City: Analysis of Urban Trends, Culture, Theory, Policy, Action*, 16, 299–312.

Madanipour, A. (2010) Whose public space? In: Madanipour, A. (ed.) *Whose public space? International case studies in urban design and development.* London, Routledge, pp. 237–242.

Martiarena (2012) Botella busca excusas para remodeler la Puerta del Sol. *La Vanguardia*, 2 October 2013. [Online] Available from www.lavanguardia.com/local/madrid/20131002/54388245301/botella-busca-excusas-para-remodelar-sol.html [23 December 2014].

Mayer, M. (2009) The 'right to the city' in the context of shifting mottos of urban social movements. *City: Analysis of Urban Trends, Culture, Theory, Policy, Action*, 13, 362–374.

Meyer, D. S. & Tarrow, S. (eds) (1998) *The social movement society: Contentious politics for a new century.* Series on People, Passions, and Power (John C. Green, editor). Lanham, MD, and Oxford, Rowman & Littlefield.

Ministry of Finance and Public Administrations (2014) *Deuda viva de los ayuntamientos a 31/12/2013.* [Online] Available from: www.minhap.gob.es/es-ES/Areas%20Tematicas/Administracion%20Electronica/OVEELL/Paginas/DeudaViva.aspx [accessed 29 November 2014].

Negri, A. (2012) *Il comune in rivolta: Sul potere costituente delle lote.* Verona, Italy, Ombre corte, UniNomade.

Noriega, D. (2014) Madrid vendió pisos públicos por 63.000 euros a empresas que ahora exigen a sus inquilinos 160.000. *Eldiario.es.* [Online] Available from: www.eldiario.es/sociedad/venta-vivienda-publica-pah-cavero_0_228527911.html [10 November 2014].

Othengrafen, F. & Sondermann, M. (2015) Konflikte, Proteste, Initiativen und die Kultur der Planung: Stadtentwicklung unter demokratischen Vorzeichen? In: Othengrafen, F. & Sondermann, M. (eds) *Städtische Planungskulturen im Spiegel von Konflikten, Protesten und Initiativen.* Planungsrundschau, no. 23 (in print).

Othengrafen, F., Reimer, M., & Sondermann, M. (2015) Planung und die Reaktion auf öffentliche Proteste, Konflikte und Initiativen: Wie, wann und warum verändern sich Planungskulturen? In: Othengrafen, F. & Sondermann, M. (eds) *Städtische Planungskulturen im Spiegel von Konflikten, Protesten und Initiativen.* Planungsrundschau, no. 23 (in print).

Pickvance, C. (2003) From urban social movements to urban movements: A review and introduction to a symposium on urban movements. *International Journal of Urban and Regional Research*, 27, 102–109.

Purcell, M. (2003) Citizenship and the right to the global city: Reimagining the capitalist world order. *International Journal of Urban and Regional Research*, 27, 564–590.

Renn, O. (2013) Partizipation bei öffentlichen Planungen: Möglichkeiten, Grenzen, Reformbedarf. In: Keil, S. I. & Gabriel O. W. (eds) *Zivile Bürgergesellschaft und Demokratie: Aktuelle Ergebnisse der empirischen Politikforschung.* Wiesbaden, Verlag für Sozialwissenschaften, pp. 71–96.

Reuber, P. (2012): *Politische Geographie.* Stuttgart: UTB.

Reuter, W. (2000) Zur Komplementarität von Diskurs und Macht in der Planung. *DISP – The Planning Review*, 141, 4–16.

Sears, A. & Cairns, J. (2010) *A good book, in theory: Making sense through inquiry* (2nd edn). Toronto, University of Toronto Press.

Segovia, C. (2013) Señora vicepresidenta, han cerrado 400.000 empresas en 2012. In: *El Mundo*, 29 October 2013. [Online] Available from: www.elmundo.es/economia/2013/10/29/526fb5660ab740c5048b456f.html [20 January 2015].

Siebel, W. (2007) Vom Wandel des öffentlichen Raumes. In: Wehrheim, J. (ed.) *Shopping Malls: Interdisziplinäre Betrachtungen eines neuen Raumtyps*, Wiesbaden, Verlag für Sozialwissenschaften, pp. 77–94.

Siebel, W. (2009) Die Welt lebenswerter Machen: Stadtplanung als Gesellschaftspolitik. *Mittelweg 36 – Zeitschrift des Hamburger Instituts für Sozialforschung*, 18, 26–48.

Sotiris, P. (2010) Rebels with a cause: The December 2008 Greek youth movement as the condensation of deeper social and political contradictions. *International Journal of Urban and Regional Research*, 34, 203–209.

Youkhana, E. & Jüssen, L. (2015) Soziale Bewegungen in Zeiten der Spanischen Hypothekenkrise: Ursachen und Folgen für Stadtplanung und – gestaltung. In: Othengrafen, F. & Sondermann, M. (eds) *Städtische Planungskulturen im Spiegel von Konflikten, Protesten und Initiativen*. Planungsrundschau, no. 23 (in print).

Part III

Urban planning and the economic crisis in Southern European cities

9 Urban planning and territorial management in Portugal

Antecedents and impacts of the 2008 financial and economic crisis

Joana Mourão and Teresa Marat-Mendes

Introduction

This chapter discusses the role that the evolution in urban development and urban planning in Portugal have played with regard to the outbreak of the economic and financial crisis, and the impact that this crisis had on urban planning and territorial management in Portugal, in the short and long term.

It is an assumption that the recent developments in urban planning, territorial management, and urbanisation in Portugal have been motivated by unsustainable drivers that have also led to the financial and economic crisis, in particular relating to the real estate and financial sectors. The crisis is strongly interconnected with urbanisation processes as well with urban planning and territorial management activities. It is thus a specific objective of this chapter to discuss this interconnection, while explaining the evolution of recent urban planning and territorial management in Portugal.

In this chapter it will be shown that planning in Portugal, while finally holding the adequate instruments to properly develop Municipal Master Plans (PDM), faces the effects of the economic recession caused by the crisis and by previous development activities. This chapter also shows that such planning instruments took time to be adopted, since their legal framework has arrived late; such as the Ground Basis Law on Territorial Planning and Urbanism (LBOTBU) (PP, 1998) and the Juridical Regime of the Territorial Management instruments (RJIGT) (MEPAT, 1999) which were published a decade after the elaboration and application of the first Municipal Master Plans, shortening the possibility of preventing unsustainable activities, which in the long term fed the outbreak of the crisis. The Strategic Environmental Assessment (SEA) framework for Urban Planning also arrived late and, deriving from the European Union Directives (Directive 2001/42/CE) (Partidário, 2007), presented an opportunity of regulation which was not always concretised when applied to Portuguese planning culture (CNADS, 2012). The obligation to evaluate planning brought advantages and a better control of the results and impacts of planning, but it arrived when many unsustainable development strategies were already in motion. Within this evaluation process, however, the environmental impact of urbanisation, and those impacts related to nature conservation were progressively taken into account. Despite this, the issues of energy dependence, carbon emissions, and climate change were only inserted later in these evaluations.

After this introduction, the chapter is structured in two sections, each containing three subsections. Finally, it presents conclusions. The opening section 'Urban planning and municipal plans in Portugal from 1988–2008' presents an overview of the recent history of urban planning and territorial management in Portugal, addressing the process of elaboration of the Municipal Master Plans (PDM) from 1988 to 2008. Three specific periods will be analysed: 1988–1998 when the first Municipal Master Plans were elaborated; 1998 the year of the publication of the first Ground Basis Law on Territorial Planning and Urbanism (LBPOTU); and 1998–2008 when the second generation of Municipal Master Plans was developed under the provisions of the new Ground Basis Law, and within the framework of the Strategic Environmental Assessment (SEA), calling for consideration of new global ecological concerns. To describe the interconnection between urbanisation and the crisis it is necessary on one hand, to address the impacts of urban development and planning on the evolution of the crisis, and on another hand, to address the impacts that the crisis had on urban development and on urban development and planning. In this context, the next section 'Impacts of the crisis on the present and future of urban planning in Portugal' addresses the bilateral impacts between urbanisation and planning activities and the crisis in Portugal. It also analyses what impact urban planning and territorial management activities in Portugal had on environmental protection, on the use of energy and on mobility patterns, wherein amplifying the effects of the crisis on the municipalities and families. In the first subsection of this second section of the chapter, we shall discuss the impacts of the crisis planning needs to deal with as well the changes in planning, motivated by the current crisis, in terms of ensuring sustainability, environmental protection, and implementing SEA. In the second subsection the challenge and opportunity of 'sustainable cities' will be introduced. In the last subsection, the crisis will be addressed as a driver of 'low carbon' urban planning and territorial management, illustrating the effects that a sustainable material dynamics and restricted access to fossil fuels can have on urbanism and urban planning. The chapter ends with some conclusions, while identifying some key ideas related to the antecedents and impacts of the 2008 financial and economic crisis on urban planning and territorial management in Portugal.

Urban planning and municipal plans in Portugal from 1988–2008

This section of the chapter offers an overall portrait of the urban planning framework which defined the territorial development and management activities in Portugal during the two decades immediately before the outbreak of the economic and financial crisis (1988–2008). This portrait is presented here because it contributes to better understanding the impacts of urban development and planning on the progression of the crisis in Portugal.

Until 1998 Portugal lacked a Ground Basis Law on Territorial Planning and Urbanism, and it still relied only on the law of 1976, designed mostly to create public land stocks and to regulate the market in times of strong urban expansion (Monteiro, 2008). In the absence of a Land Law, municipal planning had an important role to play for land use planning in Portugal in the last 20 years and was responsible for the classification of land. However, although the Portuguese Constitution states that the municipalities are the entities that should define the right to land use change (ibid.), in practice the right to convert rural land into urban land is not clearly differentiated from the civil right to own private property. Citizens have believed that owning rural land automatically assures the right to convert that land into urban land, without following the restrictions of municipal planning. This wrong assumption led to the explosion of illegal urbanism in democratic Portugal and, together with other factors, opened an opportunity for the real estate sector to develop freely and rapidly.

1988–1998: the first generation of plans

The democratic local government was established in Portugal in 1976, yet in the following decades the legislation on spatial planning was insufficient and inefficient. Only in the early 1980s was urban development legislated (Decree Law No. 208/82) and the first Municipal Master Plans (*Planos Diretores Municipais* – PDM) were adopted. It has taken a further 25 years to equally develop the PDM for the whole national territory.

The PDM in force in Portugal today were practically all designed between 1988 and 1998. These represented the main tools for urban planning at the municipal level. The elaboration of the plans has been encouraged by the European Union, in particular since 1989, however, the framework for their preparation was set only after the adoption of the Ground Basis Law on Territorial Planning and Urbanism in 1998 (*Lei de Bases da Política de Ordenamento do Território e Urbanismo* – LBPOTU), ten years after the elaboration of the first PDM, when most had already been completed (Portas, Cabral, & Domingues, 2003).

The regulations for the conversion of rural land into urban land, together with the national policy on road infrastructure, were main drivers behind the PDM. The efficiency of this regulation, however, was restricted, since the distinction between urban and rural land, although existing in the plans, was not followed in reality by formal and informal territorial changes (Carvalho, 2003) and it was not recognised by the citizens. As a result, construction in several municipalities grew almost as intensively in urban areas, where it was allowed and expected, as on rural land, where it was restricted by the plan dispositions (Mourão, 2012). This caused the offer of built land and housing (either legalised or not) and for 20 years (from 1998 to 2008) urban areas for construction expanded greatly, dissociated from population needs, and from the existing infrastructure networks.

The urban expansion contributed, in the long term, to intensifying the effects of the global crisis in Portugal which would arrive later. During the economic growth of 1980–2000, the offer of urban land and of new roads all over the country, pushed by low price of fuels, thus weakened the relationships of cities with their local territories in favour of supra-local and supra-national territories, at the aegis of globalisation. The increased supply of housing, due to the unregulated conversion of rural land into urban land, ran parallel to the public policy of high accessibility infrastructures. In such a policy it was not the logic of planning the territory that presided over the decisions (Nunes da Silva, 2008) and as a consequence in the 1990s new patterns of population distribution emerged: families working in Lisbon could live in municipalities far way, driving hundreds of kilometres daily on highways. Portugal's (sub)urbanisation of the last two decades reduced the potential for a polycentric urban system, and not only fed 'Splintering Urbanism' and highways (Domingues, 2006), but it also increased energetic demand and external dependency (Campos & Mourão, 2012).

The structural role of open and green spaces was scarcely recognised at that time, and planning relied mostly on zoning procedures and construction indexes (Portas, Cabral, & Domingues, 2003). Thus, the first generation of plans defined large areas where building was allowed, justifying it by the reduction in the average size of families and the increase in secondary housing needs. This resulted in a fast increase of built-up areas, which was not followed by the low population growth (Carvalho, 2003) and led to a large housing stock surplus, which contributed to the emergence of the 'housing bubble' and to the outbreak of the crisis.

During the implementation of the PDM, individual interests overlapped collective interests and corruption and illegal urbanisation frequently occurred, both before and after the LBPOTU Law (Oliveira, 2008). The structures of local governance, which are responsible for the implementation of the plans, faced (and still face) difficulties in articulating political and technical points of view, since politicians often choose territorial development options, contradicting the prescriptions of technicians. Difficulties also emerged in the integration of different planning sectors, such as land use, housing, mobility, rehabilitation, or environmental protection, amid which the territorial development objectives and strategies did not always converge (Mourão, 2012). When the first generation of these plans was complete, among their main advantages was the fact that they provided greater knowledge of the territory and the legal constraints involving its occupation. The main disadvantages and negative impacts of these plans, however, were the creation of a surplus of urban areas and the consequent dispersal of human settlements and building construction (Carvalho, 2003). Analysis of 16 different PDMs in 2003 showed the creation of large urban areas 12 times larger than the expected increase of housing needs (ibid.). Taking this into consideration, it could be said that the first generation of municipal plans responded to the short-term housing and accessibility needs and even exceeded them, creating territorial conditions which, in the long term, contributed to the outbreak of the financial and economic crisis in Portugal.

1998: the Ground Basis Law (LBPOTU)

The contribution of urban planning and territorial management activities to importing the international crisis to Portugal is significant, and is connected with the antecedents of the planning system in Portugal. For that reason an important moment of the evolution of the planning system is considered here, namely the adoption of the Ground Basis Law which, due to its delay and limitations, can also be related to the outbreak of the financial and economic crisis in Portugal in 2008.

The Ground Basis Law on Territorial Planning and Urbanism (PP, 1998) resulted from a long process of evolution of the instruments of urban planning and territorial management in Portugal (ibid.), with the intention of creating a framework for the public regulation of territorial transformations, protecting the public realm while assuring conditions of equity for the territorial activities of the several agents of the private sector. It introduced a new framework for spatial planning in Portugal; however, it found a territory with sprawled and unregulated settlements and infrastructures, developed as the result of a lack of efficient housing and land policies.

According to LBPOTU, a Municipal Master Plan establishes the territorial development strategy, the municipal policy on spatial planning and urbanism, and the model of spatial organisation of the municipal territory (MEPAT, 1999, Art. 84). Before the introduction of this law there was no clear definition of the purposes and contents of the PDM. This law also integrated and articulated instruments of territorial management of national and regional level with those at municipal level. Even though all municipalities had prepared a PDM since 2003, however, these plans have often not reflected the territorial strategy of local development (Costa, 2008) since these strategies are generally tied to a municipal electoral mandate, lasting for only four years, a much shorter time than the 20 years covered by the PDM.

Other limitations are noted in these plans:

> The current figure of PDM is limited to the definition of the dominant uses without ensuring the formalisation of the fundamental structures of the landscape, both in terms of ecological sustainability and in terms of a structure built to ensure the testimony of the past in the construction of future.
>
> (translated from Magalhães, 2008: p. 113)

Such structuring limitations persist partly in the process of reviewing these plans, as do the limitations regarding interaction with housing policies, urban transport, or energy demand (Mourão, 2012), increasing the vulnerability of the territories and citizens to the global crisis effects.

The experience of implementing LBPOTU, and in particular of implementing the PDM, revealed difficulties in applying measures contrary to the prevailing notion of 'quality of life' among the local communities, and also among decision-makers. In fact, plans were almost always 'non-grateful' instruments or were perceived as obstacles that needed to be overcome (Oliveira, 2008). For this reason, public participation was progressively recognised as a way to overcome the divergence between administration, spatial and urban planners, and private agents, as well as to legitimise the role of planning. Indeed, public participation found a wider space in the plans of the second generation (Crespo, 2008), allowing citizens and organisations to express their points of view to the municipalities, during the time of the plans' elaboration.

1998–2008: the second generation of Municipal Plans

A survey focusing on the first PDM showed that the areas of urban expansion predicted by the Plans, did not correspond to the demographic and economic dynamics of each municipality. The effective urbanisation of the urban land predicted on the plans was thus very low (Carvalho, 2003) and many of these areas continued to expect land use changes that never occurred. This situation, in combination with other factors, created an 'unsustainable housing bubble' fed by the growing financial real estate sector. This was addressed in several PDM revisions (*second generation plans*, initiated before the crisis outbreak) which defined urban area shrinkage, while the environmental protection of natural resources gained greater importance, in particular through the Municipal Ecological Structures (EEM) (Magalhães, 2008). The EEM constitutes an important tool which emerged as a further development of the Ground Basis Law addressed in the previous subsection. These new EEM, integrated in the PDM revisions, aimed to manage ecological non-built spaces as collective resources, allowing a reduction of pressure for the construction of new buildings in certain areas. However, many of the second generation plans were only finished after the outburst of the international crisis of 2008, facing difficulties in implementation such as new EEM, due to the lack of financial resources for any kind of territorial intervention. On one hand, the tendency to shrink the urban limits and to restrict building activities derived from environmental economic purposes (Magalhães, 2008; Portas, 2008); but on another hand, it was also facilitated by the conditions offered by the decrease in pressure from the real estate sector, justified by the crisis.

In the second generation plans, due to the introduction of the SEA imposed on Portugal by the EU (Partidário, 2007; DGOTDU & APA, 2008), the environmental risks were considered in the instruments of local land management. With regard to the use of non-renewable energy, climate change, and dependence on fossil fuels, however, SEA did not lead to the introduction of more ecological options for municipal planning (Mourão & Pedro, 2007). Public transport, mobility, the modal share of road space, energy efficiency of buildings, and urban services are secondary issues in most of the PDM. Such issues would be important in helping territories and cities to adapt to the post-crisis conditions, when energy had a heavier impact on the financial management of municipal territories and of families (Mourão, 2012).

Trying to slow the urbanisation of rural areas, the second generation of PDM proposed, in general and in theory, polycentric territorial models in favour of the rationalisation of land use and of the conservation or reactivation of the productive and landscape potential (Mourão, 2012), but in their strategic aims, the PDM were often overtaken by other sectorial planning instruments at national level, as the plans from the roads and logistic sector, overlapped local plans and neglected the integration of different planning sectors. The plans from the roads and logistic sector were often seen as an opportunity to create more infrastructure for the economy, enhancing the competitiveness of Portugal; however, the crisis effects did not confirm this assumption, in for example, the face of the declining income and rising of costs of redundant highways in the country. The problems of the disarticulation of national and local plans were aggravated by the fact that the PDM revision often lasted more than ten years, with a low capacity to respond quickly to national and local political changes (Portas, 2008; Costa, 2008).

If some of the revised plans invested in the biophysical values of the territory, safeguarding nature, agriculture, and forest, others invested simultaneously in the allocation of land to large-scale tourist and road logistic activities, remaining permissive about concerns of illegal urbanisation and the construction of heavy infrastructure in high environmental value areas. These plans were pushed by the urgency of reversing the tendencies towards unemployment and loss of population, already signs of the coming crisis. Indeed, tourism, logistics, and housing were, in general, the dominant fields of investment and allocation of municipal land use in Portugal, prior to and after the outbreak of the financial crisis (Mourão, 2012).

After the 'housing bubble' the 'tourism bubble' also began to inflate, encouraged either by municipal planning or by higher level strategic planning, following the national goal of promoting Portugal as a competitive tourism destination. However, territorial development strategies based on tourism and road logistics were questionable, because tourism suffers from the impacts of coastal erosion, of urban centre congestion, and gentrification, while the use of road logistics declines because trade flows slow down. Such planning options, however, have already left infrastructure, as well as planning instruments, which still persist today. Some of this infrastructure is now unsustainable, in either environmental or financial terms. Indeed, sustainability issues would have been important to consider in urban planning and territorial management in order to mitigate negative effects of the crisis, such as the insolvency of municipal territories and families.

Impacts of the crisis on the present and future of urban planning in Portugal

As shown previously, Portuguese territories suffered the impact of pre-crisis urban development based on unsustainable trends (1988–2008) which, together with global drivers, triggered the crisis. From 2008 on, these territories were exposed to the impacts of the global crisis which aggravated the impact of the unsustainable urban development. The crisis also evidenced the inadequacy of several infrastructures, such as highways and mass housing for a small number of users, exceeding needs and representing costs with no economic return. Addressing this second period of territorial development in the country, and the future, the next subsection analyses how the 2008 crisis impacted, in the short term, both positively and negatively, urban development, urban planning, and territorial management activities in Portugal. Addressing the long term, the second and third subsections below will discuss how planning activities can evolve in Portugal in the near future, profiting from the opportunities brought by the general concept of 'sustainable cities' and the specific targets of 'low carbon urban planning'.

Short-term impacts of the economic and financial crisis on urban planning in Portugal

In Portugal the model of urban expansion brought advantages in the short term, while satisfying housing and accessibility needs (Nunes da Silva, 2008) in a country that had still shortages in these areas, and bringing relevant social impacts which were initially seen as positive (Portas, Cabral, & Domingues, 2003), and which contributed to reinforce the importance of urban planning. However, urban planning began to be questioned (Domingues, 2006) when the model of growing urban networks (expanded by financial interests relating to infrastructure such as buildings, roads, water, waste, and energy) led to the emptying of urban centres and their degradation; when credit dependence led to the insolvency of municipalities and families; when oversized investment in motorway and logistics and private concessions of infrastructure was neglecting environmental and affecting social values; or, when excessive conversion of rural land into urban land led to the undervaluation of the countryside (Mourão, 2012). In Portugal, as worldwide, overall accessibility had increased energy demand and consumption, environmental contamination, and climate change (Stern, 2007), bringing new problems to urban planning and territorial management.

After 2008, the financial crisis further exposed the negative social impacts of the unsustainable development and planning model previously adopted. The breakdown of employment, the insolvency of families and increased levels of poverty, the rise of 'ghost neighbourhoods', the privatisation of urban services with prejudice against the state, and the weakening of institutional structures responsible for territorial management (Portas, 2008) were results of external control over the country and municipality budgets and funding, but also results of the antecedents of urban planning and territorial management. Although the crisis had devastating impacts for territories and citizens, from the point of view of planning, some changes with regard to territorial development patterns can thus be identified as positive impacts, since they allowed the rethinking of the former planning and management practices, which in some sectors had proved to be inadequate for the long-term evolution of the country, in terms, for example, of demography and ageing. Examples of such positive impacts, with regard to territorial development patterns, are the slowdown of the civil construction sector and reduction of its pressure on the governance structures, the reduction of the oversized role of the real estate sector, the changing of mobility and housing patterns to patterns spatially more concentrated, the reactivation of traditional urbanity based on agglomeration, the rise of resource-efficiency, the reoccupation of public space, together with a broader institutional space for public participation (Crespo, 2008), and for environmental and energetic commitment (e.g. *Covenant of Mayors* in JRC, 2009).

The opportunity of sustainable cities

Cities as agglomerations started facing a 'crisis' long ago, with the increase and generalisation of accessibility led by the industrial revolution and capitalism (Lefebvre, 1970). During the accelerated economic growth of 1980 to 2000, with energetic low priced resources, accessibility became widespread and cities and territories were in conflict. As recalled by Naredo (2003) and Cuchí, Marat-Mendes and Mourão (2010) this caused an environmental crisis and later an economic and financial crisis. The problem of suburbanisation has thus dominated the urbanisation agendas for the last three decades, contradicting traditional polycentric territorial systems, feeding *Splintering Urbanism* (Graham & Marvin, 2001) and stimulating debates on sustainable urban form (Talen, 2011; Marat-Mendes, 2002).

The debate of compact urbanisation versus sprawl, and its inherent impacts on a city's sustainability is not new (see, for example, Frey 1999; Jenks, Burton, & Williams, 1996; Urban Task Force, 1999; Williams, Burton, & Jenks, 2000). The implications of the urban form of our cities in the environment have strongly emphasised the issue of the sustainable city, while finding strong support, for example, within the European Union (Marat-Mendes & Scoffham, 2000). This situation is even more evident since the publication of the Urban Task Force by Lord Rogers of Riverside in 1999 (Urban Task Force, 1999), which has also had repercussions in Portugal (see, for example, Portas, Cabral, & Domingues, 2003, 2011). This also finds agreement in Echenique et al. (2012), who argue that in recent years the paradigm of urban planning has been to promote the compact city as a reaction against the sprawl induced by the newer universal use of private automobiles. However, as argued by Echenique et al. there is no clear evidence that such a compact urban model induces greater environmental, economic, or social effects, or more sustainable cities. Attention is paid to the economic and social costs of the process of urban compaction, which needs to be better understood and considered in future cost–benefit analyses, as it is being done in Portugal by Carvalho (2013). Finally, Echenique et al. (2012) conclude that there is not a clearly superior spatial urban form solution in terms of sustainability. Changes in lifestyles and the associated population growth have a far greater impact on the natural environment and resources than that attributed to spatial urban forms (Marat-Mendes, 2013). The consequences of the social and economic costs that the current financial crisis might have produced in terms of changes of lifestyles should therefore be considered. These changes must be the main elements of analysis in any urban policy.

The relationship between urban form solutions, urban planning, and their implications for environmental problems still seems to be an open discussion. Nevertheless, if one accepts that changes of lifestyles are crucial to the achievement of sustainability, and that sustainability is an important social goal (WCED, 1987), the study of the relationship between lifestyles, population growth, urban form, and the impacts of these factors on the natural environment seems to be an urgent task, to be followed by urban planning.

The crisis as an opportunity for low carbon urban planning

In a time when planning is under pressure to better respond to the financial crisis, and to the sustainability agenda which has been imposed at an international level since the publication of the Brundtland Report in 1987 and has been committed in several agreements and charts (consider, for example, the International Kyoto Agreement of 1997, or the European Water Directive of 2000), calls have been made for attention to a revision of the urban planning models and the available planning tools and methodologies to better achieve the signed commitments. In consequence, there is an ongoing debate about the integration of the necessary actions to achieve more sustainable development in the field of urban planning, and on how planning must change in order to develop cities and territories, as expressions of a society, based on a sustainable economic model. As already explained by Cuchí, Marat-Mendes, and Mourão (2010) this debate is only taking place now because there is social recognition of the environmental impact caused by the productive industrial system that is still in operation.

The continuous waste and atmospheric emissions dump generated by the productive and consumer systems generates environmental impacts, therefore Cuchí, Marat-Mendes, and Mourão (2010) argue for new methodological planning approaches that take into account tools that allow monitoring of the material flows that operate within the productive system and their relationship with sustainability. One alternative proposal is to explore the relationship between urban material dynamics and sustainability as the elementary tool through which to approach territorial and urban planning. Cuchí, Marat-Mendes, and Mourão (2010) understand this as a useful vision for sustainable urban planning. Urban material dynamics represents a tool for the recognition of new roles of the urban space, spreading ecological regeneration from the green spaces to the entire city. Green strategies can begin on the green fields, but they should finish on the 'grey' infrastructure of the city. In that sense, at the international level (Newmann, 2006; Cuchí, Marat-Mendes, & Mourão, 2010) and also in Portugal (Pinho et al., 2013) research on urbanism has identified study of the energy-carbon flow, among other flows of the *urban metabolism*, as a relevant field of research to achieve more ecological urbanisation. Several authors define *urban metabolism* as the group of material flows which enter and leave a certain urban system in order to enable its activity. Thus, studies of urban metabolism frequently use material flow accounting as has also been done for Lisbon (Niza, Rosado, & Ferrão, 2009).

'Low carbon cities' are understood as urban systems that demand fewer fossil fuels and produce less carbon emissions, thus mitigating climate change (Stern, 2007). 'Low carbon urban planning' should propose spatial scenarios of low fossil fuel consumption, envisioning scarcity or the internalisation of environmental and climate change costs. Although few 'low carbon cities and territories' exist as yet, territorial and urban administrations all over Europe, and in Portugal, are committed to the 'low carbon goal' (e.g. *Covenant of Mayors* in JRC, 2009).

The theme of 'low carbon development' entered Portuguese public institutions slowly, in particular through the work of the Environment National Agency (APA), responsible for the application of the Kyoto Protocol and for the delivery of reports to the International Panel for Climate Change (IPCC). Some Portuguese authors have researched 'low carbon buildings and cities' in Portugal in terms of climate change mitigation (Fernandes, 2009), of bioclimatic urban design and sustainable building principles (Mourão & Pedro, 2012) or in terms of the management of low carbon cities and territories (Pinho, 2009; Pinho et al., 2013), approaching the need and the strategies to reduce energy demand and the consumption of urban areas directly, and, therefore, to reduce CO_2 emissions. A route to take towards Low Carbon Economy until 2050 (APA, 2012) and a strategy for climate change adaptation (PCM, 2010) have been developed at an institutional level. A new version of a national plan for climate change is also being designed (PNAC 2020). However, 'low carbon planning' approaches in Portugal are still limited, partially due to the fact that the importance of climate change adaptation for vulnerable cities and territories has been increasing and crossing over with the concerns about climate change mitigation (Santos, Forbes, & Moita, 2002).

Portuguese academic research shows that the characterisation of carbon emissions from an urban system on the basis of nationally and locally produced data, although complex and demanding specific information (Cuchí, Mourão, & Pagés, 2009; Mourão, 2012), enables to account and to restrict carbon emissions of urban origin (buildings, mobility and sanitation emissions, considering delocalised emissions). This quantitative knowledge, although still incomplete, can help to identify options on territorial and urban form transformations, and to develop a balance between 'high carbon' and 'low carbon urbanisation', particularly relevant for post-crisis urban planning and development. 'Urban Carbon Balance' can be relevant for ecological territorial and urban form regulation aiming at higher resilience in the current crisis, but it is not yet incorporated in an operative territorial and urban regulation method which could serve urban planning in Portugal. Indeed, traditional instruments of urban planning and territorial management can address neither urban energy demand nor urban carbon emissions (Mourão, 2012).

Conclusions

This chapter discussed the role that urban development, urban planning, and territorial management activities have played on the evolution and outbreak of the financial and economic crisis in Portugal, over two decades. It also addressed the impacts that the crisis, from 2008 on, is having on urban development, urban planning, and territorial management in this country.

The assumption that evolution in urban development, urban planning, and territorial management in Portugal in the last decades before 2008 was motivated by drivers that also led to the financial and economic crisis, such as the oversized real estate sector, was verified. It was shown that the crisis is strongly interconnected with urbanisation processes as well with permissive urban planning and territorial management activities.

It is possible to conclude that the evolution of planning in Portugal was significant in recent decades; however, it is also possible to identify a time lag between this evolution and the evolution of urban dynamics, since the period of higher urban dynamics has preceded the availability of the Ground Basis Law on Territorial Planning and Urbanism, and of the arrival of conditions for its accomplishment. This contributed, in the long term, to the outbreak of the crisis in Portugal, as well to aggravating its effects.

Suffering from inefficiency in the implementation of plans and their rules, planning has had little control over its long-term consequences. The aims of planning were oriented to the short term, and the long-term environmental and economic impacts on energy demand, mobility patterns, and green fields conservation have not been properly considered. The delay in the legislation of urban planning and of environmental impact assessment, together with the inefficiency in planning accomplishment, further exposed the Portuguese urbanised territories to the drivers and to the effects of the financial crisis. For example, urban areas remain dependent on the automobile and are vulnerable to rises in the price of fossil fuels, to environmental contamination, to climate change effects, and to the sudden change in mobility patterns and housing needs connected to the change of employment conditions deriving from the crisis.

During the second generation of Municipal Plans, the tendency to reduce the expansion of urban areas showed a positive evolution in terms of environmental goals, to which the crisis is also related. However, some of these plans still allow construction in areas with high environmental value and do not face yet the challenge of sustainable mobility, ecological construction, or of the consideration of social and economic costs of lifestyle changes, which happened as a result of the crisis. Along these lines it should be noted that, as a result of the reduced pressure from the real estate sector, there has also unfortunately been a lack of pressure to conclude the revisions of the Municipal Plans and to implement their ecological structures. In consequence, many of the second generation plans are now on 'standby' leaving municipalities without strategies with which to face the crisis.

Municipal Master Plans were thus affected by the crisis due to a lack of resources and the weakening of planning institutional structures, in the face of the external control of the country and budget reductions, but also due to uncertainty about the right strategies of territorial development to be adopted, in particular in the face of the growing concepts of 'sustainable cities' and 'low carbon economy'. Questioning pre-crisis urban planning models made space for methodological discussions and renovation but, at the same time, the deadlock of the revisions of the Municipal Master Plans reduced the chances for motivating territorial and urban planning and its public participation actions, as predicted by the *second generation plans*.

It was argued in this chapter that to face the consequences of unsustainable urban development in Portugal, aggravated by the crisis, planning practice should use tools and methodological approaches that incorporate the urban material dynamics, valuing and protecting endogenous resources, such as water and energy, and assuring a higher resilience to crisis scenarios for territories. Compromises in climate change mitigation play an important role in such innovation and, although the debate on sustainable urban form continues, there is already agreement about the importance of considering lifestyle changes, together with territorial and urban form analysis of the elaboration of strategies for 'low carbon territorial and urban development'.

References

APA (Agência Portuguesa do Ambiente) (2012) *Roteiro Nacional de Baixo Carbono 2050: Opções de transição para uma economia de baixo carbono competitiva em 2050.* Amadora, APA.

Campos, V. & Mourão, J. (2012) Desenvolvimento de Sistemas territoriais de Baixo Carbono: Uma perspectiva de investigação aplicada às metodologias de avaliação de Planos de Ordenamento do Território. *Jornadas de Inovação e Investigação do LNEC Digital Proceedings.*

Carvalho, J. (2003) *Ordenar a cidade.* Coimbra, Quarteto.

Carvalho, J. (ed.) (2013) *Ocupação dispersa, custos e benefícios à escala local.* Lisbon, Direcção-Geral do Território.

CNADS (Conselho Nacional do Ambiente e do Desenvolvimento sustentável) (2012) *Parecer sobre avaliação ambiental estratégica.* [Online] Available from: www.cnads. pt/ [accessed 15 June 2014].

Costa, J. P. (2008) A revisão dos Planos Directores Municipais de primeira geração. In: *Adurbem Annual Meeting (LNEC, Lisbon), Proceedings*, pp. 323–329.

Crespo, J. (2008) A participação pública no sistema de planeamento e gestão do uso do solo municipal. In: *Adurbem Annual Meeting (LNEC, Lisbon), Proceedings*, pp. 247–258.

Cuchí, A., Mourão, J., & Pagés, A. (2009) A framework to take account of CO2 restrictions on municipal urban planning. *45th Isocarp Congress Low Carbon Cities*, Oporto, non-published Proceedings.

Cuchí, A., Marat-Mendes, T., & Mourão, J. (2010) Urban material analysis and sustainability: A new methodological approach towards urban planning. In: Pinho, P. & Oliveira, V. (eds) *CITTA – Planning in Times of Uncertainty.* Oporto, FEUP Proceedings, pp. 109–122.

DGOTDU (Direcção Geral do Ordenamento do Território e Desenvolvimento Urbano) & APA (Agência Portuguesa do Ambiente) (2008) *Guia metodológico para a avaliação ambiental estratégica (AAE).* Lisbon, DGOTDU.

Domingues, Á. (ed.) (2006) *Cidade e democracia.* Lisbon, Argumentum.

Echenique, M. H., Hargreaves, A. J., Mitchell, G., & Namdeo, A. (2012) Growing cities sustainably: Does urban form really matter? *Journal of the American Planning Association*, 78, 121–137.

Fernandes, E. O. (2009) Cities as natural resources processing systems: The energy case. [Keynote speech] *45th Isocarp Congress Low Carbon Cities*, Oporto.

Frey, H. (1999) *Designing the city: Towards a more sustainable urban form.* London, Spon.

Graham, S. & Marvin, S. (2001) *Splintering urbanism: Networked infrastructures, technological mobilities and the urban condition.* London, Routledge.

Jackson, T. (2009) *Prosperity without growth: Economics for a finite planet.* New York, Earthscan.

Jenks, M., Burton, E., & Williams, K. (1996) *The compact city: A sustainable urban form?* London, Spon.

JRC (Joint Research Centre), European Commission (2009) Covenant of Mayors. *Committed to urban sustainable energy.* [Online] Available from: www.covenantofmayors.eu/index_en.html [accessed 15 June 2014].

Lefebvre, H. (1970) *La révolution urbaine.* Paris, Gallimard.

Magalhães, M. (2008) Comentários no âmbito dos dez anos da LBPOTU. In: *Adurbem Annual Meeting (LNEC, Lisbon) Proceedings*, pp. 105–120.

Marat-Mendes, T. (2002) *The sustainable urban form: A comparative study in Lisbon, Edinburgh and Barcelona.* PhD thesis, University of Nottingham, UK.

Marat-Mendes, T. (2013) Sustainability and the study of urban form. *Urban Morphology*, 17 (2), 123–124.

Marat-Mendes, T. & Scoffham, E. (2000) Urban sustainability and the ground rules that govern urban space. *Urban Morphology*, 9, 45–46.

MEPAT (Ministério do Equipamento, do Planeamento e da Administração do Território) (1999) *Regime jurídico dos instrumentos de gestão territorial* (RJIGT) Decreto-Lei no. 380/99 – DR no. 222, 22 September 1999.

Monteiro, C. (2008) A função social da propriedade dos solos urbanos: Tópicos para a revisão da Lei dos Solos. In: *Adurbem Annual Meeting (LNEC, Lisbon), Proceedings*, pp. 57–60.

Mourão, J. (2012) *Planeamento do metabolismo urbano: Uma via para a restrição de emissões urbanas de gases com efeito de estufa.* PhD thesis, Oporto University, Portugal.

Mourão, J. & Pedro, J. B. (2007) Sustainable housing: From consensual guidelines to broader challenges. In: *Sustainable Construction. Materials and Practices, Portugal SB07 (IST, Lisbon) Proceedings*, pp. 27–34.

Mourão, J. & Pedro, J. B. (2012) *Princípios de edificação sustentável.* Lisbon, EPUL/ LNEC.

Naredo, J. M. (2003) Instrumentos para paliar la insostenibilidad de los sistemas urbanos in Ecología y Ciudad: Raíces de Nuestros Males y Modos de Tratarlos 'Ciudades para un Futuro más Sostenible'. *Boletín CF+S2002*.

Newmann, P. (2006) The environmental impact of cities. *Environment and Urbanisation*, 18, 275–295.

Niza, S., Rosado, L., & Ferrão, P. (2009) Urban metabolism: Methodological advances in urban material flow accounting based on the Lisbon case study. *Journal of Industrial Ecology*, 13 (3), 384–405.

Nunes da Silva, F. (2008) Comentários à 3ª Sessão: Âmbito. In: *Nacional Adurbem Annual Meeting (LNEC, Lisbon), Proceedings*, pp. 387–390.

Oliveira, A. (2008) O âmbito municipal do sistema de gestão territorial. In: *Adurbem Annual Meeting (LNEC, Lisbon), Proceedings*, pp. 241–246.

Partidário, M. R. (2007) *Guia de boas práticas da Agência Portuguesa do Ambiente.* Lisbon, APA.

Pinho, P. (2009) Low carbon cities: A Southern European perspective. International Society of City and Regional Planners. *Isocarp Review 05 Low Carbon Cities.*

Pinho, P., Oliveira, V., Santos Cruz, S., & Barbosa, M. (2013) Metabolic impact assessment for urban planning. *Journal of Environmental Planning and Management*, 56 (2), 178–193.

Portas, N. (2008) Evolução e desenvolvimento do sistema de gestão territorial: Uma perspectiva crítica. *Adurbem Annual Meeting (LNEC, Lisbon), Proceedings*, pp. 401–408.

Portas, N., Cabral, J., & Domingues, Á. (2003) *Políticas urbanas I, tendências, estratégias e oportunidades.* Coimbra, Fundação Calouste Gulbenkian.

Portas, N., Cabral, J., & Domingues, Á. (2011) *Políticas urbanas II, transformações, regulação e projectos.* Lisbon, Fundação Calouste Gulbenkian.

PP (Portuguese Parliament) (1998) *Lei de bases da política de ordenamento do território e de urbanismo* (LBPOTU) Law no. 48/98 – DR no. 184 I A, 11 August 1998.

PCM (Presidência Do Conselho De Ministros) (2010) *Estratégia nacional de adaptação às alterações climáticas.* ENAAC Resolução de Conselho de Ministros n°24/2010 Diário da República, 1.ª série No. 64 1.04.2010.

Santos, F. D., Forbes, K., & Moita, R. (eds) (2002) *Climate change in Portugal: Scenarios, impacts and adaptation measures – SIAM project.* Lisbon, Gradiva.

Stern, N. (2007) *The economics of climate change: The Stern review.* Cambridge, Cambridge University Press.

Talen, E. (2011) Sprawl retrofit: Sustainable urban form in unsustainable places. *Environment and Planning B*, 38, 952–978.

Urban Task Force (1999) *Towards an urban renaissance: Final report of the Urban Task Force chaired by Lord Rodgers of Riverside.* London, Spon.

Williams, K., Burton, E., & Jenks, M. (2000) *Achieving sustainable urban form.* London, Spon.

WCED (World Commission on Environment and Development) (1987) *Our common future.* Oxford, Oxford University Press.

10 Greek cities in crisis

Context, evidence, response

Athanasios Papaioannou and
Christina Nikolakopoulou

Introduction

Greek cities have been through a crisis that is apparent in a broad variety of sectors, either directly or indirectly. The credit crunch, beyond causing straitened economic circumstances, brings up social reformation at all decision-making levels. Drastic public spending cuts strongly affect health care and social services, education, and local government services. Social segregation (Maloutas, 2003), population displacement due to acute 'brain drain' movements of young qualified people abroad, and insecurity are only some of the risks that affect urban centres.

In this context, the chapter draws on the impacts of the crisis in Greece and examines the potential synergies between economy shrinkage and quality of life. In particular, spatial planning is introduced in the research methodology and through its evaluation as a decision-making instrument; both pre-crisis challenges and new emerging issues are revealed. Greek cities can constitute a good background for the investigation of the interaction between a crisis phenomenon and spatial planning weaknesses. The selection of the scale may contribute to the overview of bottom-up processes that have taken place in the development of Greek space, while spatial planning is examined as a process with high potentiality for urban resilience and improvement in the quality of life.

The chapter begins with a reference to the general conditions pertaining to the emergence and diffusion of the crisis in Greek cities, as well as extraneous impositions. With the aim of introducing the reader to the complex of problems, socio-economic indices are evaluated and the dramatic changes resulting from the crisis are linked to the quality of life across the country. Having addressed the interaction of spatial planning in the crisis response, the chapter ends with a critical overview of the institutional framework of urban planning in Greece, pointing to the need for reform and the launch of bottom-up initiatives to enhance the resilience and the comprehensive post-crisis development of Greek cities.

Scene setting: general implications

All of the processes that have taken place throughout the financial crisis in Greece have uncovered prior conditions. A high percentage of self-employed people in the labour force and a high homeownership rate made up an economic environment that did not have the potential to maintain economic stability when households and businesses were faced with increasing taxation. Moreover, state functions were insufficient considering that policies and strategic planning in the last decade were oriented mainly towards consumption rather than production. Greece has also to deal with emigration and immigration at the same time; this, combined with poor social welfare provisions, characterised by structural and distributional imbalances, makes the country's transition stage even more dangerous.

Political stagnation appears to be a basic reason for the meltdown. The lack of instrumental practice by local governors and the parallel requirement for democratically elected officials perpetuates the mismanagement of the public sector. In particular, on the one hand, political disorientation and election alliances move the focus away from community matters and, on the other hand, the public sector prevails, whereas the private sector is falling short. It is clear that socio-political relationships have been impaired and abnormal due to corruption (Koptsis, 2013). In addition, mistrust in public institutions, due to favouritism and unclear relations derived from the entanglement of political parties, has provided a bad mix, causing controversy in society. Moreover, the country has experienced decades of short-term policies and, most importantly, policy plans with no consistency and an absence of focus on real local needs (Sklias & Tzifakis, 2013; Tasopoulou et al., 2013).

In the big picture, the financial and banking debts as well as the fiscal debt of the public sector have led to a meltdown that has struck administrations on various scales due to loss of revenue. In an attempt to address these new conditions, authorities have responded with the application of (untested) recovery plans imposed by the International Monetary Fund. These measures have resulted in a situation in which local and central government are becoming even more indebted (Council of European Municipalities and Regions, 2009) as they are facing increasing taxation coupled with the lack of liquidity and the shrinkage of all economic sectors.

The current state of affairs evolved in an urban crisis, in which the bond ratings hint at effects on the business climate and the efficiency of the economy, but also investment tax credits provide the characterisation of the current time period as an era of stagnation and decline. The restructuring of public bodies responsible for urban and regional planning has been limited to a focus on collecting and regulating fines rather than progressive planning and territorial cohesion. With regard to funding resources, the government failed to set appropriate metrics for the use of European Union funds, for example in the National Strategic Reference Framework and LEADER programme, while funding has not always corresponded to the scale of urban problems addressed.

One of the most important results of the economic crisis is that the meltdown has led to higher numbers of unemployment due to the loss of working positions in all parts of the productive system. The transformation of the economy has led to a shift in perspectives and a rise in the numbers of citizens working freelance and experiencing job insecurity (Vaughan-Whitehead, 2005). Greece is the perfect case study of an economy in recession as the difficulties of this hard situation are so obvious; this is a situation that is even more severe considering the existence of a large shadow economy and of concomitant tax evasion. The prevalence of the public sector and the fragility of the local economy are combined and territorial impacts are magnified (Tasopoulou et al., 2013). The slowdown of entrepreneurial dynamics, poverty risk, and the immense increase in income and property taxes are only a few of the expressions of the depression (Petrakis, 2012).

Debt also led to a decline in the construction sector, a cornerstone of the national economy for decades (Tasopoulou et al., 2013). The increasing demand for housing and low-interest mortgages created the space for growth in the construction sector until 2010 and this, together with inefficiency in land governance, led to decades of urban sprawl. Today, a number of incomplete housing developments accompanied by redundancy in the real estate market and the bankruptcy of enterprises and job losses provide a toxic mix that is hard to manage.

As globalisation comes into play, cities have also become the collectors of diverse ethnicities and people have learned to coexist. In Greece, multicultural societies are now beginning to be formed and, as a result, the urban crisis has acquired a racial discourse and multiculturalism is intensely contested. Therefore, migrants are settled in certain parts of the medium-sized Greek cities and at the same time there is a moving stream of the middle class to the suburbs – factors that influence both social stability and the diversity of local cultural identity (Tzonis & Rodi, 2013). The social impacts appear to be taking the form of a mode of external social change. Such is the case of Athens, a city that stands as an example of the polarisation caused by a surplus of real estate products generated when the market was booming during the last decade (Maloutas, 2003).

Hence, political leadership is moving towards finding solutions to problems on the national scale and it unavoidably has to deal with problems on the urban scale. From now on, Greek society has to come to terms with a number of new challenges that require a fuller interpretative understanding of the collective experience of the past and a focus on social objectives. The lack of evaluation mechanisms makes Greek cities an interesting case study in examining the efforts made and the processes followed to mend the problems created by the crisis.

On the one hand, the scale of the problems detected on the national level needs to be determined in order to draw conclusions for the general situation in Greece; on the other hand, a focus should be placed on household economics to reveal the real economic decline, as it is experienced by citizens. The effects of the crisis have significantly affected the quality of life in Greece while deprivations and challenges are now evident at all levels of society, hindering the well-being of cities. Thus, it is necessary to examine in detail how the quality of life has been influenced by the crisis, examining how this recession is expressed in unemployment, poverty risk, and consumption indexes.

The impacts of the crisis on the quality of life in Greek cities

All of the above changes radically amended the quality of life in Greek cities. People, trying to adapt themselves to the altered circumstances, have to deal with the imposed pay cuts, dismissals, and a generalised impoverishment in the absence of supporting networks. In addition, the current lack of state capital decreases the state capacity to receive unregulated immigrants from other countries. This adds to the already high unemployment rates of the country intensifying the social and economic problems already caused by the meltdown.

In an effort to examine practically the impacts of the credit crunch on the regional level, the GDP (gross domestic product) index course through time will be taken into consideration as this provides credible information about the quality of life in different areas of Greece. However, GDP cannot be analysed in isolation but we should also consider the consumption expenditure, the income distribution, the unemployment trends, and poverty rates, the study of which can provide useful inputs.

It is a fact that there is a notable interrelation between economy and space (Figure 10.1). The two metropolitan regions of Attiki and Thessaloniki, that include the two biggest cities of Greece, show by far the highest values of GDP index, in comparison to the rest of the country. It is of particular interest that the existing difference has widened even more between 2008 and 2012, revealing the increasing internal imbalances within the country. To this point, it is worth mentioning that, except Athens and Thessaloniki, the other regions' GDP does

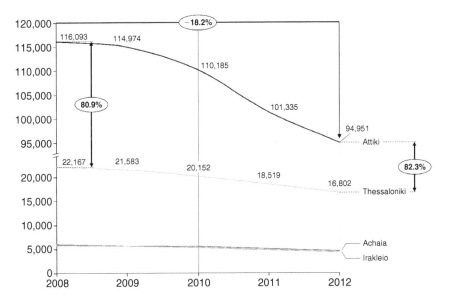

Figure 10.1 Gross domestic product in major Greek regions (€ million, at current prices) (sources: EL.STAT (2015a), author's own elaboration).

not show extensive discrepancies, making these seem more defenceless to the urban crisis compared to the latter.

Unfortunately, data for consumption expenditure on the city level does not exist. However, substantial conclusions can be drawn if the evolution of expenditure differences between urban and rural areas is examined (see Figure 10.2). In 2009 the average difference in expenditure was 32.7 per cent. In 2013 it could be observed that the gap between the two groups decreased up to 21.6 per cent. This is the result of the decline in expenditure in urban areas by 28.6 per cent, from €2.232 per month in 2009 to €1.595 per month in 2013. In the same period expenditure in rural areas fell by 16.8 per cent to €1.250.

Examining the economic perspective, there has been a constant decrease in consumption expenditure. The Hellenic Statistical Authority (EL.STAT, 2014a; see also Figure 10.3) monitoring the income and expenditure patterns of Greek

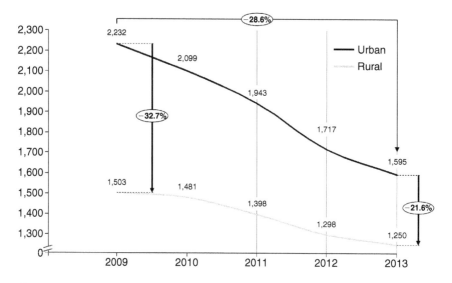

Figure 10.2 Average monthly expenditure of households in urban and rural areas (€) (sources: EL.STAT (2014a), author's own elaboration).

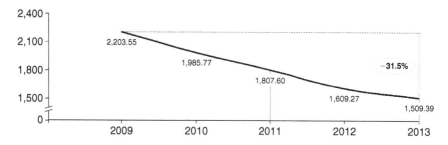

Figure 10.3 Average monthly expenditure of households (€, at constant prices) (sources: EL.STAT (2014a), author's own elaboration).

households nationwide recorded a decrease of 31.5 per cent (at constant prices) of the average monthly expenditure between 2009 and 2013.

Between 2012 and 2013 there is a notable change in the consumption patterns (in current prices) of Greek households. The shift is mostly related to a considerable cut in expenses in transport, durable goods, housing, hotels, cafés and restaurants, services, education, and communications whereas expenses related mainly to health and medication, alcoholic drinks, tobacco, and nutrition are changing in a lower rate as a percentage of the family budgets (EL.STAT, 2014a; see also Figure 10.4).

Analysing the changes between 2009 and 2013, there is a clear trend in declining expenses in all categories. However, the biggest decrease is noted in clothing, durable goods, and cafés and restaurants. In the contrary, the smallest decrease can be observed in alcoholic drinks, housing, and nutrition (EL.STAT, 2014a; see also Figure 10.5).

When looking at the distribution of total income in the different households, a generalised impoverishment of the population could not be noticed. Figure 10.6 illustrates the income quartiles. It seems that the crisis does not present a differentiating factor regarding income distribution. Taking into account also the development of the Gini Index, as a popular tool that is frequently used to measure income inequality as one number (Shkolnikov, Andreev, & Begun, 2003), between 2009 and 2013, it could be noticed that Greece remains a highly polarised country, but the crisis has not contributed to a significant change in either direction (see Figure 10.7).

However possible different findings arise when considering the portion of the population at risk of poverty or social exclusion by age group. By definition, poverty risk is defined as the percentage of people living in households where the total equalised disposable income is below 60 per cent of the national median income (Eurostat, 2015). However, it should be borne in mind that specific population groups which are presumably poor, like homeless people, illegal economic migrants, Roma, etc., are not included in the survey. In Greece in 2009 almost

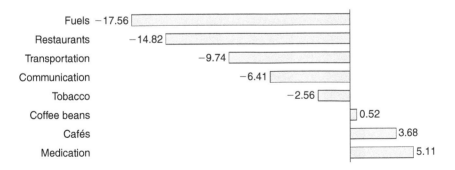

Figure 10.4 Differences in the average expenditure per household: subcategories with greater expenditure increases and reductions (between 2012 and 2013, %) (sources: EL.STAT (2014a), author's own elaboration).

one-third of the population was regarded as population at risk of poverty. It seems that the crisis has contributed to a steep rise in the percentages, especially for specific age groups, such as children and population aged between 18 and 64 (see also Figure 10.8).

Other useful findings for the degradation of lifestyle may be made when studying the trend in the unemployment rate. Greece can be an interesting case study as unemployment has soared in cities, regardless of the community and national funds raised to this purpose, such as subsidy programmes for enterprises and unemployed people. Over time, unfortunately, job opportunities in Greece

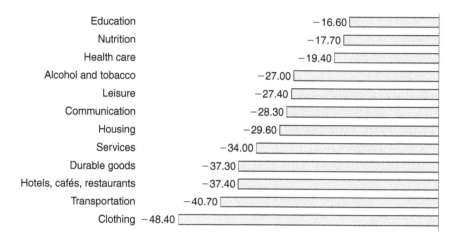

Figure 10.5 Percentage change in monthly household expenditure for goods and services (between 2009 and 2013, %) (sources: EL.STAT (2014a), author's own elaboration).

	2009	2010	2011	2012	2013
1st quadrant	9.8	9.9	9.4	8.7	8.9
2nd quadrant	18.0	17.9	17.7	17.9	17.8
3rd quadrant	25.5	25.7	26.2	26.4	26.3
4th quadrant	46.7	46.5	46.7	47.0	47.1

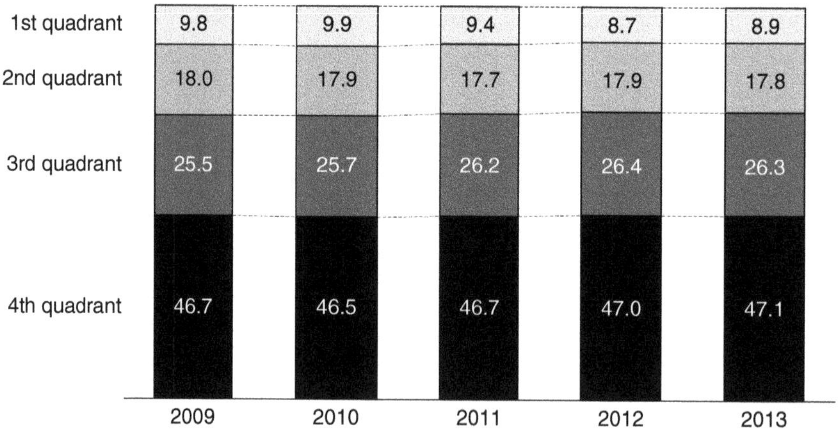

Figure 10.6 Development of the income quartiles in Greece (between 2009 and 2013) (sources: EL.STAT (2014b), author's own elaboration).

are not at all ameliorated; unemployment is constantly growing, without providing room to boost the local economy (see Figure 10.9).

Although the most obvious reasons for the rise of unemployment seem to be the austerity measures applied in the course of the economic crisis, others are to be found also in a variety of chronic dysfunctions in the state structure. The Greek labour market cannot any more provide high-productivity jobs while the education system produces high-skilled and overqualified people, demonstrating

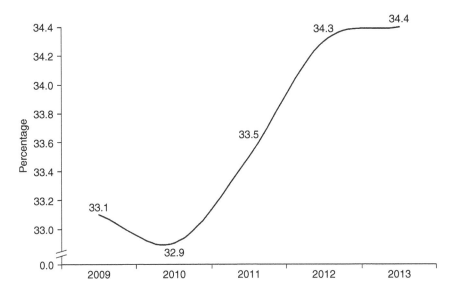

Figure 10.7 Unequal income distribution Index (Gini Index) (sources: EL.STAT (2014b), author's own elaboration).

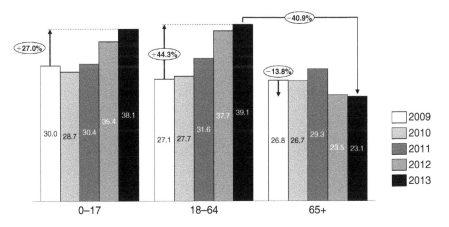

Figure 10.8 Population at risk of poverty or social exclusion, by age groups (sources: EL.STAT (2014b), author's own elaboration).

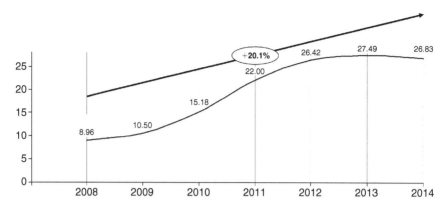

Figure 10.9 Unemployment rate (aged 15–74) in Greece (sources: EL.STAT (2015b), author's own elaboration).

that the skills developed are different from the skills demanded. This mismatch reveals the lack of an effective strategic planning that the state should implement in order to structure properly qualified society regardless of the ongoing financial crisis. To this point, attention should be drawn to the dual nature of the concerns, both economic and social ones (Monastiriotis & Martelli, 2013), that are raised by the high rates of unemployment and that require an immediate policy mobilisation.

Referring to the current credit crunch and its social impacts in the cities, we further have to consider immigration trends, although they are not covered by statistics on income inequalities or poverty. The geographical position of the country, the current turmoil in the Middle East, and the inefficient border control provide preconditions for the receiving of such numerous groups of immigrants. Up until 2008, the 'foreign population' that arrived in the country, contributed to the population increase and served the employment needs of the seasonal industries such as agriculture and tourism. Since then, these population groups have been treated as a threat (Mediterranean Migration Observatory, 2004). Nowadays, the unauthorised entry of migrants from Africa and Asia raises the portion of undocumented expatriates and makes cities, especially on Greek islands, experience economic and cultural awe. In addition, the state remains incapable of implementing a succinct integration policy and has not sufficient infrastructure to take care of this new population (Triandafyllidou, 2014). In this way, the lack of efficient policies and the bureaucracy in deportation procedures have led to both sides' dissatisfaction. On the one hand, immigrants cannot resort to an immediate exodus and, on the other hand, Greek society's cohesion is threatened.

Regarding this, it should be pointed out that the extent of this problem was the main reason for the rise of the ultra-right party of Golden Dawn. This party focused on racism, xenophobia, and the stranded feeling of security, trying to persuade voters by promoting a stricter policy towards foreign population. Also many conservative political groups have focused on anti-immigrant campaigns, ignoring any positive influences these foreign groups may bring to the country (Ellinas, 2013).

The shocking depravity of the country's issues found its expression in the results from the last national elections. The population, drained economically and mentally by austerity, in an effort to defend a decent quality of life, was attracted by the left-wing government of Syriza for the very first time in Greek political history. Greek people were totally convinced by the anti-austerity argument of Syriza, supporting his approach of setting in question the 'over-valued', according to them, Greek debt (Vasilopoulou & Halikiopoulou, 2015).

Since 2008, recession has been continuous and is still evolving. The changes that occurred as a result of the crisis in the political, economic, and social system of the country and finally in the production model itself have led to a radical deconstruction of the traditional model of business development and living conditions that prevailed in various versions since the post-war era and the dictatorship (Psycharis, 2011). The degradation is manifested in two ways. First, indirectly, by the depreciation of small and medium entrepreneurship and property that were once the pillars of Greek economic development and, second, directly by the systematic promotion of a new business model, that until at least the election of Syriza to government, has been radically diverging from the traditional model of the Greek 'compact capitalism'. Employment prospects in the public sector, lending, as well as income from subsidies and tax exemptions, had orientated households in channelling much of the rising income in the purchase of land and property as a form of investment. The new model is based on the use of large public or private land, mainly in the form of organised receptors for residential and business activities; gradually devaluing the traditional small Greek construction companies (Giannakourou & Kafkalas, 2014). From now on, political decisions will show if Syriza will be able to implement immediate measures, trust local people, respect the lenders, and improve state organisation structures.

Against the background of the conducted analysis it could be concluded that quality of life is entwined with economic prosperity in Greek cities. Unemployment and risk of poverty affect directly the life of people, excluding them from any social and professional activities. Differences between urban and rural areas, as well as between urban areas themselves, are key points of an underlying spatial differentiation in Greece. Prior key characteristics of the system, such as a high percentage of self-employed people and high homeownership, were immediately affected by the crisis and created a new economic and social environment that was not in a position to deal with the acute consequences of the crisis. Previous structural problems as well as considerable underestimation of strategic planning and policies, combined with poor social welfare provisions, were only enhanced by the crisis (Kotios, Galanos, & Roukanas, 2012).

The retraction of the social welfare state, in combination with the inability of the traditional Greek supporting network, mainly family and friends, because of their own vulnerable position, brought up other types of supporting networks (Sotiropoulos & Bourikos, 2014). The volunteer networks that have emerged are organised in an informal way and cover various fields of the social welfare provisions, ranging from providing shelter and food to people in need, to establishing infirmaries, pharmacies, or supporting centres for families.

The question is how spatial policies are to address the issues discussed. The deterioration of living conditions and quality of life in general is affecting all levels of administration. However in most cases the key responsibility for confronting the immediate effects of the crisis remains within the limits of regional authorities. Their limited resources however do not provide a sustainable framework for enhancing the quality of life, as the focus is restricted to damage control actions such as maintenance, while in the meantime new plans are abandoned. From this perspective, it remains questionable whether the crisis will allow spatial planning to fulfil its basic aims as described in the following section or not.

Spatial planning in Greece: structures and enablers of a new paradigm

Spatial planning plays a critical role in providing the tools and the solutions for economic, social, and environmental stability and growth. Spatial planning creates an important framework by enabling horizontal and vertical coordination across policies and sectors and by developing a vision and a common path of effort for all stakeholders. In its strategic character it can become an important lever for improving the quality of life, by managing change efficiently, and for promoting sustainable development by the smart allocation and use of resources.

The spatial specificities in Greece along with the effects of the current crisis on spatial planning and their contribution to the quality of life are a matter worth further analyses. The newly drafted laws and the new reality of deteriorating living conditions and policy priorities are changing the framework within which planners practice. Shifts in legislation, new tools, and new strategic decisions regarding development policies are influencing spatial planning at various levels.

The main characteristic of these changes is the failure to incorporate in the strategic and conceptual dimension of planning the manifestation and implications of the crisis. Planning as an organised logical effort to choose the best alternatives and means to achieve specific goals (Angelidis, 2010) is clearly not embedded in this new legal framework (Klampatsea, 2011). The core values of spatial planning in Greece have traditionally been to ensure equal living conditions and employment opportunities, to improve quality of life, to regenerate cities, and to coordinate public policies with spatial impacts, *inter alia* (L. 2742/1999). However structural deficits often act as a hindrance. This includes, besides spatial elements such as the fragmentation of landownership, also other important aspects such as inefficient and highly hierarchical and bureaucratic relations among public authorities as well as strategies without internal and external cohesion and complementarity (Evangelidou, 2004).

One example, which tried to eliminate planning gaps and mitigate intense differentiations caused by the high number of small municipalities, many of which were mainly rural and non-functional, a second considerable reform, after the Kapodistrias reform of 1997, was implemented in 2011. At the early stages of the crisis, Greece came to ameliorate its spatial and administrative organisation and built a more flexible and effective state by the adoption of L. 3852/2010, known as the Kallikratis Programme.

Characteristically, the Kallikratis Programme reduced the number of municipalities from 1,033 to only 325 and bridged 51 prefectures (NUTS III) to 13 regional units (NUTS II), while a 50 per cent decrease was applied to this level of public administration employees. The reform of national level administration included merging the 13 former administrative districts into seven new ones (OECD, 2014). These kinds of changes aimed at the restoration of transparency as well as reinforcement of citizens' trust and accessibility to public affairs.

Nevertheless, structural deficiencies still remain. As pointed out by Souliotis (2013) this decentralisation is just a means of transferring fiscal cuts to the low levels of administration structure; the devolution of responsibilities to subnational entities was not accompanied by allocation of the necessary funds and their capacity (especially in spatial planning) persists to be limited (Akrivopoulou, Dimitropoulos, & Koutnatzis, 2012).

Planning in Greece has always had a lesser role in comparison to other policies (Papaioannou, 2009) and the flexibility of the new planning instruments, as described later, and their fragmented nature constitute a paradigm shift, where the crisis is used as a 'Trojan horse' rather than as a reason for redefining the priorities and the instruments for spatial planning. The main aspect of this shift is the change in definition of the concept of public land and public property in general from being a public good to being a commodity owned by the state (Klampatsea, 2012). The new role of spatial planning, as defined by public officials, is to act as a facilitator for the government's privatisation programme by enabling real estate development and providing instruments for the exploitation of the Greek public sector's private properties. The circumvention of the basic concepts and the total redefinition of spatial planning further degrade its role to that of merely a support mechanism for pre-judged decisions, thus entirely neglecting the social and environmental dimensions traditionally part of planning. Terms such as 'sustainability' and 'social justice' are absent from modern day planning and governance in Greece (Sotiropoulos, Featherstone, & Karadag, 2014). There is, therefore, a need for a review of the basic doctrines and principles of spatial planning in order to facilitate market interests and private initiatives (Giannakourou & Balla, 2012).

As it stands, spatial planning represents two totally different fragmented aspects. On the one hand, on a national/regional scale, spatial planning is regarded as a mechanism of delay, blocking any major investments through its regulatory slant regarding land use or environmental protection; on the other hand, on a city/neighbourhood scale, spatial planning has long been focused on damage control, mitigating the effects of uncontrolled city expansion, a lack of social infrastructure, and environmental problems.

With regard to the role of spatial planning in hindering progress, to bypass barriers, and in light of the experiences of the Olympic Games and the projects associated with them, new concepts such as holiday and tourist housing are being introduced as distinct categories regarding location and the permit process. Moreover, substantive legislation in recent years has provided the state and investors with instruments to fast-track processes in implementing strategic investment projects (L. 3894/2010; L. 4146/2013). These 'fast-track' instruments enable the direct circumvention of any type of spatial, social, or environmental obstacle and cover both private and PPP-type projects in various fields, such as industry, tourism, energy, and transportation. To qualify for the status of a 'fast-track' project, it has to meet some minimum requirements in generating quantitative and qualitative results of major significance for the national economy overall. The projects that have gained fast-track status thus far include projects in the fields of energy, mining, tourism, and retail (Enterprise Greece, 2014).

These new tools aim to accelerate procedures and avoid costly administrative activities. Thus, for example, approval of the environmental impact assessment study in planning is granted directly by ministerial decision, rather than requiring the issuance of opinions by authorities and organisations (L. 3894/2010, art. 6), and there are specific and special deviations from applicable terms and restrictions foreseen in land use and urban plans (L. 3894/2010, art. 7). These derogations may relate to any condition or restriction applicable under approved plans, i.e. the distance of the buildings from the boundaries of the plot, the distances between buildings and other facilities, the building coefficient, the coverage coefficient, and the maximum height. Recently, the adoption of Special Spatial Development Plans of Strategic Investments, as a new type of plan outside the official planning legislation in Greece, has enabled investors and landowners to override any different or opposing restriction by any type of plan and has thus succeeded in creating an investors' oasis inside the present planning system (L. 4146/2013).

Turning to the city/neighbourhood scale, spatial planning has historically been the means of mitigating the damage caused by uncontrolled processes of city expansion, addressing the lack of social infrastructure and remediating environmental problems. The main aspects requiring attention traditionally were the fragmentation of landownership, illegal dwellings, and land use management. Strategic or regulatory decisions and plans were sparsely developed and implemented.

Because of the crisis, urban planning has seen its resources and role shrink. The misconception of the meaning of planning and the persistence in associating planning with urban design, along with a significant cut from the municipalities in expenditures regarding planning activities, have limited the role of planning and its ability to fulfil its remit. Parallel to these problems, old institutional fragmentation and a lack of coordination have intensified the situation. Despite efforts to improve decision-making procedures by decentralising resources and enabling governance in urban centres, the same notorious Greek problems in policy coordination on both horizontal and vertical levels still remain (Pagonis, 2013). Moreover antagonism between the ministries has played a catalytic role in reinforcing these problems.

Currently, two clear trends can be identified (Zifou et al., 2011). First, there is the emergence of point interventions and regeneration following a 'decorative' logic in continuation of the urban design tradition of spatial planning in Greece. The lack of experience and tradition in strategic planning has clearly shifted the focus solely to the 'architectural dimension' of planning. New projects, such as the pedestrianisation of central Athenian streets, with a total budget of approximately €110 million, follow no clear plan to deal with the crisis and have no social or environmental substance, depriving other projects of resources and funds (Pagonis, 2013; Zifou et al., 2011). The European Commission, noticing the complementary nature of these point interventions, has recently decommissioned the projects from receiving EU funds (Hemikoglou, 2014).

Second, another trend emerging is the strengthening of non-institutional or private actors in the production and development of space. The focal point of government policy, as a tool to address the crisis, is the exploitation of public property. In this context, the state has transferred competences to state-owned private entities, which operate under opaque conditions outside the established state structures in search of possible investors. Alongside private investors, private entities (e.g. institutions) finance specific studies and projects, which are often not in harmony with official planning priorities.

Having documented the shift in the priorities of spatial planning policy – because of and during the crisis – it could be noted that spatial planning has been transformed from an instrument dedicated to the enhancement of the quality of life and to guarantee equal living conditions, to a secondary activity. Major determinants, such as the social and natural environment and transportation, have seen their role neglected in formulating new priorities.

Conclusions: unravelling the threads of hope

Since 2008, Greece has been experiencing a socio-economic crisis, the impacts of which have resulted in a drop in quality of life in a variety of ways. Households are dealing with heavy taxes, municipalities with great cuts, and policy reform is limited to tax collection. Will Greece finally be able to use austerity to effective ends?

Localism, meritocratic political leadership and powerful social capital, and a reliable planning system could become tools to release pressure on cities in crisis and make them more resilient to crises. Professional discourse concerning territorial, economic, and social affairs has to take place following educational schemes designed to create strong social capital (United Nations World Tourism Organization & International Labour Organization, 2013). Increased volunteering and collective action, the action of NGOs, citizens' groups, and local initiatives seem to be promising tools for assimilating the damaging consequences and accelerating recovery in the future aimed at social cohesion (Tasopoulou et al., 2013). In the case of Greek cities, the development of social services based on volunteerism seems to be a remarkably positive side-effect of the crisis in urban society, where there was no such practice in the past. The needs to be addressed are varied and the effects of the crisis are aggravated by the state acting not as an enabler but as an obstacle to civilians and industry. It is clear that private interests can no longer be the first priority and state needs to be in the forefront of change. The emergence of social solidarity networks constitutes a seed of hope for Greek cities, provided that the relevant novel structures prove to be a legacy for the future and not a contingent phenomenon.

However, all the hardships the country has undergone thus far provide lessons to be learned. Reformation is necessary but evaluation has to precede it. It has become clearer than ever that Greece has to re-evaluate its objectives and come up with new ideas and models. The current situation offers the country a chance to reconsider decision-making at all levels and focus on regional and urban planning through visionary development. Resilience requires long-term planning as decisions should be based on a common community vision. Policy evaluation can reveal shadow processes and vocational training programmes can add value to the territorial aspects of development and growth.

On the strategic level, spatial planning has shifted from being an instrument of problem solving through participatory processes to being a platform for enabling foreign investment and facilitating the transfer of state resources to private owners. Moreover, planning has failed to take into account the deteriorating living standards of the majority of the Greek population and has not yet provided any concept or solution for overcoming these negative tendencies. The long-term consequences of such a policy shift might have various impacts on the structure and function of Greek cities and regions and the socio-environmental consequences are worthy of further investigation. It is from now on that it shall be seen if Greece can manage to return to economic growth, albeit by unpopular political decision-making.

References

Akrivopoulou, C., Dimitropoulos, G., & Koutnatzis, S. (2012) *The 'Kallikratis Program': The influence of international and european policies on the reforms of Greek local government.* [Online] Available from: www.regione.emilia-romagna.it/affari_ist/ Rivista_3_2012/Dimitropoulos.pdf [accessed 15 May 2015].

Angelidis, M. (2010) *Spatial planning and sustainable development.* Athens, Symmetria.

Council of European Municipalities and Regions (2009) *Financial and economic crisis.* [Online] Available from: http://urbact.eu/fileadmin/corporate/doc/News/CEMR%20 CCRE.pdf [accessed 7 May 2015].

Ellinas, A. (2013) The rise of golden dawn: The new face of the far right in Greece. *South European Society and Politics*, 18 (4), 543–565.

EL.STAT (2014a) *Household budget survey.* Hellenic Statistical Authority (in Greek). [Online] Available from: www.statistics.gr/portal/page/portal/ESYE/BUCKET/A0801/ PressReleases/A0801_SFA05_DT_AN_00_2013_01_F_GR.pdf [accessed 18 May 2015].

EL.STAT (2014b) *Income and living conditions of households.* Hellenic Statistical Authority (in Greek). [Online] Available from: www.statistics.gr/portal/page/portal/ ESYE/BUCKET/A0802/Other/A0802_SFA10_TS_AN_00_2010_00_2013_02_F_ GR.xls [accessed 18 May 2015].

EL.STAT (2015a) *Gross domestic product by region and county.* Hellenic Statistical Authority (in Greek). [Online] Available from: www.statistics.gr/portal/page/portal/ESYE/PAGE-themes?p_param=A0703&r_param=SEL48&y_param=TS&mytabs=0 [accessed 18 May 2015].

EL.STAT (2015b) *Workforce.* Hellenic Statistical Authority (in Greek). [Online] Available from: www.statistics.gr/portal/page/portal/ESYE/PAGE-themes?p_param=A0101 [accessed: 18 May 2015].

Enterprise Greece (2014) *Confirmed investment projects.* [Online] Available from: www.investingreece.gov.gr/default.asp?pid=173&la=1 [accessed 17 December 2014].

Eurostat (2015) *People at risk of poverty or social exclusion.* [Online] Available from http://ec.europa.eu/eurostat/statistics-explained/index.php/People_at_risk_of_poverty_or_social_exclusion [accessed 25 May 2015]

Evangelidou, M. (2004) Institutional conditions for exercising a policy for stimulating the international role of Athens. *Geography.* Issue 7.

Giannakourou, G. & Balla, E. (2012) Privatizing urban planning in Greece: Current trends and future prospects. Presentation at *International Conference – Platform of Experts on Planning Law*, Lisbon, October 2012. [Online] Available from: www.icjp.pt/sites/default/files/cursos/documentacao/_privatizing_urban_planning_in_greece.pdf [accessed 12 November 2015].

Giannakourou, G. & Kafkalas G. (2014) Rethinking spatial planning in times of crisis: Necessity, content and conditions of the reform. In: Masourakis, M. & Gortsos, C. (eds) *Competitiveness for growth: Policy proposals.* Athens, Greek Bank Association, pp. 511–522 (in Greek) [Online] Available from: www.hba.gr/5Ekdosis/UplPDFs//sylltomos14/511-522%20Giannakourou-Kafkalas%202014.pdf [accessed 25 May 2015].

Hemikoglou, A. (2014) *Tombstone in Faliron and Panepistimiou: To Vima* (in Greek). [Online] Available from: www.tovima.gr/society/article/?aid=653015 [accessed 17 May 2015].

Klampatsea, R. (2011) *Spatial fingerprints and design challenges in a crisis: The Greek case.* Greek Congress on Regional Development and Economic Crisis, Greek Society of Regional Science, Athens.

Klampatsea, R. (2012) The city at the time of the crisis and the prospects for sustainability (in Greek). Presentation at *Human Environment and Sustainable Management*, Medies, Athens, 13 November 2012. [Online] Available from: www.medies.net/_uploaded_files/desd_manmade_2012/klabatsea.pdf [accessed 8 June 2015].

Koptsis, G. (ed.) (2013) *Restoring public debt sustainability: The role of independent fiscal institutions.* Oxford, Oxford University Press.

Kotios, A., Galanos, G., & Roukanas, S. (2012) The Greek crisis and the crisis of the Eurozone governance system. *Research Series*, 18 (1): 1–26. Volos, University of Thessaly.

L. 2742/1999 (Hellenic Government Gazette Issue A 207/07-10-1999) Spatial planning, sustainable development and other provisions.

L. 3852/2010 (Hellenic Government Gazette Issue A 87/07-06-2010) Kallikratis Programme.

L. 3894/2010 (Hellenic Government Gazette Issue A 204/02-12-2010) Acceleration and transparency regarding the realization of strategic investments.

L. 4146/2013 (Hellenic Government Gazette Issue A 90/18-04-2013) Creation of a friendly development environment for strategic and private investments and other provisions.

Maloutas, T. (2003) Contextual parameters for promoting social sustainability: The case of Athens. *Discussion Paper Series*, 9 (5), 77–94.

Mediterranean Migration Observatory (2004) S*tatistical data on immigrants in Greece: An analytic study of available data and recommendations for conformity with European Union standards.* [Online] Available from: www.mmo.gr/pdf/general/IMEPO_Final_Report_English.pdf [accessed 15 May 2015].

Monastiriotis, V. & Martelli, A. (2013) Beyond rising unemployment: Unemployment risk, crisis and regional adjustments in Greece. *GreeSE - Hellenic Observatory Papers on Greece and Southeast Europe*, 80. Hellenic Observatory, LSE.

OECD (2014) *OECD regional outlook 2014 regions and cities: Where policies and people meet.* [Online] Available from: https://books.google.gr/books?id=ir2zBAAAQBAJ&pg=PA242&hl=el#v=onepage&q&f=false [accessed 15 May 2015].

Pagonis, A. (2013) The evolution of metropolitan planning policy in Athens over the last three decades: Linking shifts in the planning discourse with institutional changes and spatial transformation. In: *Changing Cities: Spatial, Morphological, Formal and Socioeconomic Dimensions*, University of Thessaly, Skiathos Island, 18–21 June 2013.

Papaioannou, A. (2009) Spatial development between competitiveness and cohesion policies: The case of Athens and the consequences for the spatial structure of Greece. In: *2nd Greek Congress in Urban Planning and Regional Development*, University of Thessaly, Volos, 24–27 September 2009.

Petrakis, P. (2012) *The Greek economy and the crisis*: *Challenges and responses.* Berlin, Springer.

Psycharis, I. (2011) *Study on the impact of the economic crisis on the regional economy of in Greece.* Final Report, Panteion University of Social and Political Sciences, Institute of Regional Development, Athens, September 2011.

Shkolnikov, V., Andreev, E., & Begun, A. (2003) Gini coefficient as a life table function: Computation from discrete data, decomposition of differences and empirical examples. *Demographic Research*, 8 (11), 305–358.

Sklias, P. & Tzifakis, N. (eds) (2013) *Greece's horizons: Reflecting on the country's assets and capabilities.* Centre for European Studies, Konstantinos Karamanlis Institute for Democracy. Athens, Springer Science & Business Media.

Sotiropoulos, D., Featherstone, K., & Karadag, R. (2014) *Sustainable governance indicators: 2014 Greece report.* Gütersloh, Bertelsmann Stiftung.

Sotiropoulos, D. & Bourikos, D. (2014) Economic crisis, social solidarity and the voluntary sector in Greece. *Journal of Power, Politics and Governance*, 2 (2), 33–53

Souliotis, N. (2013) Athens and the politics of the sovereign debt crisis. In: Fujita, K. (ed.) *Cities and crisis: New critical urban theory.* Chandigarh, Sage Publications, pp. 237–270.

Tasopoulou, N., Andrikopoulou, E., Kafkalas, G., & Kakderi, C. (2013) Coping with the crisis: Understanding resilience in a Greek region. *9th International Urban and Regional Studies Conference, Europe and the World: Competing Visions, Changing Spaces, Flows and Politics*, University of Sussex, Brighton, UK, 10–12 July 2013.

Triandafyllidou, A. (2014) *Migration in Greece recent developments in 2014.* ELIAMEP, Athens. [Online] Available from: www.eliamep.gr/wp-content/uploads/2014/10/Migration-in-Greece-Recent-Developments-2014_2.pdf [accessed 15 May 2015].

Tzonis, A. & Rodi, A. (2013) *GREECE modern architectures in history.* London, Reaktion Books.

United Nations World Tourism Organization & International Labour Organization (2013) *Economic crisis, international tourism decline and its impact on the poor.* World Tourism

Organisation, Madrid, Spain. [Online] Available from: https://pub.unwto.org/WebRoot/ Store/Shops/Infoshop/5154/3532/B855/6F7A/95FA/C0A8/0164/763A/130328_ economic_crisis_excerpt.pdf [accessed 13 May 2015].

Vasilopoulou, S. & Halikiopoulou, D. (2015) *The Golden Dawn's 'nationalist solution': Explaining the rise of the far right in Greece.* New York, Palgrave Macmillan.

Vaughan-Whitehead, D. (ed.) (2005) *Working and employment conditions in new EU member states.* Geneva, International Labour Organization.

Zifou, M., Kalantzopoulou, M., Samarinis, P., & Chatzikontstantinou, E. (2011) *Planning for the center of Athens, in the context of crisis.* [Speech] Encounter Athens, Initiative for the Center of Athens, Discourse and Demands for a Fair City, Athens, 16 May 2011.

11 Crisis and urban shrinkage from an Italian perspective

*Carlo Salone, Angelo Besana, and
Umberto Janin Rivolin*

Introduction

This chapter discusses the concept of urban shrinkage from an analytical perspective, a concept widely addressed in international debates but much less so in Italy, bearing in mind the spatial trends seen in the country. The findings will be discussed with consideration of two main aspects: with regard to the recent economic crisis, which originated from the burst of the housing bubble but rapidly evolved, as abroad, into a generalised recession throughout the country; and in light of the domestic spatial planning system, its traditional features, and more recent changes. An attempt will thus be made to understand the extent to which spatial policies in Italy have been made to face the recent global crisis and the possible urban shrinkage resulting from it.

The main purpose of this contribution is to show the extent to which the recent dynamics of the Italian urban system reflect the idea underpinning the 'urban shrinkage model' as a generalised phenomenon of contraction in cities affected by industrial decline throughout Europe. In particular, the shrinkage has affected the less industrialised cities of southern Italy, but it is not perceived in the large- and middle-sized cities of the northern and central part of the country. It will also be suggested that strong diversification of the spatial planning system at the regional and local level should favour a flexible and 'place-based' approach towards this diversified process of spatial transformation. Unfortunately, the generalised and persisting 'conformative' approach to spatial planning in Italy tends to counteract the flexibility that is needed to face the effects of the current crisis.

The current chapter is then structured into six sections. The next section presents a theoretical framework structuring the analysis of recent Italian urbanisation processes. It revives the currently neglected literature on the urban life cycle, trying to avoid an overestimation of the part played by the real estate/ financial crisis of 2007–2008 in the shrinkage processes, whilst emphasising the need for more tailored interpretations that take into account the structural differences among urban regions across Western countries. The third section contains some conceptual definitions that contribute to setting the methodology used in this analysis. The fourth section offers a preliminary survey of demographic and economic processes taking place in Italian urban systems through a detailed retrospective examination. The fifth section then sums up the limitations of the application of concepts drawn from specific spatial processes, such as urban shrinkage, to situations that are structurally different, such as the case of Italy, and supports the need for further theoretical and interpretive elaboration in the country. The sixth section describes the overall organisation, traditional features, and current trends of the Italian spatial planning system, referring to the ability of planning tools to deal with the spatial effects of the crisis. The final section recaps the main content and findings of the chapter.

Urban shrinkage and the recent economic crisis

The term 'urban shrinkage' was suggested (Haase, Rink, & Grossmann, 2014) to indicate the processes of physical abandonment and economic decline in many old industrial urban areas affected by the production crisis during the transition to post-Fordism. It is therefore a multidimensional phenomenon, which needs to be observed while paying particular attention to demographic and employment dynamics and their implications in terms of urban intervention policies.

'Urban shrinkage is not a new phenomenon' (Martinez-Fernandez et al., 2012a: p. 213), but it represents a specific subject in an ample scientific literature that since the late 1960s has attempted to describe and model the general process of transformation and sprawl in urban systems of Western countries (Gottman, 1964; Berry, 1976; Hall & Hay, 1980; Van den Berg et al., 1982; Hall, 1984; Cheshire & Hay, 1989; Fielding, 1982; Gottman & Muscarà, 1991; Friedrichs, 1993; Cheshire, 1995; Soja, 2000; Champion, 2001; Sassen, 2001; Scott & Storper, 2003; Oswalt, 2006; Baron et al., 2010).

The different development paths of cities are thereby placed in a broader, complex and diversified process of spatial transformation, characterised by events of concentration and functional upgrading at a global and continental scale and, simultaneously, by a continuous search for new areas to be exploited at a regional and local level. The growth and decline of metropolitan and urban systems are therefore a manifestation of the temporal and spatial cycle of the global economy and markets driven by actors constantly looking for rent positions (Harvey, 2000, 2005; and, for a broader conceptualisation of urban shrinkage see Haase, Rink, & Grossmann, 2014).

There are many significant examples of studies focusing on the abandonment of the industrial cities of the so-called North American Rust Belt (Buffalo, Cleveland, Youngstown, Pittsburgh, etc.), dominated by the production cycle of the steel and metal industry; of the urban centres of the former German Democratic Republic, 'victims' of the 1990 reunification and the post-socialist transition (Wiechmann & Pallagst, 2012); of the Polish urban systems (Nowak & Nowosielski, 2008); and of metropolitan Japan (Flüchter, 2008). Many attempts have also been made to include French and British industrial cities in these reflections (Cunningham-Sabot & Fol, 2009), whose decline is related to the emergence of new regional specialisations as a response to globalisation, resulting in the relocation of private investment from heavy industry to high-tech sectors.

From Nord-Pas-de-Calais to the Ardennes, from Lorraine to the belt of industrial centres of the Massif Central, from the Scottish conurbations (Greater Glasgow, the Western Isles) to the Black Country, the process of abandonment appears to be generalised, increasing migratory flows towards capital cities and urban centres that are more active in technologically advanced industries.

Although there are different forms of 'urban contraction',[1] the definition of urban shrinkage used in this chapter is that drawn from the international literature on the topic (Pallagst, 2008; Wolff, 2010; Plöger, 2012; Martinez-Fernandez et al., 2012b; Wiechmann & Pallagst, 2012): a phenomenon characterising densely populated areas that record a population loss and, at the same time, undergo a transformation of their economic base, showing symptoms of structural crisis. The 'crisis-contraction' combination dominates the reflections of international research and deserves to be expanded upon accordingly.

Crisis and urban shrinkage: an economic link?

The nature of the 'crisis' concept appears to be controversial. Going beyond the nevertheless useful original meaning of the ancient Greek term *krisis* – 'the action of deciding, dividing, breaking, transitioning' – a sharpened perception and a subsequent definition of empirical evidence of the crisis phenomenology could be observed during the most intense phase of the unfolding of globalisation, the years spanning the 1980s and 1990s. With the disruption of the bipolar world order, the Western capitalist systems as well as the socialist regimes of old Europe have experienced an intense restructuring of social structures, economic systems, and mechanisms for political regulation. These processes are frequently associated with the terms 'decline', 'decadence', and, of course, 'shrinkage', and are projected against the backdrop of the advent of neoliberalism.

For several years, Western sociology has been conducting analyses of social disintegration generated by the spread of neoliberalism. This, like any form of modernisation, produces 'human waste' (term used by Zygmunt Bauman, 2004) put into circulation by the emergence of new production paradigms and new social and economic structures that exclude those who do not have adequate skills to enter the labour market and who represent a 'cost' to public welfare systems (Dietzsch, 2009).

Along these lines, within certain limits, the phenomenon of urban shrinkage might be seen as an epiphenomenon of a structural shift, a 'crisis', in fact, that more generally produces *urban waste*, a conceptual category that not only includes the material rubble of (parts of) cities that have become *dispensable*, no longer necessary, and therefore abandoned to physical degradation, but also includes the roles they have had and the people who played them.

The structural crisis highlighted by international research is generally measured by indicators such as the employment rate and the per capita income of residents. When these show negative variations and, at the same time, when a negative demographic trend is observed the urban area is considered a shrinking city. The phenomenon of demographic contraction is therefore related to restructuring processes aimed at a drastic downsizing of the local production base, and is associated with high unemployment rates, a growing dependence on public welfare, and the decay of the urban environment caused by the mass departure of the population and the abandonment of residential assets (Plöger, 2012). The link between 'crisis' and 'shrinkage' is always noted in the introductory remarks of essays on the topic, but is rarely developed from a conceptual and interpretive point of view.

Italian accounts

In general, Italian cities are not the 'protagonists' of international studies, although there are many explicit references to demographic decline recorded in urban centres of the peninsula, for example in Plöger (2012) and Wiechmann and Pallagst (2012), classified within a general tendency towards shrinkage. It is impossible to ignore the fact that the relationship between urban shrinkage and the recurring crises of the capitalist regime of accumulation is not a topic in Italian debates on the subject. An exception in this regard is the successful work of Alessandro Coppola (2011), although this focuses on the United States.

In the macro- and regional-economic literature in Italy attention has been correctly paid to the derivatives 'crisis', associated with subprime mortgages granted in support of the housing market between 2007 and 2008 (Bruni, 2008; Percoco, 2010; Presbitero, 2009) and to the late yet violent impacts this has had on the societies and economies of Southern Europe, such as Spain, Portugal, and Greece. International analyses provide many accounts of the uneven geography of the crisis (Martin, 2011; Hadjimichalis and Hudson, 2013) but until now, Italian territorial research has not been able to address this issue using its own analytical categories. This issue is more relevant than ever if the persistence of recessionary phenomena and the stark material evidence of their effects on settlement patterns are considered.

Only recently, have some works addressed the economic crisis and its impact on Italian cities, discussing not only the negative performances recorded in the construction industry sector (Girardi, 2012), but also investigating the chain effects of the mortgage crisis across the various economic activities characterising the largest cities in the country (Staricco, 2010). These studies witness the collapse of construction activities owing to the burst of the real estate bubble and the consequent credit crunch, along with the later effects on the real economy and the fall in the provision of health services (see Figure 11.1). Examining the data for the main Metropolitan Areas of the country, the evidence from the GDP variations, as well as the productivity and unemployment rates, testify to a generalised downturn, which can be seen even in wealthy urban economies, such as Milan, Bologna, or Turin.

Despite this, it appears useful to focus on Italian urban systems, especially in light of recent census data that, as discussed later in the text, provides a picture of an Italy that is split in two by a north–south divide, but with characteristics that differ greatly from the post-war division.

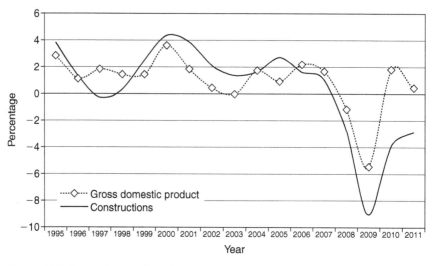

Figure 11.1 Economic growth and construction sector (% variation) (source: Girardi, 2012: p. 9).

Methodological issues and limits of generalisation

In order to give an initial view of the evolution of Italian urban systems with respect to urban shrinkage, the demographic component at both a temporal and spatial scale has been considered. The urban decline has been interpreted through the concentration of population, given that data on economic activities for the last census (2001–2011) is yet not available in detail. For this purpose the present study has calculated the percentage change in the resident population at the different dates of General Census of Population, 1951 to 2011. This period is long enough to highlight structural spatial dynamics and show the supposed 'cyclic' performance, where the observation is divided into consecutive intervals, even if they are affected by the arbitrariness of the date of the census. During the last decade, there has been in-depth observation of natural and migratory patterns. With regard to the geographical scale, reference to a double dimension has been made: national and local. The national level is an unavoidable political-institutional and economic framework of spatial differentiation of the analysed phenomena. The local scale is also relevant, because at this scale specific factors of differentiation of the territorial systems operate in combination with the dynamics of the global economy, which can contribute more than others to triggering their growth or decline.

The spatial level of the statistical analysis

More precisely, the territorial units of reference are the 'Local Labour Systems' (LLSs) used by Istat, the Italian National Institute of Statistics. These are areas of the daily commute, drawn up on the basis of census data, statistical territorial units that group several municipalities into one central municipality that attracts a working daytime population. The boundaries of 2001 were used because the subdivision of the last census survey is not yet available. To ensure uniformity in the use of definitions, the indications provided by Istat (2008) in its *Rapporto 2007* (2007 report) were used.

This definition of a local labour system is 'functional' as it interprets the relationship between work and home as a form of interdependence that allows the identification of relatively homogeneous urban areas of gravitation. However, in addition to this approach, there are at least two others: one that interprets the city in morphological terms, taking into account the built area *continuum*, in this case the area where buildings follow one another with intervals not exceeding 200 metres; and another that looks at the city as a social organism with administrative, productive, and commercial functions. Similar reflections are developed in the ponderous study 'Villes et régions en contraction', carried out by an international research team in 2010 (Baron et al., 2010).

If applied separately, these three criteria provide partial results that vary greatly from one another, and are therefore generally inadequate for explaining the entire urban aspect of spatial dynamics. Consequently, it seems to be more reasonable to use them jointly as 'filters' that allow a selection to be made, out of the 686 LLSs covering Italian territory, of those that can be truly considered urban systems. This method has obvious advantages: it results in broader and more complex territorial divisions compared to the simple municipal jurisdictions, respects the typically urban vocation of tertiary and administrative activities, and also takes into account the 'perception' of physical density as a criterion for defining the urban phenomenon (the density/variety combination mentioned by Lévy, 1997) (Figure 11.2).

Three categories of 'urban systems'

In this preliminary study, Istat identified 162 local systems throughout the country that were considered 'urban' for various reasons. Of these, 41 satisfied both the morphological and vocation criteria, 90 only the morphological criteria, and 31 only the vocation criteria. In Figure 11.2 you can see the overall coverage of LLSs, in which the 162 urban systems are represented by three different graphic patterns. These latter systems account for 25 per cent of the total number of LLSs, including 40 per cent of all Italian municipalities, cover 30 per cent of the national territory, and are home to 66.5 per cent of the 2011 population (more than 38.9 million inhabitants). Within these urban systems, based on the prevalence of one of the three criteria, a distinction between morphologically urban LLSs, vocationally urban LLSs, and 'metropolitan regions' can be made:

* *90 morphologically urban LLSs*: characterised by high population density (454 inhabitants per km^2, more than twice the national average), with employment mainly in the manufacturing sector (e.g. Turin, Bergamo, Busto Arsizio), located predominantly in the north-west (31) and in the

south (41). In 2011 approximately 14.5 million residents lived in these areas (24.5 per cent of the entire population). These are cities that had or still have a prominent role in the national industrial system, but with a generally lower supply of 'rare' services than other cities of comparable size.

- *31 vocationally urban LLSs*: the population density (136 inhabitants per km²) and the urbanisation density are below the national average, the main

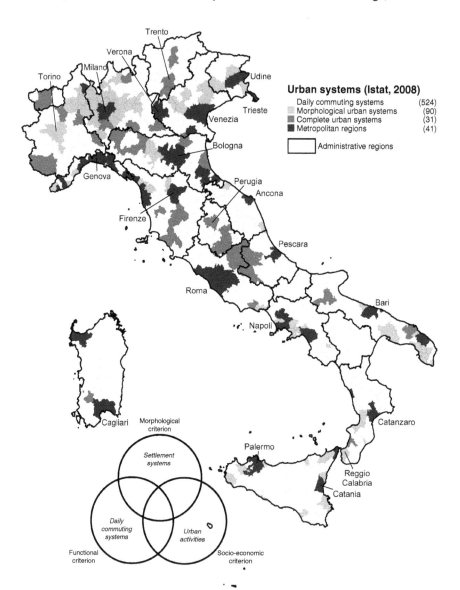

Figure 11.2 Local labour systems 2001, by type of urbanisation (source: own elaboration of Istat data 2008).

centres are Parma and Piacenza in the north, and Perugia in central Italy. Overall these areas are home to 6.6 per cent of the Italian population, equal to 3.9 million inhabitants. In this case the cities offer 'urban' services that are relatively superior compared to their dimensional size.

*   *41 'metropolitan regions'*: these systems combine a relevant size and service characteristics; they have on average 500,000 inhabitants, with high population density (657 inhabitants per km^2). More than 20.4 million Italians live in these areas (34.4 per cent of the total population). These cities are more commonly situated in the south and those located in the north have an overall greater population (approximately 8.4 million compared to 6.8 million in the south). The main urban systems are Rome (3.6 million), Milan (3.1 million), and Naples (2.2 million).

Between 2001 and 2011 the different types of Italian local labour systems grew in varying degrees: the category with the most evident growth was that of the morphologically urban systems (+6.4 per cent), closely followed by the vocationally urban systems (+6.2 per cent). The metropolitan regions grew by 3.5 per cent whilst the non-urbanised systems grew the least (+3.3 per cent). Despite not being the most dynamic systems in the country, metropolitan regions experienced greater growth in southern and central Italy.

As illustrated in Figure 11.2, however, the northern metropolitan regions, and Milan in particular, are practically surrounded by morphologically urban systems: this means that they have maintained and probably reinforced their centrality as highly ranking regional/national centres with 'superior' functions, but demographic growth in the area has particularly affected the suburbs, according to the well-known mechanisms of suburbanisation and sprawl, which in Italy is referred to as *città diffusa*.

Another interesting aspect involves the varying attractiveness of the systems in terms of migratory flows: the vocationally urban systems are the most attractive (10.5 new arrivals for every 1,000 inhabitants), followed by the metropolitan regions (7.6) and the morphologically urban systems (6.5 per 1,000 inhabitants). If in north-east and central Italy the metropolitan regions have very high values (respectively 14 and 13.4), net migration to the urban systems in the south is weaker and even slightly negative in most urbanised areas.

A general overview of the demographic evolution of urban systems in Italy

Before focusing on the last decade, a retrospective glance at the post-Second World War period is useful not only for summarising, but also for explaining some interpretive issues that have occurred in more recent times. As pointed out, in recent works on the same topic, any consideration that focuses solely on contemporary times is likely to provide an incomplete and misleading picture of current trends (Grasland & Sessarego Marques da Costa, 2010).

The percentage variations in the population of urban systems in the decade 1951–1961 confirm already recognised trends (Figure 11.3): during this period all peripheral and rural local systems lost a large part of their population in favour of the urban systems and, in particular, of the metropolitan regions. The drainage was especially acute in the systems located along the Apennines ridge and marginal areas of the north: Polesine, Mantua, the Alpine systems, etc. This was the decade of the most intense industrialisation, with an overall increase of employees of almost 29 per cent. This process affects the prevailing urban systems (31 per cent), particularly metropolitan poles (35 per cent), and particularly concerns some areas of northern and central Italy (central-east Lombardy, Veneto, Emilia-Romagna, Marche, and north-central Tuscany). These phenomena have noted the start of the so-called *peripheral industrialisation* of the *Terza Italia* (*Third Italy* – Bagnasco, 1977). Industrial growth in the rest of the peninsula was sporadic and mainly related to the coastal poles and some regional areas, such as Apulia and Sardinia.

The demographic phenomena was accentuated in the following decade – 1961–1971 – with a massive depopulation (from –30 to –20 per cent) of systems located in internal mountainous areas, especially in the Apennines. Conversely, notable demographic growth in metropolitan regions (from +20 to +30 per cent) was accompanied by a significant increase of non-metropolitan urban systems. Regarding the processes of industrialisation, during this decade peripheral growth was even more evident, although the general increase of manufacturing workers had a strong slowdown (18 per cent). The non-urban systems saw the strongest relative increase (over 26 per cent), while that of the metropolitan poles was less intense (13 per cent). The spatial distribution of these phenomena confirms and reinforces the centrality of Third Italy.

During the decade 1971–1981, the slowdown of industrial development that began in the second half of the 1960s was reflected by certain population trends: the growth rate in northern Italy, characterised by large industrial concentrations, clearly decreased, whilst positive trends persisted in certain peripheral systems, where district economies were consolidated or strengthened. The hypothesis that this was due to development of the industrial districts seems to be corroborated by the positive dynamics characterising both central Italy and the Adriatic Corridor.

Conversely, in southern Italy the tumultuous metropolitan growth was accompanied by a strengthening of the urban systems affected by state-led aid and the establishment of public and subsidised industry. This caused the first clean break between the northern metropolitan systems undergoing a phase of economic slowdown and the southern metropolitan systems that were draining population from inland areas. This decade completed the post-war industrialisation of Italy. The systems not classified as urban had the most intense values of growth (more than 33 per cent) while the Metropolitan Areas were still growing less intensely (7 per cent). Central Italy was the heart of these processes, which also tended to extend to the southern regions. The industrial triangle of the north-west was, conversely, characterised as an area of decrease: Milan (–10 per cent), Turin (–6 per cent), and Genoa (–3 per cent).

Figure 11.3 Per cent change in population, 1951–1961 (source: own elaboration of Istat data).

Between 1981 and 1991 these dramatically opposed dynamics underwent a major change, with a significant and generalised contraction in many northern and central urban systems and the continuation of the demographic crisis in the southern peripheral systems, with particular emphasis on the local systems situated along regional boundaries or in the outskirts of macro-regions (Friuli-Venezia Giulia, Eastern Veneto, the Ligurian coast, non-metropolitan Piedmont). During this period an important phase of decentralisation and delocalisation of industrial production began. This was important, especially in the Metropolitan Areas and in the northern industrial poles (–12 per cent of employees), but also in some of the district systems of the Third Italy, although to a lesser extent. Conversely, the southern regions experienced a rather widespread growth, which was centred particularly in some local systems in the borders of Campania, Basilicata, and Apulia, where public industrial investments and government incentives for the localisation of private facilities stimulated positive demographic dynamics.

Between 1991 and 2001 an element of novelty arose: the country's metropolitan systems all appeared to be in a demographic crisis while the local urban and non-urban systems of the peripheral areas of northern and central Italy started to grow again, albeit not dramatically. The crisis of the southern Metropolitan Areas – an entirely new Italian demographic trend – was matched by an even more accentuated crisis of the local systems located in the inland areas of southern Italy. In this context the migratory component was mainly directed towards the more dynamic systems in the north, where there was also a natural demographic increase (notably the areas in Eastern Lombardy and Central Emilia).

This was a very important decade for the Italian economy due to the privatisation of several large public companies, the strong international delocalisation of production phases by district systems, and the growth of tertiary activities. It opened a period of profound transformation of the national economy and the industrial fabric, which led to a functional and spatial requalification again driven by the urban and metropolitan and district systems of the northern and central regions.

Finally, during the recent decade (2001–2011) (Figure 11.4), the inland areas of southern Italy were most affected by demographic haemorrhage: while Calabria and Basilicata were almost entirely in demographic deficit (the situation in Basilicata particularly confirms the observations made by Schmoll et al., 2010), inland Sicily, northern Apulia, inland Molise, and Abruzzo are not in a better condition.

Most of these processes overlap with the regional boundaries, in peripheral systems rather than central areas of economic and administrative life, especially in the south, but also along the regional boundaries between Emilia-Romagna and Tuscany, Liguria and Piedmont, and northern Veneto and Friuli.

The demographic growth of the systems that make up the Po Valley is particularly striking and has a positive, in some cases even an extremely positive, balance. This contrasts with the urban crisis of the southern regions, where metropolitan regions and many urban systems are losing population.

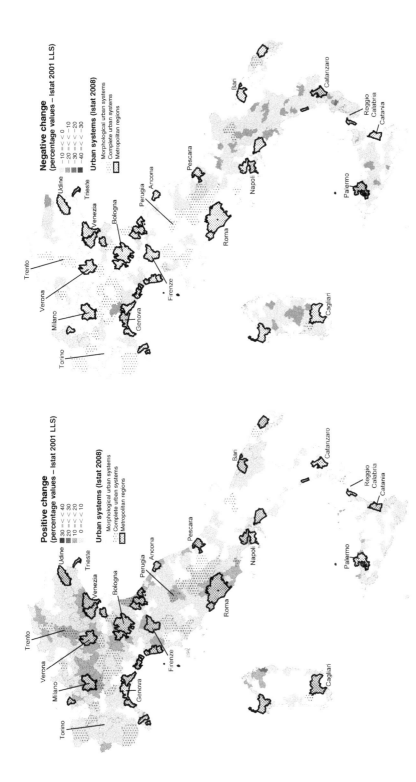

Figure 11.4 Per cent change in population, 2001–2011 (source: own elaboration of Istat data).

Over this decade, evidence from the scarce national literature about the recession and its impact on major Italian cities suggests a dramatic decrease of the GDP and of employment (Staricco, 2011), only partially counterbalanced by the social security provided by the public sector to companies hit by the crisis. It is therefore worth focusing on the trends verified in urban systems over the last decade, in order to formulate interpretative hypotheses and compare them with the reflections provided by international literature on the theme of urban shrinkage.

The diversified path of Italian urban systems

Following the above synthetic review of the demographic dynamics of Italian urban systems in the last 60 years and consideration of the increase/decrease processes of the last decade, some interpreting hypothesis will now be presented. These will be compared to the main findings of international research on the topic of urban shrinkage. This does not mean, of course, reassuming the dichotomous model as a dominant perspective in the interpretation of Italian spatial evolution, but rather recognising that the ancient divisions, as such, persist as structural elements in spite of the significant changes that have occurred on the Italian peninsula since the second half of the twentieth century. The point, therefore, is to offer a plausible explanation for this process of diversification in terms of spatial dynamics, attempting to make a distinction between contingent factors and effects and long lasting ones.

First, the 'reappearance' of the north–south divide has been highlighted, which seems considerably mirrored in the distinctive behaviours of urban and Metropolitan Areas. Without exception, all northern metropolitan systems have a 'plus' sign, however, the rhythms of this demographic growth differ according to the nature of the systems: the cores grow slowly, while the rings have far higher scores. If the phenomenon is observed at a national scale, the picture describes the strong suburbanisation which features the spatial dynamics in many industrialised areas – and not only in Italy – between 1990 and 2010, and which is most likely one of the various faces of metropolitisation. On the other hand, the loss of population in the south is general and also concerns many urban systems, which had previously been attractive, with some exceptions: Bari and some of Apulia's systems, such as Lecce, Catania.

The links between the demographic dynamics and the economic structure should be highlighted. In particular, considering the economic specialisation of the local systems (Istat, 2006; Figure 11.5) and comparing them to the demographic and manufacturing dynamics of 2001–2011 (Figures 11.6 and 11.7), some general considerations could be made:

- Urban systems that grew due to both natural and migration increase are concentrated in northern regions, notably along the Milan–Venice axis, where many studies highlight the dynamic role played by innovative medium-sized firms (Coltorti, 2007, 2010). The same positive trend can be seen in central Emilia, the Adriatic coast, and the Rome systems (Figure 11.6).

- While all internal areas have declined in the southern regions, in most of the systems of the north and the centre both internal and coastal areas have grown, thanks to a positive migration rate (Figure 11.6): these systems are those where the Italian districts and the SME local clusters are the dominant means of industrial organisation, and they remain attractive for migratory flows despite the overall downsizing process of the industrial structure of the country (Figure 11.7).

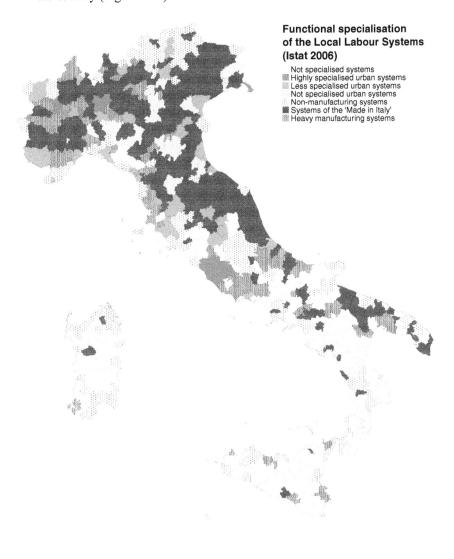

**Functional specialisation
of the Local Labour Systems
(Istat 2006)**

Not specialised systems
Highly specialised urban systems
Less specialised urban systems
Not specialised urban systems
Non-manufacturing systems
Systems of the 'Made in Italy'
Heavy manufacturing systems

Figure 11.5 Economic and territorial typologies of the Istat 2001 LLS (source: Istat, 2006).

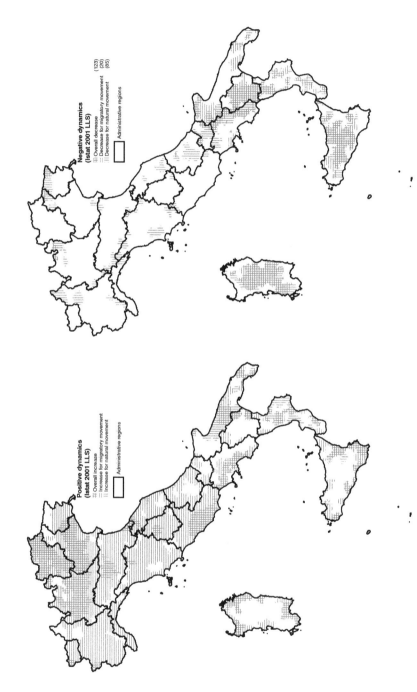

Figure 11.6 Demographic dynamics, 2001–2011 (source: own elaboration of Istat data).

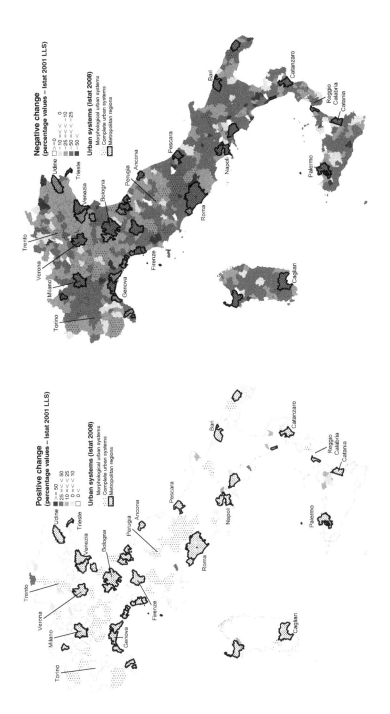

Figure 11.7 Manufacturing dynamics, 2001–2011 (source: own elaboration of Istat data).

The Italian spatial planning system: suitable to face the crisis?

As argued in Chapter 4 of the present book, the organisation of the spatial planning system (i.e. the ensemble of devices addressed to the public control of space in a given institutional context) is a crucial aspect both to interpret the spatial effects of a crisis, and to reflect on possibilities for new strategies and approaches for cities and regions that are affected by the crisis. This appears to be of particular interest for a country, such as Italy, that does not have a homogeneous urban structure but, as discussed in previous sections, 'diversified paths' of urban and regional development that, in times of crisis, may even lead to questioning the general notion of 'urban shrinkage'.

Embedded within an administrative and legal structure belonging to the 'Napoleonic family' (Newman & Thornley, 1996), characterised by strongly hierarchical power relationships between the state and municipalities, a 'modern' planning culture emerged in Italy between the nineteenth and twentieth centuries. This was the background of the first national 'urbanism' law of 1942 (*Legge urbanistica nazionale*, Law no. 1150), which is still in force despite various successive amendments (CEC, 2000). This law established, first and foremost, that the planning system should focus on the municipal plan for zoning existing land uses and future developments (so-called *Piano regolatore generale*, or 'General regulative plan'). The Italian spatial planning system is still today thus closely associated with the so-called 'urbanism' tradition, characterised by 'a strong architectural flavour and concern with urban design, townscape and building control', and by regulations 'undertaken through rigid zoning and codes' (CEC, 1997: p. 37).

Various problems of development control arose during the post-war reconstruction period, when building activity recorded an unprecedented boom in Italy, however, without achieving the political aim of improving housing conditions for the weakest social groups. Within a highly agonistic social and political context (Ginsborg, 2003) 'reformist planning practices (and their culture) ... constituted the hegemonic discourse on planning' after the 1950s, with an increasing influence of economics and social sciences (Vettoretto, 2009: p. 193). This led to a partial reform of the planning system in 1967 (Law no. 765 – so-called *Legge 'ponte'* or 'bridge law'), alluding to its then supposed provisional character. Coherent with the consolidated prescriptive approach, this introduced more precise zoning typologies, quantitative indicators, and minimum standards for public services and infrastructure provision.

A decade later, a major change in the structure of the Italian planning system culminated in the extension of certain legislative powers (including urban planning) to the regions, as a late consequence of the application of the Italian Constitution that was approved in 1948. On the one hand, this gave rise to a more extensive development of regional (NUTS 2) and provincial (NUTS 3) plans, and greater prescription for certain sectoral policies (e.g. infrastructure networks, environment and landscape preservation) in addition to local rules established by zoning plans. On the other hand, this progressive regionalisation (Putnam, 1993) has accentuated the differentiation of regional planning systems under a common national framework. Since then, most planning practices and their working cultures 'vary significantly, in a way, among regions (the institutional setting of spatial planning) and among communities of practice' (Vettoretto, 2009: p. 190).

Apart from a few exceptions, however, the widespread prescriptive approach has led to typical planning practices becoming even more bureaucratic, such as 'a formal obligation, where social interactions have been reduced to formal ones defined by laws and regulations and/or ... affected by patronage negotiations' (ibid.: p. 196). As a consequence, in a country where spatial planning is 'practically non-existent at the national level, merely a guideline at the regional level, and implemented at the local level' (CEC, 2000: p. 97), land use planning has often become a powerful instrument for political and electoral consensus building, contributing to the realisation of massive low-density urban regions and sprawl in the long run (Clementi, Dematteis, & Palermo, 1996). This culminated in an epochal political crisis in the early 1990s (called by the national press *Tangentopoli* or 'Corruption city'), which led to the collapse of the country's political system.

Major problems in controlling spatial development and a widespread lack of spatial strategies began to be seriously questioned in the last two decades by a new generation of planners and scholars. Public authorities were meanwhile concerned with new challenges that traditional planning instruments were unable to manage, such as inter-municipal coordination, environmental and landscape concerns, the integration of sectoral policies, the involvement of private stakeholders and resources in spatial planning implementation, and vertical and horizontal coordination in territorial governance processes. The emergence of European spatial planning and the progressive establishment of the European Union (EU) territorial governance agenda in the same years (Dühr, Colomb, & Nadin, 2010) is not a coincidence, and the influence of European integration on more recent innovations concerning spatial planning in Italy has attracted the interest of scholars with different standpoints and perspectives (Gualini, 2001; Palermo, 2001; Janin Rivolin, 2003; Janin Rivolin & Faludi, 2005). Overall, a 'Europeanisation' of Italian domestic planning was thus triggered at that time, although it did not occur via direct 'transposition' of legal obligations, for which the EU does not retain powers in the field of spatial planning (Dühr, Colomb, & Nadin, 2010), but through more indirect 'cultural' types of influence (Cotella & Janin Rivolin, 2011).

In recent years Italian spatial planning has therefore undergone an institutional renovation that is perhaps unprecedented in its post-war history. One clear example is the substitution of the term *urbanistica* (urbanism) by the wording *governo del territorio* (government of the territory) in the Italian Constitution (art. 117) in 2001. As much as the former has been exposed to a 'weak' or at least uncertain planning culture (Zucconi, 1989; Mazza, 2002), the new institutional expression emphasises the centrality of the use of space with respect to public development strategies and, as an implicit consequence, the need for effective government tools to deal with this issue. Spatial planning legislation reforms occurring since the late 1990s in various Italian regions (while the claim for a national reform of the planning system was a recurring *leitmotiv*) have introduced significant innovation in respective spatial planning tools, such as the distinction between 'structural-indicative' and 'operative-regulative' plans, the establishment of collaborative planning processes, and procedures for the transfer of development rights (so-called *perequazione* or 'equalisation'). The recent 'fashion' of strategic spatial plans, experienced spontaneously by various cities and local communities in the last decade (despite the absence of specific legislation) is perhaps the clearest sign of a widespread attempt to capitalise on the experimental 'innovation' process (Palermo, 2006). In a scenario characterised by the progressive consolidation of spatial development programming alongside more traditional forms of land use planning, 'a sort of hybridisation of mere old regulative styles and new perspectives' characterises spatial planning in Italy at present, without, however, neglecting that 'a traditional culture of planning, as essentially a command and control activity, is still vital and influential' (Vettoretto, 2009: pp. 201–202).

Ultimately, despite more recent innovation and the influence of other European planning cultures (Knieling & Othengrafen, 2009), Italy still demonstrates a tangible dependence to its 'urbanism tradition', a 'conformative' model of the planning system, which is based on preventive binding zoning and that, despite theoretical expectations, is thus the cause of continuous multiplication of property rights and incomes, and of the impairment of public strategies (Janin Rivolin, 2008). This may have somehow contributed to amplify the effects of the current crisis, especially in the absence of a shared understanding of the diversified trends concerning the Italian urban system, as they have been described in previous sections. As for the opportunity for new strategies and approaches in the future, three considerations are possible:

1   On the one hand, the progressive diversification of the Italian spatial planning system at subregional and local levels in the long run (Figure 11.8) is potentially favourable to a flexible and 'place-based' approach to development (Barca, 2009), in the face of a process of spatial transformation that, as it was shown, is all but generalised within the country.

2   On the other hand, a generalised and persisting 'conformative' approach to spatial planning – as recalled above – tends to counteract the required flexibility in practical terms.

3   Overall, continuing weak attention to spatial planning in the political agenda at a central level, despite more recent evolutions, inhibits the hope that more comprehensive observations, such as those developed in the previous sections, can have any effect in terms of national guidelines for more strategic and effective local planning.

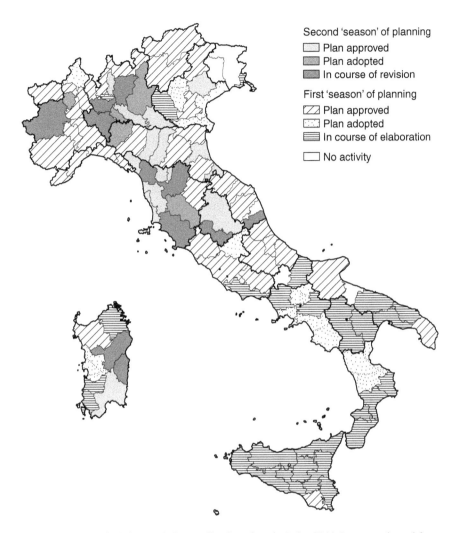

Figure 11.8 Provincial (NUTS 3) coordination plans in Italy, 2010 (source: adapted from INU, 2011).

Conclusions

Despite the preliminary nature of these notes, which deserve to be further developed with additional statistics and spatial analysis, particularly regarding the relationships between the demographic and economic dynamics, the recent dynamics of the Italian systems seem to contrast with the idea of an 'urban shrinkage model', applicable to any industrialised country. At least in the Italian peninsula, the shrinkage affects the less industrialised cities of the south, and it is not as perceivable in the large- and middle-sized cities of the north and centre.

Compared to the post-war period, when the rural south experienced an exodus towards the most industrialised areas of northern Italy and Western Europe, but the large southern urban areas still showed significant demographic growth, the demographic decline today spreads throughout the entire urban and non-urban south, albeit with some important exceptions (Bari, Salerno, Catania), whilst the urban north is massively growing.

It is possible that the organisational differences of the Italian urban structure, which have established themselves over a long historical period – mainly poly-centric in the centre-north and hierarchical in the south – are the cause of the different 'response' to the changes taking place in the economic and productive structure of late capitalism. Indeed, the affirmation of the dominant role of cities in Italian history dates back much further than industrial development, while in other European and non-European contexts the process of urbanisation has been closely connected to industrialisation.

The overall framework of population dynamics reveals that in the period of 20 years, 1981–2001, the main urban systems, particularly situated in northern and central Italy, experienced a period of crisis. This should be further investigated, taking into account the differences between the dynamics in the cores and those in the rings. Over these two decades, the Italian economy has experienced a major transformation period with the end of the system of large state-holding enterprises and special financial aid to the south, the emergence of new models of flexible production, and the beginning of important processes of industrial decentralisation and delocalisation. It could be in these processes, perhaps, that some traces of urban shrinkage according to the features indicated by the international literature could be identified.

Against this backdrop, a still immature spatial planning system, especially as far as technical culture and multilevel policy coordination are concerned, accentuates the risk that rhetorical fashions, such as the 'urban shrinkage model', can prevail over more careful analyses in guiding the Italian political agenda for spatial planning in face of the crisis. A clearer understanding of urban dynamics in Italy after the effects of the current crisis, especially as far as possible urban shrinkage is concerned, might help to address domestic spatial policies at various levels. This opportunity, however, is also related to the renovation of the national planning system, in order to improve its capacity for reaction to varying circumstances.

Note

1 A classification, for example, has been outlined by Cunningham-Sabot and Fol in the work mentioned above (2009).

References

Bagnasco, A. (1977) *Tre Italie: La problematica territoriale dello sviluppo italiano.* Bologna, Il Mulino.

Barca, F. (2009) *An agenda for a reformed cohesion policy: A place-based approach to meeting European Union challenges and expectations.* Independent Report prepared at the request of Danuta Hübner, Brussels, EU Commissioner for Regional Policy.

Baron, M., Cunningham-Sabot, E., Grasland, C., Rivière, D., & Van Hamme, G. (2010) *Villes et régions européennes en décroissance: Maintenir la cohésion territoriale?* Paris, Éditions Hermès.

Bauman, Z. (2004) *Wasted lives: Modernity and its outcasts.* Cambridge, Polity Press.

Berry, B. J. L. (1976) *Urbanization and counterurbanization.* Beverly Hills, CA, Sage Publications.

Bruni, F. (2008) Contro la crisi: Cultura e regole. In: Shiller, R. J. (ed.) *Finanza shock: Come uscire dalla crisi dei mutui subprime.* Milano, Egea, pp. 121–158.

CEC (Commission of the European Communities) (1997) *The EU compendium of spatial planning systems and policies.* Luxembourg, Office for official publications of European Communities.

CEC (Commission of the European Communities) (2000) *The EU compendium of spatial planning systems and policies: Italy.* Luxembourg, Office for official publications of European Communities.

Champion, A. (2001) A changing demographic regime and evolving polycentric urban regions: Consequences for the size, composition and distribution of city populations. *Urban Studies*, 38 (4), 657–677.

Cheshire, P. (1995) A new phase of urban development in Western Europe? The evidence for the 1980s. *Urban Studies*, 32 (7), 1045–1063.

Cheshire, P. & Hay, D. (1989) *Urban problems in Western Europe.* London, Unwin Hyman.

Clementi, A., Dematteis, G., & Palermo, P. C. (eds) (1996) *Le forme del territorio italiano* (2 vols). Rome-Bari, Laterza.

Coltorti, F. (2007) Un nuovo protagonista economico: La media impresa. In: Berta, G. (ed.) *La questione settentrionale: Economia e società in trasformazione.* Milano, Fondazione Giangiacomo Feltrinelli, pp. 379–416.

Coltorti, F. (2010) *Le medie imprese industriali italiane.* Milano, Ufficio Studi Mediobanca.

Coppola, A. (2011) *Apocalypse town: Cronache dalla fine della civiltà urbana.* Roma-Bari, Laterza.

Cotella, G. & Janin Rivolin, U. (2011) Europeanization of spatial planning through discourse and practice in Italy. *disP – The Planning Review*, 47 (186), 42–53.

Cunningham-Sabot, E. & Fol, S. (2009) Shrinking cities in France and Great Britain: A silent process. In: Pallagst, K., Aber, J., Audirac, I., Cunningham-Sabot, E., Fol, S., Martinez-Fernandez, C., Moraes S., Mulligan, H., Vargas-Hernandez, J., Wiechmann, T., & Wu, C. T. (eds) *Future of shrinking cities: Problems, patterns and strategies of urban transformation in a global context.* Berkeley, Center for Global Metropolitan Studies, Institute of Urban and Regional Development (IURD) and the Shrinking Cities International Research Network (SCiRN), University of California, pp. 17–27.

Dietzsch, I. (2009) Perceptions of decline: Crisis, shrinking and disappearance as narrative schemas to describe social and cultural change. *Anuarul Institutului de Istorie 'George Baritiu'*, VII, 7–22.

Dühr, S., Colomb, C., & Nadin, V. (2010) *European spatial planning and territorial cooperation.* London and New York, Routledge.

Fielding, A. J. (1982) Counterurbanization in Western Europe. *Progress in Planning*, 17, 1–52.

Flüchter, W. (2008) Shrinking cities in Japan: Between megalopolises and rural peripheries. *Electronic Journal of Contemporary Japanese Studies*, III, 3–8.

Friedrichs, J. (1993) A theory of urban decline: Economy, demography and political elites. *Urban Studies*, 30 (6), 907–917.

Ginsborg, P. (2003) *A history of contemporary Italy: Society and politics, 1943–1988.* New York and Houndmills, Palgrave Macmillan.

Girardi, D. (2012) *The construction sector in Italy, crisis and change.* MPRA Paper No. 49901. [Online] Available from: http://mpra.ub.uni-muenchen.de/49901/ [accessed 1 December 2014].

Gottmann, J. (1964) *Megalopolis: The urbanized northeastern seaboard of the United States.* Cambridge, MA, MIT Press.

Gottmann, J. & Muscarà, C. (eds) (1991) *La città prossima ventura.* Bari, Laterza.

Grasland, C. & Sessarego Marques da Costa, N. (2010) Le temps long des phénomènes démographiques. In: Baron, M., Cunningham-Sabot, E., Grasland, C., Rivière, D., & Van Hamme, G. (eds) *Villes et régions européennes en décroissance: Maintenir la cohésion territoriale?* Paris, Éditions Hermès, 43–66.

Gualini, E. (2001) 'New programming' and the influence of transnational discourses in the reform of regional policy in Italy, *European Planning Studies*, 9 (6), 755–771.

Haase, A., Rink, D., & Grossmann, K. (2014) Conceptualizing urban shrinkage. *Environment and Planning A*, 46, 1519–1534.

Hadjimichalis, C. & Hudson, R. (2013) Contemporary crisis across Europe and the crisis of regional development theories. *Regional Studies*, 48 (1), 208–218.

Hall, P. (1984) *The world cities.* London, Weidenfeld & Nicolson.

Hall, P. & Hay, D. (1980) *Growth centres in the European urban system.* London, Heinemann Educational.

Harvey, D. (2000) *Spaces of hope.* Edinburgh, Edinburgh University Press.

Harvey, D. (2005) *A brief history of neoliberalism.* Oxford, Oxford University Press.

INU (Istituto Nazionale di Urbanistica) (2010) *Rapporto dal territorio 2010.* Roma, INU edizioni.

Istat (1951) *III Censimento dell'industria e dei servizi.* Roma, Istat.

Istat (1951) *IX Censimento della popolazione e delle abitazioni.* Roma, Istat.

Istat (1961) *IV Censimento dell'industria e dei servizi.* Roma, Istat.

Istat (1961) *X Censimento della popolazione e delle abitazioni.* Roma, Istat.

Istat (1971) *V Censimento dell'industria e dei servizi.* Roma, Istat.

Istat (1971) *XI Censimento della popolazione e delle abitazioni.* Roma, Istat.

Istat (1981) *VI Censimento dell'industria e dei servizi.* Roma, Istat.

Istat (1981) *XII Censimento della popolazione e delle abitazioni.* Roma, Istat.

Istat (1991) *VII Censimento dell'industria e dei servizi.* Roma, Istat.

Istat (1991) *XIII Censimento della popolazione e delle abitazioni.* Roma, Istat.

Istat (2001) *VIII Censimento dell'industria e dei servizi.* Roma, Istat.

Istat (2001) *XIV Censimento della popolazione e delle abitazioni.* Roma, Istat.

Istat (2006) *Rapporto annuale 2005.* Roma, Istat.

Istat (2008) *Rapporto annuale 2007.* Roma, Istat.

Istat (2011) *IX Censimento dell'industria e dei servizi.* Roma, Istat.

Istat (2011) *XV Censimento della popolazione e delle abitazioni.* Roma, Istat.

Janin Rivolin, U. (2003) Shaping European spatial planning: How Italy's experience can contribute. *Town Planning Review*, 74 (1), 51–76.

Janin Rivolin, U. (2008) Conforming and performing planning systems in Europe: An unbearable cohabitation. *Planning Practice and Research*, 23 (2), 167–186.

Janin Rivolin, U. & Faludi, A. (eds) (2005) Southern perspectives on European spatial planning, special issue. *European Planning Studies*, 13 (2), 195–331.

Knieling, J. & Othengrafen, F. (eds) (2009) *Planning cultures in Europe: Decoding cultural phenomena in urban and regional planning.* Farnham, Ashgate.

Lévy, J. (1997) *Europe: Une géographie.* Paris, Hachette.

Martin, R. (2011) The local geographies of the financial crisis: From the housing bubble to economic recession and beyond. *Journal of Economic Geography,* 11, 587–618.

Martinez-Fernandez, C., Audirac, I., Fol, S., & Cunningham-Sabot, E. (2012a) Shrinking cities: Urban challenges of globalization. *International Journal of Urban and Regional Research,* 36 (2), 213–225.

Martinez-Fernandez, C., Kuto, N., Noya, A., & Weyman, T. (eds) (2012b) *Demographic change and local development: Shrinkage, regeneration and social dynamics.* OECD-LEED Working Paper Series, OECD Publishing. [Online] Available from: [accessed 19 May 2015].

Mazza, L. (2002) Technical knowledge and planning actions, *Planning Theory,* 1 (1), 11–26.

Newman, P. & Thornley, A. (1996) *Urban planning in Europe: International competition, national systems and planning projects.* London and New York, Routledge.

Nowak, M. & Nowosielski, M. (2008) *Declining cities/developing cities: Polish and German perspectives.* Poznań, Instytut Zachodny.

Oswalt, P. (ed.) (2006) *Shrinking cities. Volume 1: International research.* Ostfildern-Ruit (DE), Hatje Cantz Verlag.

Palermo, P. C. (ed.) (2001) *Il programma Urban e l'innovazione delle politiche urbane* (3 vols). Milano, Franco Angeli/Diap.

Palermo, P. C. (2006) *Innovation in planning: Italian experiences.* Barcelona, APRO.

Pallagst, K. (2008) Shrinking cities: Planning challenges from an international perspective. Special Issue on Cities Growing Smaller. *Urban Infill,* 1, 6–16.

Percoco, M. (2010) La dimensione spaziale della crisi del 2008–2009. *Scienze Regionali,* 9 (2), 101–104.

Plöger, J. (2012) Learning from abroad: Lessons from European shrinking cities. In: Mallach, A. (ed.) *Rebuilding America's legacy cities: New directions for the industrial heartland.* New York, American Assembly, Columbia University, pp. 295–321.

Presbitero, A. (2009) The 2007 financial crisis: Facts, causes and future scenarios. *MoFiR Working Paper* 27, Pavia.

Putnam, R. D. (1993) *Making democracy work: Civic traditions in modern Italy.* Princeton, NJ, Princeton University Press.

Sassen, S. (2001) *The global city: New York, London, Tokyo.* Princeton, NJ, Princeton University Press.

Schmoll, C., Baron, M., Groza, O., Salaris, A., & Ysebaert, R. (2010) Vieillissement et migrations, réflexions à partir de la Basilicate et de la Bretagne. In: Baron, M., Cunningham-Sabot, E., Grasland, C., Rivière, D., & Van Hamme, G. (eds) *Villes et régions européennes en décroissance: Maintenir la cohésion territoriale?* Paris, Lavoisier, pp. 161–186.

Scott, A. & Storper, M. (2003) Regions, globalization, development. *Regional Studies,* 37 (6/7), 579–593.

Soja, E. (2000) *Postmetropolis: Critical studies of cities and regions.* Oxford, Blackwell.

Staricco, L. (2010) Gli effetti socioeconomic della crisi sulle città mertopolitane italiane: Il caso di Torino. *Archivio di Studi Urbani e Regionali,* 99, 50–69.

Van den Berg, L., Drewett, R., Klaassen, L., Rossi, A., & Vijverberg, H. (1982) *Urban Europe: A study of growth and decline.* Oxford, Pergamon Press.

Vettoretto, L. (2009) Planning cultures in Italy: Reformism, laissez-faire and contemporary trends. In: Knieling, J. & Othengrafen, F. (eds) *Planning cultures in Europe.* Farnham, Ashgate, pp. 189–204.

Wiechmann, T. & Pallagst, K. M. (2012) Urban shrinkage in Germany and the USA: A comparison of transformation patterns and local strategies. *International Journal of Urban and Regional Research*, 36 (2), 261–280.

Wolff, M. (2010) Urban shrinkage in Europe: Benefits and limits of an indicator-based analysis. *Working Paper*, 6, Dresden, Dresden University of Technology.

Zucconi, G. (1989) *La città contesa: Dagli ingegneri sanitari agli urbanisti (1885–1942)*. Milano, Jaca Book.

Part IV

Crisis as driver of change?

12 Potentials and restrictions on the changing dynamics of the political spaces in the Lisbon Metropolitan Area

João Seixas, Simone Tulumello, Susana Corvelo, and Ana Drago

Introduction

The current chapter supplies empirical evidence to extract and a critical analysis of how the economic crisis and its political management has affected the evolution of European urban regions. This will be carried out through an analysis of the recent evolution, both geographical and socio-political, of the main Portuguese urban region, the Lisbon Metropolitan Area (LMA). The chapter proposes some insights into the ongoing discussion about the relevance of territorial and urban dimensions to the knowledge and interpretation of the present European crisis, that is, the economic crisis and its socio-political consequences. It emphasises the importance of the differentiated spatial impacts of the crisis but also of the pressures and conflicts resulting from the intersection of the reactions of the different political stances and scales (Othengrafen et al., this volume; Pinho, Andrade, & Pinho, 2011; Hadjimichalis, 2011; Werner, 2013).

These are particularly painful times for Southern European territories and societies due to the conjunction of the financial crisis and the political responses of the European Union (EU) and individual nation states. The reaction was to put in place austerity measures that deeply disrupted social, economic, and territorial fabrics as well as the fundamentals of inclusive and sustainably driven societies. This clearly shows that the crisis is no longer, if it ever was, mainly driven by public and financial reasons, but it has instead multidimensional and structural political bases.

Amongst several contemporary crisis landscapes, European cities are the *locus* where pressures and changes are most evident. A relevant part of the European crisis shows to be the result of the crash of an old economic order, supported on large amounts of non-secured urbanisation credit (financial, territorial, and environmental credit), with growingly unregulated financial markets. At the same time, and not surprisingly, it is the urban fabrics that witness the materialisation of new political and civic cultures. If this is true in the wider European landscape, the history and position of the Mediterranean urban territories makes their present role particularly relevant. The European Commission (2011) itself recognises that cities will reinforce their crucial role as main drivers for transition. Their very nature makes them places for connectivity, citizenship, creativity, and innovation; all fundamental characteristics for facing the challenges ahead. However, 'the European model of sustainable urban development is under threat' (ibid.: p. 14): one that is not only arising from the upheaval of the crisis, but also from the mainstream political and financial responses to the crisis. This threat brings new pressures to bear on the urban socio-economic and environmental ecosystems and particularly on the growing spatial polarisation, both in income and in access to urban functions. Moreover, it hides other difficulties for the effective development of new models of social and economic progress, in parallel with the need for ecological regeneration.

This chapter will study the links between the European crisis, its urban impacts, and the applied austerity measures, and will discuss selected innovative policies in their different scales. These links will be studied against the background of the (re)shaping of the political spaces of the LMA. The main hypothesis is that the urban trends within (and beyond) the crisis have to be dissected along three different dimensions. First, how the spatial impacts of the economic recession are transforming inclusion and exclusion patterns within the urban system. Second, how related 'anti-crisis' policies are expanding those patterns, and how the political economics for austerity are reshaping capacities and priorities at the local scale. Third, how the city's political and civic realms react and reconfigure themselves, thus changing urban political systems, possibly in an enduring way. Lisbon will thus be shown as an illustrative example of the emergence of new political culture(s), whose characteristics are especially complex and inherently contradictory.[1]

Beyond this introduction, the text is structured in five sections. In the nex section, a critical perspective on the crisis and the applied austerity measures is introduced, complementary to the understanding provided by geographical and longitudinal analyses. The third section analyses the context of political responses to the crisis in Portugal to give a critical understanding of connections between national, austerity-driven pressures and local reactions. The fourth section includes some variables to serve as a basis for exploring the nature of the various impacts of, and their distribution within, the LMA. In the fifth section, a critical analysis of the main drivers of change at the institutional, political, and civic level will be conducted, before some concluding remarks in the final section.

The European crisis: a critical perspective

Most of the European political-institutional discourses explain the origins and the persistence of the Southern European components of the crisis as being the result of decades of profligate and under-accountable public spending, connected with allegedly unsustainable welfare systems (Blyth, 2013). From these perspectives arose the main justifications for the present austerity-driven political economics, considered as the only way to consolidate national budgets and to create future conditions for economic recovery (Krugman, 2012).

According to Blyth (2013), the ongoing crisis should not be understood as a public sector one, but instead as a crisis of the private sector, which is being paid for by public funds. The sovereign debt crisis is thus seen, above all, as a *consequence* of the use of public funds in order to bail out financial institutions and save the European financial system. Prior to the crisis, sovereign debt in countries such as Spain and Ireland were well below critical thresholds, amounting in 2007, to 26 and 12 per cent debt/Gross Domestic Product (GDP) ratio respectively (Blyth, 2013). Other Southern European countries, such as Italy, Greece, and Portugal historically had high debts. Yet, there exist different reasons for the economic crisis in the Southern European countries and in Ireland. These are to be found, on the one hand, in the explosion of large real estate bubbles and correspondent banking systems considered as 'too big to fail' and, on the other hand, in the consequences of low growth since the year 2000, ageing societies, and political-institutional incapacity for structural changes.

In the months following the Wall Street collapse of 2008, after the fall of some of the so-called 'too big to fail' banking institutions and public revelations of malpractice in the financial markets, far-reaching analyses on the unsustainability of the financial systems came to the fore, together with two main recommendations to national governments: to sustain and intervene in banking institutions at risk, reassuring financial markets, and preventing public panic; and to launch large amounts of public investment to allow faster economic recovery. By the end of 2008, the EU had approved an ambitious Recovery Plan (Commission of the European Communities, 2008), envisioning a €170,000 million investment from member states. However, only a few months after the debate about the need to regulate markets was over, the need for austerity was advocated by international institutions, governments, and mainstream think-tanks (Peck, 2013). Austerity is

> a form of voluntary deflation in which the economy adjusts through the reduction of wages, prices, and public spending to restore competitiveness, which is (supposedly) best achieved by cutting the state's budget, debt and deficits. Doing so, its advocates believed, will inspire business confidence.
>
> (Blyth, 2013: p. 2)

However, the cuts in the welfare state and the fiscal pressures on the labour market expanded inequalities and poverty, neither reducing national debts nor easing the recession and stimulating economic growth (Krugman, 2012).

Roitman (2014) explores the narratives about the risk of the collapse of political and economic systems as the justification for devaluation, hence austerity. If the current crisis is one of the neoliberal economy and of its financialisation, austerity may be understood as the way for neoliberalism to survive its own crisis: 'what might be incautiously labelled "the system" was brazenly rebooted with more or less the same ideological and managerial software, complete with most of the bugs that had caused the breakdown in the first place' (Peck, 2013: p. 135). From a critical perspective, understanding the neoliberalism narrative is necessary to understand the European crisis. According to Harvey (2005), neo-liberalism is a project for the restructuring of capitalism and the restoration of the conditions for capital accumulation. However, the specificity of the neolib-eral dynamics is showing that the state is not being reduced, as in classical liberal conceptions, but rather re-engineered in order to enable particular forms of competition (Wacquant, 2012). A contradictory mix of regulation and deregu-lation patterns are therefore coexisting (Brenner, Peck, & Theodore, 2010; Rod-rigues & Teles, 2011): (financial) markets are deregulated and, at the same time, nation states intervene both in financial and economic landscapes in order to primarily favour capital accumulation, through the management of public ser-vices and new forms of public–private partnerships.

A critical understanding of neoliberal dynamics is relevant to understand why crisis and austerity matter so much for cities, for two reasons. On the one hand, the central role of urban (re)production and of territorial space restructuring has been at the heart of the development of neoclassical and neoliberal approaches since the 1980s, a deeply debated issue (Brenner, 2004). The vast production, and consumption, of urban, suburban, and peri-urban territories is understood by many as a coherent and long-term strategy (Peck, Theodore, & Brenner, 2013). Although there is a significant variety in local and regional trends, mostly related to the landscape of institutional, governance, and political contexts, which has justified several critiques of the usefulness of neoliberalism as a generalised theoretical concept (Baptista, 2013), some common trends in urban governance can be discerned, stemming around concepts such as territorial competitiveness, city marketing, public–private partnerships, outsourcing, and privatisation (Sager, 2011).

On the other hand, many see the economic crisis (especially in Southern Europe) as the culmination of long-term uneven development paths driven by neoclassical policy-making (Hadjimichalis, 2011; Blyth, 2013), clearly exempli-fied by housing policies characterised by the shift from the provision of both leasing and public housing to the support of private ownership (i.e. the Thatcher-ite 'right to buy'). This, together with the erosion of welfare,

> forced people in the United States and elsewhere to rely ever more on home-ownership as a substitute for social risk-sharing mechanisms. Individual efforts to replace public cash and public services with homeownership pushed home prices up to clearly unsustainable levels.
>
> (Schwartz, 2012: p. 53)

The resulting private debt and housing bubble allowed enormous leverage in fin-ancial markets, hence triggering the financial bubble to burst (Blyth, 2013).

It can be seen that the main categories currently being applied to an economy in times of crisis are basically the same as they were before 2008: an emphasis on the need to attract foreign investment with a globally competitive discourse, following international organisational trends (Oosterlynck & González, 2013). Production and consumption are not solely within the urban/metropolitan space in the global economy, but the mainstream political agenda takes the city as a nodal element for commodity creation: urban renewal projects, real estate development, state incentives towards homeownership, privatisation of public spaces, and the key role of financial institutions in new urban regimes (Peck, Theodore, & Brenner, 2013). In this sense, it could be argued that the interpretation of the nature of the present crisis could also imply a critical examination of territorial government institutions.

Setting the context: the austerity agenda and its impact in Portugal

The outbreak of the financial crisis in 2008 marked the beginning of a profound change in Portuguese society and politics. As far as the political responses to the crisis are concerned, different or even contradictory approaches, as well as different sequential phases, can be identified (Pedroso, 2014): policies to sustain the 'system' and to relaunch the economy, the implementation of austerity measures and financially driven policies, and the development of austerity to a complete, and now ideologically driven, scale.

Aligned with early political reactions to the crisis by European institutions (see previous section), the Portuguese government issued public debt guarantees to the private banking sector and took control of investment banks, whose subprime and further unaccounted for financial activities were made public. A seemingly neo-Keynesian agenda was presented for the 2009 budget:[2] public servants were given a 2.9 per cent wage increase, and an ambitious programme of public works was announced, mostly concerning transport infrastructure. However, by 2010, all that came to an end: public works investment was stopped, tax revenue shrank considerably, and public spending in automatic stabilisers (namely unemployment benefits) increased. As the euro crisis was unfolding, Portuguese public debt interest rates climbed and the fiscal deficit grew. Portugal was officially in crisis.

As 2010 went by, austerity policies made their way in, and a sequence of fiscal adjustment policies were implemented: taxes were raised, pensions and public sector salaries frozen, and new legislation was adopted which limited access to social benefits. In April 2011, due to Parliament's rejection of a new adjustment package, the Socialist Prime Minister requested external financial aid, and the so-called 'Troika' of external borrowers, the International Monetary Fund, the European Commission, and the European Central Bank, imposed a large-scale and severe budgetary and political-administrative memorandum on national politics. Two months later, a right-wing government was elected. The full-scale austerity that allowed Portugal to access financial assistance had to be justified by a political narrative of Portuguese economic and public policy inability. The diagnosis was built on a distorted representation of public and household spending patterns that allegedly led to unsustainable national indebtedness.

However, this interpretation could be easily refuted by a closer look at the main figures of the national debt (Abreu et al., 2013). Portuguese public debt rose steadily since the mid-1990s, reaching the EU's average by 2005. However, the major indebtedness happened only after 2008, much of which was due to the international financial crisis. At the same time, it could be seen that household indebtedness remained relatively limited: in 2010, about 63 per cent of the Portuguese population had no credit debt and 80 per cent of household debts were related to mortgage loans. Despite the current economic crisis, in 2013, only 6.6 per cent of those loans reported a credit default. This shows that the Portuguese banking system mainly contracted mortgage loans to middle-class families.

Over the last decade, Portugal suffered from major shocks that had a profound impact on its ability to compete internationally: the adoption of a strong currency, the euro, the impacts of global liberalisation and of Chinese exports on traditional Portuguese export markets, and the oil shock in the mid-2000s. All this led to the so-called 'lost decade' (as it was commonly termed in the media) for the Portuguese economy. From 2000 to 2010, Portuguese GDP grew at an annual average rate of 1 per cent. According to Reis and Rodrigues (2011) the reason was that Portugal had been responding to external shocks through a progressive shift towards an economic model grounded on low wages and growing inequality rather than on investments in sectors with high added value.

Without acknowledging this last issue, the Troika's therapy consisted mainly of drastic cuts in public spending/investment as well as restructuring and liberalisation policies. State administration, public services, and public salaries were to be significantly cut and reduced, public spending on health and education was drastically reduced, and a programme for civil service redundancies was implemented, resulting in a reduction of around 50,000 posts. Poverty and inequality reduction policies, as well as unemployment benefits, were also cut. A mix of tax increases was imposed over work and pension revenues as well as on consumption. Furthermore, a vast privatisation programme was implemented in strategic economic sectors: public transport, energy and communications, postal services, and airports.

The main social and economic effects of the 'adjustment programme' imposed by the Troika cannot be understated (Abreu et al., 2013): from 2011 to 2013 Portuguese GDP has fallen 5.9 per cent. In 2013, private consumption returned to the level it was at in 2000 and public consumption fell to the level of 2002. As far as investment rates are concerned, both public and private, there is no memory (i.e. no statistical data) of such a collapse. In the first trimester of 2013, the net investment in the Portuguese economy was 20 per cent lower than in 1995, when this indicator was collected for the first time. From 2011 to 2013, national available income dropped by 4 per cent, whereas work income suffered a significant reduction of 9.7 per cent.[3] These figures could be interpreted as a lowering-wage pressure typical for a recessive economy, but were certainly induced both by the continuous wage cuts in the public sector, undertaken by the government since 2010, and the effects of massive unemployment.

The next section will focus on the LMA for our empirical analysis. Economic, territorial, and socio-demographic trends will be presented, thus interpreting the effects of the economic crisis and corresponding political reactions through corresponding data analyses.

The Lisbon Metropolitan Area: crisis in motion[4]

Economic performance and territorial effects

As a capital city of a centralised and relatively small country, the LMA has always been a stronghold for the performance of an entire nation (Table 12.1). Its concentration of population, production, and consumption has attracted the most national resources and Research and Development (R&D) investment. The LMA gathers a significant part of Portugal's productive resources: 27 per cent of the country's inhabitants,[5] 26.2 per cent of its employment, and 37.2 per cent of national Gross Value Added (GVA).

The LMA has been strongly affected by the economic crisis and the subsequent austerity measures, but this has happened in apparently contradictory ways, as evident in the trends of the Regional Development Composite Index[6] (see Table 12.2), when taking into account the years prior to and after the beginning of the implementation of austerity measures (2010 onwards). The competitiveness component of the Index shows a slight improvement pattern up until the year 2010, clearly contradicted by the cohesion and environmental quality components. A more careful analysis of the competitiveness component helps to understand its apparent recovery. All variables (per capita GDP, qualified personnel, exports growth, R&D intensity, or the prevalence of knowledge intensive activities) are less reactive, taking into account the LMA specialisation profile,[7] whereas an internal market dependence is markedly balanced by the exports

Table 12.1 Some data on Lisbon Metropolitan Area (LMA)

2011	*Portugal*	*LMA*
GVA (€ millions)	149,268	55,483
Employees (thousands)	3,843	1,369
Exports (€ millions)	42,870	14,168
GDP % (PT=100)	100	139.6
Productivity (€ thousands – 2010)	30.7	38.7

Source: elaboration of authors on data: INE; CCDR-LVT.

Table 12.2 Regional Development Composite Index

		RDCI	*Competitiveness*	*Cohesion*	*Environmental quality*
Portugal		100	100	100	100
Lisbon Metropolitan Area	2011	**105.33**	113.26	103.99	98.01
	2010	**106.48**	113.93	104.64	100.20
	2008	**106.79**	113.18	106.57	100.00
	2006	**107.21**	113.01	107.78	100.27

Source: Portugal: 100. Elaboration of authors on data INE.

profile, thus giving a sense of growth, while the behaviour of macroeconomic variables is not so positive.

During the first phase of the economic crisis (2007–2010), rather moderate growth was registered in the LMA before the economy started to contract: export sectors and a still contained unemployment growth (8.4 per cent in 2007; 9.2 per cent in 2009) meant better performing variables when compared to the national average. Also, the predominance of the service sector and tourism activities in the region seemed to have contributed to balancing the economic depressors. It was during the second phase, after 2010, when all components of the Index were lowered.

The analysis of further economic performance variables helps to understand the real effects of the economic crisis and then those of the applied austerity measures: major private and (especially) public investment drops, while the austerity discourses grew, together with cuts in public spending to supposedly restore competitiveness. The trend of investment is evident in the figures of Gross Fixed Capital Formation,[8] which dropped by almost 20 per cent from 2008 to 2011. Around 65,000 companies (17.6 per cent) disappeared between 2008 and 2012, shifting the survival rate to below the national average.

The real estate and construction sector was one of the first to suffer from the crisis, as evident in the drop in building sale contracts (Figure 12.1). Today, the LMA is a densely urbanised system as the result of several decades of prevalence of urbanisation economics. This is quite noticeable from the levels of growth in terms of inhabitants and dwelling stock. According to the census, between 2001 and 2011, a 6 per cent population growth resulted in a growth of the built area of around 14.2 per cent. After a sustained growth in the early 2000s, construction works in both districts of the LMA (Lisbon and Setúbal) dropped by half over a few years (2007–2012). It should be noted that the financial breakdown intervened in an ongoing process (Figure 12.1): the number of building sale contracts stopped growing in 2006 because of the burst of the construction bubble and the growing effectiveness of planning regulations after decades of unregulated urbanisation (Fernandes & Chamusca, 2014). The contraction of the building sector strengthened regional polarisation, especially in the Setúbal district where, 'municipalities characterised by low education and skill levels, with structural issues of social inclusion and job insecurity, dependent on job segments in contraction,... show a stronger sensibility to early effects of crisis' (Ferrão, 2013: p. 256, translated).

At the same time, mortgage insolvencies rose by 49.5 per cent from 2009 to 2013. Although recent political discourses have been pinning the blame for the Portuguese crisis on families for their excessive indebtedness, the growth of private debt can largely be explained by the lack of an overall public housing policy for decades. In 2010, housing loans accounted for 80 per cent of family indebtedness, and homeownership was encouraged by tax benefits and a state-subsidised credit system for house purchase that lasted for more than 30 years until 2010. This pervasive system created a specific articulation, linking state policies, family investments/indebtedness, and credit-financial institutions (Santos, 2013).

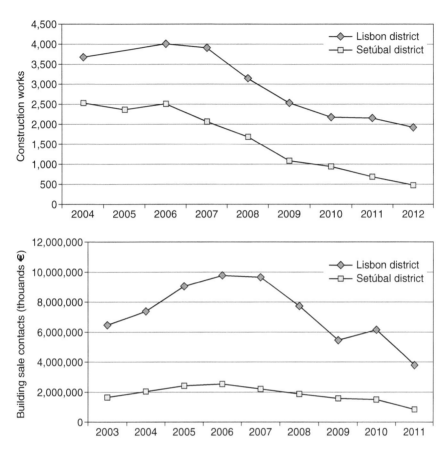

Figure 12.1 Construction and real estate in Lisbon Metropolitan Area (source: authors' elaboration on data from INE).

Socio-demographic trends

The LMA is a highly skilled region, with the largest universities in the country, the highest number of R&D centres and a considerable number of innovative companies. With 16.8 per cent of inhabitants holding higher education degrees (against a national average of 11.8 per cent), and a slight increase in the proportion of young people in the population (from 14.9 per cent in 2001 to 15.5 per cent in 2011), it is nonetheless an ageing region with declining birth rates. Over the last ten years, the percentage of the elderly (65 and over) rose from 15.4 to 18.2 per cent of the overall population, notwithstanding a fairly young immigrant population. These trends are just as significant when looked at from the perspective of labour market figures and their intensified characteristics throughout the crisis years. In fact, the effects of the crisis and the political responses to them are very clear here, with a reduction of *c.*180,000 employees between 2008 and 2013. The unemployment rate more than doubled in the 2008–2013 period (from 7.9 to 17.3 per cent), and the increase became steeper since the 2011 bailout (Figure 12.2), confirming the depressive effects of austerity. In particular, the youth unemployment rate grew from 16.9 per cent in 2007 to 22.7 per cent in 2010, then ballooned to 42.4 per cent in 2013. The figures of registered unemployed at public employment services, which are updated monthly and allow trends to be captured more quickly, are consistent with these findings: registered unemployment in the LMA[9] started to rise at a low pace just after 2008, growing drastically after 2010/2011, when the cut off measures by central government started.

Furthermore, risk of poverty has been rapidly increasing since 2009, rapidly inverting a slightly positive trend traced since the beginning of the decade as a result of steady social policies. According to the 2013 EU Statistics from the Income and Living Conditions survey, 18.7 per cent of the population of Portugal was at risk of poverty, notwithstanding social transfers in 2012, as against 17.9 per

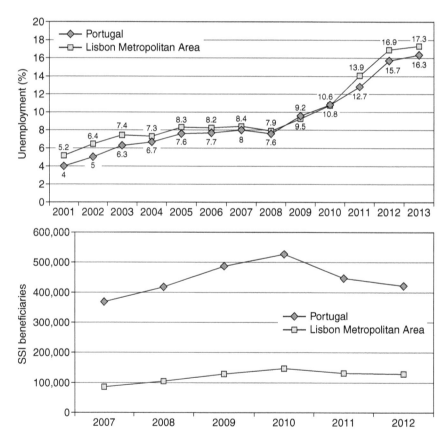

Figure 12.2 Unemployment rate and beneficiaries of Social Integration Income (SII) (number) (source: authors' elaboration on data from INE, II/MSESS (http://www4.seg-social.pt/estatisticas)).

cent in 2009. The growth is much more significant when using a time-anchored rate (Table 12.3).[10] The risk of poverty rate for the unemployed population in the country was 40.2 per cent in 2012, a rise of almost four points when compared to 2009. Under the austerity agenda, a renewed rise of asymmetry in income distribution since 2010 has inverted the trends of the previous decade, which were characterised by a steady reduction in economic inequalities (Alves, 2014).

Even though there is no consistent data for poverty at the regional level, sufficient knowledge exists of the fact that urban areas have been comprehensively affected. In the first phase of the crisis, there was a significant increase (approximately 66 per cent) in the number of beneficiaries of Social Integration Income (SII, a social security benefit for poorer families) in the LMA. Since 2010, however, the austerity measures[11] have reduced these figures drastically, in paradoxical contrast with the growth in unemployment (Figure 12.3). Moreover, significant ageing trends among the LMA's population, a subsequent rise in the number of pension beneficiaries, and the low value of average pensions in the Social Security system (€426) (Comissão de Coordenação e Desenvolvimento Regional de Lisboa e Vale do Tejo, 2013) makes the elderly a highly vulnerable social group, at high risk of poverty. The deep cuts to the 'Complemento Solidário para Idosos' (an important social benefit for the elderly), which the central government has imposed since 2011, have increased the percentage of the population over 65 years old exposed to poverty.

The austerity measures and the lowering of wages and family income have also hugely affected mobility, especially in a wide and dispersed urbanised region like the LMA. The LMA is characterised by significant daily commuting and semi-polycentric travels: Lisbon-City's population (*c.* 600,000 residents)

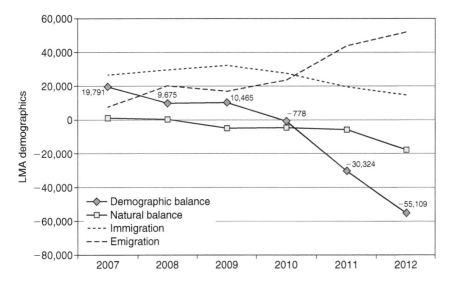

Figure 12.3 Demographic trends in Lisbon Metropolitan Area (source: authors' elaboration on data from INE).

Table 12.3 Portugal indicators (EU-SILC, 2010–2013)

	2009	2010	2011	2012 (estimated)
At risk of poverty rate before social transfers (%)	43.4	42.5	45.4	46.9
At risk of poverty rate after social transfers (%)	17.9	18.0	17.9	18.7
Time-anchored at risk of poverty rate (reference income=2009) (%)	17.9	19.6	21.3	24.7
Severe material deprivation (%)	9.0	8.3	8.6	10.9
At risk of poverty population (%)	25.3	24.4	25.3	27.4
Gini coefficient	33.7	34.2	34.5	34.2
Inequality on income distribution (S80/S20)	5.6	5.7	5.8	6.0
Inequality on income distribution (S90/S10)	9.2	9.4	10.0	10.7

Source: elaboration of authors on data: INE/Eurostat. Po: estimated value.

almost triples during working days. Between 2008 and 2010, the number of urban and suburban journeys on public transport were stable while, in the 2010–2012 period, a drop of 23 per cent happened. It could be assumed that, among the reasons for this, are the purchasing power loss caused by the economic crisis, the cutbacks in the public metropolitan transport offer, and the significant fare increases (*c.*24 per cent in the period 2010–2012), which in the LMA's case, were decided by the central government.

Finally, the emergent emigration flows should be pointed out for their potential consequences. Since 2010, there has been a complete inversion of migration trends in the LMA: immigration flows have fallen drastically (the values of 2012 being half of those in 2009), whilst emigration, especially among young people, has risen abruptly. In 2012, the number of emigrants was three times higher than in 2009. In 2011, a negative demographic balance was recorded for the first time in decades. These trends prefigure a potential further consequence of the crisis: loss of human capital because of the increasingly ageing population and especially because of the net emigration of skilled and educated workers.

Recent political and civic changes in the Lisbon Metropolitan Area

This section will provide an overview of parallel patterns of socio-political and civic reactions, changes, and restructuring dynamics in the LMA. Caught between European and national austerity pressures and multiple local and civic differentiated responses, the LMA shows a complex, if not contradictory, political landscape.

Between national reforms and local responses

Portugal remains one of the most politically centralised societies in Europe. It is the second most non-micro EU country (after Greece) with the lowest proportion of subnational (i.e. regional plus local) public expenditure. This accounted for around 15 per cent of public expenditure in 2011, a number lying well below the European Union average of *c*.25 per cent (Dexia & Conseil de Communes et Régions d'Europe, 2012). Moreover, the regions, accounting for around 4.5 per cent of public expenditure, have no politically autonomous governments, but are localised bodies of the national government (Nanetti, Rato, & Rodrigues, 2004). This centralised pattern is the main reason for the constant weakness in the local administrations (Seixas & Albet, 2012). The scarce resources are now even more curtailed by the fiscal stress induced by the economic crisis and, above all, by the reduction of national transfers since 2010. As a result, municipal budgets within the LMA have seen, with few exceptions, steep reductions since 2009/2010 of 20–30 per cent.[12]

In addition to the budget cuts, the national government has been carrying out fiscal and administrative reforms of territorial powers within the framework of austerity policies. First, a cut of municipal economic and real estate taxes is envisaged in the medium and long term. Second, Laws 22/2012 and 75/2013 represent further centralised steps towards the curtailment of local government capacities and autonomy. Law 22/2012, regarding administrative reorganisation of municipalities, targets expenditure cuts through the elimination of 27 per cent of the existing 4,260 parishes.[13] The Law gave municipal assemblies 90 days to elaborate a proposal for internal reorganisation and establish the parameters for it. The national association of parishes has contested the reform, advocating that the reorganisation should have been grounded on voluntary aggregations rather than on demographic parameters (Associação Nacional de Freguesias, 2012). Fourteen of the 18 municipalities in the LMA decided against the administrative reorganisation and two (Sesimbra and Sintra) did not submit any proposal within the given terms. As a result, a working group established by the national parliament imposed administrative restructuring on 14 municipalities, whereas in two cases (Sesimbra and Alcochete) the former organisation has been kept because these two abided by the parameters. In other words, protests and resistance had no effect. Lisbon and Amadora chose a different approach and outlined reorganisation proposals. In Amadora, the reorganisation was based on a demographic study, which aimed to achieve an equitable distribution of public services, and also on a consultative process that received around 1,000 contributions (Câmara Municipal de Amadora, 2012). The municipality of Lisbon had been working on administrative reform since 2009 and could thus forestall the national law with its own temporal terms (see the preliminary study, developed by a multidisciplinary scientific team in Mateus, Seixas, & Vitorino, 2010). The reduction of the number of parishes (from 53 to 24) was just one step towards an all-round enhancement of urban governance quality. The main aim was to transfer competences to the parishes, which previously had very little administrative and public management capability: management and maintenance of public spaces, issue of permissions and licences, planning and management of neighbourhood services, and promotion of cultural and social programmes. The municipal reform underwent a consultative process, which received more than 7,000 contributions (Mateus, Seixas, & Vitorino, 2010; Câmara Municipal de Lisboa, 2011).

Law 75/2013 has four main aims: decentralisation, strengthening of municipal power, backing of voluntary associations of municipalities, and promotion of territorial cohesion and competitiveness. The Law envisages the delegation of competences from the national level to the local and the inter-municipal one. However, metropolitan boards (Lisbon and Porto, instituted in 2003) and municipal associations (instituted in 2008) have been kept as coordination bodies without actual competences, further resources, or elected boards (Crespo & Cabral, 2010). In fact, discourses about 'decentralisation' are not resulting in any evident measures.

Along with the national–local confrontation about political-administrative reforms described above, the application of innovative governance instruments can also reveal complex patterns of institutional and local responses to the challenges within and beyond the crisis, as well as efforts to build accountability for local expenditure in times of constraint. Several instruments have been developing, such as Agenda 21[14] (implemented in five municipalities of the LMA), participatory budgeting (the most diffused tool, used by nine of the 18 municipalities), and a number of consultative and digital tools for citizen–government communication (Lisbon, Cascais). However, it is not always in the most stable fashion; for example, the recent Portuguese history of participatory budgeting is characterised by much experimentation with some inherent instability (Alves & Allegretti, 2012). Some municipalities had to cut budgets (Lisbon and Cascais), others have used participatory budgeting without any regularity (Odivelas, Oeiras and Sesimbra), and, in further cases, what was called participatory budgeting has actually only been the use of simple consultative tools (Alcochete and Palmela).

Lisbon-City: between innovation and contradictory trends

Different local governments in the LMA, in terms of their partisan and ideological components, have been trying to develop robust policies and new practices to respond to the crisis and its main urban problems. Amongst these, Lisbon-City is an especially interesting case. Since 2007, efforts to be innovative have been made possible thanks to a stable political background, supported by a centre-left government. The efforts towards sustained reform and political empowerment have been shaped around the principles of innovation and participation. In addition to the above-mentioned administrative reform and participatory tools, two policy areas can be analysed: urban regeneration and strategies for fostering economic recovery.

First, a new emphasis has been put on building rehabilitation and urban regeneration, as this is seen as a cornerstone of planning policy for investor-friendly action, and fiscal and edification incentives. As a result of 30 years of demographic contraction, a significant volume of vacant dwellings (around 50,000) is available in Lisbon-City, particularly in its historic centre. Political discourse has, since the 1990s, emphasised the need for public policy that would encourage the rehabilitation of buildings, but few results were achieved until recent years. With the impact of the crisis on the construction sector, the rehabil-itation of derelict buildings has become a more tangible activity, both in public and private strategies. Just recently, the central government introduced a new regulation (Law 53/2014) to reduce technical requirements, with the aim of redu-cing rehabilitation costs by over 30 per cent (Ministério do Ambiente, Ordena-mento do Territorio e Energia, 2014). In addition to a stimulus for the requalification of private dwellings, the Lisbon municipality has elaborated a strategic plan for the requalification and management of council housing (around 30,000 flats) with the final aim of transferring ownership of the stock over the next few decades (UrbanGuru, 2011). However, political critiques have high-lighted the risk that only real estate investors will be able to respond to the chal-lenge because of the credit crunch that is affecting middle-class families and their housing strategies. In fact, regeneration policies in central districts have already boosted gentrification trends (Mendes, 2013), which may keep growing in the near future as a consequence of tourism-friendly policies.

On the other hand, attention paid to grass-roots planning in Lisbon-City was complemented by a programme about priority intervention neighbourhoods, BIP/ZIP or 'Bairros e Zonas de Intervenção Prioritaria'.[15] The BIP/ZIP promotes micro-actions for urban regeneration funded by an annual competitive process and implemented by coalitions of local grass-roots participants. Although the scheme is an innovative one, the scarcity of the already allocated funds (€1 million a year, around 0.25 per cent of the municipal budget) cannot fully influ-ence the regeneration of deprived areas.

Also, several strategies to foster economic activity and employment have been developed, particularly with the advent of the crisis. Urban entrepreneur-ship support schemes have been launched: business incubators, incentives for new businesses, and support of retail initiatives. The strategy of designing urban policies to attract international tourism flows has also been at the core of the efforts of the municipal government. Globally, Lisbon-City suffered the impact of a global tourism recession in the first phase of the crisis (a reduction of 8.9 per cent in the number of overnight stays for the period 2007–2009), but emerged as an important tourist destination among Europe's cities in the follow-ing years (an increase of 19.4 per cent in the number of overnight stays for the period 2009–2012) (Câmara Municipal de Lisboa, 2014). The town councillor for planning has recently launched a proposal for a non-tax area for hotels in the downtown area of the city and a major investment is programmed for upgrading Lisbon Cruise Terminal so that it can accommodate larger numbers of arrivals. New services and economic activities, as well as new multi-sectoral approaches to city living itself, are popping up, not only in the city centre but in other his-toric areas.

Civic participation within and beyond the crisis

As far as political-electoral patterns are concerned, the last three rounds of municipal polls (2005, 2009, and 2013) show a consistent trend in growing disaffection with politics (Table 12.4), especially in 2013, when the number of voters dropped by around 15 per cent in comparison to the 2009 elections. Contextually, blank and spoilt votes have shown a significant increase in 2013, accounting for 8 per cent of the total number of votes. Moreover, a significant increase in the number of independent parties can be observed, a phenomenon almost non-existent until 2009. Overall, the traditional parties lost significant portions of their constituencies: the centre-right coalition experienced a breakdown in 2013, correlating with the national mood of discontent for austerity policies implemented by the national government, but the votes did not move towards other traditional political forces. The only exception was the centre-left 'Partido Socialista' in Lisbon-City. Here, in 2013, the party of Mayor António Costa received the absolute majority in the municipal board and in the municipal assembly, as well as in the boards of 17 out of 24 parishes. Meanwhile, the polls from May 2014 for the European Parliament elections have confirmed the trends towards reduced participation and fragmentation of constituencies in the LMA.

The growing disaffection with politics seems to parallel an emergence of civic participation and protests. In 2006, the landscape of civic dynamics in Lisbon Metropolitan Area (formal grass-roots organisation and further forms of mobilisation) was small but expanding (Seixas, 2008). An enquiry conducted in 2009 (the main results of this can be found in Mateus, Seixas, & Vitorino, 2010) highlights the emergence of new socio-political cultures, mainly amongst the most educated and younger people but spreading within denser urban areas. In times of crisis and austerity politics, some signs of renewed civic participation are evident from two perspectives. On the one hand, protests against austerity measures have been organised since 2011 by non-party organisations, such as 'Que se Lixe a Troika!'.[16] Although they are not quantitatively comparable to the

Table 12.4 Municipal polls in LMA, 2009–2013 (%)

	District	2005	2009	2013	Relative variation 2005–2013
Total voters	Lisboa	53.05	52.11	44.54	−16.04
	Setúbal	50.20	49.60	41.67	−16.99
Votes for traditional parties*	Lisboa	90.82	92.18	80.85	−10.98
	Setúbal	93.96	93.66	86.37	−8.08
Votes for independent parties	Lisboa	2.76	3.67	7.43	169.20
	Setúbal	0.06	1.23	1.97	3,183.33
Blank and spoilt votes	Lisboa	5.17	3.03	8.21	58.80
	Setúbal	4.90	3.15	8.23	67.96

Source: elaboration of authors on data General Directorate for Internal Affairs (www.dgai.mai.gov. pt/?area=103&mid=001&sid=003).

Note
* Parrtido Social Democrata (PSD); Partido Popular (CDS-PP); Partido Socialista (PS); Bloco de Esquerda (BE); Partido Comunista Português (PCP); Partido Ecologista 'Os Verdes' (PEV); and their coalitions.

protests in Spain and Greece, they have been the biggest mass protests in history of democratic Portugal. On the other hand, a number of alternative urban movements were born. Habita,[17] for example, is the first network to offer advice and support to dwellers about evictions-without-rehousing on shanty towns and against rent increases in council housing. 'Plataforma Gueto'[18] promotes immigration inclusion, analysis of laws and policies, and provides assistance to families of victims of police violence in several peripheral areas of Lisbon.

Conclusions

The analysis of both geographical and socio-political developments in the LMA during the economic crisis and of the mainstream political austerity measures, as well as of the more localised responses, has illustrated not only the existence of different phases and drivers for the crisis, but also the emergence of a geopolitical conflict.

The manifold impacts of the economic crisis in the LMA suggest that a series of diverse consequences have followed the global financial breakdown and that three temporal phases are to be highlighted. In the first phase (2008 to 2010) the structural financial crisis deeply affected the economic fabric of the country, especially in territories mostly dependent on the urbanisation and space production economies. In this phase, the LMA, as the main Portuguese urban hub, seemed to show some resilience, due to its relative socio-economic and urban diversity and characteristics, albeit considerably increasing its internal socio-spatial polarisation. The second phase, marked by the implementation of austerity policies in 2011, led to the widening of the impacts over larger areas of the socio-economic inner urban fabric. The effects have been particularly significant, not only on the poorer classes most dependent on social transfers, but also on middle-class families and public employees, as well as on the elderly population, leading to increased economic depression and an increase in poverty. The correlation between the austerity measures and the social impacts of the crisis are evident, although more in-depth analyses will be necessary to accurately discern more specific causation relationships, as well as spatial concentration impacts. In addition, the LMA now seems to enter a third phase of the crisis (since 2013/2014), with migration trends boosting the drainage of not only poorer but also younger and more skilled people, prefiguring serious demographic shifts and a fundamental loss of human capital.

The drivers of socio-political change debated in this chapter form a complex socio-political framework made of responsive, contradictory, and clashing trends. Two main socio-political restructuring trends can be identified as influencing the evolving patterns in the LMA: on the one hand, the financially driven central state policies, especially as a consequence of the 2011 bailout; on the other hand, the more socially and territorially driven urban political strategies. As far as institutional processes are concerned, a clash between the top-down austerity curtailment and the bottom-up urban transformation dynamic is clearly ongoing and developing, through a complex frame of multi-scalar intersections.

The case of the parishes' administrative reorganisation is quite revealing: although the national law had aimed at expenditure and institutional cuts rather than actual decentralisation, some municipalities have been able to be innovative in their governance and administrative dynamics, whereas protests and inertia have almost always shown no results. The historical, and now renewed, pressure for austerity localism in Portugal are colliding with local self-empowerment and resistance, shifting urban regimes towards a still unknown future. Furthermore, a steady evolution of grass-roots activism and civic participation adds further pressure on the top-down institutional approaches.

To sum up, several conflicting layers are reshaping the socio-political dynamics of the Lisbon Metropolitan Area, both within the crisis and beyond it. Understanding which pressures will be the strongest will be a crucial task; framing the right questions is thus an urgent need. If some individual local governments and communities are developing different narratives, will these be able to overrule secular path dependencies? Or will growing socio-spatial fractalisation foster socio-political splintering? If building new patterns of urban equity (and quality) within the political-economic framework is curtailed following, or justified by, the crisis, what is the aim and which are the political spaces to be built, or reinforced?

Although these questions were set out from an analysis of the LMA, several hints from this volume suggest a generalisation of them to the field of cities in crisis. In this respect, Southern Europe could be seen as a privileged space and place because of its common trends and characterisation in urban governance and (geo)politics (Nel.lo, 2001; Chorianopoulos, 2002; Leontidou, 2010; Seixas & Albet, 2012; Tulumello, 2013): many Southern European urban areas have witnessed a distinctive path of development and restructuring, as well as distinctive modes of governance, at least throughout a major part of the twentieth century. This is reflected, not only in the specific urban production processes (clearly understood in major trends such as the peri-urbanisation of vast Mediterranean urban and coastal areas), but also in the curtailing of city characteristics and competitiveness.

In conclusion, a preliminary outline can be drafted upon some dimensions for a research agenda. This agenda should have both theoretical and policy-making relevance for (Southern European) cities in crisis. Looking at the impacts of, and the ways out from, the crisis in different urban fabrics, such an agenda should explore the (re)production of the crisis and its socio-spatial patterns in different times, drivers, and contexts. The dimension of politics and policies, hence of institutional and political community landscapes and dynamics, should be addressed through an exploration of how different political cultures and regimes are reshaped in vertical and horizontal relationships, around subsidiarity patterns and government/governance capacities. A focus on the reactions and responses to the crisis implemented at the local level would be the key to questioning whether urban regimes are shifting towards incremental internal resilience to external shocks or structural changes that may have the capacity of questioning global commonplaces about economic regimes. A call is hence made here for scholars, practitioners, and activists to build networks able to link places and rescale urban studies from this perspective.

Notes

1 Although the object of study of the chapter is the Lisbon Metropolitan Area, some sections focus on Lisbon-City, which is the core municipality of the Metropolitan Area, because it is characterised by special socio-political dynamism in recent years (cf. the fifth section of the chapter, 'Lisbon-City: between innovation and contradictory trends').
2 Law 64-A/2008.
3 Elaboration by authors on data from Pordata (www.pordata.pt/).
4 Unless otherwise specified, data comes from the Portuguese Institute for Statistics (www.ine.pt).
5 A total of 2,821,876 inhabitants in 2011.
6

> The Regional Development Composite Index is a statistical study of annual frequency and national coverage.... Data collection is indirect and the variables used to compute the composite index result from administrative procedures and from statistical operations within the National Statistical System.... It relies on the basis of a 65 statistical indicators matrix, for the 30 Portuguese NUTS 3 level regions, properly normalized ... distributed by three components – competitiveness, cohesion and environmental quality – subsequently aggregated by a non-weighted average, for the components level as well as from the components level to the overall index level, four composite indicators are produced – competitiveness, cohesion, environmental quality and overall index of regional development.
>
> (Instituto Nacional de Estatistica, 2014: p. 8)

7 According to its GVA, the Lisbon Region specialises in services, transport and logistics, energy and environment, tourism, and the chemical, electronic, and mechanical industries.
8 Gross Fixed Capital Formation is a GVA component and a macroeconomic indicator used to measure how much of the new value added in the economy is invested rather than consumed.
9 That is, 2009 – 113,168; 2010 – 129,206; 2011 – 129,540; 2012 – 156,420; 2013 – 167,413 (Instituto de Emprego e Formação Profissional, various years).
10 The at-risk-of-poverty rate is statistically dependent on a percentage of the national average income. When national average income is reduced, as has happened in the present context, the at-risk-rate income is reduced as well. It is possible to have the absurd situation of a massive impoverishment and still register a statistical reduction in at-risk-of-poverty. To avoid this misleading effect, some experts have experimented with a 'time-anchoring' analysis, using the national average income from 2009 as a benchmark (cf. Rede Europeia Anti-Pobreza/Portugal, 2014).
11 A measure called 'condição de recursos' has been included in the first national austerity package (known as PEC 1). It has imposed cuts in the number of beneficiaries with property ownership evidence, obtained through fiscal analysis. After 2011, the lowering of the reference income value enabling access to the SII has caused a reduction of the number of poor households able to apply for it.
12 Elaboration by authors, screening municipal budgets of all municipalities in the LMA, 2009–2013.
13 The following elaboration stems from the analysis of original documents by the working group established by Parliament (Unidade Técnica para a Reorganização Administrativa do Territorio, 2012), the national association of parishes (Associação Nacional de Freguesias, 2012), and the websites of municipalities which submitted proposals or decided against reorganisation.
14 Agenda 21 is a scheme developed by the United Nations, which consists of local action plans, participatory in nature, for sustainable developments.

15 For more details, see http://bipzip.cm-lisboa.pt/.
16 For more details see http://queselixeatroika15setembro.blogspot.pt/.
17 For more details see www.habita.info/.
18 For more details see http://plataformagueto.wordpress.com/.

References

Abreu, A., Mendes, H., Rodrigues, J., Gusmão, J. G., Serra, N., Alves, P. D., & Mamede, R. P. (2013) *A crise, a troika e as alternativas urgente*s. Lisbon, Tinta da China.

Alves, M. L. & Allegretti, G. (2012) (In)stability, a key element to understand participatory budgeting: Discussing Portuguese cases. *Journal of Public Deliberation*, 8 (2), article 3.

Alves, S. (2014) Welfare state changes and outcomes: The cases of Portugal and Denmark from a comparative perspective. *Social Policy and Administration*. [Online] Available from: doi 10.1111/spol.12075.

Associação Nacional de Freguesias (2012) *Proposta de lei n° 44/XII/1.ª (GOV): Aprova o regime jurídico da reorganização administrativa territorial autárquica. Parecer.* [Online] Available from: www.anafre.pt/freguesias-associadas/reorganizacao-administrativa/parecer-anafre [accessed 1 December 2014].

Baptista, I. (2013) The travels of critiques of neoliberalism: Urban experiences from the 'borderlands'. *Urban Geography*, 34 (5), 590–611.

Blyth, M. (2013) *Austerity: The history of a dangerous idea.* New York, Oxford University Press.

Brenner, N. (2004) *New state spaces: Urban governance and the rescaling of statehood.* Oxford, Oxford University Press.

Brenner, N., Peck, J., & Theodore, N. (2010) After neoliberalization? *Globalizations*, 7 (3), 327–345.

Câmara Municipal de Amadora (2012) *Reorganização administrativa territorial do município da Amadora.* September 2012. [Online] Available from: http://ra.cm-amadora.pt/PageGen.aspx?WMCM_PaginaId=29188 [accessed 1 December 2014].

Câmara Municipal de Lisboa (2011) *Reforma administrativa da cidade de Lisboa: Relatório da discussao pública.* April 2011. [Online] Available from: www.youblisher.com/p/120029-Relatorio-da-Consulta-Publica-da-Reforma-Administrativa-da-Cidade/ [accessed 1 December 2014].

Câmara Municipal de Lisboa (2014) *A economia de Lisboa em numeros. 2014: Turismo.* [Online] Available from: www.cm-lisboa.pt/fileadmin/INVESTIR/logos_areas/economia_cidade_imagens/Turismo_012014.xls [accessed 1 December 2014].

Chorianopoulos, I. (2002) Urban restructuring and governance: North–south differences in Europe and the EU urban initiatives. *Urban Studies*, 39 (4), 705–726.

Comissão de Coordenação e Desenvolvimento Regional de Lisboa e Vale do Tejo (2013) *Plano de ação regional de Lisboa 2014–2020 (diagnóstico prospetivo).* [Online] Available from: www.ccdr-lvt.pt/pt/documentacao-ja-produzida/7906.htm [accessed 1 December 2014].

Commission of the European Communities (2008) *Communication from the Commission to the European Council: A European economic recovery plan.* COM (2008) 800 final. [Online] Available from: http://ec.europa.eu/economy_finance/publications/publication 13504_en.pdf [accessed 1 December 2014].

Crespo, J. L. & Cabral, J. (2010) the institutional dimension to urban governance and territorial management in the Lisbon Metropolitan Area. *Análise Social*, 197, 639–662.

Dexia & Conseil de Communes et Régions d'Europe (2012) *Subnational public finance in the European Union: Summer 2012.* [Online] Available from www.ccre.org/docs/ Note_CCRE_Dexia_EN.pdf [accessed 1 December 2014].

European Commission (2011) *Cities of tomorrow: Challenges, visions, ways forward.* [Online] Available from: http://ec.europa.eu/regional_policy/sources/docgener/studies/ pdf/citiesoftomorrow/citiesoftomorrow_final.pdf [accessed 1 December 2014].

Fernandes, J. R. & Chamusca, P. (2014) Urban policies, planning and retail resilience. *Cities,* 36, 170–177.

Ferrão, J. (2013) Território. In: Cardoso, J. L., Magalhães, P., & Machado Pais, J. (eds) *Portugal social de A a Z: Temas em aberto.* Paço de Arcos, Expresso, pp. 244–257.

Hadjimichalis, C. (2011) Uneven geographical development and socio-spatial justice and solidarity: European regions after the 2009 financial crisis. *European Urban and Regional Studies,* 18 (3), 254–274.

Harvey, D. (2005) *A brief history of neoliberalism.* Oxford, Oxford University Press.

Instituto de Emprego e Formação Profissional (various years) *Informação mensal do mercado de emprego.* [Online] Available from: www.iefp.pt/estatisticas [accessed 1 December 2014].

Instituto Nacional de Estatistica (2014) *Regional development composite index.* [Press release] 11 April 2014. [Online] Available from: www.ine.pt/ngt_server/attachfileu. jsp?look_parentBoui=216075440&att_display=n&att_download=y [accessed 1 December 2014].

Krugman, P. (2012) *End this depression now!* New York, W. W. Norton & Company.

Leontidou, L. (2010) Urban social movements in 'weak' civil societies: The right to the city and cosmopolitan activism in Southern Europe. *Urban Studies,* 47 (6), 1179–1203.

Mateus, A., Seixas, J., & Vitorino, N. (eds) (2010) *Qualidade de vida e governo da cidade: Bases para um novo modelo de governação da cidade de Lisboa.* Lisbon, ISEG. [Online] Available from: www.reformaadministrativa.am-lisboa.pt/fileadmin/ MODELO_GOVERNACAO/Documentos/ISEG_governacao_abril2010.pdf [accessed 1 December 2014].

Mendes, L. (2013) Public policies on urban rehabilitation and their effects on gentrification in Lisbon. *AGIR – Revista Interdisciplinar de Ciências Sociais e Humanas,* 1 (5), 200–218.

Ministério do Ambiente, Ordenamento do Territorio e Energia (2014) *Regime excecional para a reabilitação urbana (RERU).* 24 February 2014. [Online] Available from: www.portugal.gov.pt/media/1351721/20140224%20regime%20excecional%20recupe- racao%20urbana.pdf [accessed 1 December 2014].

Nanetti, R. Y., Rato, H., & Rodrigues, M. (2004) Institutional capacity and reluctant decentralization in Portugal: The Lisbon and Tagus Valley region. *Regional and Federal Studies,* 14 (3), 405–429.

Nel.lo, O. (2001) *Ciutat de ciutats.* Barcelona, Editorial Empúries.

Oosterlynck, S. & González, S. (2013) 'Don't waste a crisis': Opening up the city yet again for neoliberal experimentation. *International Journal of Urban and Regional Research,* 37 (3), 1075–1082.

Peck, J. (2013) Explaining (with) neoliberalism. *Territory, Politics, Governance,* 1 (2), 132–157.

Peck, J., Theodore, N., & Brenner, N. (2013) Neoliberal urbanism redux? *International Journal of Urban and Regional Research,* 37 (3), 1091–1099.

Pedroso, P. (2014) *Portugal and the global crisis: The impact of austerity on the economy, the social model and the performance of the state.* Lisbon, Friederich Ebert

Stiftung. [Online] Available from: http://library.fes.de/pdf-files/id/10722.pdf [accessed 1 December 2014].

Pinho, C., Andrade, C., & Pinho, M. (2011) Regional growth transition and the evolution of income disparities in Europe. *Urban Public Economics Review*, 13, 66–103.

Rede Europeia Anti-Pobreza/Portugal (2014) *Indicadores sobre a pobreza: Dados Europeus e nacionais: Atualização Março 2014*. [Online] Available from: www.eapn.pt/documentos_visualizar.php?ID=322 [accessed 1 December 2014].

Reis, J. & Rodrigues, J. (eds) (2011) *Portugal e a Europa em crise: Para acabar com a economia de austeridade*. Lisbon, Actual.

Rodrigues, J. & Teles, N. (2011) Portugal e o neoliberalismo como intervencionismo de mercado. In: Reis, J. & Rodrigues, J. (eds) *Portugal e a Europa em crise: Para acabar com a economia de austeridade*. Lisbon, Actual, pp. 34–46.

Roitman, J. (2014) *Anti-crisis*. Durham, NC, Duke University Press.

Sager, T. (2011) Neo-liberal urban planning policies: A literature survey 1990–2010. *Progress in Planning*, 76 (4), 147–199.

Santos, A. C. (2013) Temos vivido acima das nossas possibilidades? In: Soeiro, J., Cardina, M., & Serra, N. (eds) *Não acredite em tudo o que pensa: Mitos do senso comum na era da austeridade*. Lisbon, Tinta da China, pp. 17–30.

Schwartz, H. (2012) Housing, the welfare state, and the global financial crisis: What is the connection? *Politics and Society*, 40 (1), 35–58.

Seixas, J. (2008) Estruturas e dinâmicas do capital sócio-cultural em Lisboa. In: Cabral, M. V., Silva, F. C., & Saraiva, T. (eds) *Cidade e Cidadania: Governança Urbana e Participação Cidadã*. Lisbon, Imprensa de Ciências Sociais, pp. 177–210.

Seixas, J. & Albet, A. (eds) (2012) *Urban governance in Southern Europe*. Farnham, Ashgate.

Tulumello, S. (2013) Panopticon sud-Europeo: (Video)sorveglianza, spazio pubblico e politiche urbane. *Archivio di Studi Urbani e Regionali*, 107, 30–51.

UrbanGuru (2011) *Programa de intervenção estratégica no património habitacional municipal e nos devolutos municipais: Relatório final*. Lisbon, CML. [Online] Available from: http://habitacao.cm-lisboa.pt/documentos/1323729521D4qVS7sl3Eu87LY5.pdf [accessed 1 December 2014].

Unidade Técnica para a Reorganização Administrativa do Territorio (2012) *Proposta concreta de reorganização administrativa do territorio* [one document for each municipality of the national territory]. [Online] Available from: http://app.parlamento.pt/utrat/Municipios/Abrantes/Abrantes_Proposta.pdf [accessed 1 December 2014].

Wacquant, L. (2012) Three steps to a historical anthropology of actually existing neoliberalism. *Social Anthropology*, 20 (1), 66–79.

Werner, R. A. (2013) Crises, the spatial distribution of economic activity, and the geography of banking. *Environment and Planning A*, 45 (12), 2789–2796.

13 Rethinking Barcelona

Changes experienced as a result of social and economic crisis

Joaquín Rodríguez Álvarez

Introduction

The economic and social crisis experienced by Spain over the last few years has had consequences that can largely be defined as ideological, institutional, and material, although the political response to the crisis has been articulated mainly through the material and institutional field, to manage the ideological changes that society has experienced. This chapter studies how and to what extent the Metropolitan Area of Barcelona (AMB) has suffered from the impacts of the crisis and the responses and mechanisms which have been applied in an attempt to overcome these impacts.

The chapter starts with a short overview of the 'Spanish Crisis', giving special importance to the housing bubble and the institutional system that has facilitated this situation. It then analyses how the crisis has affected the AMB and its city model. In this context the situation of Barcelona is analysed and the main differences between the context of Barcelona and Spain are discussed to explain the management of the crisis in the material, ideological, and institutional fields. Then the analysis focuses on some of the most important policies applied by the City Council in response to the crisis impacts. Finally, in the conclusions, the new tendencies of Barcelona in the aftermath of the crisis are presented and some new lines of research are proposed.

Overview of the crisis in Spain: its origins and consequences

The Spanish context

It could be argued that up to the year 2007 Spain was in a period of economic boom, which had started in the 1990s and had led the government of President José Luis Rodríguez Zapatero to a state of semi-euphoria because of exponential decline in unemployment rates and even talk of full employment (CincoDias, 2007). His government conducted a set of legislative actions that represented a real social revolution and modernisation of the state. Among these initiatives were permission for same-sex marriage, the law of dependence that secured financial support from the state for all those with degrees of dependence, and a new abortion law (the most progressive ever). At that time Spain was, as it were, in the middle of a dream from which no one wanted to wake up. This dream had shaky foundations, however. It could be argued that this is one of the main reasons why the outbreak of the crisis had such serious ideological consequences in Spain; it not only shattered the economic dream, but also seriously affected social progress.

Analysing the foundations of Spanish growth to identify the elements that helped to create a national crisis greater than the international one, it could be argued that the reasons were threefold. First, the primacy of the construction and real estate business, second the predominance of the tourism sector, and third the underground economy that was estimated in 2008 as 23 per cent of the GDP (GESTHA, 2011). The developments in all these sectors were essential to manage Spain's dizzying rate of progress. Yet today most scholars agree (Echeverría, 2008; Redondo, 2007; Romero, 2010) that the real estate and the housing bubble in Spain played the most important role in the Spanish crisis. This will be the focus of the following subsection.

The housing bubble in Spain

The importance of the real estate market in the Spanish crisis is proven by the available data from the National Institute of Statistics (INE), which show that the rate of construction (both residential and non-residential) in the Spanish GDP increased from 11.7 per cent in 1996 to 17.9 per cent in 2007 (INE, 2014). Other experts using more inclusive methodologies to calculate GDP consider the economy even more dependent on the construction sector and argue that in 2007 this number was close to 39.4 per cent (BDE, 2008).

The exponential growth of the real estate sector in relation to GDP was made possible by the action of the government of the Popular Party (1996–2004) of José María Aznar, who launched a massive liberalisation of land through Law 6/1998 on land use and ratings (BOE, 1998). This law aimed to go much further than the one approved in 1990 by the socialist government of Felipe González that was a first step in converting rural land to urban land. The law of 1998 further liberalised and simplified land types into urban, developable, and undevelopable land, besides setting the premise that unless specifically prohibited by a provision of law, all land was now developable. The aim was to achieve a huge increase in the supply of land, which, according to the then Minister of Public Works, Arias-Salgado, should in the medium term reduce the price of land and therefore housing (El País, 1997). But the reality once again was not in line with the government's public speeches.

The consequences of the new law have been dramatic. Between 1998 and 2007, the housing stock grew by 5.7 million, an increase of almost 30 per cent. In the third quarter of 2007, construction accounted for 13.3 per cent of total employment, well above that of Germany (6.7 per cent) and the United Kingdom (8.5 per cent). With regard to prices the revaluation of housing in Spain between 1997 and 2007 was 191 per cent (*The Economist*, 2005). In 2013, this was the second largest rate in the OECD and was higher than in countries where there was no doubt of the existence of a bubble, such as the United Kingdom (168 per cent) and the United States (85 per cent) (*The Economist*, 2005, 2013).

It is also necessary to underline that in the period 1998–2005 the banking system played a key role in the generation and extension of the boom phase of the residential market. The banks gave abundant credit to acquirers and promoters of housing and undoubtedly contributed decisively to the record levels of both demand for and offer of residences. High liquidity was owed mainly to three factors: a huge expansion in the number of savings banks, substantial bank competition, and low interest rates. The housing bubble created as a consequence of this process became responsible for a period of growth, but in turn weakened the resilience of the state to deal with potential setbacks (Romero, 2010).

At this point, it is necessary to understand that what Spain experienced was not a result of the international financial and economic crisis but a combination of international crisis and internal factors, which, as explained above, helped to amplify the magnitude of the catastrophe, generating a scenario that few other countries faced during the crisis years. It could be argued that the Spanish crisis was mainly caused by Spanish misrule and the patronage networks between political and economic power that allowed the housing bubble to arise in a context in which the economy and the institutional system were incapable of providing a framework of accountability, and where corruption was identified as a lesser evil by a large part of the citizenry (Metroscopia, 2014). The institutional factors that have enabled the current crisis situation are analysed in the next subsection.

The institutional problem

In order to understand the real dimension of the Spanish crisis with the problems outlined above, other issues should also be considered such as the complexity and opacity of the public administration and the multiplicity of institutions and agencies, most of which duplicated functions already assigned to other agencies. In this sense it can be assumed that Spain suffered a lack of institutional rationalisation on all levels (Royo, 2014). This, together with the lack of confidence of citizens in institutions during the crisis period expressed repeatedly in the Metroscopia polls (Metroscopia, 2014), represents one of the most serious challenges facing Spain.

The institutional problem started with the so-called 'transition' period (1975–1982), when the figures of the Franco regime (heirs of the dictatorship) and the opposition leaders designed the current institutions and constitution. What was supposed to be the end of the dictatorship did not represent a real new beginning for Spaniards. Military pressure forced the leaders of the opposition to accept the maintenance of some old institutions, and allowed the old guard to occupy important positions in the administration (Martínez-Conde, 1979; Rodríguez de Arce, 2014).

Another ongoing key discussion at that time was between the defenders of the central state and the supporters of a decentralised or federal state. This discussion is still ongoing and is important when it comes to understanding the institutional problems of Spain today. Some regions such as Catalonia and the Basque Country, whose languages were banned during the dictatorship, and where repression was especially strong, wanted to develop a federal system to recognise the different nationalities that exist inside Spain (Solanes & Molinero, 2014). However, the reluctance of the conservative sector and heirs of the dictatorship to recognise the uniqueness of these regions forced the selection of an intermediate system, the Autonomous Communities, a system that is in the spotlight today because it keeps alive the struggle between centralising and decentralising tendencies, and does not protect the competences of the different autonomous communities. This system allows the inference of the state in many policies such as education, the responsibility for which was theoretically transferred to the autonomous communities, but it does not guarantee autonomous communities the necessary financial resources, the allocation of which is a state decision (Montaner, 1996; Ysàs, 1994).

In the context of the recent economic crisis this has led to a situation where the state, given its need to reduce its debt, has made budget adjustments and transferred the budget cuts to the autonomous communities while initiating a new recentralising effort through different sets of legislative actions like the new education law that gives the central government the capacity to design the content of the primary and secondary education curricula, something that was previously the autonomous communities' legal right, and the new Organic Law 2/2012 of 27 April (BOE, 2012) governing budgetary stability and financial sustainability that allows the central government to intervene in the Autonomous Communities when they exceed the budgetary restrictions. It came thus into conflict with territories such as Catalonia, whose people wanted to deepen their self-government, and now, as a reaction against the recentralising strategy of the state, are also claiming independence. The referendum of 9 November 2014 made this clear, when more than 80 per cent of the participants voted for independence (*LaVanguardia*, 2014).

Socio-spatial impacts

The economic and financial crisis has had serious and multiple consequences in Spain. These impacts are illustrated by a series of indicators such as the unemployment rate, the gross domestic product (GDP), and the consumer price index (CPI). The unemployment rate, for example, which hit a record low in the spring of 2007 with 1.76 million people (7.95 per cent of the active population) unemployed, went on to register a record high in the first quarter of 2013 with more than 6.2 million unemployed (27.16 per cent) with a youth unemployment (unemployed and under 25 years of age) of more than 960,000 people (57.2 per cent) (INE, 2014). GDP also steadily declined during the last half of 2008 as a result of which Spain, for the first time in 15 years, entered a period of recession. The country did not come out of it until the second quarter of 2010. However, this recovery did not last for long, since in 2011 Spain experienced a decrease in

GDP. This series of recessions seriously affected the GDP per capita and it went from 105 per cent of the average of the European Union in 2006 to 95 per cent in 2013 (INE, 2014).

Other data that helps to explain the impacts of the crisis is the new unemployment dynamics in terms of the number of people that have completed a year of job searching without success. The Statistical Agency of Catalonia (IDESCAT, 2014) confirms the significant increase in long duration unemployment both in the Barcelona area and in Catalonia, a tendency that also exists in the rest of the country. In the AMB, the number of unemployed people looking for a position for 12 months or even longer doubled between 2006 and 2011, increasing from 33.7 to 60 per cent. This trend is especially obvious for those over 50 years of age, whose chances of finding a job again are limited or non-existent. This is accompanied by serious psychological effects, expressed in the form of disaffection, pessimism, and lack of confidence. It is very important to underline that the crisis has led to two lost generations: young people who are unable to enter the labour market, and those over 50 who have been excluded without any chance of reintegration.

Along with the decrease in employment and GDP, the crisis affected prices as well. Throughout the second half of 2007, prices started to increase significantly, placing the annual CPI in December of that year at 4.2 per cent. However, a study by the bank Catalunya Caixa claimed that the CPI was actually 7.9 per cent and that the everyday consumer goods suffered an even greater increase, especially milk (31.0 per cent), gasoline (16.2 per cent), bread (14.4 per cent), and eggs (9.6 per cent) (Catalunya Caixa, 2010). This has had serious consequences for the population, generating new typologies of poverty, such as energy poverty as families cannot afford to pay for fuel.

In the crisis years the public debt was also seriously affected. In 2007 it represented 36.1 per cent of GDP but doubled in the following three years, reaching 60.1 per cent in 2010 and even 93.4 per cent in 2013 (INE, 2014). This brought serious consequences with regard to the maintenance of the welfare state, which suffered huge cuts in order to control the public deficit, cuts that among others resulted in a loss of quality in the health and education systems.

All these developments have had an enormous impact on the ideological field, and Spain like many other Southern European countries affected by the crisis has seen a loss of confidence in institutions and traditional political parties. This new situation has led to the creation of new social movements, many protests against the status quo, and a decline of the traditional political opinion in favour of new ones, which in many cases represent new forms of populism.

A study conducted by the Centre for Sociological Research on the assessment of the economic and political situation of citizens provides some key clues to understanding this phenomenon. The survey from 2014 shows that the four major concerns of Spaniards are unemployment (82.3 per cent), corruption (41 per cent), economic problems (28.2 per cent), and political parties (26 per cent) (Metroscopia, 2014), whereas in the pre-crisis context terrorism was among the major concerns. This change clearly shows that the concern about politicians and corruption has overtaken terrorism. This is mainly because many Spaniards consider traditional parties largely responsible for the current crisis, casting doubt on many other state institutions like the monarchy or the administration of justice, which they consider politicised. The situation has resulted in a crisis of trust and the consequent loss of votes by the traditional parties, as well as the creation of a new leftist party, *Podemos* (We can), which currently ranks first in voting intentions (CIS, 2014).

Bearing in mind the above overview of the Spanish context the following section focuses on analysis of the situation in Barcelona and of the extent to which the crisis has affected its Metropolitan Area.

Barcelona and the consequences of the crisis for its Metropolitan Area

Barcelona remains one of the most dynamic cities in Spain, thanks to a diversified economic system which includes a knowledge economy, design, industry, tourism, and construction. The capital of Catalonia, the most industrialised region of Spain, it has its own dynamics that have had a major impact on the management of the crisis. The impacts of the crisis on the city of Barcelona cannot be seen in isolation from what happened in the Spanish context. It is, however, necessary to conduct a specific analysis to explain why the effects of the crisis on the city were not as devastating as they were in other parts of the country. In this line it is important to identify those factors that have helped to mitigate the impacts of the crisis on the city and then to focus on analysis of the responses undertaken in the entire Metropolitan Area of Barcelona.

A look at the data reveals that the situation of Barcelona is not as critical as that of other Spanish cities, such as Madrid, which remains the most indebted city in the country, with passive public debts according to the Excessive Deficit Procedure (EDP) that totalled €7.036 million at the end of the fourth quarter of 2013; according to the latest statistics of the Bank of Spain the debt of Barcelona, in this same period, was €1.110 million (*El Economista*, 2014). This situation is undoubtedly directly related to the institutional framework (organisations, norms, and transparency) and the confidence that citizens have in their institutions. In this regard it can be assumed that Madrid is much closer to the previously identified problems of the Spanish institutional system (Villoria & Jiménez, 2012) than Barcelona. The city of Barcelona has been ruled by the Catalan Socialist Party (PSC) and is now governed by Catalan nationalist conservative parties (CiU), which are less close to the patronage networks of Spain (but have problems with corruption), whereas since 1991 Madrid has been ruled by the Popular Party.

The study of a set of variables can provide a picture of the situation in Barcelona and the impacts of the crisis on the city. Among the most important indicators is the rise of unemployment, which in January 2014 reached 16.2 per cent in terms of unemployed jobseekers registered at the Public Employment Service offices in the province of Barcelona (IDESCAT, 2014). These numbers indicate that unemployment has doubled since the beginning of the crisis. In relation to unemployment it should be noted that the sectors with the highest percentage of job losses are the construction (–30 per cent) and the real estate (–47 per cent) sectors (ibid.). In the rest of Spain unemployment has tripled in the same period.

In relation to the real estate sector the Department of Fiscal Studies of the City Council of Barcelona has provided a set of data that helps to visualise the evolution of the housing market. Based on this data it can be pointed that the price declines are widespread in every district. There are neighbourhoods with significant falls (e.g. Les Corts, with a decrease of 40 per cent in prices) and others where the prices fall more slowly, such as Eixample and Sant Martí, with declines of 3.3 and 4.1 per cent (Ara, 2012). This situation has led to a profound change in the dynamics of the real estate sector, as many citizens now prefer renting to buying, something entirely new to Spanish society.

Along with the social impacts the crisis has had on the city and its inhabitants, the crisis has also affected the city budget. For example, in 2014 almost half of the yearly budget (€903.1 million out of €2,574 million) has been allocated to protection policies and social development and is also meant to ensure the quality of life of people in all city districts (Barcelona City Council, 2014a). An example of these new spending priorities is food subsidies, which allow children from families at risk of social exclusion to eat free at schools. In 2014 there were 549 more families than in 2013 that were included in this category (BTV, 2014a), which shows that the crisis has increased social spending.

Another point to take into account is that contrary to many other parts of Spain where a crisis of trust and consequent loss of votes of the traditional parties is obvious, this is not the case in Catalonia and Barcelona, where traditional political parties remain stable, albeit with a transfer of votes from the centre right to the centre left. Currently the polls predict a victory for ERC, a centre-left independent party, with more than 80 years of history, whereas the benchmark CiU, the nationalist centre-right party, which currently is in government, remains in second position (Metroscopia, 2014). This is because even though political corruption in Catalonia exists and it has affected the nationalist parties in many cases, it is not as blatant as in Spain in general, where cases of corruption that affect the Crown abound, such as the case of the governing party itself, which is currently under investigation for illegal financing and double counting, but also cases involving the opposition and the trade unions.

The fact that people consider the Catalan government and institutions as more transparent is a key point in crisis management. It should not be forgotten that Transparency International gave Catalonia a score of 100 out of 100 for government transparency whereas Madrid scored 56 (Transparency International, 2014). The government of Spain was denounced by Amnesty International for torture and ill-treatment of demonstrators (Amnesty International, 2014). The factor of trust can also be related to the economic situation of Catalonia, which has been perceived as more stable, a perception that is important for generating trust in public institutions.

The trust factor is, in consequence, one of the key factors that made the difference between the Spanish crisis and the situation in Barcelona, where there is still confidence in the Catalan institutions but not in the Spanish ones. This confidence has given the right to the government to implement a series of measures aimed to increase transparency and social participation, but has also led to an unprecedented situation of tension and estrangement between the two governments (the Catalan and the Spanish one).

The management of the crisis

Following the line of argumentation about the impacts of the crisis on the society both in Spain and Barcelona this section analyses the actions taken by the local administration in an attempt to mitigate the effects of the crisis and to generate new synergies and resilience factors to take Barcelona one step beyond the crisis. The analysis focuses on the different kinds of responses implemented by Barcelona as a consequence of the global economic crisis and the Spanish one. In the following the responses are studied in three categories in order to provide a structured overview of recent developments. The first of these categories refers to material capacities, which could be natural resources as well as technological, economic, or organisational skills that could be affected by the crisis. The second one is the ideas, understood as intersubjective beliefs or collective conceptions of social order, which could be influenced by the city administration through adaptation of the institutional system to the new claims of the citizens. The third category is the institutions or institutionalisation, which work as a means for the stabilisation of a certain order. It should be noted at this point that the presented categories are interdependent and a phenomenon observed in one category could have important consequences in another one. This is the main reason why the institutional and ideological response is discussed in a single paragraph.

The material management of the crisis

The economic impacts, as illustrated above, have been among the most visible of the crisis. In the following it is discussed how the economic recession and rising unemployment have materialised in the AMB.

As seen in the contextualisation of the crisis, the impacts on the economy can be easily related to a decline in tax collection, which has provoked a reaction from the public administrations because of their need for more resources in order to respond to the new demands of their citizens. For this reason, in a first stage the City and the Catalan governments have chosen a strategy based on increased prices for public services such as public transportation and have applied different taxes such as property tax or water or electricity taxes in order to get money to provide the basic social services. These strategies were accompanied by new forms of urban exploitation such as the increased licensing of the construction of luxury hotels, which ultimately evoked criticism from neighbours, port expansion (both commercial and industrial), the sale of public buildings, and the cancellation of public works that were under construction or planned.

It is worth mentioning that in order to continue the implementation of key projects the government of Barcelona has established public–private partnership(s) (PPP), a strategy that is studied here as it is seen as a consequence of the lack of public resources. This strategy, although already well known and established in many English-speaking countries, is quite new to Barcelona.

In this context it should be noted that the City Council has also tried to rationalise the public spending through establishing new protocols in order to pay providers in 30 days as well as concessions for the opening of new business (*El Mundo*, 2011).

In relation to the rationalisation of public spending several examples of public works that have been affected by the crisis in a different way can be mentioned here. Among these are the Blue Museum, the Cultural del Born Centre, and the dissenyHub. It should be highlighted that traditionally in Barcelona the public administration has been responsible for planning, designing, and implementing public works. In the middle of the crisis a move to a new scenario was observed, whereby private companies shared responsibilities with the city government in the administration and construction of facilities, providing new resources to face the new challenges of the city. It should be underlined, however, that different advantages as well as disadvantages have been observed. The biggest negative effect related to PPP is the impact on people. Citizens feel that they are losing control over the city, and see private participation as an invasion of the public sphere, in a field traditionally monopolised by public administration. Mainly because this process has been simultaneous with the privatisation of buildings and services it has suggested the dissolution of public administration at a time when corruption is a principal concern and as such new strategies generate mistrust (*El País*, 2011). Yet these strategies have important benefits such as the new commitment of local companies to the city. The PPP seems to generate quite positive synergies, although the novelty of the strategy makes in-depth analysis of all the consequences impossible.

Furthermore, it should be emphasised that Barcelona examined other possibilities for the acquisition of additional resources. An example in this regard is the use of venues in the city which are sold to private companies, as is the case with the Statue of Columbus at the end of the Ramblas. The City Council allowed Nike to dress the statue of Columbus with an FC Barcelona jersey (Ediciones La Vanguardia, 2013) for promotional reasons. This sparked numerous protests which forced the Council to dismiss the strategy. Yet it has been used in other Spanish cities like Madrid, where the City Hall has allowed the sale of names of city venues such as the name of subway stations. An example in this regard is Puerta del Sol, which now bears the name Vodafone Sol (EuropaPress, 2013).

The discussed impacts on the material sphere (and the responses to these) led, at first, to a change of mind on the part of many citizens.

Ideological and institutional changes

All these changes (political dissatisfaction with national policies and protests against the government) have had a real impact on municipalities, mainly because they are the closest administration, where attempts are made to combat political disaffection by implementation of new policies and strategies that can generate confidence, a set of strategies that usually appears in new ways of public participation and new forms of transparency and accountability. That is, the government has tried to respond to the ideological shift of the population mainly through institutional reforms.

In this sense it could be argued that Barcelona has spent years experimenting with different approaches to participatory democracy. Among these was the involvement of stakeholders in the decision-making process and the establishment of district councils or other arenas/platforms for discussion about public policies and urban planning (Casellas, 2007). The crisis has disrupted these traditional strategies, however, mainly because citizens are looking for more direct participation without the intervention of intermediate actors, and this is having effects on the traditional stakeholders of the civil society. A clear example of this situation is that one of the key traditional actors, the neighbour associations that were acting as a privileged partner of the local government (Huertas, 1997), seem no longer to be preferred by the citizens, increasing thus a trend that began earlier this century. This situation has become one of the biggest challenges for the city, because now there is no structured representation by civil society of the concerns of citizens.

Importantly, these associations played a key role in the anti-Franco struggle, and the first decades of democracy in the whole of Spain, especially in Madrid and Barcelona. It was in the 1980s and 1990s when their social involvement and mobilisation capacity reached their highest levels (Blanco, 2009). At that time Barcelona's Council began to include them in almost all discussions related to the implementation of policies especially in relation to urbanism. Yet now the situation has changed and it seems that citizens no longer see these associations as useful in the defence of their interests, either because of excessive politicisation, whereby many of the leaders are active in political parties, or because of a lack of modernisation (they use practically no new technologies, have no social networks, their meetings are held at private places at times impossible for working people to make, and many of them have no young people involved).

An analysis of the survey conducted in 2012 among the 86 neighbour associations of the FAVB (Federation of Neighbour Associations of Barcelona) shows that the total number of members was 43,672 with an average of 424 people for every association (FAVB, 2012). From the data it can be assumed that only a small number of citizens are now members of these associations. When compared with the overall population of Barcelona (1,620,943), 43,672 represent only 2.6 per cent of the citizens. In conclusion, it should be obvious that the participatory process should go beyond these organisations. This becomes clear from participatory processes led by civil society, like the BarcelonaDecideix, an unofficial consultation about the independence of Catalonia. This was held in Barcelona in 2011 and had a participation of 21.37 per cent of the population of the city (BarcelonaDecideix, 2001).

Changes in the perception and behaviour of citizens are obvious also from the fact that after the emergence of the crisis citizens created new platforms to support the weakest members of society. An example in this regard is the platform of people affected by the evictions (*PAH*) or the *StopPujades* dedicated to opposing the rising price of public services (Castells, 2013), as well as movements with a strong presence in the social networks, less organised or not organised at all, and in general without a clear leadership.

This ideological change entailed the need for updating the strategies of the government, and, of course, for renewal of the institutions. In the case of Barcelona's transformation it led to a model of decision-making, especially related to planning decisions, and new instruments for participation, some of the most important starting in 2014 such as the new open governance project.

The combination of the previously described facts has forced local governments to be the first to implement changes in organisational models to adapt to the new requirements of citizens as well to make rational use of resources in order to serve more people with less money, simplifying the bureaucratic steps in order to provide more fluid communication. In this context the following subsections describe the changes experimented in relation to the participatory process in the city, a field that is between the ideological and the institutional one, as well as the institutional changes that converged in the creation of the Metropolitan Area of Barcelona.

Public participation challenges

In this subsection, two processes, the referendum of La Diagonal and the new open governance project of Barcelona, are presented. The consultation process for the future of La Diagonal, one of the main avenues of the city, was considered one of the biggest experiments with regard to public participation. This pioneering initiative intended to directly involve the residents in the decision-making process about the urbanisation of the avenue, surpassing the existing stakeholder model described in the previous paragraph. This process was one of the first initiatives undertaken by the public institutions in order to address the citizens' new claims for deeper participation, which arose as a result of the crisis. The result was far from expected and had an enormous influence on the strategies developed thereafter (Corrochano, 2014). This process explains how the government of Barcelona has been trying to apply new tools of communication between the administration and the citizens in the middle of the crisis as a possible solution to reconnect with the citizens and combat political disaffection, one of the biggest ideological impacts of the crisis.

The consultation process was an unprecedented case of the exercise of participatory democracy in Barcelona. It took place between 10 and 16 May 2010, one of the worst points of the crisis, and aimed to involve all residents aged over 16 years and registered in the city in the decision on the future of the diagonal. The process was handled in the following manner:

The city government presented three options designed by the city technicians in collaboration with stakeholders such as neighbour associations or commerce associations, organising a huge publicity campaign in order to inform the citizens about the process (*LaVanguardia*, 2010). But the referendum had little pulling power and the registered participation was 12.17 per cent of the people eligible to vote. The option C got 137,474 votes in the consultation issue, which means that about four out of five people voted against the reform of La Diagonal. The option supported by the mayor was option A, which got 11.38 per cent support and the consequences were that after the resignation of some members of the city government the mayor lost the elections after 32 years of socialist government (Barba, 2014).

This experience has been a key point in the development of current participatory processes. No other public consultation has been conducted locally again because of the risks this could pose to local government. The principal conclusions of the process indicate the difficulty of sensitising the message to the public in a society where it is not normal to consult the cities outside the traditional electoral process. Many of the public saw the referendum or public consultation as an opportunity to blame the local government, transforming the vote into a vote against the mayor, similar to the process that occurred in France when the European constitution was voted on (Hawes, 2012). We have to take into account that the popularity of the mayor at that time was very low and in addition many of the public did not understand the importance of the reform of La Diagonal in a context marked by the crisis.

Four main lessons can be drawn from this process. First, the risk taken by the local government in participatory processes when it opts for one of the proposals, as Barcelona's mayor did. Second, the difficulties in making people see the real utility of the vote instead of a global referendum about the city management. Third, there are strong possibilities for political opposition to turn a participatory process with such features into a motion of censure against the government. Finally, in countries with little democratic tradition and no training on the importance of a binding referendum it is not recommended to carry out such processes in contexts of social tension and without the necessary pedagogic effort.

The new mayor of Barcelona chose not to undertake a consultation process because of the risks explained before, instead generating a new methodology that he called Open Government, which tries to fight against political disaffection by including citizens in the decision-making process.

The Open Government project, created in the first quarter of 2014, is a digital initiative on the City Council web page which has tried to meet some of the ideological challenges created by the crisis, such as the lack of confidence and the demand for a more participative democracy. It provides citizens with a tool that lets them follow the current status of the approved municipal budget or the evolution of the debt and the solvency of the city. Through this tool the City Council also publishes a series of indicators that enable the citizens to understand how the council functions, and it contains information on grants and subsidies granted by the council and grouped by category, as well as an annual list of companies that have received major contracts from the administration. Xavier Trias, mayor of Barcelona, has described the project as 'a new way of doing politics to serve the people' (BTV, 2014b; Barcelona City Council, 2014b).

The Open Government initiative could be described as a major attempt at transparency and accountability, as well as a tool of bureaucratic simplification because it allows people to track all open participatory processes, obtain information on completed processes, participate online, follow the contributions of other residents, and make arrangements online thanks to a new application called MobileID. This is an attempt to curb the phenomenon of disaffection and build confidence in institutions, but it is still too early to make an assessment of its results. Apart from its positive side, however, the tool can also create problems like the digital exclusion of people from social segments that have no knowledge about technology, like elderly people or people at risk of social exclusion. Apart from this initiative, efforts have also been dedicated to finding other ways of rationalisation and transparency, such as the creation of the Metropolitan Area of Barcelona.

The Metropolitan Area of Barcelona

The creation of the Metropolitan Area of Barcelona (AMB) in July 2010, two years after the beginning of the crisis, was considered to be one of the most ambitious plans for the institutional reform of Barcelona (Muñiz & García-López, 2013). The AMB can be defined as the public administration of the metropolitan Barcelona. It occupies $636 \, km^2$ and comprises 36 municipalities with a population of more than 3.2 million. It is the largest metropolitan sprawl in the western Mediterranean, and generates half of the yearly GDP in Catalonia (IDESCAT, 2014). This new civil metropolitan administration was created to replace the three entities that had existed until 2011 (the Union of Municipalities of the Metropolitan Area of Barcelona, the Environmental Agency, and the Metropolitan Transport). The introduction of the single administration was meant to simplify the existing administrative levels that as shown above were one of the causes of the amplification of the international crisis in the national context.

The creation of this new institution has been accompanied by a new legal framework that has also reinforced the new metropolitan government by awarding it new powers and objectives. The new law (DOGC, 2010) envisions that the metropolitan urban master plan is elaborated by the new administration, which provides spatial planning instruments tailored to the needs and requirements of the different municipalities included in the new institutions. The Metropolitan Area also has a Planning Commission, which ensures that all subjects of interest to the 36 urban municipalities are analysed according to a joint planning group (AMB, n.d. a).

In addition, the AMB has also played a role in the sphere of environmental preservation. It includes for instance provisions for preservation of natural areas and also manages 30 km of the metropolitan beaches and has developed a comprehensive maintenance network of the 31 metropolitan parks (ibid.). In relation to mobility aspects it prepares and approves the Metropolitan Urban Mobility Plan. AMB now coordinates the transport in 36 metropolitan municipalities. It has also acquired competencies in the field of economic and social development to promote economic activity and strategic planning and promote employment and entrepreneurship.

The new governing body of the new administration is the Metropolitan Council, which currently comprises 89 metropolitan advisers. Each of the 36 municipalities has a number of members in proportion to their demographic weight. The mayors of the municipalities are ex officio members of the council, in addition to the councillors appointed by the city councils up to the number stipulated for each municipality (AMB, n.d. b).

The new administration, created in the middle of the worst period of the economic crisis, has been a key factor in Barcelona's recuperation. It provides a legal and institutional framework that allows Barcelona to face the future in a coherent and rational way, integrating the city and the adjacent municipalities in a new administration that only reflects a reality that already existed. This is because the Metropolitan Area has been a territorial, social, demographic, economic, and cultural entity that has been forming over the last century as a product of growth and connection of urban systems surrounding the city of Barcelona. The AMB is considered one of the biggest institutional changes undertaken as a consequence of the rationalisation process needed to manage the crisis. It saves resources and streamlines operations in the Metropolitan Area, but it also has some problems that should be considered, especially with regard to public knowledge and transparency. Few people really know how it works, and the fact that its organs of government are not elected directly but indirectly through municipal voting in different cities could generate problems of accountability and transparency. In fact, one of the biggest problems we face when we study the impact of the AMB, is that there are no studies about the perception of citizens. That is why it is a very interesting topic for further research. We need more time for a deeper analysis of the success or failure of these initiatives.

Conclusions

The crisis Spain has experienced has not been caused only by international factors, but has also occurred because of institutional weaknesses bequeathed by the Spanish transition process. The emergence of the international financial and economic crisis caused a number of factors that helped to accelerate the bursting of the housing bubble, which had dramatic consequences for Spanish society. It is from this time that Barcelona City Council began to rethink Barcelona, applying new tools and updating some policies to the needs of the new era. These responses to the crisis are in three fundamental areas.

The material one, which has been mainly structured through a reformulation of municipal budgets, aimed at meeting the basic needs of citizens and maximising the pre-existing resilience to the crisis. Also, new ways of financing public works, such as the PPP route, have also generated new synergies in civil society.

The ideological one is characterised by the recognition of the new demands of the population. The City Council is trying to answer these demands through reforms towards greater transparency and public participation surpassing the existing mechanisms and opening possibilities for new ways of governance.

Finally, the institutional level, heavily influenced by the previous two, is living a transformation, trying to adapt itself to the new demands of the society through the open government project and the creation of a new administration that seeks to rationalise the previous administrative levels, avoiding duplication and simplifying interaction with citizens. Although it is too early to assess some of these changes, the reality is that Barcelona seems to be generating a breeding ground for future growth, understanding that the institutional factor, transparency, and accountability are key elements of resilience.

The novelty of many of these projects, processes, and institutions suggests the need for further analysis to check their actual impact not only on society but also on the efficiency of the city. Analysis of the impact of the new Open Government strategy is a good example of a topic for further research.

References

AMB (n.d. a) Metropolitan area: Urban planning. [Online] Available from: www.amb.cat/s/web/territori/urbanisme/planejament-urbanistic.html [accessed 21 October 2014].

AMB (n.d. b) Governance of the metropolitan area of Barcelona. [Online] Available from: www.amb.cat/web/amb/govern-metropolita [accessed 21 October 2014].

Amnesty International (2014) *Malos tratos y torturas*: *Report about abuse and torture*. [Online] Available from: www.es.amnesty.org/paises/espana/tortura-y-malos-tratos/ [accessed 16 October 2014].

Ara (2012) La situació del mercat immobiliari a Barcelona. *Diari Ara*. [Online] Available from: http://emprenem.ara.cat/opendata/2012/04/26/la-situacio-del-mercat-immobiliari-a-barcelona/ [accessed 24 October 2014].

Barcelona City Council (2014a) *Barcelona's budget 2014*. [Online] Available from: http://premsa.bcn.cat/wp-content/uploads/2013/10/Presentaci%C3%B3-Pressupost-2014.pdf [accessed 7 November 2014].

Barcelona City Council (2014b) Open government. [Online] Available from: http://governobert.bcn.cat/en [accessed 21 October 2014].

BarcelonaDecideix (2001) 21, 37% Barcelona decides makes history. *BarcelonaDecideix*. [Online] Available from: www.barcelonadecideix.cat/noticia/4132/21-37-barcelona-decidex-fa-historia [accessed 7 November 2014].

Barba, C. C. (2014) Urbanismo participativo: Realidad teórica y ficción práctica. *Boletín CF+ S*. [Online] Available from: http://habitat.aq.upm.es/boletin/n56/nred.html [accessed 19 May 2015].

BDE (Bank of Spain) (2008) *Annual report 2008*. [Online] Available from: www.bde.es/f/webbde/SES/Secciones/Publicaciones/PublicacionesAnuales/InformesAnuales/08/cap5.pdf [accessed 22 October 2014].

Blanco, I. (2009) Gobernanza urbana y políticas de regeneración: El caso de Barcelona. *Revista Española de Ciencia Política*, 20, 125–146. Madrid, Trama Editorial.

BOE (official gazette of the Government of Spain) (1998) B-A-1998–8788. [Online] Available from: www.boe.es/buscar/doc.php?id=BOE-A-1998-8788 [accessed 16 October 2014].

BOE (official gazette of the Government of Spain) (2012) Organic Law 2/2012. 27 April 2012. [Online] Available from: www20.gencat.cat/docs/portaljuridic/02-Actualitat/ Documents/LO_2_2012.pdf [accessed 1 December 2014].

BTV (Barcelona's Broadcast service) (2014a) The City Council increased the budget for food subsidies to 5.7 million. *Barcelona Televisió*. [Online] Available from: www.btv.cat/ btvnoticies/2014/05/23/l%E2%80%99ajuntament-incrementa-el-pressupost-per-a-beques-menjador-fins-als-57-milions-d%E2%80%99euros/ [accessed 7 November 2014].

BTV (Barcelona's Broadcast service) (2014b) Barcelona presents the Open Government portal, which includes indicators of the functioning of the city. *Barcelona Televisió*. [Online] Available from: www.btv.cat/btvnoticies/2014/02/21/barcelona-presenta-el-portal-govern-obert-que-aplega-indicadors-del-funcionament-de-la-ciutat/ [accessed 1 September 2014].

Casellas, A. (2007) Gobernabilidad, participación ciudadana y crecimiento económico: Adaptaciones locales a estrategias globales. *Scripta Nova*, XI (243). [Online] Available from: http://ddd.uab.cat/pub/artpub/2007/113552/scripta_a2007m7d10vXIn243a13.pdf [accessed 17 December 2014].

Castells, M. (2013) *Networks of outrage and hope: Social movements in the internet age.* Cambridge, John Wiley & Sons. Ed. Polity Press.

Catalunya Caixa (2010) Report on the consumer and family economics. *Caixa Catalunya*, (59). [Online] Available from: www.catalunyacaixa.com/docsdlv/Portal/Ficheros/ Documentos/informe_es3.pdf [accessed 20 October2014].

CincoDias (2007) Zapatero announced that Spain will achieve 'full employment' in the next legislature. [Online] Available from: http://cincodias.com/cincodias/2007/07/03/ economia/1183598608_850215.html [accessed 7 November 2014].

CIS (Centre of Sociological Studies) (2014) *Barometer October 2014.* [Online] Available from: www.cis.es/cis/opencms/ES/index.html [accessed 7 November 2014].

Corrochano, C. (2014) Urbanismo participativo: Realidad teórica y ficción práctica. *Boletín CF+ S*, 51. [Online] Available from: http://habitat.aq.upm.es/boletin/n56/nred. html [accessed 16 October 2014].

DOGC (official gazette of the Government of Catalonia) (2010) Law 31/2010. Metropolitan Area of Barcelona. *DOGC*. 3 August 2010. [Online] Available from: http://gov-ernacio.gencat.cat/web/.content/mon_local/documents/arxius/llei31_metropolitana.pdf [accessed 21 October 2014].

Echeverría, J. (2008) *La burbuja inmobiliaria española.* Barcelona, Ed. Marcial Pons.

Economist, The (2005) The global housing boom: In come the waves. *The Economist*. [Online] Available from: www.economist.com/node/4079027 [accessed 22 September 2014].

Economist (2013) Housing in Spain: Mortgaged to the hilt. *The Economist*. [Online] Available from: www.economist.com/news/europe/21576717-after-house-price-crash-come-repossessionsand-angry-response-mortgaged-hilt [accessed 16 October 2014].

Ediciones La Vanguardia (2013) Nike, remove the Barca shirt, off the statue of Columbus. [Online] Available from: www.lavanguardia.com/vida/20130609/54375824951/ nike-retira-camiseta-barsa-colon.html [accessed 24 October 2014].

El Economista (2014) The debt of the City of Madrid is six times greater than that of Barcelona. [Online] Available from: www.eleconomista.es/economia/noticias/5788439/05/14/-La-deuda-del-ayuntamiento-de-Madrid-es-seis-veces-mayor-que-la-de-Barcelona.html [accessed 7 November2014].

El Mundo (2011) Trias wants to reduce to 30 days the payment to suppliers and licensing. [Online] Available from: www.elmundo.es/elmundo/2011/09/14/barcelona/1316011195. html [accessed 7 November 2014].

El País (1997) Fomento dice que la ley del Suelo acabará con la especulación de los ayuntamientos. [Online] Available from: http://elpais.com/diario/1997/03/14/economia/ 858294019_850215.html [accessed 16 September 2014].

El País (2011) Trias last full privatization of funeral services of Barcelona. [Online] Available from: http://ccaa.elpais.com/ccaa/2013/09/05/catalunya/1378408472_535941. html [accessed 20 October 2014].

EuropaPress (2013) Metro Station 'Sol' renamed 'Vodafone Sol' over the next three years. [Online] Available from: www.europapress.es/madrid/noticia-estacion-metro-sol-pasara-denominarse-vodafone-sol-proximos-tres-anos-20130601090014.html [accessed 14 October 2014].

FAVB (2012) *Report: Neighbors associations in Barcelona.* [Online] Available from: www.favb.cat/ [accessed 18 September 2014].

GESTHA (Technicians' Union of the Ministry of Finance) (2011) Reduce tax evasion and the underground economy. [Online] Available from: www.gestha.es/archivos/ informacion/monograficos/2011/reducir-el-fraude-fiscal-y-la-economia-sumergida.pdf [accessed 20 October 2014].

Hawes, D. (2012) Political allegiance after European integration. *Journal of Contemporary European Studies*, 20 (3), 409–410.

Huertas, J. (1997) El moviment ciutada a Barcelona i l'aparicio del Pla General Metropolita. *Regió Metropolitana de Barcelona: Territori, estratègies, planijament*, 28. [Online] Available from: www.raco.cat/index.php/PapersIERMB/article/viewArticle/ s102596/0 [accessed 20 September 2014].

IDESCAT (2014) Idescat. Statistical Agency of Catalonia. [Online] Available from: www.idescat.cat/es/ [accessed 10 September 2014].

INE (Spanish National Institutute of Statistics) (2014) [Online] Available from: www.ine. es/ [accessed 16 October 2014].

LaVanguardia (2010) The failure of the consultation of the Diagonal is carried forward to the Deputy Mayor. [Online] Available from: www.lavanguardia.com/vida/20100516/ 53928946995/el-fracaso-de-la-consulta-de-la-diagonal-se-lleva-por-delante-al-primer-teniente-de-alcalde.html [accessed 20 September 2014].

LaVanguardia (2014) Results 9N: Support for independence achieved 81%. [Online] Available from: www.lavanguardia.com/politica/20141110/54419122198/resultados-9n.html [accessed 2 December 2014].

Martínez-Conde, F. (1979) Las fuerzas armadas en la constitución española. *Revista de Estudios Políticos*, 12. [Online] Available from: http://dialnet.unirioja.es/servlet/articul o?codigo=1273154&orden=0&info=link [accessed 20 October 2014].

Metroscopia (2014) *Report: Polls and social and opinion research. Social climate.* [Online] Available from: www.metroscopia.org/datos-recientes/climasocial [accessed 6 October 2014].

Montaner, L. (1996) Los estatutos de autonomia y los pactos autonómicos. *Revista de Estudios Regionales*, 44, 47–68. [Online] Available from: http://dialnet.unirioja.es/ servlet/articulo?codigo=252208&orden=186611&info=link [accessed 6 October 2014].

Muñiz, I. & García-López, M. (2013) Anatomía de la dispersión urbana en Barcelona. *EURE*, 39 (116), 189–219. [Online] Available from: www.scielo.cl/scielo. php?pid=S0250-71612013000100008&script=sci_arttext [accessed 20 November 2014].

Redondo, J. (2007) Crecimiento y especulación inmobiliaria en la economía española. *Principios, Estudios de Economía Política.* [Online] Available from: www.academia. edu/download/31010114/Crecimiento_y_Especulacion.pdf [accessed 6 October 2014].

Rodríguez de Arce, I. (2014) *La España contemporanea (1975–2012): Evolución política y marco constitucional.* Milano, EduCatt.

Romero, J. (2010) Construcción residencial y gobierno del territorio en España: De la burbuja especulativa a la recesión: Causas y consecuencias. *Cuadernos Geográficos de La Universidad de la Universidad de Granada*, 47 (2), 17–46.

Royo, S. (2014) Institutional degeneration and the economic crisis in Spain. *American Behavioral Scientist.* [Online] Available from: http://abs.sagepub.com/content/early/20 14/05/28/0002764214534664.abstract [accessed 6 October 2014].

Solanes, P. & Molinero, C. (2014) *La cuestión catalana: Cataluña en la transición española.* Barcelona, Grupo Planeta.

Transparency International (2014) *Index of transparency of the Spanish Autonomous Communities.* [Online] Available from: www.transparencia.org.es/INCAU_A%C3%91OS_ ANTERIORES.htm [accessed 16 October 2014].

Villoria, M. & Jiménez, F. (2012) La corrupción en España (2004–2010): Datos percepción y efectos. *Revista Española de Investigaciones Sociológicas*, 138 (1), 109–134.

Ysàs, P. (1994) Democracia y autonomía en la transición española. *Ayer.* [Online] Available from: www.jstor.org/stable/41320059 [accessed 7 November 2014].

14 From crisis to crisis

Dynamics of change and emerging models of governance in the Turin Metropolitan Area

Nadia Caruso, Giancarlo Cotella, and Elena Pede

Introduction

The global financial and economic crisis started in 2008 and continues to date in the form of a sovereign debt crisis that has added a further dimension to the increasing social and economic complexities of contemporary urban life (Cash et al., 2006; Gibson, Ostrom, & Ahn, 2000; Holling, 2004). The crisis has generated growing challenges for territorial governance, as it has been traditionally conceived in the different European Union (EU) member states. Answers had to be developed within the ongoing process of consolidation of a so-called multi-level governance model that, since the advent of globalisation, redefines the distribution of powers and competences from the local to the EU scale, from public authority to the private sector (ESPON, 2013).

The crisis, the development of complex cooperation and competitive relations between cities, the emergence of a new form of territorial governance, and the process of globalisation itself have put cities at the heart of the turmoil in multiple ways. On the one hand, public administrations have experienced a crisis of the tools that have been traditionally adopted to manage territorial transformation and which, in the majority of the contexts, consisted of local land-use plans now ill-equipped to interpret the heterogeneity and fluidity of contemporary urban phenomena. On the other hand, cities and their regions have quickly become key institutional laboratories for restructuring territorial governance, and for experimental policy-making. Nowadays, confronted with a further wave of austerity urbanism, politicians and urban managers continue to look for new strategies to cope with the intensified contradiction between shrinking resources on the one side, and the need to guarantee development and cohesion on the other.

To shed some light on this process, it is worth trying to link the evolution of territorial governance arrangements in a specific territory to the contextual conditions that may have influenced them. This chapter discusses the various territorial governance initiatives that have emerged in the context of the Turin Metropolitan Area[1] in the last 20 years,[2] reading them in the light of the two crises that affected the city in the 1980s and in the late 2000s. The case of Turin has been chosen due to its peculiar history in the Italian framework, characterised by waves of crisis and recovery that started in the early 1980s, when the shift from Fordism to post-Fordism undermined the economy of the most successful Italian one-company town (Bagnasco, 1986; Governa, Rossignolo, & Saccomani, 2009). Building on the recent literature about 'planning with soft spaces and fuzzy boundaries' (Allmendinger & Haughton, 2009, 2010; Haughton et al., 2011), the authors show how traditional territorial governance has been increasingly paralleled by a heterogeneous set of 'softer' policies and tools for boundaries that vary 'fuzzily' in relation to the issues at stake, the actors involved, and other factors.

After a brief introduction to the ongoing debate over the tensions between 'hard' and 'soft' spaces in territorial governance, and to the methodology of analysis in the second section of this chapter, the text in the third section presents the evolution dynamics of Turin's Metropolitan Area, starting from the local crisis of the 1980s up to the recent global economic crisis. The analysis in the fourth section then focuses on the territorial governance models that emerged during the last 20 years, subdividing them into 'hard' and 'soft' geographies and reflecting upon their characteristics in terms of scale, statutory character, actors involved, and geographical and thematic scope. A concluding section rounds off the contribution, discussing the presented results in light of an additional territorial layer, which will be introduced to the Italian institutional system in 2015: metropolitan cities. As will be shown, this process derives more from reasons of economic austerity than from a thorough analysis of actual territorial governance needs.

Territorial governance between 'hard' and 'soft' tensions facing new challenges

The systems of institutions regulating territorial development are both path-dependent and context-dependent. They are centred on those spatial organisation models that have characterised each peculiar context through the ages. Territorial governance models developed incrementally, through the juxtaposition and evolution of answers developed to tackle the negative effects of urban and territorial transformations.

In particular, since the 1970s, as a consequence of the rise of globalisation, spatial interdependencies between cities and territories increased rapidly (Veltz, 1998) and development became more and more embedded in the local–global dialectic of a new 'space of flows' (Castells, 1989), characterised by hyper-connectivity and fragmentation at the same time. In turn, this brought along a series of dramatic challenges for institutions, spatial policies, and processes, aimed at steering urban development, and led to their progressive redefinition (Bagnasco & Le Galès, 2001; Le Galès, 2002; ESPON, 2007, 2013). Traditional territorial governance models proved to be ill-equipped to efficiently cope with challenges that were barely manageable within fixed administrative borders. Although this process did not lead to the end of traditional territorial governance, however, it allowed for the consolidation of two overlapping models, as described in the work of Hooghe and Marks on multilevel governance (2001,

2003). On the one hand, a first type of (multilevel) territorial governance continued to insist upon non-intersecting, general-purpose territorial jurisdictions
arranged in a hierarchical way. On the other hand, a second type of (multilevel)
territorial governance started to emerge as a complex, fluid patchwork of
innumerable, overlapping jurisdictions, defined case by case in relation to specific problems, tasks, or types of territory. While the former continues to be
strongly related to territorial borders and jurisdictions, nested in the traditional,
hierarchical fashion, in the latter it is not the jurisdictional borders that determine
governance arrangements, but the problems or issues at stake, which are very
much related to the individual characteristics of a specific place or territory.

In contraposition to the 'hard' character of the space, commonly regulated by
traditional territorial governance, a new, 'softer' set of processes emerged,
grounded in territories defined through 'fuzzy' boundaries that vary in relation to
the policy issue at stake (Allmendinger & Haughton, 2009, 2010; Faludi, 2011;
Haughton et al., 2011; Adams, Cotella, & Nunes, 2011). As a matter of fact:

> even though many implementation networks are situated at the regional or
> local level, their boundaries often do not converge with any administrative
> delineations. In addition, they are often of a more ephemeral nature.... In
> that sense, functional need ... is the key concept.
>
> (Conzelmann, 2008: p. 26)

The concept of 'soft spaces' that is the basis of the territorial governance
arrangements of the second type described by Hooghe and Marks signals an
attempt to understand the implications of relational and non-state-centric geographies for spatial planning and territorial governance, and refers to the emergence
of 'alternative administrative geographies' in the context of new governance
arrangements for spatial planning and development (Haughton & Allmendinger,
2008: p. 143). Here, soft spaces are viewed both as a policy tool facilitating the
cross-sectoral policy coordination ambitions of strategic spatial planning, as well
as an attempt to break away from the constraints of the formal scalar hierarchies
of traditional spatial planning systems:

> There is also an emergent resort to new multi-area subregions for strategy
> making and policy delivery, evident at various scales of regeneration, plan-
> ning, and other domains, breaking away from the rigidities associated with the
> formal scales of statutory plan-making. The emergence of these 'soft spaces'
> is an important trend, which alongside the tactical use of 'fuzzy boundaries' is
> related to a policy impetus to break away from the shackles of pre-existing
> working patterns which might be variously held to be slow, bureaucratic, or
> not reflecting the real geographies of problems and opportunities.
>
> (Allmendinger & Haughton, 2009: p. 619)

The elements highlighted in the above discussion constitute a useful starting
point for exploration of the way external pressures impact the urban system, and,

particularly, ways to deal with the challenges these changes have caused. In more detail, one may assume that the occurrence of a crisis, such as that which recently struck the developed economies, generates dramatic framework changes that punctuate the equilibrium[3] of urban regimes (Mossberger & Stoker, 2001), thus leading to the emergence and consolidation of new models of territorial governance. The new answers may be 'harder' or 'softer' in nature, more institutionalised, or take the shape of ad hoc responses to critical challenges and to emerging opportunities. They constitute, at the same time, (i) a consequence of the new conditions (positive or negative) and opportunities that characterise the evolving scenario, and (ii) a series of attempts to deal with the challenges brought by the latter. In any case, they move away from traditional territorial governance tools grounded on the existing administrative jurisdictions, and require the introduction of new, overlapping scales of governance, often delimited by fuzzy boundaries, and obeying, above all, two main complementary logical requirements: (i) an increase of the efficiency of territorial governance processes, and (ii) a better reflection on the real geographies of the issues under consideration.

Building on these assumptions, it is interesting to explore the chronological evolution of the territorial governance initiatives that characterise a specific territory, and to try to build some casual links between these initiatives and the contextual conditions that may have triggered their initiation. As the experience of Turin will show, although responses to the crisis may be drawn from a very heterogeneous array of potential policies, nowadays the concepts of austerity and investment containment are mostly applied to both hard and soft spaces.

The crises of Turin, from local to global

The case of Turin has many elements of interest. First of all, the city is the most famous one-company town in Italy. Until the 1970s, most of the economic development of its Metropolitan Area was linked to the car industry, and the actions of the local authorities suffered from the hegemonic influence of the will of the leading company, FIAT.[4] In the beginning of the 1980s, the area was hit by a deep car industry crisis that continued throughout the 1990s and caused dramatic social and economic structural changes. During this period the local governments initiated and led a series of innovative governance processes. These were more similar to the processes led by generally European cities facing similar conditions than to the actions undertaken by other Italian towns/cities. Nowadays Turin, as most of the cities in the Mediterranean countries, faces a new crisis, the origin of which is not local, but global. Once again the city is suffering from a weak economic system that is still based around the industrial sector, and is looking for a new economic vocation.

It should be noted that the local crisis of the 1980s and 1990s and the efforts to overcome it, running in parallel with a crucial constitutional reform of Italian local public administration, has contributed to strengthening the political ability to tackle a crisis. On the other hand, the present global crisis evolved under different conditions, including less public funds and a recentralisation of public policies. The current crisis, in fact, is a financial crisis, whereas the crisis of the 1980s to 1990s was much more related to a specific sector (car industry crisis, post-Fordism transition). A chronological overview of the two crisis periods allows for a better understanding of the changes in the framework conditions and provides a useful background against which to read the models of governance that emerged in response.

Life and decline of a one-company town

As already argued, Turin was the most popular Fordist city in Italy, whose development and international identity were based on the car industry. From the last quarter of the nineteenth century until the 1970s, the social and economic structure of the city and many aspects of its life in particular were organised in subordination to the company (Saccomani, 2003). As a consequence of FIAT's success in the post-war period, Turin's population almost doubled in 20 years (1951–1971), growing by around 50,000 inhabitants each year.[5] Most of the new inhabitants were migrants from the south of Italy. They first settled in the new residential districts of the city, and then spread towards other municipalities in the Metropolitan Area. This became possible because of the establishment of several mechanic and automotive components factories belonging to the FIAT supply chain.

City life followed the industry strategies and the economic sectors and the policies of the local government were all also influenced by FIAT. Municipal authorities were a keen sponsor of Turin's industrial expansion and in many cases they adopted a laissez-faire attitude towards the company's decisions and actions. For its part, the company did not operate towards the general improvement of the city and its citizens' conditions. It exerted its strong influence on specific urban areas following business-oriented logics. This led to spiralling rents and to unregulated private housing constructions that were understandardised (Winkler, 2007). Workers' living conditions and the poor quality of public services caused regular strikes and a strong working-class activism. The 'hot autumn' of strikes of 1969 marked the prologue to FIAT's slow decline. In the following years, the number of strikes and demonstrations reached the peak, with students and workers fighting together, claiming civil rights and better working conditions. In the 1970s and 1980s the crisis hit the whole automotive sector, and FIAT started a dramatic phase of work termination and redundancy payments.[6]

While the national government continued to support FIAT through the introduction of public subsidies as state 'CIGS' benefits[7] to laid-off workers, this was no longer sufficient to maintain the company's competitiveness and productivity. The decline of the car industry quickly affected the whole supply chain, hitherto the main economic engine of the region, leading to exponentially increasing unemployment rates and to a diffuse feeling of social insecurity (Bagnasco, 1990). The strong specialisation of the regional economic system, centred exclusively around the car industry, at once revealed its dramatic weakness, starting a domino effect that brought the majority of other satellite activities down with it. The demission of the industrial sector reached its peak in 1983 and 1984 and culminated in a generalised crisis for the whole Metropolitan Area.

From crisis to crisis

As a consequence of the industrial crisis, the Metropolitan Area of Turin had to reinvent its economic future under post-Fordist auspices. During the 1990s the concomitance of various factors allowed for the consolidation of a new paradigm of urban development, relying on 'softer' territorial governance tools. First of all, a set of reforms, promoted by the Italian government in 1993, introduced, among other things, the direct election of mayors, thus increasing their power and resources (Law 81/1993). On the wave of this local government resurgence, two major activities were undertaken the success of which served as a framework for the progressive recovery of the city: the elaboration and the implementation of the First Strategic Spatial Plan (2000) and the successful candidacy to host the 2006 Winter Olympic Games. Both activities gained the necessary political will and the resources for the transformation of Turin's heritage of industrial brownfields, mostly located in the inner town.[8] Although projects related to Turin's 2006 Olympic Games were added to the Strategic Plan only in its closing phase, it is undeniable that the Olympic event and the media attention acted as a virtuous sounding board for the urban transformation of the city and played a crucial role in the promotion of a new identity for the whole Metropolitan Area (Bondonio et al., 2007). In this light one could argue that, despite the usual problems accompanying large-scale events,[9] the real success of the Olympics in Turin was the cultural change that they triggered. Turin was no longer the traditional Fordist city, but a vivid, attractive area able to attract investments and tourists.

The change of perspective mentioned allowed for a period of relatively slow growth, which saw the consolidation of the local creative industry in parallel to the hosting of several large-scale events (the XXIII International Congress of Architects in 2008, the 150th anniversary of the unification of the country in 2011, as well as several other sports events), all to the benefit of the economic development of the city. The city continued to benefit from the outcomes of the activities undertaken during the 1990s as a consequence of the industrial crisis. During this period, various networks of local stakeholders, more or less consolidated, started to cooperate in different issues. Even if the First Strategic Plan did not take into account the whole Metropolitan Area, the Winter Olympic Games allowed for a focus on a wider dimension, linking the city and the surrounding mountain areas, thus creating the illusion of a sound amalgamation of the urban area and its surroundings that was missing in previous Turin-centric policies.[10] It must be said that all events and ceremonies were hosted in Turin, whereas only some of the competitions took place in the mountains.

However, while the Olympics marked the greatest moment of fame for the city, they also represented the end of the vibrant renewal. In the continuous search for new vocations and economic development, the Metropolitan Area's transforming economic structure was still vulnerable, and it was hit harder by the global financial crisis than the economies of other Italian areas. Whereas the whole country was stricken by increased social-economical vulnerability, rising unemployment, growing social and territorial inequalities, and the almost complete withdrawal of public investments, Turin faces a more severe situation. It has become the poorest city in northern Italy, with the highest young unemployment rate in the area. The current crisis and the heavy burden of public debt decrease the capacity of the city to react. The economic reconversion measures promoted in recent decades did not effectively shield the economy of the Metropolitan Area from the financial crisis. The relatively slow growth experienced during the first half of the 2000s, thanks to the continuous organisation of international events, melted like ice in the sun as soon as the crisis hit home, preventing the hope for transformation to an international cultural service hub, and leaving the area once again at the mercy of its industrial heritage. The main reason could be identified in the timing of the current crisis: it struck too soon, while the economic structure of the city was still changing. Turin was struck heavier because it was in the middle of a reconversion process, with the new activities (promoting growth) that were not solid enough to survive the crisis.

It should be noted, however, that the framework conditions of the current situation differ substantially from those of the past. From the second quarter of 2007 to 2012 the Italian GDP fell by –8.8 per cent (Eurostat data), the unemployment rate in January 2014 was 12.9 per cent, and since 2005 the number of poor people in the country has doubled (and tripled in the north) (ISTAT data). The crisis had stronger impacts on the regions with strong reliance on the industrial and export sectors. In the Piedmont region (Turin's region), in 2009 GDP decreased by 7.7 per cent, the worst loss in the north of Italy, thus the economic recovery process has been slower and harder than in other areas (Table 14.1). The annual report on Turin (Davico & Staricco, 2013) underlines a decrease of 1.4 per cent of income per person and a higher bankruptcy of business and lower birth rate than the other Metropolitan Areas of Italy.

Another difference relates to the financial assets of Italian municipalities. In 1999 the national Financial Law introduced the Internal Stability Pact (ISP), a tool aimed at preventing an uncontrolled increase in public expenditure and, in

Table 14.1 Development of economy in the Piedmont Region: average annual rates compared with the reference year 2000 (%)

	2001–2007	2008	2009	2010	2011	2012
Gross domestic product	0.8	–2.0	–7.7	2.0	0.5	–2.0
Domestic consumption	2.2	2.4	1.7	–0.8	–0.8	–1.5
Domestic demand	1.0	–2.0	–4.3	1.2	–0.2	–3.6
Value added	0.8	–2.1	–7.9	2.4	0.8	–1.9

Source: authors' elaboration on: I-trend 2013, www.regione.piemonte.it/industria/sist_info/dwd/2014/i_trend.pdf.

turn, in the national public debt. The ISP has important consequences for municipalities, as it poses rigid norms in relation to expenditure, strongly limiting public investment in development. In addition, the relatively high flow of funds running from the state and regional governments to the municipalities in the 1990s decreased by some 70 per cent during the 2000s, further worsening the situation for local budgets (website of Comune di Torino). As recently as 2013 the Municipality of Turin had more than €35 million funding cuts compared to the previous year from the state and regional governments. This important funding reduction is barely justified by the aim of decreasing the national debt. In fact, the debts of municipalities count for only 5.4 per cent of the national debt.

In recent years, the city of Turin has had to face the described scarcity of local public resources, on top of the huge financial debt derived from the loans obtained to sustain the Winter Olympic Games, and has therefore been unable to promote any relevant development programme.[11] Similarly, due to the economic sufferings of the majority of the other municipalities, as well as of the private sector, and to the lack of external funding opportunities, the activation of virtuous partnership aimed at territorial development is barely possible, and with it replication of the development strategies that characterised the 1990s.

Although there seems to be a general consensus regarding the need to come up with new ways to foster development in the face of the current global financial crisis, the path to follow appears uncertain. On the one hand, the general current conditions of the crisis hamper the capacity of local institutions to react through the creation of ad hoc 'soft spaces' as they did in the 1990s; on the other hand, the solution proposed by the central government is based on the creation of new 'hard spaces', hoping to reduce costs and to provide, at the same time, new input to the local system to tackle the crisis.

Geographies of governance in the Metropolitan Area of Turin

By virtue of the described sequence of crisis and recovery periods and of their various features, Turin's Metropolitan Area constitutes an interesting case study. In particular, the various attempts developed by the municipalities of the Metropolitan Area, as well as by other actors, to overcome the challenges that the periods of crisis brought with them, gave birth to a heterogeneous array of territorial governance initiatives. A first analysis of these episodes of cooperation shows how their characteristics vary widely in relation to different parameters, including (i) the temporal phase when they emerged; (ii) the issue(s) at stake; (iii) the territorial scale at which they originated; and (iv) the number of municipalities involved. In particular, it is possible to undertake a preliminary differentiation between 'hard' and 'soft' geographies of territorial governance as follows:

* *Hard geographies* of territorial governance are those forms of cooperation introduced by the government, often through national or regional law, in

order to manage social and territorial factors (services, public goods, etc.) through the introduction of new authorities, with specific competences within defined borders. Each group of hard geographies covers the entire territory of Italy (or of a region, in the case of those instituted by regional law) and could, for instance, be in charge of the management of public services such as health care, water provision, garbage collection, waste disposal etc., or focus on more general purposes, such as the Mountain or Hill Communities. These geographies have designed various geometries that depend on the issue at stake, and vary from one issue to another.[12]

- On the other hand, *soft geographies* of territorial governance are forms of cooperation between municipalities and other possible partners (different public authorities or private actors), created to address specific needs, to promote and implement projects and/or programmes, to exploit funding opportunities, etc. They are often path-dependent and influenced by territorial specificities, institutional capacities, and the long-term strategies and political will of the actors involved. This kind of geography may last for decades, transforming themselves, becoming more or less institutionalised, enlarging their boundaries, opening up or varying their aims. Alternatively, they may last only for the duration of a project and, built on temporary opportunities (often funding) by a precarious group of partners, disappear at the end of their purpose.

The following paragraphs build upon this classification and present an overview of the 'hard' and 'soft' territorial governance initiatives that have emerged in Turin's Metropolitan Area during the last 25 years.

Hard geographies of governance

As well as regions, provinces, and municipalities, the main hard geographies of governance that cover all the territory of the country as allowed by national laws are: associations of municipalities (the so-called Mountain Communities and Ensembles of Municipalities), water management authorities, waste management authorities, health authorities, and parks and natural areas managing bodies. All are public institutions and manage different types of public services or utilities. Although they were created at different times and not as consequential responses to crisis episodes, they mainly aim to guarantee the more efficient management of a specific area according to a sector of competence or a geographical matter (such as the Mountain Communities), and therefore to rationalise expenditure in times of financial scarcity.

It was possible to identify various types of hard geographies of governance, responsible for portions of the Metropolitan Area of Turin: those mentioned above and others that originate from context-specific aspects. For instance, Hill Communities represent place-specific institutions linked to the morphology of the Piedmont Region, and have similar duties and jurisdiction to the Mountain Communities and to the Municipality Ensembles. Due to the large number of

Italian municipalities with a low number of inhabitants, various regions are working on this type of grouping in order to reduce public expenditure and to improve the efficiency of public service delivery. An analysis of these geographies of governance shows how they form different shapes of territory, focusing on a variable number of involved municipalities (Table 14.2).

Although hard geographies are mainly developed by law, some may also be shaped as partnerships between institutions willing to improve their efficiency in dealing with a specific issue or managing a public service for citizens. In this case, the organisation of specific public service takes over the traditional divisions of duties and powers among several municipalities and managing authorities. This is, for instance, the case for the so-called Mobility Agency, a place-specific institution created in 2003 to address mobility and transportation issues in the Metropolitan Area of Turin. It is geographically shaped around Turin and covers several rings of municipalities, representing an exception in the Italian context, and the first experience of its kind that goes beyond the central municipality's boundaries.

All in all, although the institution of hard geographies does not represent a direct reaction to either of the two crises described in the previous paragraph, these geographies of territorial governance somehow aim to improve (in some cases preserve) the efficiency of public services in times of increasing financial scarcity for local budgets.

Soft geographies of governance

Moving to the soft geographies of governance that emerged in Turin's Metropolitan Area in the past 25 years, it is possible to identify as many as 44 forms of cooperation among public and private actors.[13] These governance initiatives were classified according to the prevalent goals they address when taken from a list of six general themes/fields:[14] (i) rural development; (ii) economic development and

Table 14.2 Hard geographies of governance in Turin's Metropolitan Area

Type	Number of hard geographies	Min.–max. number of municipalities
Mountain communities	11	11–43
Hill communities	17	2–22
Municipalities' ensembles	6	3–10
Water agencies	19	1–43
Waste agencies	8	1–108
Health agencies	20	1–65
Tourism agencies	3	20–46
Mobility agencies	1	32
Protected natural Areas	12	3–37
Landscape authorities	40	1–14

Source: authors' elaboration.

innovation; (iii) public transport and mobility; (iv) urban regeneration and social inclusion; (v) sustainability and renewable energy; (vi) tourism, culture and heritage, environment and landscape, international events. Furthermore, they were subdivided in relation to the year they were instituted, in three time-spans: pre-2000, 2000–2006, and 2007–2013 (Table 14.3).

The territorial priorities of each aggregation are a consequence of various elements, among which are socio-economic, territorial, or political specificities, but also the funding opportunities that characterise a specific time-span. It should also be noted that the aggregations around different themes cover different areas: since soft geographies depend on the will of local actors to aggregate in the framework of a programme or a project, the soft governance arrangements do not cover the complete territory of the region as most of the hard geographies do.

Be that as it may, the increased number of soft geographies demonstrates the attention of the public actors of Turin's Metropolitan Area on experimenting with new governance models to deal more efficiently with the emergencies brought about by the crises. In more detail, the local crisis of the 1980s and 1990s forced the local authorities to put new tools in place to respond to its dramatic consequences. These years were characterised by high shares of resources, derived both from the decentralisation of portions of the national budget as well as from an increase of EU Structural Funds dedicated to territorial priorities (Janin Rivolin, 2003, 2004). The activation of numerous EU and national funding programmes triggered a heterogeneous set of innovative institutional processes at the local scale, allowing at the same time for a comprehensive reaction to the local crisis, built around strategic priorities. For instance, the

Table 14.3 Soft geographies of governance in Turin's Metropolitan Area

Thematic Fields	Number of geographies pre-2000	Number of geographies 2000–2006	Number of geographies post-2007	Total number of geographies
Rural development and fishing	2	3	–	5
Economic development and innovation	6	5	2	13
Public transport and mobility	1	2	3	6
Urban regeneration and social inclusion	–	3	2	5
Sustainability and renewable energy	–	2	–	2
Tourism, culture and heritage, environment and landscape, international events	3	8	2	13

Source: authors' elaboration.

integrated approach promoted by EU initiatives (URBAN, LEADER, INTER-REG) also influenced national and regional programmes that funded various forms of cooperation (such as Territorial Pacts, 'Patti Territoriali') that were created in different decades (e.g. in the 1990s for the Territorial Pacts). The main themes, around which the greatest number of territorial governance geographies was developed, are 'economic development and innovation' and 'tourism, culture and heritage, environment and landscape, international events'. This shows a clear attempt to exploit external funding opportunities in order to respond to the general challenge of the economic transformation process: from the traditional industrial sector to innovation, cultural heritage, landscape, and environmental values, in order to change the external image of the area through international events (as mentioned above). The local crisis was tackled through measures of cooperation launched at the local level, with the local stakeholders that developed new cooperation strategies in order to take advantage of EU, national, and regional funding programmes.[15]

The EU had great influence not only over the financial dimension, but also in relation to the strategic priorities that contributed to inspire the local policies of renovation and diversification. Numerous experiences of inter-municipal cooperation took place until the year 2000, generating a highly heterogeneous set of soft spaces. A plethora of inter-institutional processes of cooperation were implemented in the Metropolitan Area of Turin: programmes and projects concerning mobility, the environment, and socio-economic factors. These forms of coordination and cooperation between different local authorities, and between the latter and specific actors coming from the private sector, also show how difficult it is to identify a static perimeter for the Metropolitan Area, as in fact the dynamics of the challenges that need to be dealt with present, in most of the cases, a variable geometry.

Among the programmes that favoured the aggregation of local actors, an important role was played by the so-called 'Patti Territoriali' (Territorial Pacts), nationally funded programmes which generally aimed to improve the socio-economic conditions of the country. They constituted one of the first forms of bottom-up partnerships among municipalities: goals and initiatives were decided freely by the partners on the basis of their specificities. Other experimental soft geographies of governance were the result of a general local awareness and interest in the promotion of natural areas, and made possible through the EU Community Initiative LEADER. For instance, the creation of specific groups of action (LAG – Local Action Group) created a new attention on the rural environment and its socio-economic characters. Some of those LAGs still exist today, progressively improving the cooperation and integration of several sources of funding.

As Figure 14.1 clearly illustrates, the majority of cooperative initiatives undertaken in the period 2000–2006 continued to focus upon the issues that were topical during the 1990s; however, the number of initiatives increased drastically, and their scope broadened, touching upon other issues such as environmental sustainability and energy security, as well as urban renewal and social cohesion. As noted above, this period lies at the crossroads of the partial emancipation from the effects of the

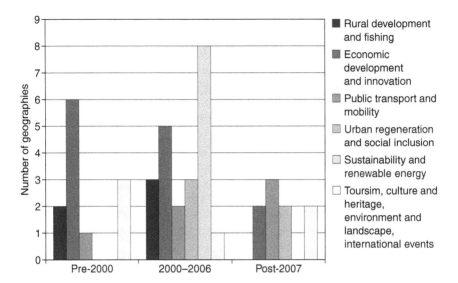

Figure 14.1 Number of soft geographies of governance per issue for the time-spans pre-2000, 2000–2006, and post-2007, for each theme during the time (source: authors' elaboration).

industrial crisis and the progressive triggering of various events and initiatives. This situation, pursued by local actors through participation in several calls for proposals of European and national importance, allowed for a wide experimentation of cooperation forms on several themes, and contributed to the progressive institutionalisation of 'softer' alternative models of territorial governance. An example of these initiatives are the so-called 'Programmi Territoriali Integrati' (Integrated Territorial Programmes) created at the regional level in 2006 to promote the social, cultural, economic, and environmental development of subregional forms of cooperation. These tools were created by the Piedmont Region to promote the cooperation among various municipalities, to value local resources, and to provide services for the citizens. These programmes cannot be considered a crisis response since the worldwide financial crisis had not yet hit Italy in that year. After 2006 the analysed initiatives decreased, those remaining constituted specific projects of cooperation implemented by the clear will and need of some local actors (mainly public authorities).

The most recent years, partially overlapping with the years of the global financial crisis having strong impacts on the territory of Turin's Metropolitan Area, have been characterised by fewer soft geographies of governance. This partly reflects the socio-economic complexity of the current period, with national and European levels that provide less input and fewer triggers in the form of direct funding for cooperation. The majority of aggregations individuated in the analysis focus on the field of transport and mobility. This sector is still well financed by the EU, as well as by the national and the regional governments, as shown by the controversial development of the high speed Turin–Lyon railway in the Susa Valley, as a segment of the Trans-European Network Corridor V.[16] This railway project is considered as soft space in this analysis since it brings along with the hard hierarchies and transformations also a strategic plan of local actions that involve the local municipalities and it was defined though their participation and empowerment. On the other hand, the lack of funding constitutes a major constraint to the bottom-up development of new soft geographies: at different levels public authorities are in severe financial conditions, struggling to maintain basic public services and ordinary activities. The various seasons of national or regional programmes supporting bottom-up cooperation among municipalities and private actors are considered over. Turin's Metropolitan Area, as explained further below, shows that after the financial economic crisis the soft geographies have been greatly reducing, while the hard ones have been modified by national priorities to cut public expenditure, and been recentralised.

In conclusion, it is worth noting how only four of the 44 soft geographies of governance identified through the analysis, were developed following top-down logic (mainly national). These projects, programmes, and plans may be seen as 'exogenous' soft geographies, and involve various municipalities as well as other public and private actors. Sectors of national interest such as transport (the Turin–Lyon high speed train) and cultural heritage (the requalification of the Royal Residence of Venaria), and of world relevance (such as the 2006 Winter Olympic Games) were the main reason for the strong involvement of the central government. The other 40 soft geographies can be defined as endogenous, as they were built around a bottom-up approach, constituting the results of the voluntary aggregation of local actors to answer the call for projects and specific local needs, using various forms of funding. This set of initiatives, highly heterogeneous in terms of scope and geographical coverage, is evidence of the will of local actors to struggle against the challenges brought about by the collapse of the Metropolitan Area economic structure during the 1980s, and to come to terms with the heritage of the latter. An increase of cooperative initiatives between the 1990s and the period 2000–2006 suggests learning by experience among municipal actors who, as time went by, learned how to deal with the new governance mechanisms and to attract the funds attached to them. However, the change in framework conditions brought about by the recent crisis (the pauperisation of public budget, the withdrawal of external funding sources, the partial recentralisation of competences) did not allow for a full capitalisation of the acquired experience, as it simply removed the conditions required for this wave of bottom-up cooperation to continue.

Concluding remarks and future governance perspective of Turin's Metropolitan Area

Due to its emblematic character – crisis over crisis, the ups of innovation and institutional activism, and downs of debacles and funding cuts – the case of Turin is a paradigmatic example of various possible ways through which crisis situations may contribute to shaping urban governance regimes.

In conclusion, it may be worth summarising the above debate in the light of the recent Italian administrative developments. These envisage another layer of complexity that will soon aggregate with the existing overlap of hard and soft geographies of governance. Following a general trend that is taking place in most European countries, as well as a response to the current crisis, the Italian administrative system will soon be reformed in an attempt to reduce and integrate local policies through a process of recentralisation which should lead, as stated in the government's aims, to a reduction in public expenditure and improved efficiency (Perulli, 2010). This last rescaling process, already approved by an Act of Law (Law 56/2014), downsizes the role of provincial governments[17] to a minimum, introducing the so-called 'Città Metropolitane' (Metropolitan Cities) at the same time. Both provinces and Metropolitan Cities were initially introduced and enforced by Law 142/1990, but, for various reasons, including concerns regarding the geographies on which this new layer should be based, no Metropolitan City has been instituted to date, despite various attempts.[18]

According to Law 56/2014 the ten main Italian cities (Rome, Milan, Turin, Genoa, Florence, Venice, Naples, Bologna, Bari, and Reggio Calabria) will introduce the Metropolitan City layer from 1 January 2015. The layer will cover areas that overlap with those of the respective provinces. The institutional level of the province is supposed to be substituted by those of the Metropolitan Cities in these ten cases.

The main reason for reform is to be found in the financial conditions of the public administration budgets, read in the framework of the challenges generated by the global financial crisis. In particular, the lack of public funds has had a dramatic impact on the Italian public authorities. On the one hand, it created the necessary momentum to pursue a reform of the hard geographies of governance, but, on the other hand, the reform mainly followed the logic of public expenditure rationalisation, without any specific attention on the socio-economic and territorial specificities of the new configuration. As a result, despite aiming at steering the territorial development of a wide area, the new geographies that are soon to be born are not linked to any spatial relationships. In the case of Turin, for instance, the new Metropolitan City will contain 315 municipalities, including various urban municipalities, hills, and countryside areas as well as a good number of mountain territories that do not have much in common. One could argue that the insertion of Metropolitan Cities is closely related to a downsizing of the role of the provinces so that, regarded as expensive and inefficient, they will be relegated to secondary entities.[19] It is true that the decentralisation undertaken in the 1990s has brought some cases of economic inefficiency, but the changes pursued today seem more related to the political need to show a strong reaction to the financial crisis rather than representing a real way to decrease public expenditure. The provinces will lose their political role, but will be maintained as a secondary entity of government in the whole Italian territory except for the ten Metropolitan Areas chosen by law (56/2014). The decrease in expenditure is therefore only partially effective, it is more a political declaration than a real saving.

How will the forthcoming institutional changes impact the constellation of hard and soft geographies of territorial governance in Turin presented above? Despite the absence of a connection to the existing socio-economic and territorial specificities, the implementation of the Turin Metropolitan City is likely going to affect territorial governance policies and practices. The challenge of the shift from province to Metropolitan City not only concerns the realm of institutional relations, but particularly the new administrative configuration of the government of the latter, radically different from that of the province. The upcoming changes may indeed have an impact on the political relationships between institutions and on the cooperation procedures.[20] Furthermore, Law 56/2014 will have consequences on Mountain and Hill Communities as well as on Municipality Ensembles. Municipality groupings will be allowed according to new conditions, and the new configuration process will influence the geometry that these agreements will adopt.

When it comes to soft geographies the impact the administrative reform will have is less clear, due to the number and heterogeneity of the cooperation initiatives. As shown in Figure 14.2, the higher density of cooperation is visible in some zones around Turin, and in the central city that seems to be less willing to cooperate than the neighbouring municipalities. It is possible to argue that the hegemonic role of the Turin municipality over its surrounding has raised a clear barrier against cooperation processes with the rest of the municipalities. These prefer to group among themselves and develop a critical mass, enabling them to compete with the centre and to make their voice heard. The dynamics of the main

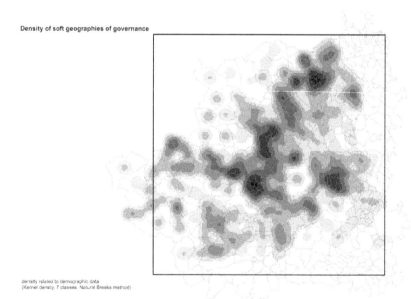

Density of soft geographies of governance

density related to demographic data
(Kernel density, 7 classes, Natural Breaks method)

Figure 14.2 Density of soft geographies of governance in Turin's Metropolitan Area (source: AA.VV., forthcoming).

city of the Metropolitan Area are obviously stronger when compared to those that characterise the small municipalities surrounding it: the core attracts strengths and weaknesses. Social needs, financial resources, and policies implemented by Turin therefore have a greater impact not only inside the borders of Turin, but also in the rest of the area. In particular, the density of soft geographies shows four groups of municipalities around Turin (in the west, north-west, north, and east directions) that cooperate more than the other municipalities. This means that these groups of small cities are often part of soft geographies, socio-economic territories reacting to every chance of cooperation and funding with a bottom-up approach.

These trends could easily influence the political life of the future Metropolitan City. The ten new Metropolitan Cities will be affected by the dynamics taking place in their territory and they will have to promote strategies and policies for all the municipalities grounded inside their borders, understanding their specificities and strengthening positive trends.

On the one hand, a new season of national funding should be promoted to activate a local response to the current financial crisis. As seen in the 1990s, Italian territories can trigger development opportunities insisting upon their place/based specificities (Barca, 2009). On the other hand, local political arenas will be competing to achieve as much as they can from the new equilibrium that will consolidate within the reorganisation process of the Metropolitan City. The elected mayors of the municipalities in Turin's Metropolitan Area are already contemplating and debating the role and the weight of the central city compared to the other territories around it. Be this as it may, soft geographies of territorial governance may well be identified as the main innovative vector of the past two decades, able to channel a large amount of EU, national, and regional funds to the territory of Turin's Metropolitan Area, and leading to an experimentation with innovative modes of interaction, practices, and goals. However, they cannot be considered an easy way out of the crisis; the case of Turin showed how different the use of these forms of cooperation is, during different type of crisis situations. On the other hand, innovative approaches, funding, and the ability of public and private actors to cooperate can be considered fruitful conditions to promote new policies and practices needed in a time of crisis. For this reason, whereas hard geographies will continue to constitute the main structure of territorial governance, programmes, plans, and projects insisting on soft spaces seem to be the more advisable tools with which to experiment in the forthcoming Metropolitan Cities.

Acknowledgements

The authors would like to express their gratitude to the whole research team of the project 'Post-metropolitan territories as emergent forms of urban space: coping with sustainability, habitability, and governance', financed by the Italian Ministry of Education, University and Research (MIUR) and led by Politecnico di Milano. In particular, we are grateful to Umberto Janin Rivolin, Cristiana Rossignolo, Silvia Saccomani, and Carlo Salone for their continual proactive debate throughout the research work.

Notes

1 Analysing the Turin Metropolitan Area leads to a complete picture of territorial governance processes. The central city constitutes the core of a more complex territory with different morphological features, and towns and villages with various forms of relationships. Whereas the Metropolitan Area of Turin was defined in different ways in numerous studies over the decades, in this chapter we refer to the area of competence of the Metropolitan City that will be instituted in 2015, i.e. the current province.

2 The presented information is part of the interim results of the research project 'Post-metropolitan territories as emergent forms of urban space: coping with sustainability, habitability, and governance', financed by the Italian Ministry of Education, University and Research (MIUR), for the period 2013–2015.

3 See Baumgartner and Jones (1993, 2002), True, Jones, and Baumgartner (1999), Meijerink (2005) and Adams, Cotella, and Nunes (2011) for various interpretations of the concept of 'punctuated equilibrium'.

4 FIAT, 'Fabbrica Italiana Automobili Torino' was established in 1899. It became the main factory of the country and the first labour power after the Second World War. Between 1949 and 1959 production increased from 71,000 to 425,000 units and in the following decade the number of workers amounted to 150,000. FIAT drove the post-war 'economic miracle' also thanks to financial and political support. For instance, after the Second World War $22 million (30 per cent) of the $58 million of Marshall Plan funds was earmarked for the entire Italian engineering sector. The national automobile market expanded rapidly, turning Turin into Europe's most specialised region (Winkler, 2007).

5 Turin's population peaked at over 1.2 million in 1975, and then, also as a result of the FIAT crisis, it started to decrease (Bagnasco, 1990).

6 To provide evidence of the magnitude of the crisis, it is worth mentioning that the Metropolitan Area lost more than 100,000 jobs between 1975 and 1984.

7 CIGS 'Cassa Integrazione Guadagni Straordinaria' is a long-term benefits programme that pays workers 60 per cent of their previous wage from funds, paid by the state, workers, and companies.

8 Moreover, various other parallel projects were undertaken by the municipality during the 1990s. Of particular relevance is the 'Progetto Speciale Periferie' (Special Suburbs Project): from 1997 to 2005 a programme for urban and social regeneration of suburbs, built during the Fordist housing boom, which needed green areas, new transportation, and social services.

9 Such as public and private investments, and their 'weight' on public expenditure (public debts load), the environmental impacts of new buildings and infrastructures, the financial and physical management of the Olympic heritage, etc.

10 The organisation of the Games was a complex mix of hard and soft governance: traditional public authorities (region, province, municipalities, Mountain Communities) were paralleled by two ad hoc instituted bodies – TOROC and the Agency Torino 2006. TOROC was a private foundation that acted as a local organising committee responsible for setting the programme of the event and then monitoring its execution. Agency Torino 2006 was responsible for implementing the Olympic programme defined by TOROC. TOROC and the Agency were dismantled after the end of the event and of its monitoring process respectively.

11 From 2011 the Municipality of Turin economic policy aimed at debt reduction. The debt in 2011 amounted to €3.28 billion; in 2012 it decreased to €3.20 billion and to €3,086 billion in 2013. In 2014 it should be under the threshold of €3 billion (website of Comune di Torino).

12 In case of those geographies instituted by national laws for the whole country, it is interesting to note that in recent decades each region was given the chance to modify them in order to ensure consistency with its territorial specificities, in so doing allowing for an even greater heterogeneity.

13 The soft geographies of governance were chosen according to the following criteria: (i) they should take place in Turin's Metropolitan Area; (ii) they should feature a partnership involving at least two municipalities.

14 These themes were grouped building on the EU Structural Funds priorities for the periods 2000–2006 and 2006–2013. This approach, as well as the selected time-spans, were chosen to allow for a more comfortable exploration of the causal links between funding sources (EU, state, region) and the analysed cooperation initiatives that they triggered.

15 As already briefly mentioned above, the most important reform concerns the change in the procedure for appointing the cities' mayors. Since 1993, the latter are elected directly by the cities' inhabitants, and therefore their actions are provided with greater legitimacy and accountability.

16 The original train line project is actually older, but the strategic plan involving the municipalities of Susa Valley that was approved in 2008 constitutes its most recent development. This project is part of the Mediterranean Corridor, designed by the EU. The high speed train has become a battlefield between the local population and national priorities (authorities?). More information about this conflict can be found at: www.nytimes.com/2014/03/18/world/europe/italy-divided-over-rail-line-meant-to-unite.html?_r=0.

17 Provinces are an additional territorial level, provided with self-elected government, that lies in-between the regions and the municipalities.

18 For instance, the Piedmont Region started a revision of the metropolitan level in 1972, proposing an area corresponding to 54 municipalities. This, however, never led to any real action. A proposal, developed in 1995, which included only 33 municipalities, shared a similar fate.

19 Province governments will no longer be elected, but will remain in place as public authorities virtually emptied of any political power.

20 For instance, the mayor of the Metropolitan City will be elected in the central city.

References

AA.VV. (forthcoming) *Atlante dei territori post-metropolitani*. Milano, Politecnico di Milano.

Adams, N., Cotella, G., & Nunes, R. (eds) (2011) *Territorial development, cohesion and spatial planning: Knowledge and policy development in an enlarged EU*. London and New York, Routledge.

Allmendinger, P. & Haughton, G. (2009) Soft spaces, fuzzy boundaries, and metagovernance: The new spatial planning in the Thames Gateway. *Environment and Planning A*, 41, 617–633.

Allmendinger, P. & Haughton, G. (2010) Spatial planning, devolution, and new planning spaces. *Environment and Planning C: Government and Policy*, 28, 803–818.

Bagnasco, A. (1986) *Torino un profilo sociologico*. Torino, G. Einaudi.

Bagnasco, A. (1990) *La città dopo Ford: Il caso di Torino*. Torino, Bollati Boringhieri.

Bagnasco A. & Le Galès, P. (eds) (2001) *Le città nell'Europa contemporanea*. Naples, Liguori.

Barca F. (2009) *Agenda for a reformed cohesion policy: A place-based approach to meeting European Union challenges and expectations*. Brussels, Report for the European Commission.

Baumgartner, F. R. & Jones, B. D. (1993) *Agendas and instability in American politics*. Chicago, IL, University of Chicago Press.

Baumgartner, F. R. & Jones, B. D. (eds) (2002) *Policy dynamics*. Chicago, IL, University of Chicago Press.

Bondonio, P., Dansero, E., Guala, C., Mela, A., & Scamuzzi, S. (2007) *A Giochi fatti: L'eredità di Torino 2006*. Roma, Carocci.

Cash, D. W., Adger, W. N., Berkes, F., Garden, P., Lebel, L., Olsson, P., & Young, O. (2006) Scale and cross-scale dynamics: Governance and information in a multilevel world. *Ecology and Society*, 11 (2), 8.

Castells, M. (1989) *The informational city: Information technology, economic restructuring, and the urban regional process*. Oxford and Cambridge, MA, Blackwell.

Conzelmann, T. (2008) Efficient and legitimate? Reflections on multi-level governance. In: Conzelmann, T. & Smith, R. (eds) *Multi-level governance in the European Union: Taking stock and looking ahead*. Baden-Baden, Nomos, pp. 11–30.

Davico, L. & Staricco, L. (2013) *Liberare il future: Quattordicesimo rapporto 'Giorgio Rota' su Torino*. Torino, Centro Einaudi.

ESPON (European Spatial Planning Observation Network) (2007) *ESPON project 2.3.2: Governance of territorial and urban policies from EU to local level*, Final report. [Online] Available from: www.espon.eu/export/sites/default/Documents/Projects/ESPON2006Projects/PolicyImpactProjects/Governance/fr-2.3.2_final_feb2007.pdf [accessed 30 January 2015].

ESPON (European Spatial Planning Observation Network) (2013) *ESPON TANGO: Territorial approaches for new governance*. Final Report. ESPON, Luxembourg.

Faludi, A. (2011) *Cohesion, coherence, cooperation: European spatial planning coming of age?* London and New York, Routledge.

Gibson, C. C., Ostrom, E., & Ahn, T. K. (2000) The concept of scale and the human dimensions of global change: A survey. *Ecological Economics*, 32 (2), 217–239.

Governa, F., Rossignolo, C., & Saccomani, S. (2009) Turin: Urban regeneration in a post-industrial city. *Journal of Urban Regeneration and Renewal*, 3 (1), 20–30.

Haughton, G. & Allmendinger, P. (2008) The soft spaces of local economic development. *Local Economy*, 23, 138–148.

Haughton, G., Allmendinger, P., Counsell, D., & Vigar, G. (2011) *The new spatial planning: Territorial management with soft spaces and fuzzy boundaries*. London, Routledge.

Holling, C. S. (2004) From complex regions to complex worlds. *Ecology and Society*, 9 (1), 11. [Online] Available from: www.ecologyandsociety.org/vol. 9/iss1/art11/ [accessed 30 January 2015].

Hooghe, L. & Marks, G. (2001) *Multilevel governance and European integration*. Oxford, Rowman & Littlefield.

Hooghe, L. & Marks, G. (2003) Unraveling the central state, but how? Types of multi-level governance. *American Political Science Review*, 97 (2), 233–243.

Janin Rivolin, U. (2003) Shaping European spatial planning: How Italy's experience can contribute. *Town Planning Review*, 74 (1), 51–76.

Janin Rivolin, U. (2004) *European spatial planning*. Milano, Franco Angeli.

Le Galès, P. (2002) *Le città europee: Società urbane, globalizzazione, governo locale*. Bologna, Il Mulino.

Meijerink, S. (2005) Understanding policy stability and change: The interplay of advocacy coalitions and epistemic community, windows of opportunity and Dutch coastal flooding policy 1945–2003. *Journal of European Public Policy*, 12 (6), 1060–1077.

Mossberger, K. & Stoker, G. (2001) The evolution of urban regime theory: The challenge of conceptualization. *Urban Affairs Review*, 36 (6), 810–835.

Perulli, P. (2010) Politiche locali tra decentralizzazione e ricentralizzazione. *Stato e Mercato*, 90, 365–394.

Saccomani, S. (2003) La governance metropolitana e la tradizione postfordista nell'area metropolitana torinese. *Urbanistica Informazioni*, Dossier, 128–133.

True, J. L., Jones, D., & Baumgartner, F. R. (1999) Punctuated equilibrium theory, explaining stability and change in American policy-making. In: Sabatier, P. (ed.) *Theories of the policy process*. Boulder, CO, Westview Press, pp. 73–93.

Veltz, P. (1998) Economia e territori: Dal mondiale al locale. In: Perulli, P. (ed.) *Neoregionalismo*. Torino, L'economia arcipelago, Bollati Boringhieri, pp. 128–151.

Winkler, A. (2007) *Torino city report.* CASE report, 41. London, Centre for Analysis of Social Exclusion, London School of Economics and Political Science.

Websites

www.regione.piemonte.it

www.comune.torino.it

www.regione.piemonte.it/ambiente/coronaverde/

www.comune.torino.it/periferie/

www.mtm.torino.it

www.lavenaria.it

www.istat.it

http://ec.europa.eu/eurostat

www.nytimes.com/2014/03/18/world/europe/italy-divided-over-rail-line-meant-to-unite.html?_r=0

15 Urban rescaling

A post-crisis scenario for a Spanish city: Valencia and its megaregion

Josep Vicent Boira and Ramon Marrades[1]

> The urban question has been widely rearticulated in the form of a scalar question.
>
> (Brenner, 2009a: p. 69)

> The rehierarchization of the urban and regional system is only partly explained by economic factors (crisis-induced industrial restructuring, the rise of flexible production systems, new spatial divisions of labour); just as important are political factors (centrally orchestrated state strategies to promote transnational investment in major urban regions, governmentalized remapping of state spaces, the political-construction of an elite top hierarchy of cities and urbanized regions within national and international circuits of capital).
>
> (Harrison, 2015: p. 7).

Introduction

The present economic crisis, experienced during the first decade of the twenty-first century, encompasses three different dimensions in Spain: an economic dimension linked to the explosion of the construction bubble, a social dimension represented by the loss of confidence in public institutions and in traditional political parties, and a third dimension that questions the territorial model of governance. Spanish cities have already initiated processes of reorientation, but those processes appear almost exclusively in terms of economic orientation towards post-industrial and post-real estate models, but do not show any significant change in spatial governance. Since the economic crisis has been reinforced by the governance framework, any institutional post-crisis scenario should consider not only the reorientation of the economy but should also rethink how the urban, regional, and national spaces are governed.

Spanish cities and regions should tackle what Neil Brenner (1999, 2000, 2004, 2009a, 2009b, 2013) has defined as urban and regional rescaling, following examples of regions and countries that have already responded to this process in terms of institutional reforms (the UK, Germany, the United States). A new territorial vision of the role of cities, Metropolitan Areas and regions appears as a key issue, because, as already mentioned, the urban crisis in Spain is not only an economic crisis but also a crisis of territorial governance.

The need for reforms in terms of territorial governance in Spain will be linked in this study to Neil Brenner's theoretical framework of urban rescaling. Spanish cities have not tested so far, with a few exemptions, metropolitan agreements or implemented multilevel governments. Local governments are seated at the administrative boundaries of municipalities.

The Valencian region and its capital are an appropriate example of the need for rescaling governance. It is the third biggest Spanish city, it has one of the most dynamic ports in the Mediterranean, and it is part of the economic and cultural megaregion called the Mediterranean Axis or Mediterranean Arch, defined empirically as a megaregion (Ferras, 1986; Trullén et al., 2010a) and recognised by the European Union as a priority area in the Trans European Transport Network TEN-T (European Commission, 2013).

As rescaling is already taking place as a change in territorial and economic dynamics, the lack of institutional response to the phenomenon has reinforced the effects of the crisis. In this chapter it will be shown that the new post-crisis scenario in Spanish cities, specifically in the case of Valencia, should involve not only an economic reorientation to overcome the real estate bubble but also a reorientation of territorial and urban governance. It will be demonstrated that the interaction of scales and multilevel governance is so far an unresolved matter. It will be asserted that Valencia and its region already manifest some of the preconditions that are necessary to finally initiate a process of re-territorialisation of urban, metropolitan, and regional governance. The proposal discussed is that the present crisis can create momentum for an urban transformation with new premises, which as per Galiana (2013) and Subirats (2014) make it necessary to rethink and assess urban policies in a framework that includes different mechanisms of territorial intervention at supra-local and multilevel scales, so far not really developed in Spain.

This chapter will be structured as follows. In the second section the territorial dimension of the crisis in Spanish cities is assessed. In the third section the changes already happening in several Spanish cities, focusing on economic reorientation, are discussed. In the fourth section the theories of territorial rescaling mainly by Neil Brenner are evaluated. In the fifth section the case of Valencia and the potential to initiate a process of governance rescaling in the megaregion of the Mediterranean Axis is studied. The chapter ends by concluding that public policy must adapt to the new territorial dynamics.

A territorial crisis in Spanish cities

The social, economic, and political effects of the crisis in Spanish cities, as discussed in the chapters 'The neoliberal model of the city in Southern Europe: a comparative approach to Valencia and Madrid' and 'Rethinking Barcelona: changes experienced as a result of social and economic crisis' will be complemented here with an assessment of the scalar and territorial perspectives of the crisis and the need for multilevel governance.

The starting point of this chapter is the multidimensional characteristics of the crisis in Mediterranean societies and specifically in Spanish society. It is not only an economic and social crisis, but also a crisis of political representation and of territorial governance. The crisis that Spanish cities face can be understood as a 'sum of vulnerabilities' (Martí-Costa, García, & Iglesias, 2014: p. 137).

Focusing primarily on the economic dimension but pointing out the need for changes in territorial governance Lois and Miramontes (2014) note that the current economic downturn has affected urban reality in three fundamental ways. First, the crisis has accelerated the reorientation of the productive structure. Second, a period of speculative excesses of contemporary urban practice in Spanish cities came to an end. Third, the consequences of the crisis have not only questioned, but have also demanded a rethinking of the notions of urban centres and centralities. These three different aspects have led to two major inflection points that will be emphasised in this chapter. The first relates to the fact that the post-crisis scenario in Spanish cities is characterised by a productive shift and the second points to the fact that the crisis has forced the redefinition of theoretical concepts of urban studies, such as the definition of cities and their policies.

Navarro et al. (2014: p. 85) identify a clear correlation between urban crisis and governance: 'Local political societies, especially in big cities, have been really vulnerable to the governance crisis, understood as the inability to respond in a collective way to the demands and tensions inherent to the socio-political dimension of the urban space.' Specific manifestations of this crisis are: urban government fragmentation; the dependence of the city on both the government economic flows and the real estate sector; and the assumption of improper powers (when regional and national governments cannot respond to the urgent demands of citizens, municipal governments are pressured to do so, without having enough resources or the legal framework allowing it).

The urban crisis and the crisis of governance that Valencia and other Southern European cities face, which profoundly affects essential aspects of people's life, requires rethinking public policy in a significant way. This is particularly important in the urban arena, because urban policies have a strong effect on everyday life and welfare. Local public policies are known for their low coordination, being predominantly segmented and specialised. Despite the constant influence and interrelation of the different levels of government (European, national, and regional), multilevel coordination is hardly common, with notable contradictions and duplications between policies implemented by different governments (Romero, 2012). In Spain, there are almost no public policies formulated at the supra-local or inter-governmental scale.

The central government did not develop any national policy of metropolitan realignment, but focused instead on reinforcing the centrality of Madrid (Bel, 2011). In Spain, the 'city-centric capitalism strategy' that also characterises other European countries (Harrison, 2014: p. 20) becomes 'Madrid-centric capitalism' generating territorial tensions (Albalate, Bel, & Fageda, 2012). Furthermore, each region (Spanish Autonomous Communities) has implemented policies according to their own independent criteria. Several scholars from human geography academia assert that territorial ordering of state, regions, and cities is missing in Spain, while calling for a deep territorial reform and reform of the model of governance (Gómez, Lois, & Nel.lo, 2013).

New models of territorial governance become crucial. The following section will consider whether and what new models have been applied in Spanish cities following the economic crisis. It will be argued that cities and urban areas that advance in social and urban sustainability are those that learn from their own experience, keep open channels of innovation with their supra-local and international presence, and combine new approaches to urban challenges (environmental sustainability, social cohesion, etc.) with new governance models ingrained in the territory (coordination, multilevel governance, citizen participation, etc.).

Spanish cities right after the crisis: economic reorientation but not urban rescaling

A recent paper by Precedo and Míguez (2014) serves as a starting point to assess the present situation of the Spanish system of cities. The data provided allows an overview of the period 2007–2012 and is based on evaluation of the results of questionnaires, sent to a group of geographers in 22 urban areas in Spain in order to detect changes in a period of intersection between crisis and post-industrialism. The Spanish urban areas (and the associated experts) were selected on the basis of two criteria: a population of the central municipality more than 200,000 inhabitants and the location of any of the 500 largest private companies in Spain in the Metropolitan Area. The 22 selected urban areas account for a total of 425 municipalities, with 34,451,310 inhabitants, 34.56 per cent of whom live in a central municipality and 65.44 per cent in peripheral municipalities.

In their study Precedo and Míguez (2014) analyse four key issues: urban structure and spatial organisation, urban development and planning, urban economics, and urban competitiveness (image, representation, and city-branding). Several of the insights gained can be highlighted.

An economic reorientation is already taking place, which seems coherent with a post-industrial stage. A total of 75 per cent of the 22 surveyed cities had developed a strategic plan in 2012 and 40 per cent have even prepared two successive plans. Fifteen per cent of the cities have launched financial planning schemes, mainly associated with tourism (although 12 per cent of these schemes are inclined to reindustrialisation objective). The mere existence and rhetoric of these plans, however, say very few things about how effective public policies are or even whether they have been implemented at all. The main implemented reorientation policies are summarised in Table 15.1.

Cities are generally service-oriented, as obvious from the statement 'the interest in adapting cities to the post-industrial economy force the majority of plans to aim the reorientation to a service economy' (Precedo & Míguez, 2014: p. 28). Based on the information gathered, the authors differentiate between two models of tertiarisation: a first generation of service-oriented cities (strong

Table 15.1 Reorientation policies in Spanish cities

Re-orientation area	Main re-orientation policies
Economic re-orientation	Strategic plans Financial planning schemes Tertiarisation policies
Infrastructures	Transport infrastructures Waterfront redevelopment Large urban green spaces
Urban competitiveness	Cultural and sporting big events Tourism promotion and city branding Heritage protection and cultural policies

Source: authors' elaboration.

business content, promotion of tourism, new commercial areas, leisure) as in the cases of Bilbao, Valencia, Malaga, and Barcelona; and a second model, that appears later, aimed at strengthening the productive system adapting to the new economy (knowledge activities, industries, ICT, international logistics activities) such as the cases of Pamplona, Bilbao, Vitoria, Malaga, Granada, and Seville. It is worth noting, however, that the strategic plans analysed aimed at promoting tourism (16.5 per cent of the plans), commercial sales (13.8 per cent), city brand-ing (11.2 per cent), and service business (11.2 per cent). Other scenarios resulted in less consensus, such as reindustrialisation (6.4 per cent), ICT (6.4 per cent), or international logistics hubs (5.6 per cent).

According to the consulted experts, the most important Spanish urban areas already have a good supply of equipment and infrastructure. The public sector has heavily invested in architectural improvement and transport infrastructure (Boira, 2013; Cruz, 2013). Even though most of this infrastructure is currently underused due to the lack of proper management or even simply unnecessary, it could be used for social or economic purposes.

The highest percentage of these infrastructure provisions (26.5 per cent) is transport infrastructure (new metro lines in Seville, Bilbao, Madrid, and Ali-cante, new highways in Valladolid, Cádiz, Madrid, and Zaragoza, new railway stations in Malaga, Pamplona, and Zaragoza, new airport terminals in Malaga, Madrid, and Alicante-Elche). The second is waterfront operations (18.5 per cent) (in Malaga, Palma, La Coruña, San Sebastián, Alicante, Vigo, Valencia), and the third corresponds to large urban green spaces (10.2 per cent) (the Green Ring of Vitoria, Zaragoza, and river parks Pamplona, etc.). When it comes to building new infrastructure, most Spanish cities have complemented their (intended) pro-ductive reorientation with the realisation of large architectural projects such as in the case of the Guggenheim in Bilbao, the City of Arts and Sciences in Valencia (Figure 15.1), La Ciudad de la Luz in Alicante, the Island of Innovation in Avilés, the convention centres in San Sebastian, Pamplona, Zaragoza, La Coruna, or Vigo. Many of these interventions have not achieved their objectives

Figure 15.1 La Ciutat de les Arts i de les Ciències or City of Arts and Sciences and adjoining development along the former bed of the River Turia in Valencia (source: Emilio García, 2007 (creative commons)).

and others have done so, but at a very high economic cost. For instance the Guggenheim is recognised worldwide as a model of urban development, La Ciudad de la Luz is completely bankrupt, and the City of Arts and Sciences, in spite of being one of the most visited tourist attractions in Spain, is currently in a privatisation process.

In the transition to a post-industrial model Spanish cities intended to enhance their urban competitiveness. Somehow, it was (not always effectively) assumed that the post-industrial development model had to be associated with new components of productive activity, which led to the realisation of cultural or sporting events (31 per cent of the cities surveyed), tourism promotion and city branding (30 per cent), heritage protection and (macro) cultural policies (13 per cent, five Spanish cities have achieved distinction of World Heritage of UNESCO and three of Cultural City). There were even plans associated with film festivals, literature, or gastronomy. It could be assumed that many large and medium-sized Spanish cities already have a significant amount of physical and intangible infrastructure. The challenge is to use this in an efficient and cohesive way. At the same time, city governments indeed wrote plans to achieve the reorientation to service economy, but the simple existence of these plans does not guarantee their effectiveness, their contextualisation, or their relationship to endogenous factors. It is possible that these are rhetorical rather than practical. A total of 28 per cent of the experts consulted by Precedo and Míguez (2014: p. 37) note that the great urban renovation projects undertaken in recent years are characterised by 'a greater cost than benefit' albeit 38 per cent of the same group of experts assert that the benefit was greater than the cost.

In summary, most medium and big Spanish cities have already started to implement public policy that aims to reorient their economic structure towards sectors that differ from real estate, with notable developments in strategic planning, service orientation (including technology, tourism, and innovation), and developing their cultural activities. At the same time, those cities are already well equipped concerning infrastructure and big architectural projects that can eventually be used for new economic, entrepreneurial, and civic activities. It should also be noted that most cities are implementing policies that aim at the reorientation of economic activity, but with limited territorial visions, without developing any process of multilevel governance, territorial governance, or policy responses to urban rescaling.

It is almost impossible to find supra-local policies in Spain. In order to face territorial transformations that respond to the new territorial dynamics, policies are still attached to the municipal scale (Nel.lo, 2010, 2011). For the time being, urban policies are characterised by the absence of territorial planning at metropolitan and regional scales (Galiana, 2013) and for low articulation and integration (Subirats, 2014). Until 2006, none of the urban areas with a population greater than 500,000 inhabitants had developed any instrument of territorial planning at the metropolitan scale (Hildebrand, 2006) and only more recently have some Spanish Metropolitan Areas been provided with such instruments as in the case of the Bilbao Metropolitano (2006), the urban agglomerations of Seville and Malaga (2009), and the Barcelona Metropolitan Area (2010). In brief, there exists dissociation in Spain between urban and territorial (Galiana, 2013) or, put another way, there is a clear mismatch between institutional geography and territorial dynamics (Romero, 2010). Because of this, the need to incorporate supra-local and international influences in urban policies and to implement new forms of city governance seated on principles such as the integration of multilevel governance seems essential.

In this context, Neil Brenner (1999) formulated several theoretical principles for the new territorial dynamics described. The main one with regard to the aim of this chapter is the relationship between new forms of capital circulation and urban dynamics which appears in the assessment of re-territorialisation (cities and nations) as a process of reconfiguration and rescaling linked to the present phase of globalisation. This concept will be explained in the following section.

On urban and territorial rescaling

As a theoretical framework for the main proposal of this chapter the concept of urban rescaling developed by Neil Brenner will be used and linked to the numerous academic reflections that have called for the need to rethink traditional territorial concepts such as the concept of the 'region' in Spain.

From the 1990s onwards a great amount of literature assessing the impact of globalisation on urban agglomerations has been developed. This literature, from the fields of geography and political science, is heterogeneous, but it can be grouped into two main categories: the new regionalism and the rescaling or re-territorialisation approach (Tomàs, 2014). In this chapter, the second approach is presented as an explicative theory of the impact of globalisation on urban agglomerations as part of the transition to a post-industrial state. As in Brenner (2004) the globalisation of markets and the changes in productive models involve a restructuring of the levels of government, configuring a new hierarchy that encourages metropolitan agglomerations as centres of production. In this case, territorial restructuring influences metropolitan governance, pushing public actors to reset their strategies towards the goal of economic development, but in the Spanish case, these changes have not been addressed in terms of territorial governance.

As stated in Brenner (2000: p. 15) 'The multiscalar methodologies are now absolutely essential for grasping the fundamental role of cities as preconditions, arenas and outcomes of the current round of global capitalist restructuring'.

Moreover 'the urban question has been widely rearticulated in the form of a scale question' (ibid.: p. 2). Any post-crisis scenario for Spanish cities (and also possibly for other Mediterranean cities) will therefore involve a discussion about the appropriate scales of intervention. In this discussion, Brenner's rescaling per-spective is fundamental, 'the urban question has been reconceptualised in reflex-ively scalar terms in the context of debates on worldwide urban and regional restructuring' (Brenner, 2009a: p. 61). Three main aspects of Brenner's analysis are relevant to this reflection: first, that 'the concern with settlement typologies (nominal essences) must be superseded by the analysis of sociospatial processes (constitutive essences)' (Brenner, 2013: p. 98); second, that reflection on the scalar question (Brenner, 2004) comes from the idea of a 'politics of scale', a transition that has not yet been developed in Spain; and, finally, the need to understand the concept of scale 'as produced, contested and therefore malleable arenas and prod-ucts of political-economic relations' (ibid.: p. 4). By combining these principles a conclusion could be drawn that is applicable to the case presented in this chapter: 'supraurban geographical scales are not merely external parameters for the urban question' but 'crystallizations of diverse, overlapping political-economic processes' (Brenner, 2009a: p. 7). In Spanish cities there has been no political response to the emerging relevance of supra-urban geographical scales.

Linking global restructuring to rescaling is the initial theoretical framework that enables an assessment of Valencia (and other Spanish and Southern Euro-pean cities). In Spain, territorial visions have not yet evolved. A special issue of *Boletín de la Asociación de Geógrafos Españoles* (2001), has pointed out the conceptual conservatism, in this case about the concept 'region'. Abet (2001) showed that nation states, provinces, and counties should not be the single objects of study, because they have to be overcome for deep spatial reorganisa-tion. Gómez (2001) stated that the boundaries of territorial institutions are a product rather than a cause. Farinós (2001) pointed out the need for territorial reorientation to respond to the new challenges of a rapidly changing environ-ment and Sánchez (2001) called for combining traditional territoriality with a networked one. More recently Solís and Troitiño (2012) noted that emerging global processes (technological revolution, global competition, business restructuring) are related, also through public policy, to new territorial forms (urban upscaling and national rescaling). They called for linking urban policies with a 'new regionalism' conception. The rethinking of regions as a concept can be translated to the urban scale.

In fact, there are already some innovative responses to Brenner's theory on rescaling. The traditional view of the municipality is complemented by new approaches to subregional governance (Pemberton and Morphet, 2014) and new forms of the supra-local scale (Harrison, 2014), such as the megaregions. Sassen (2012) asserts that the megaregion becomes a scale that includes both globalised and provincial cities and areas. In this case, cities have to be actively involved within what Harrison and Hoyle (2014: p. 2) define as megaregions: 'In certain spatial contexts, the expansion of large cities into larger city-regions is being superseded by transmetropolitan landscapes comprising two or more city-regions.'

In this regard other examples could also be pointed out: the global city-regions (Scott, 2001) or the polycentric urban corridors (UN-Habitat, 2011). According to UN-Habitat (2011), megaregions are natural economic units that result from the growth, convergence, and spatial spread of geographically linked Metropolitan Areas and other agglomerations and urban corridors characterised by linear systems of urban spaces linked through transportation networks. Other dynamic and strategic cities are extending beyond their administrative boundaries and integrating their hinterlands to become full blown city-regions. These new formulations are related to the need for an appropriate scale for a global world, despite their diversity they all emphasise the urgency for political responses to the shifts in scale (RPA, 2006; Dewar & Epstein, 2006; Rodríguez-Pose, 2008; McCann, 2008; McCann & Acs, 2011; Florida, 2014a; Clark & Clark, 2014).

In summary, Spanish cities and policies cannot stay out of the process of urban rescaling and the new mosaic of regional economies; the lack of political response so far may have amplified the territorial effects of the crisis (Solis & Troitiño, 2012). Research must look at the polycentric urban regions associated with an urban rescaling, which needs action-oriented strategic planning. Spain as a nation, but also Spanish cities, must learn from foreign experiences. Examples are numerous, from the Ocean Gateway (north-west England) that focuses on urban dynamics in the spatial corridor between cities (Dembski, 2014) to the policies of regional restructuring in China (for instance in Guangzhou and the south-east of the country), a leap in scale (Shin, 2014) as a negotiated policy to link the urban, regional, and macroregional realities with the global. Most of these policies come from a European tradition, as Harrison (2014) points out, such as the case of Britain and Germany. In Germany, the federal government made a strategic choice of six urban agglomerations to become European Metropolitan Regions, rescaling policies and visions. The European Commission (2014), through its macroregional strategies, has also joined those integrated visions about the classic territorial units. In the next section the case of Valencia is analysed and the potential benefits of addressing rescaling dynamics with policies are pointed out.

The case of Valencia: the need for rescaling urban governance

Few cities embody the engagement of urban process with globalisation and European integration better than the Mediterranean city of Valencia (Prytherch & Boira, 2009). Valencia is Spain's third largest city (after Madrid and Barcelona) with more than 1.5 million residents within the Metropolitan Area. This traditionally agrarian and provincial city has become capital of the Spanish Autonomous Region, the Comunitat Valenciana, Mediterranean cultural and economic centre, and a major destination for foreign visitors. Indeed, the University of Valencia is now the second most popular destination for European exchange students. This metamorphosis is seen in the city's changing landscape, embodied in the monumental cultural-entertainment complex Ciutat de les Arts i les Ciències (City of the Arts and Sciences), a new conference centre, the growing container port, gentrification and immigration in the city centre, and the newly renovated harbour. The urban fabric of the city is presented in Figure 15.2.

Valencia is a Mediterranean city transformed by two decades of rapid change. If this transformation was initially guided by territorial planning under socialist administrations, in the past decade the process has been accelerated within the free-market entrepreneurialism of the conservative Partido Popular. This shift

Figure 15.2 Map of Valencia (source: our figure, University of Valencia, 2013).

has produced a clear and characteristically postmodern model of transformation, in which creative change is unrestrained by laws. Unlike Barcelona, change in Valencia has not been guided by a social-democratic but rather a neoliberal regime. After two decades of aggressive entrepreneurialism and dizzying urban change, Valencia may be slowing down to digest its growth (Cucó, 2013).

Many challenges remain for Valencia, however. From an endogenous perspective, these include integration of the city's rapidly growing immigrant population, the planning of the city's maritime facade, and the development of advanced public services. From an exogenous perspective, the main issue is the governance of urban rescaling. On the one hand, this includes the urgency of implementing strategies of metropolitan governance, which are absolutely absent nowadays (Ponce, 2013). Valencia needs to develop a strategic vision of the city's place in the urban networks of supra-local scale and metropolitan governance (Prytherch & Boira, 2009). On the other hand, urban rescaling is also about the understanding of what it means to belong to a wider megaregion: the urban Mediterranean Axis. Thirty years ago, a French study of Spanish regional geography (Ferras, 1986) showed the existent megaregions, one of them being the Spanish subset of the Mediterranean Axis: connected by its cities and infrastructure. The results of this research have been updated recently by Trullén et al. (2010a) again showing the expansive megaregion that stretches from Valencia to Lyon (France), using assessment techniques based on light intensity (Figure 15.3), as Florida (2014b) does for the American case.

A central challenge facing Valencia is ensuring its strategic situation and connectivity within Spain and a wider network of European cities. Valencia is destined to occupy a strategic position in the economic megaregion of the Mediterranean Axis (Boira, 2002, 2009). It is close to Mediterranean shipping routes and connected to Madrid (to the west) and Barcelona (to the north). Infrastructure improvements remain important, including a project developing a freight corridor (the Mediterranean Corridor). While high velocity trains connected Valencia and Madrid a few years ago, it would be necessary to build a similar freight and passenger rail link through Barcelona to Europe. These ideas reflect growing efforts to organise a network of cities and territories as a megaregion that could adapt to globalisation's challenges.

A great effort is being made to connect the megaregional European network of cities promoting the Trans European Transport Network (TEN-T), intended to provide the single market with integrated modern transport networks (Martellato, 2011). This project creates a map of connections between urban agglomerations defining a dual layer approach to the TEN-T. The basic layer, or 'Comprehensive Network', should ensure accessibility to all regions of the Union. The second layer, the 'Core Network' is constituted of the strategically most important parts of the Comprehensive Network, identified according to a specific methodology, transparently and coherently applied to decide which project development and implementation will be supported with priority (European Commission, 2013). In this second layer, the Mediterranean Corridor will link the south-western Mediterranean region up to the Ukrainian border with

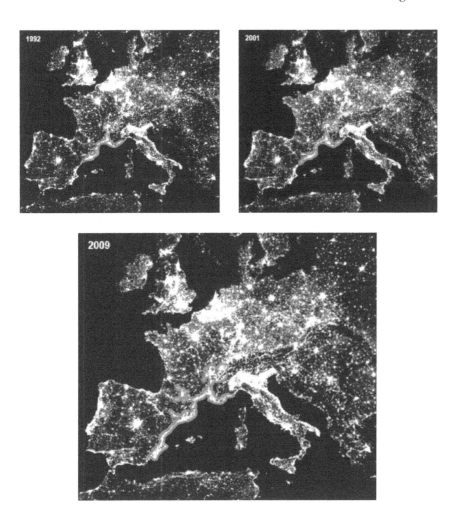

Figure 15.3 Mediterranean axis defined through light intensity assessment (source: Trullén et al., 2010b).

Hungary, following the coastlines of Spain, France, and crossing the Alps eastwards through Italy, Slovenia, and Croatia. This corridor of about 3,000 km, will provide a multimodal link to the ports of the western Mediterranean with the centre of the EU. It is important to talk about connections between cities as related to this corridor (European Commission, 2013).

The Mediterranean Corridor runs across four densely populated regions of Spain: Andalusia, Murcia Region, Valencian Community, and Catalonia. In 2009 there were approximately one million companies registered in the area, producing textiles, shoes, toys, furniture, tiles, and ceramics. Modern agriculture is another important engine of economic activity. The economy of the area is strongly oriented towards exports, both in agricultural and industrial products: in 2009 the value of exports and imports amounted respectively to €70 and €91 billion in the area, both corresponding to about 44 per cent of the national trade (CENIT, 2012). Trade activity is favoured, in particular, by the presence of a large number of ports along the southern coast of Spain (including Barcelona, Tarragona, Valencia, Cartagena, and Algeciras). Tourism is another important generator of wealth, accounting for approximately half the tourists visiting Spain each year. The location of the corridor, stretching from west to east Spain and crossing some of its most highly populated and developed regions, makes it a potentially important multimodal axis connecting Spain to the rest of Europe through the Pyrenees and the world via the numerous ports (ibid.). Policy efforts at a European level in terms of rescaling have not been reciprocated at national, regional, or urban levels.

Valencia should not only develop strategic policies related to its position in the Mediterranean Axis megaregion but also develop new tools of metropolitan governance in order to take advantage of its privileged geographical location and the emerging territorial dynamics.

The benefits of implementing new tools of governance to address urban rescaling will involve fostering the alliance between infrastructure and the productive economy, as the scale of intervention would be a product of the existing economic dynamics; exactly the opposite of what has happened in Spain where administrative boundaries act as a precondition (and sometimes as an obstacle) and where the reinforcement of Madrid centrality has come at the cost of a lack of investment and governance tools in the economic corridors and megaregions. Responding to rescaling would mean taking an advantage of the revalorisation of location (McCann, 2008); and would imply taking into account a broader spectrum of agents (citizens, business, and governments) involved in urban development at different scales.

Valencia will remain an interesting and perhaps emblematic case study of Mediterranean urban change, how European places distinguished by unique landscapes and regional identities navigate the complexities of the global economy, and can remake themselves in the process. On the other hand, a rigid or null reaction to the changes described would not come without cost.

Conclusions

Using Neil Brenner's words as conclusion (2009b: p. 458)

> the field of urban governance has continued to evolve in the first decade of twenty-first century, as new institutional and scalar configurations are introduced though diverse forms of regulatory experimentation in neighbourhoods, metropolitan regions and intercity networks across the European urban system.

Agreeing to this, it seems reasonable to imagine a post-crisis scenario characterised by rescaling processes that will pull the development of new governance models that are able to include all agents involved in urban development. As Rozenblat (2012) says, it is not easy, conceptually, to articulate the different scales of organisation if these are considered as given objects a priori. On the contrary, they can be a posteriori, the result of cohesive interaction within broader networks. Globalisation demands simultaneously taking into account the multidimensional aspect of economic agent strategies and the multilevel territorial dynamics (ibid.).

Spain must follow foreign experiences of rescaling: the national government has a role in promoting new governance models at urban and supra-local scales (Fariña, 2014). In Harrison's (2014) examples the state intervened to create new, or modify existing, socio-spatial infrastructures at the urban and regional level to, first, create the necessary conditions for capital accumulation, and, second, to make their major urban region(s) more attractive to transnational capital than their international competitors.

This is unfinished business in Spain. As in the UN-Habitat (2011) report, new urban configurations are being created (cities in clusters, corridors, and regions) that are becoming the new engines of both global and regional economies; the lack of political adaptation to this process may have amplified the territorial effects of the crisis. Spanish cities cannot avoid this process. The case of the Mediterranean Axis and freight corridor follows the incipient steps of the Euroregion Galiza-Norte de Portugal and the Atlantic Axis strategy, with a conference on cities and a research joint programme (Figueiredo, Peña, & Varela, 2012).

Spain and its regions must learn from projects like the 'City Growth Commission', established in the United Kingdom in October 2013 to understand how complementary growth between cities can be achieved and what governance arrangements are needed (CGC, 2014). This chapter has shown how important it is for city leaders (and for the central government) to work with one another as part of a connected Spanish system of cities. The future of cities, the future urban scenarios, are linked to a 'pan-regional investment for a more productive system of cities' (ibid.: p. 7) and the responsibility of the Spanish government is fundamental. The Mediterranean Axis, with Valencia as a key player, can be an example of a stronger, megaregional strategy for Spain and of flexible and innovative territorial governance.

Any future post-crisis scenario for Spanish cities (and Valencia in particular) must resolve the three main questions that Neil Brenner's research has raised: first, to differentiate between settlement typologies and socio-spatial processes; second, to observe scale as a product of economics, and social and political dynamics and not as a precondition; and, third, to design new politics for these new scales.

Note

1 Ramon Marrades research has been funded by the Spanish Ministry of Economy and Competitiveness in the benchmark of the National R&D&i Plan 2008–2011 (project CSO2012-39373-CO4-3).

References

Abet, A. (2001) Regiones singulares y regiones sin lugares? Reconsiderando el estudio de lo regional y lo local en el contexto de la geografía postmoderna. *Boletín de la Asociación de Geógrafos Españoles*, 32, 35–52.

Albalate, D., Bel, G., & Fageda, X. (2012) Beyond the efficiency-equity dilemma: Centralization as a determinant of government investment in infrastructure. *Papers in Regional Science*, 91 (3), 599–615.

Bel, G. (2011) *España, capital París*. Barcelona, La Campana.

Boira, J. V. (2002) *Euram 2010: La via Europea*. Valencia, Edicions Tres i Quatre.

Boira, J. V. (2009) El corredor de la Mediterrània en l'horitzó del 2025: Fluxos, infraestructures i escenari global. *Idees: Revista de temes contemporanis*, 32, 103–112.

Boira, J. V. (2013) Infraestructuras y financiación en España: Hacia un nuevo paradigma. In: Gómez, M. J., Lois, R., & Nel.lo, O. (eds) *Repensar el estado: Crisis económica, conflictos territoriales e identidades políticas en España*. Santiago de Compostela, Universidad de Santiago de Compostela, pp. 101–109.

Brenner, N. (1999) Globalisation as reterritorialisation: The re-scaling of urban governance in the European Union. *Urban Studies*, 36 (3), 431–451.

Brenner, N. (2000) The urban question: Reflections on Henri Lefebvre, urban theory and the politics of scale. *International Journal of Urban and Regional Research*, 24 (2), 361–378.

Brenner, N. (2004) *New state spaces: Urban governance and the rescaling of statehood*. Oxford, Oxford University Press.

Brenner, N. (2009a) Restructuring, rescaling, and the urban question. *Critical Planning*, 16 (4), 60–79.

Brenner, N. (2009b) Cities and territorial competitiveness. In: Rumford, C. (ed.) *The SAGE handbook of European studies*. London, SAGE, pp. 462–463.

Brenner, N. (2013) Theses on urbanization. *Public Culture*, 25 (1), 85–114.

CENIT (Centre for Innovation in Transport) (2012) *Ex post evaluation of investment projects co-financed by the European regional development fund (erdf) or cohesion fund (cf) in the period 1994–1999: The Mediterranean Corridor*. Paper prepared for European Commission Directorate-General Regional Policy Policy Development Evaluation, Barcelona. [Online] Available from: http://ec.europa.eu/regional_policy/sources/docgener/evaluation/pdf/projects/mediterranean_corridor.pdf [accessed 12 February 2014].

City Growth Commission (CGC) (2014) *Connected cities: The link to growth*. RSA. 2020 Public Services. [Online] Available from: www.thersa.org/_data/assets/pdf_file/0010/1545247/RSA-City-Growth-Commission-report-Connected-Cities.pdf [accessed 3 April 2014].

Clark, G. & Clark, G. (2014) *Nations and the wealth of cities: A new phase in public policy*. Centre for London, London. [Online] Available from: http://centreforlondon.org/publication/nations-wealth-cities/ [accessed 12 February 2014].

Cruz, J. (2013) Las infraestructuras del transporte: Magnitud y contrastes de una transformación histórica. In: Gómez Mendoza, M. J., Lois González, R., & Nel.lo, O. (eds) *Repensar el Estado: Crisis económica, conflictos territoriales e identidades políticas en España*. Santiago de Compostela: Universidad de Santiago de Compostela, pp. 93–100.

Cucó, J. (2013) *La ciudad pervertida: Una mirada sobre la Valencia global*. Barcelona, Anthropos.

Dembski, S. (2015) Structure and imagination of changing cities: Manchester, Liverpool and the spatial in-between. *Urban Studies*, 52, 1647–1664.

Dewar, M. & Epstein, D. (2006) Planning for megaregions in the United States. *Conference of Association of Collegiate Schools of Planning*, Fort Worth, TX, USA. New version in *Journal of Planning Literature*, 2007, 22 (2), 108–124.

European Commission (2014) *Report from the Commission to the European Parliament, the Council, the European Economic and Social Committee and the Committee of the Regions.* COM (2014) 284 final.

European Commission (2013) *The core network corridors: Trans-European transport network 2013.* European Commission. [Online] Available from: www.tentdays2013. eu/Doc/b1_2013_brochure_lowres.pdf [accessed 10 December 2014].

Fariña, J. (2014) Ciudad global *versus* ciudad local. *Papers*, 57, 17–25.

Farinós, J. (2001) Reformulación y necesidad de una nueva geografía regional flexible. *Boletín de la Asociación de Geógrafos Españoles*, 32, 53–71.

Ferras, R. (1986) Ecrire de la geographie regionale sur l'Espagne. *L'Espace Géographique*, 4, 283–288.

Figueiredo, A., Peña, J., & Varela, E. (2012) Para gobernar y liderar las ciudades del Eixo Atlantico con el horizonte de 2020. In: Vazquez, X. (ed.) *Retos de la acción de gobierno para las ciudades del siglo XXI: Desafíos da governação das cidades do século XXI.* Vigo-Porto, España-Portugal, Eixo Atlântico da Noroeste Peninsular, pp. 9–13.

Florida, R. (2014a) *The mega-regions of North America.* Martin Prosperity Institute. [Online] Available from: http://martinprosperity.org/2014/03/11/the-mega-regions-of-north-america/ [accessed 24 September 2014].

Florida, R. (2014b) *The economic data hidden in nighttime views of city lights.* Citylab. [Online] Available from: www.citylab.com/tech/2014/05/the-economic-data-hidden-in-satellite-views-of-city-lights/371660/ [accessed 24 September 2014].

Galiana, L. (2013) La revisión del Plan General: Planificar la ciudad en ausencia e una estrategia territorial regional. In: Vinuesa, J. (ed.) *Reflexiones a propósito de la revisión del Plan General de Madrid.* Madrid, Universidad Autonóma de Marid-Grupo TryS, pp. 129–143.

Gómez, J. (2001) Un mundo de regiones: Geografía regional de geometría variable. *Boletín de la Asociación de Geógrafos Españoles*, 32, 15–33.

Gómez, M. J., Lois, R., & Nel.lo, O. (2013) *Repensar el estado: Crisis económica, conflictos territoriales e identidades políticas en España.* Santiago de Compostela, Universidad de Santiago de Compostela.

Harrison, J. (2014) The city-region: In retrospect, in snapshot, in prospect. In: Shields R., Lord, A., & Jones, K. (eds) *The city-region in prospect.* Montreal, Canada, McGill/Queens University Press. [Online] Available from: https://dspace.lboro.ac.uk/dspace-jspui/bitstream/2134/15829/3/HarrisonHoyler2014.pdf [accessed 19 May 2015].

Harrison, J. (2015) Cities and rescaling. In: Paddison, R. & Hutton, T. (eds) *Cities and economic change.* London, SAGE Publications, pp. 38–56.

Harrison, J. & Hoyle, M. (2014) Governing the new metropolis. *Urban Studies*, 51 (1), 2249–2266.

Hildebrand, S. A. (2006) La política de ordenación del territorio de las Comunidades Autónomas: Balance crítico y propuesta para la mejora de su eficacia. *Revista de Derecho Urbanístico y Medio Ambiente*, 230, 79–139.

Lois, R. & Miramontes, A. (2014) Introducción. In: Lois, R. & Miramontes, A. (eds) *Reflexiones sobre las ciudades y el sistema urbano en tiempos de crisis.* Santiago de Compostela, Universidad de Santiago de Compostela, pp. 9–14.

McCann, P. (2008) Globalization and economic geography: The world is curved, not flat. *Cambridge Journal of Regions, Economy and Society*, 1 (3), 351–370.

McCann, P. & Acs, Z. J. (2011) Globalization: Countries, cities and multinationals. *Regional Studies*, 45 (1), 17–32.

Martellato, D. (2011) TENT-T priority projects: Where do we stand? *European Research Studies*, 3, 52–66.

Martí-Costa, M., García, A., & Iglesias, M. (2014) Conclusiones: La crisis como suma de vulnerabilidades. In: Subirats, J. & Martí-Costa, M. (eds) *Ciudades, vulnerabilidades y crisis en España*. Sevilla, Factoría de Ideas, Junta de Andalucía, pp. 137–146.

Navarro, C., Rodríguez, M. J., Herrera, M. R., & Mateos, C. (2014) Gobernabilidad y crisis urbana: Causas, manifestaciones y estrategias. In: Subirats, J. & Costa, M. (eds) *Ciudades, vulnerabilidades y crisis en España*. Sevilla, Factoría de Ideas, Junta de Andalucía, pp. 85–108.

Nel.lo, O. (2010) El planeamiento territorial en Cataluña. *Cuadernos Geográficos*, 47, 131–167.

Nel.lo, O. (2011) La ordenación de las dinámicas metropolitanas: El Plan Territorial Metropolitano de Barcelona. *Scripta Nova. Revista Electrónica de Geografía y Ciencias Sociales*, XV (362). Barcelona: Universidad de Barcelona. [Online] Available from: www.ub.es/geocrit/sn/sn-362.htm [accessed 12 February 2014].

Pemberton, S. & Mophet, J. (2014) The rescaling of economic governance: Insights into the transnational territories in England. *Urban Studies*, 51 (11), 2249–2266.

Ponce, G. (2013) Estrategias de metropolización de la ciudad de Valenia en la etapa autónomica: La centralidad cuestionada en el modelo postchristaller de ordenación del territorio. *Boletín de la Asociación de Geógrafos Españoles*, 62, 147–172.

Precedo, A. & Míguez, A. (2014) Una radiografía de las ciudades españolas: Una evaluación del modelo postindustrial. In: Lois, R. & Miramontes, A. (eds) *Reflexiones sobre las ciudades y el sistema urbano en tiempos de crisis*. Santiago de Compostela, Universidad de Santiago de Compostela, pp. 15–72.

Prytherch, D. & Boira, J. V. (2009) City profile: Valencia. *Cities*, 26 (2), 103–115.

Rodríguez-Pose, A. (2008) The rise of the 'city-region' concept and its development policy implications. *European Planning Studies*, 16 (8), 1025–1046.

Romero, J. (2010) Sobre el buen gobierno de las áreas metropolitanas y las regiones urbanas en Europa. In: Pascual, J. & Goldás, X. (eds) *El buen gobierno 2.0: La gobernanza democrática territorial: Ciudades y regiones por la cohesión social y una democracia de calidad*. Valencia, Tirant Lo Blanch, pp. 434–458.

Romero, J. (2012) España inacabada: Organización territorial del Estado, autonomía política y reconocimiento de la diversidad nacional. *Documents d'Anàlisi Geogràfica*, 58 (1), 13–49.

Rozenblat, C. (2012) Las aproximaciones multidimensionales y multinivel a los sistemas urbanos. In: Delgado, C., Juaristi, J., & Tomé, S. (eds) *Ciudades y paisajes urbanos en el siglo XXI*. Madrid, Estudio, pp. 220–235.

RPA (Regional Plan Association) (2006) *America 2050: A prospectus*. [Online] Available from: www.america2050.org/pdf/America2050prospectus.pdf [accessed 12 February 2014].

Sassen, S. (2012) *Novel spatial formats for urban inclusion: Megaregional and global cities*. [Online] Available from: www.booksandideas.net/Novel-Spatial-Formats-For-Urban.html [accessed 6 March 2014].

Sánchez, J. L. (2001) La región y el enfoque regional en geografía económica. *Boletín de la Asociación de Geógrafos Españoles*, 32, 95–111.

Scott, A. J. (2001) *Global city-regions: Trends, theory, policy*. Oxford, Oxford University Press.

Shin, H. B. (2014) Urban spatial restructuring, event-led development and scalar politics. *Urban Studies*, 51 (14), 2961–2978.

Solís, E. & Troitiño, M. A. (2012) El paradigma de la red: Bases para una nueva interpretación del territorio y de los procesos escalares de la urbanización. *Boletín de la Asociación de Geógrafos Españoles*, 60, 141–164.

Subirats, J. (2014) Introducción: ¿Cambio de época?. In: Subirats, J. & Costa, M. (eds) *Ciudades, vulnerabilidades y crisis en España*. Sevilla, Factoría de Ideas, Junta de Andalucía, pp. 9–18.

Tomás, M. (2014) We want our city back! Estrategias y valores ante las reformas metropolitanas. *Scripta Nova. Revista Electrónica de Geografía y Ciencias Sociales*, XVIII (489). [Online] Available from: www.ub.es/geocrit/sn/sn-489.htm [accessed 30 July 2014].

Trullén, J., Galletto, V., Boix, R., & Marull, J. (2010a) La Catalunya futura: Bases economicoterritorials del nou model de desenvolupament: Ampliant l'escala cap a la gran megaregió Barcelona-Lió. *Revista Econòmica de Catalunya*, 62, 46–63.

Trullén, J., Galletto, V., Boix, R. & Marull, J. (2010b) With methodology of Doll, C., Muller, J. P. & Elvidge, C. D. (2000) Night-time imagery as a tool for global mapping of socioeconomic parameters and greenhouse gas emissions. *AMBIO – A Journal of the Human Environment*, 29 (3), 157–162.

UN-Habitat (United Nations Human Settlements Programme) (2011) *State of the world's cities report 2010/11*. New York, UN-Habitat.

16 Urban decline, resilience, and change

Understanding how cities and regions adapt to socio-economic crises[1]

Thilo Lang

Introduction

Urban decline in a sense of demographic shrinkage combined with weak economic development has been a topic for scholars in urban and regional studies for many years. A lot has been written about cities in crisis, urban decay, shrinking cities, and old industrial regions since the end of the Fordist Age in the Western world, but also under post-socialism with the impacts of political and economic transformation as well as increasing globalisation. East Germany, the West German Ruhr area, the US Rust Belt, and some Southern European regions, such as the Mezzogiorno in Italy, have been widely used examples for studying decline, regeneration, and change. Whereas there is a lot of research into the reasons, processes, and impacts of urban and regional decline, there is less research into regeneration and very little into change. A more recent approach is linked to the adaptation of the resilience concept to urban and regional studies. Resilient cities and regions are said to hold specific capacities, making them less vulnerable to crisis and able to recover more quickly after periods of external stress.

This chapter draws together the concepts of decline and resilience and discusses their explanatory value for understanding urban and regional change in times of crisis. In the next section, forms of the current crisis in European cities and regions will be discussed against the background of diverse urban and national developments and socio-spatial polarisation in the European Union (EU). This will open up perspectives to a better understanding of the conditions, facilitators, and limitations of change as a precondition for regeneration. In the third section, I develop an understanding of urban and regional resilience in economic terms. This is followed in the fourth section by a critical discussion of the limitations of the resilience approach when it comes to researching how cities and regions adapt to socio-economic crisis.

In the fifth section, before concluding with some recommendations for future research, I develop a research approach based on new institutional thinking. I suggest including a perspective on dominant norms, routines, and practices which are crucial when it comes to understanding the local room for manoeuvre and change under conditions of crisis.

Decline, socio-spatial polarisation, and urban crises

In Western Europe there is a strong connection between the literature on urban decline and the economic restructuring in old industrialised areas. In the globalised economy, only a few global cities and metropolitan regions are said to be the 'control points of the global economic system' (Dicken, 2003: p. 240). Within the international system, 'networked' cities and agglomerations (especially capital cities) are said to be the number one location for headquarters of multinational companies and big national enterprises or subcontractors, in particular in the financial sector. In this way, current processes of internationalisation and global inter- and intra-firm relations tend to concentrate much of the world's most important trading activities in a relatively limited number of subnational regions or agglomerations (Krätke, 2014; Scott & Storper, 2003; Beaverstock, Smith, & Taylor, 1999). Amin and Thrift suggest that capital cities and core metropolitan regions can derive competitive advantage from the presence of many organisations in economic, political, and cultural life (1994: p. 105). Current tendencies of globalisation are likely to promote concentrated economic and demographic development in some metropolitan regions, which thereby dominate national urban and economic systems, to the disadvantage of other old industrialised agglomerations or smaller non-metropolitan regions. As a consequence of this spatial polarisation, many regions based on traditional (or old) economies are still struggling to find their role in the globalising economy and to respond to this form of socio-economic crisis.

Indeed, in the past years, regional disparities within the EU have increased (EC, 2010), and the European Union has witnessed a new form of socio-spatial polarisation, with often economically dynamic capital and second-tier metropolitan regions with population and GDP growth on the one hand and less dynamic smaller metropolitan and non-metropolitan regions on the other hand (EC, 2013). The recent economic and financial crisis brought to an end a period during which regional disparities (measured in regional GDP per head and regional unemployment rates) within Europe were generally shrinking (with the exception of the new Eastern European member states) (Lang, 2011). Despite the strong overall performance of the bigger agglomerations in the EU, most of them saw their GDP per head drop between 2007 and 2010 relative to the national level. Smaller agglomerations lost most ground; three out of four declined relative to their country average. The capital regions showed a stronger performance with only 30 per cent of them losing ground (EU, 2013: p. 22).

Looking at employment figures, similar to the GDP per head changes, the capital regions in general outperformed the rest of their respective countries: nine out of ten had a stronger employment performance, nine EU capital regions even achieved employment growth despite increasing national unemployment (ibid.: p. 23). Hence, throughout the EU, there has been a general trend favouring the biggest metropolitan and capital regions. One could argue that these city regions have shown high resilience because they recovered quickly after short turbulences in the fate of the financial and economic crisis throughout the past years. On the other side of the coin, however, this crisis has added a new dimension to the struggles of third-tier city regions and non-metropolitan regions, in particular under the conditions of a longer lasting and ongoing economic and financial crisis in the Southern European countries.

Having identified the reasons for the crisis to be to a large degree at the level of the national economic and financial systems (see also Gambarotto & Solari, 2014), it would be naive to explain the different performances of city regions by analysing the properties of urban and regional socio-economic systems. A more integrated and multilevel perspective would be needed, which is, however, often neglected, as the following brief review of various attempts to explain regional development shows.

The question of why some cities' and regions' economic performance is better than others is an enduring one. It has been addressed by many scholars in recent decades, with interpretations linked, *inter alia*, to industrial districts (Marshall, 1920; Pyke, Becattini, & Sengenberger, 1990), innovative milieus (Aydalot, 1986), clusters (Porter, 1998), the creative class (Florida, 2002), performance within the information age (Castells, 1996), or cities' and regions' networking function within global flows (Beaverstock, Smith, & Taylor, 1999) allowing them to link up with the global economy. However, none of these attempts seems to recognise the role of the state when it comes to moderating and regulating the globalised economy. The debate around urban and regional economic resilience bears similarities to these attempts to sufficiently explain economic performance (Hudson, 2010) but it similarly does exclude a conceptualisation of the role of the state and of present-day capitalism.

In the light of this initial criticism, it has to be discussed whether resilience can be seen as a property which can be 'learned' through particular forms of governance and institutional learning and whether a resilience perspective could include a critical take on the political economy of globalisation. In terms of the management of uneven development and decline, Painter and Goodwin point out that local governance can only be effective if it is part of a multi-scale system of regulation. As the causes for uneven development often, to a large extent, lie outside the local sphere of influence, local governance at best 'can influence only the local half of the (unequal) relationship between global flows and local conditions' (Painter & Goodwin, 2000: p. 43). Local governance must be seen as limited in its stabilising capacity in a multi-scale mode of regulation.

Nevertheless, in particular in Southern Europe, cities and regions have to find answers to the challenges of multi-scale and overlapping forms of socio-economic crises and the question of how cities and regions can recover after external shocks has become even more relevant.

Developing an understanding of urban and regional resilience

Recently, the notion of resilience has become very popular to analyse the ways cities and regions recover after extraordinary events, internal or external shocks, and disasters or any other form of stress. In the context of urban and regional economic development, such events can range from European or global economic crises to periodic national recessions, as well as from general economic transformations to unexpected plant closures. In recent years, many scholars have been concerned with how regions performed differently during and after the crisis of the late 2000s (e.g. Jones, Clark, & Cameron, 2010; Gorzelak & Goh, 2010). It thus seems worthwhile to analyse how the concept of resilience has been utilised in such studies and to develop an understanding of urban and regional resilience.

A comprehensive understanding of the term has yet to be developed in urban and regional studies (Bürkner, 2010; Hudson, 2010). The only basic agreement across most writing on resilience is systemic thinking. Another common position is to apply a kind of equilibrium model linking resilience to the 'ability' of a system – in this context, an urban or regional economy – to return to its earlier, pre-crisis equilibrium state or to be transformed into a new stable version of the system. In this chapter, the interest is in the strand of the academic debate which examines the ways in which a system can adapt to changing conditions from an institutional or evolutionary economics perspective (e.g. Simmie & Martin, 2010). As with an eco-system, urban and regional socio-economic systems cannot be seen as working within given boundaries and their multi-scale interdependencies have to be acknowledged along with their complex specific institutional environments (Lang, 2009: pp. 194ff.). Such institutional environments encompass, besides particular local institutional frameworks, the interplay with national forms of regulation, the wider policy context, and the (local interpretation of) European and global framework conditions.

Across different disciplines, resilience sometimes refers to contradictory characteristics (see also Medd & Marvin, 2005: p. 45). Most resilience research is rooted in post-positivistic epistemology (Walker et al., 2006) and applies an understanding of cities and regions as complex multidimensional or hybrid systems. Concepts of resilience are used to describe the relationship between the system under observation and the externally induced disruption, stress, disturbance, or crisis. In a more general sense, resilience concerns the stability of a system to resist interference. It is, however, more than a response to or the means of coping with particular challenges. Resilience can be seen as a kind of systemic property. In social psychology, for instance, some scholars see resilience as being more than the ability to cope with critical events; it is seen, for example, as 'something underneath', like the unique personal strength of children to cope with physical or social challenges (Murphy, 1974: p. 90; Welter-Enderlin, 2006); it is the capacity, motivation, will, or desire of people that allow them to cope with critical events. This thinking has been transferred to cities and regions as urban and regional resilience. The major theoretical body exploited for a conceptualisation of urban and regional resilience, however, stems from socio-ecological research. In order to develop a more qualitative take on urban and regional resilience research, it is worthwhile to review the conceptualisation of adaptation in the context of socio-ecological systems.

Holling (2001) has linked his understanding of socio-ecological resilience to questions of adaptation. He describes the complex adaptive systems of people and Nature as being self-organised, with a few critical processes creating and maintaining this self-organisation. Such systems of Nature, humans, combined human–natural systems, or social-ecological systems can be perceived as being 'interlinked in never-ending adaptive cycles of growth, accumulation, restructuring, and renewal' (ibid.: p. 392). The accumulation and transformation of resources alternate with phases creating opportunities for innovation. Understanding these cycles, their temporal and spatial scales, as well as the relevant frames of reference used to produce and value these processes would help to 'identify the points at which a system is capable of accepting positive change and the points where it is vulnerable' (ibid.). In this context, (a) resilience as 'a measure of its [the system's] vulnerability to unexpected or unpredictable shocks' (ibid.); (b) the internal controllability; and (c) the wealth of the system determining the range of possible future options, are seen as the main properties shaping the adaptive cycles and the future state of the systems (ibid.: p. 393). High resilience would allow for tests of novel combinations that trigger innovation and adaptation. Holling sees this as particularly true if controllability is low and high resilience allows for the recombination of elements in the system because the costs of failure are low. In contrast, with low resilience or vulnerability at multiple scales, revolutionary transformations would be quite rare due to the nested character of sets of adaptive cycles. A combination of separate developments would have to coincide, i.e. there would be a need for recombinations and inventions to occur simultaneously in order to open windows for fundamental new opportunities (ibid.: p. 404).

In offering an initial conceptualisation of adaptation, it is not surprising that Holling's ideas have been transferred from the study of social-ecological systems to the general sphere of urban and regional development. Hence, in urban and regional studies, socio-economic resilience can be seen as the systemic capacity to address problems in a way that generates long-term stable development paths and allows cities and regions to better adapt to external shocks and interference to the system. To operationalise the concept, some authors (e.g. Hill, Wial, & Wolman, 2008) have used a categorisation into three groups of cities and regions, being resilient, resistant, or non-resilient/vulnerable.

- Resilient regions might be seen as regions which recover after external shocks within a relatively short time span and return to their previous level of employment, economic output, or population. They might even outperform their previous development paths.
- Shock-resistant cities or regions with their development path being not at all influenced by the external event.
- Non-resilient and vulnerable places with the city or region entering a persistent phase of decline or stagnation.

To date, only a few scholars have used the concept of urban and regional resilience to investigate adaptation to urban and regional development problems (e.g.

Hill, Wial, & Wolman, 2008; Gerst, Doms, & Daly, 2009; Hassink, 2010). In these studies, the main focus is on a descriptive quantitative analysis of urban and regional development indicators to identify variations in development as a consequence of external stress. When it comes to understanding these variations, most authors turn to an analysis of structural and framework conditions or portray the ways decision-takers and firms have dealt with external economic and social disturbances.

Gerst, Doms, and Daly (2009) explore the different paths of development taken by urban IT centres in the US after the dot-com bubble burst in 2000. Impacts of decline and paths of recovery varied considerably. Using quantitative methods, their research revealed that IT centres specialised in IT services performed better than those in manufacturing because of their highly educated labour force. Some centres maintained growth due to their adjustment to changes in demand. The research, however, does not go into detail concerning the practices these centres managed to adjust.

Simmie and Martin (2010) tested their model of economic resilience, using economic development data in two British case studies (Cambridge and Swansea travel to work areas), reviewing how they came out of the recessions of the early 1980s and early 1990s. They suggest that endogenous sources of new knowledge and market-related entrepreneurial decisions combined with supportive institutional environments could be key factors for economic resilience. Further, they see a reliance on external factors (such as foreign direct investment) as a short-term solution only (ibid.: p. 42). After analysing governance and firm responses over a number of decades following an evolutionary logic of adaptive cycles, their theoretical conclusion is that the adaptive cycle model is a useful approach to analysing and better understanding regional (economic) resilience.

In addition, systemic thinking should be taken seriously. Hill, Wial, and Wolman (2008: p. 2) stressed that such a perspective helps to shift the focus to analysing the long-term structure of macroeconomic relationships and the relevant social, economic, and political institutions conditioning these structures. Hence, studying resilience should involve studying the rise, stability, and decay of institutions conditioning long-term economic success within a governance and industry/firm dimension. This perspective might help towards the better understanding of why some cities can also maintain their development paths during various forms of crises and how they adapt to changing framework conditions induced by disruption, stress, or crises. However, such a conceptualisation seems to be less suited to the understanding of vulnerabilities and why many cities and regions are non-resilient. This point leads me to a discussion of the limits of the resilience approach in the following section.

Limits of the resilience approach

When linking the notion of resilience to urban and regional studies, a number of problems inherent to the debate should be considered: in normative political contexts in particular, some scholars tend to seek specific local properties that make urban areas less vulnerable to (perceived forms of) crises, sometimes raising expectations about self-contained urban systems functioning like a perpetual motion machine. There is a risk in limiting research on urban and regional change and adaptation to internal regional properties which would be misleading. This ignores the crucial question of national regulation and the necessity to investigate the role of national frameworks and forms of intervention (Lang, 2009: p. 171) as well as political economic issues of globalisation. Hudson astutely discusses options for more resilient regions in relation to the resilience of capitalism and dominant neoliberal models of regional development which trigger national state interventions, and which have at best been partially and temporarily successful in the past (Hudson, 2010). Indeed, neoliberal thought as a dominant feature of current capitalism can be seen as having become maladaptive and a major threat to urban and regional resilience. In particular in the fate of the financial, economic, and national debt crisis, many countries have introduced austerity policies and measures prioritising the rescue of the financial systems without giving too much thought to the social consequences. These measures are usually justified by pointing out that there is no alternative and no choice. Hence, instead of working against the initial reasons, such as the deregulation of financial markets, such neoliberal policies are even strengthened, whereas cuts in the social sphere are accepted as unavoidable (see also Krätke, 2014).

In times of increasing globalisation during contemporary capitalism, cities and regions are increasingly networked across the world by means of an internationalised economy with functional specialisation, global value chains, and a spatial division of labour. Thus it becomes progressively more difficult to understand how a particular urban or regional economy works based on what happens within particular administrative boundaries. Whereas the concept of resilience seeks to explain the ways in which cities or regions adapt to socio-economic crises with certain properties of the system, the system is often defined as being an urban or regional system, instead of being a complex multi-dimensional transnational urban system. Due to the principles of how the economy currently functions, the system would have to be defined as a globally networked multilevel political economic system. Within this system, some places with particular forms of economic activities seem to be privileged while others are disadvantaged.

Therefore I would argue that, in most cases, the very reasons for urban decline and for a growing number of non-resilient cities and regions cannot be explained without referring to the ways in which present-day capitalism functions. Similarly some forms of current urban crises (in particular in Southern Europe) cannot be studied without studying the conditions of the recent financial and economic crisis affecting national economies as a whole. Here, the benefit of the resilience approach is limited as well, as it can only identify variations between cities and regions in terms of their 'performance' during and after the crisis. The reasons for these variations should again not only be sought at an urban or regional level, but are rather linked to the characteristics of this form of crisis in the current form of capitalism which favours finance-dominated models of development. For many national economies, among others, in Southern Europe, trading financial values as well as the real estate business have become cornerstones of the national value added. Both fields are highly internationalised and thus also fragile when the global financial system gets into trouble. A potential response to such forms of stress would be to focus on redirecting 'development trajectories' towards 'real economy activities' (ibid.: pp. 1660, 1674) with better local roots. This is an approach which would certainly need national policy backup and different forms of national regulation.

Opposing such radical forms of response, political ideas of promoting resilience as a normative model match currently dominant neoliberal policy agendas very well. In order to maintain the wider system, responsibility for critical developments is projected on an urban or regional level, linked to the request that places should become more resilient. Hence, resilience thinking seems to be exploited to reproduce contemporary capitalism, or at least excludes opposition to and transformation of the wider system logics.

'Resilient spaces are exactly what capitalism needs – spaces that are periodically reinvented to meet the changing demands of capital accumulation' (MacKinnon & Derickson, 2013: p. 254). Thinking about resilience as a normative, externally defined strategy would even reproduce uneven forms of development, or at least would serve to reproduce 'wider social and spatial relations that generate turbulence and inequality' (ibid.). However, such an instrumentalisation of the concept as a normative model contradicts the understanding of adaptive systems as being self-organised.

The main limitation of the concept concerning the latter two points is it being apolitical or de-politicised and thus lacking explanatory strength. A further hope projected on to the emerging resilience debate is that it provides us with a new approach for better understanding change and adaptation. Closely linked to the concept of resilience is the idea of adaptive cycles, which are portrayed as being never-ending, nested, and complex, supporting the emergence of new structures and behaviours and allowing for novel combinations which lead to innovation because the costs of failure are low. However, in a social world, the approach fails to give an idea of how this might function. This may be in particular because it lacks a conceptualisation of agency within the system perspective, including questions of understanding behaviour, collective agency, and agenda setting. Therefore, studies using the concept would need to 'move beyond emphasis upon narrow ... metrics of regional macro-economic performance ... pre- or post-shocks' (Bristow & Healey, 2014: p. 932). Otherwise results will not move beyond merely descriptive results of the ways in which cities and regions cope with external stress from a purely economic point of view, while neglecting questions of long-term social stability.

With its roots in research into coping with extreme events, the concept of resilience also has limitations when it comes to assessing urban responses to critical social and economic developments: in resilience research, questions tend to be overlooked as to why and how external events are perceived as disturbance or crisis, as well as questions on the achievable state when this crisis is over. In this context, questions of power concerning the judgement and classification of what constitutes crisis, as well as the objectives for achievable states of the system through adaptation are crucial and should be topics for further research (see also Hudson, 2010: p. 13), as should issues regarding the social construction of vulnerabilities and resilience in general (Bürkner, 2010: pp. 34ff.). In this context, the adaptation of a system does not have to correspond to widely accepted 'positive' developmental trajectories.

Adding a new institutionalist perspective to the resilience approach

To conduct research specifically into various forms of urban and regional adaptation to the ongoing crisis in Southern Europe, the previous paragraphs show that the resilience approach needs some add-ons. Understanding urban and regional resilience only in terms of structural properties is inadequate when one assumes that the world is socially constructed and that cities are part of global urban networks. So how can cities and regions become more resilient under the conditions of a complex multilevel system?

To answer the above question, the options for urban and regional change, as well as the local room for manoeuvre should be better understood. If we perceive urban socio-economic resilience as being linked to those properties of the institutional environment that maintain success and allow for 'positive' developmental trajectories, new institutionalism combined with an agency perspective could possibly help to focus research agendas in urban and regional studies. We could see resilience as a long-term systemic 'capacity', closely related to an institutional environment being supportive of the constant advancement of the system – one which also includes mobility that introduces positive feedback from the outside, circumventing lock-ins in negative development paths (and vice versa). Resilience could then be seen as being linked to a particular culture that constantly advances the key properties of the system and facilitates institutional and collective learning processes in the long run. Elements of such institutional environments would favour experimentation, risk, and innovation in response to anticipated or experienced external challenges and threats. Hence, the particular institutional environment would be supportive of foresight, developing advanced products, processes, or fields of economic activity in due time. They would also allow for alternative futures in the event of particular paths of development coming to an end. In the light of the current crisis, processes of adaptation then would allow for the creation of economic development paths less vulnerable to failures of the global financial system.

Place- and time-specific institutional environments function as strong frames of reference and serve to structure local decision-making. In particular (collective or shared) norms, routines, and practices constitute institutionalised forms of behaviour, which tend to make local policy and responses to crisis path-dependent (Lang, 2009: pp. 58ff.). Processes of governance must be seen as social processes that are shaped in a tense atmosphere of structure and agency.

As decision-makers are embedded in differing social and cultural structures (including different sets of institutions or multiple institutional environments) they 'may have to choose among competing institutional loyalties as they act' (Peters, 1999: p. 26). Such selection processes depend on individual, collective, or organisational capacities based on the ability to learn from applied strategies and tactics in other contexts and at previous times.

Such institutional environments will always be specific to place and time, although they do contain multilevel elements, i.e. in the form of specific 'translations' of super-ordinated frameworks. Acknowledging the central ideas of new institutionalism regarding a dynamic rather than static as well as a non-deterministic understanding of institutions, while still structuring social processes (Peters, 1999: pp. 25ff.; Lowndes, 2002: pp. 95ff.; Lang, 2009: pp. 54ff.), the idea of adaptive cycles should not be taken as necessary sequences of clearly identifiable phases in a mechanistic process. An institutionalist understanding of resilience does not sustain ideas of a static set of properties. Further, there might be phases which are more open and others which are more confined to adaptation and change. Hence, resilience should not be seen as a permanent feature of particular regions, but as dependent on time-specific contexts. Resilience rather describes more or less elusive circumstances in the form of particular institutional practices and orientations. These are supportive of an adaptation of the system without it becoming locked into unsuccessful development paths.

The discussion of ideas of complex adaptive systems and adaptive cycles within which resilience plays an important part (see above) reveals prominent overlaps with the concepts of path dependence (North, 1990; Pierson, 2000) and institutional thickness (Amin & Thrift, 1994), whereby functional, cognitive, or political lock-in (Grabher, 1993) sometimes hinders new forms of development. In such cases, the relevant system becomes maladaptive. Path dependence and lock-in can thus be either an enabling or constraining factor in regional economic adaptation following a crisis situation (see also Simmie & Martin, 2010: p. 32). North (1990: pp. 80f.) discusses the capacity to avoid lock-ins under the term 'adaptive efficiency', while remaining open about what such a capacity would actually mean and how it could be researched.

Conclusions

Throughout the recent financial and economic crisis in Europe, regional polarisation has become a major feature of Europe's urban and regional system. Only a few, mainly large metropolitan and capital regions, have taken the lead in economic development after the economic crisis, with an increasing number of regions 'lagging behind'. A number of regional scientists have applied the notion of resilience to explore and understand these differences. The main motivation for this chapter is to critically reflect upon and discuss the limitations of such approaches.

The resilience approach favours a prioritisation of local forms of response to urban crises and tends to neglect supralocal forces in the wider institutional system which have been crucial to understand the spatial impacts of the recent financial and economic crisis in Southern Europe and beyond. Due to the systemic organisational capacities of the state, supralocal forces must be seen as integral context for local action. There can be no doubt that the nation state plays a crucial role when it comes to local development. The national and regional levels provide (organisational, financial, discursive) mechanisms and frameworks leading to and supporting the emergence of local development initiatives and other forms of response. The state also plays a key role in the regulation of transnational relations and in mediating the impacts of a globalised economy, e.g. in the financial sector. This has to be acknowledged when doing research into urban and regional change.

By applying a multilevel conceptualisation, a new institutional understanding of urban resilience could open up promising perspectives for Social Science research on urban change. Conceptualising cities and regions as complex multidimensional or hybrid systems should encourage us to look at the interaction of different dynamics and hybrid processes intersecting at various spatial levels; the ways in which they shape and produce vulnerability, crisis, and change. Such a systemic perspective has the potential to advance governance research, which is often overloaded with normative expectations of how governance should be. From a resilience perspective, governance can be seen as purposeful collective action to sustain a stable state of the system or to transform the system into a 'better' state. Governance cannot, however, be seen as a tool to steer the system (Walker et al., 2006).

Utilisation of the resilience notion may assist researchers to address key questions relevant to urban and regional development: In what way is adaptation to socio-economic crises linked to processes of growth, accumulation, restructuring, and renewal at different scales and in different social, political, and economic contexts? Which social or discursive processes constitute a crisis situation, perceived vulnerabilities, and necessities to adapt? Who are the main drivers behind these processes? To what extent is the debate on resilience steered by political interest groups and power structures? What differences can be identified between cities and regions in their systemic capacities to adapt to crisis situations across space and time?

The conceptual and theoretical work on resilience could provide a basis for a better understanding of change in complex systems of spatial interdependencies, and thus could fill a gap in institutional theory and governance research. By suggesting analytical categories, new institutionalist notions could help to identify the properties that make the urban or regional system resilient. Understanding development as being composed of nested adaptive cycles of growth, accumulation, restructuring, and renewal (Holling, 2001: p. 392) thereby helps to conceptualise change and persistence. These cycles should not, however, be seen as mechanistic or deterministic processes. Appreciation of their nested character allows for a complex research perspective on issues of change, one that recognises adaptation as occurring at different scales and in various social, political, and economic contexts.

Social scientific attempts to conceptualise urban and regional resilience require further development, in particular on issues of agency, power, institutional constraint, and national regulation. Nevertheless it appears promising to combine concepts of resilience and systemic thinking with new institutionalist ideas that can address these oversights. The question as to whether and how change can be successfully managed remains open. In the context of urban and regional development, this question is largely linked to spatial and social justice and thus deserves more attention. The ideas presented in this chapter may assist in advancing research concepts dealing with these issues.

Note

1 The chapter is based on an earlier version (Lang, 2012).

References

Amin, A. & Thrift, N. (1994) Living in the global. In: Amin, A. & Thrift, N. (eds) *Globalization, institutions and regional development in Europe*. Oxford, Oxford University Press, pp. 1–22.

Aydalot, P. (ed.) (1986*) Milieux innovateurs en Europe*. Paris, GREMI (Groupe de recherche européen sur les milieux innovateurs).

Beaverstock, J. V., Smith, R. G., & Taylor, P. J. (1999). A roster of world cities. *Cities*, 16 (6), 445–458.

Bristow, G. & Healy, A. (2014) Regional resilience: An agency perspective. *Regional Studies*, 48, 923–935.

Bürkner, H. J. (2010) Vulnerabilität und Resilienz: Forschungsstand und sozialwissenschaftliche Untersuchungsperspektiven. *Leibniz Institute for Regional Development and Structural Planning Working Paper (Erkner)*, 43. [Online] Available from: http://irs-net.de/download/wp_vr.pdf [accessed 26 January 2015].

Castells, M. (1996) The rise of the network society: The information age: Economy, society, and culture (Vol. 1). Cambridge, Chichester, Wiley-Blackwell.

Dicken, P. (2003) *Global shift: Reshaping the global economic map in the 21st century*. New York, Guilford Press.

EC (European Commission) (ed.) (2013) *The urban and regional dimension of the crisis: Eighth progress report on economic, social and territorial cohesion*. Luxembourg, Publications Office of the European Union. [Online] Available from: http://ec.europa.eu/regional_policy/sources/docoffic/official/reports/interim8/interim8_en.pdf [accessed 26 January 2015].

EC (European Commission) (ed.) (2010) *Fifth report on economic, social and territorial cohesion*. Brussels, European Commission. [Online] Available from: http://ec.europa.eu/regional_policy/sources/docoffic/official/reports/cohesion5/pdf/5cr_en.pdf [accessed 26 January 2015].

Florida, R. (2002) *The rise of the creative class: And how it's transforming work, leisure, community and everyday life*. New York, Basic Books.

Gambarotto, F. & Solari, S. (2014) The peripheralization of Southern European capitalism within the EMU. *Review of International Political Economy*, doi: 10.1080/09692290.2014.955518.

Gerst, J., Doms, M., & Daly, M. C. (2009) Regional growth and resilience: Evidence from urban IT centers. *Economic Review*, 2009, 1–11.

Gorzelak, G. & Goh, C. C. (eds) (2010) *Financial crisis in Central and Eastern Europe: From similarity to diversity*. Warsaw, Scholar.

Grabher, G. (1993) The weakness of strong ties: The lock-in of regional development in the Ruhr area. In: Grabher, G. (ed.) *The embedded firm: On the socioeconomics of industrial networks*. London, Routledge, pp. 255–277.

Hassink, R. (2010) Regional resilience: A promising concept to explain differences in regional economic adaptability? *Cambridge Journal of Regions, Economy and Society*, 3 (1), 45–58.

Hill, E., Wial, H., & Wolman, H. (2008) Exploring regional economic resilience. *Working Papers*, Institute of Urban and Regional Development UC Berkeley 2008 (4). [Online] Available from: http://iurd.berkeley.edu/wp/2008-04.pdf [accessed 26 January 2015].

Holling, C. S. (2001) Understanding the complexity of economic, ecological, and social systems. *Ecosystems*, 4 (5), 390–405.

Hudson, R. (2010) Resilient regions in an uncertain world: Wishful thinking or a practical reality? *Cambridge Journal of Regions, Economy and Society*, 3 (1), 11–25.

Jones, A., Clark, J., & Cameron, A. (2010) The global economic crisis and the cohesion of Europe. *Eurasian Geography and Economics*, 51 (1), 35–51.

Krätke, S. (2014) Cities in contemporary capitalism. *International Journal of Urban and Regional Research*, 38 (5), 1660–1677.

Lang, T. (2009) *Institutional perspectives of local development in Germany and England: A comparative study about regeneration in old industrial towns experiencing decline*. Potsdam, Universität Potsdam. [Online] Available from: http://opus.kobv.de/ubp/volltexte/2009/3734/ [accessed 26 January 2015].

Lang, T. (2011) Regional development issues in Central and Eastern Europe: Shifting research agendas from a focus on peripheries to peripheralisation? In: Eröss, A. & Karacsonyi, D. (eds) *Geography in Visegrad and neighbour countries*. Budapest, HAS Geographical Research Institute, pp. 57–64.

Lang, T. (2012) How do cities and regions adapt to socio-economic crisis? Towards an institutionalist approach to urban and regional resilience. *Raumforschung und Raumordnung*, 70 (4), 285–291.

Lowndes, V. (2002) Institutionalism. In: Marsh, D. & Stoker, G. (eds) *Theory and methods in political science*. Basingstoke, Houndmills, pp. 90–108.

MacKinnon, D. & Derickson, K. D. (2013) From resilience to resourcefulness: A critique of resilience policy and activism. *Progress in Human Geography*, 37 (2), 253–270.

Marshall, A. (1920) *Principles of economics* (8th edn). London, Macmillan.

Medd, W. & Marvin, S. (2005) From the politics of urgency to the governance of preparedness: A research agenda on urban vulnerability. *Journal of Contingencies and Crisis Management*, 13 (2), 44–49.

Murphy, L. B. (1974) Coping, vulnerability, and resilience in childhood. In: Coelho, G. V., Hamburg, D. A., & Adams, J. E. (eds) *Coping and adaptation*. New York, Basic Books, pp. 69–100.

North, D. C. (1990) *Institutions, institutional change and economic performance*. Cambridge, Cambridge University Press.

Painter, J. & Goodwin, M. (2000) Local governance after Fordism: A regulationist perspective. In Stoker, G. (ed.) *The new politics of British local governance*. Basingstoke, Palgrave Macmillan, pp. 33–53.

Peters, G. (1999) *Institutional theory in political science: The 'new institutionalism'*. London, Pinter.

Pierson, P. (2000) Increasing returns, path dependence, and the study of politics. *American Political Science Review*, 94 (2), 251–267.

Porter, M. (1998) *The competetive advantage of nations*. New York, Free Press.

Pyke, F., Becattini, G., & Sengenberger, W. (1990) *Industrial districts and inter-firm cooperation in Italy*. Geneva, International Institute of Labour Studies.

Scott, A. & Storper, M. (2003) Globalization, regions, development. *Regional Studies*, 37 (6–7), 579–593.

Simmie, J. & Martin, R. (2010) The economic resilience of regions: Towards an evolutionary approach. *Cambridge Journal of Regions, Economy and Society*, 3 (1), 27–43.

Walker, B. H., Anderies, J. M., Kinzig, A. P., & Ryan, P. (2006) Exploring resilience in social-ecological systems through comparative studies and theory development: Introduction to the special issue. *Ecology and Society*, 11 (1), 12.

Welter-Enderlin, R. (2006) Einleitung: Resilienz aus der Sicht von Beratung und Therapie. In: Welter-Enderlin, R. & Hildebrand, B. (eds) *Resilienz: Gedeihen trotz widriger Umstände*. Heidelberg, Carl Auer Verlag, pp. 7–19.

Part V
Conclusion

17 Learning from each other

Planning sustainable, future-oriented, and adaptive cities and regions

Jörg Knieling, Frank Othengrafen, and Galya Vladova

Origins and impacts of the crisis

The current socio-economic crisis has its origins in multiple events of the preceding decades and is manifested in a series of socio-political and socio-spatial impacts. Many of the authors in this volume have sought to trace the various causes of the crisis and to provide an in-depth study of its manifold impacts in selected Southern European cities and urban regions. This allows for a comparative analysis of recent developments as well as the identification of challenges for the years ahead.

According to Chuliá, Guillen, and Santolino (in this volume) the current financial system is among the reasons for the financial and economic crisis as it allows the creation of bubbles based on speculative transactions and unrealistic expectations. Additionally, the high level of risk-taking of banks and investors has been fostered through a long period of low inflation and stable growth in most industrialised countries, including Southern European states. An example for this can be found in the irresponsible mortgage lending in the US but also in many European countries such as the UK, Ireland or Spain, Portugal, and Greece. Here, loans were distributed to 'subprime' borrowers with poor creditworthiness for building or buying houses who then struggled to repay the loans. When looking at the situation in the US, the distribution of loans was not a single event but happened in all parts of the country. It led to the burst of the real estate bubble in the country, the collapse of the investment bank Lehmann Brothers, and to far-reaching consequences for the global financial systems.

The impacts of the global financial crisis have also reached Europe and have hit Southern European countries and cities particularly hard. There seem to exist various reasons for this (see the contributions of Chuliá, Guillen, & Santolino; Romero, Melo, & Brandis; Seixas et al.; Serraos et al. in this volume). First, the long period of low inflation and stable growth in most European countries, together with the introduction of the euro as a currency, has raised capital flows from the North-western European countries to the Southern European ones and has provoked the current account deficits of the latter. As argued by Chuliá, Guillen, and Santolino (in this volume) this has resulted in a credit boom in the banking sector that has created jobs in low-skilled industries, such as the construction sector (see also the contributions of Mourão & Marat-Mendes; Rodrigez Álvarez; Romero, Melo, & Brandis; Seixas et al.). This development already indicates that the economies of most of the Southern European countries are highly specialised in sectors with low productivity and high employment.

In Spain and Portugal, for example, the financial industry has been strongly focused on the housing business as a strategy for growth (see for instance contributions of Chuliá, Guillen, & Santolino; Rodrigez Álvarez; Mourão & Marat-Mendes; Romero, Melo, & Brandis, in this volume). According to Chuliá, Guillen, and Santolino, banks provided cheap mortgage loans to investors and house purchasers, inflating house prices. As a consequence, and due to the lack of suitable policies and spatial plans or strategies in most Southern European countries to stricter control urban development, the built land and the number of housing plots has expanded enormously in the two decades preceding the outbreak of the crisis. This has provided the construction sector a possibility to increase rapidly producing a large housing stock surplus (see for instance contribution of Mourão & Marat-Mendes). The house price bubble has not been anticipated by policy-makers, and countermeasures have not been launched. 'Even worse, tax deductions were applied to the purchase of a property, inflating the bubble' (Chuliá, Guillen, & Santolino, this volume). The favourable loans granted by banks and the economic specialisation in sectors with low productivity and high employment are thus among the main reasons for the crisis in Southern European countries and might help explain the housing bubble and its eruption.

Another reason for the crisis or the strong impacts of the crisis on Southern European countries is to be found in the socially deeply embedded ambition of Southern Europeans of purchasing their own property (see Cotella et al., this volume). Due to the capital flows banks have also granted generous loans to households and borrowers with poor creditworthiness to finance housing projects. Additionally, people borrowed against overvalued houses (see Chuliá, Guillen, & Santolino, in this volume, for instance). Similar as in the US, the economic crisis, the subsequent economic contraction and the increasing unemployment rates, foreclosures, and mortgage insolvencies resulting from it have faced individuals, households, and families with difficulties repaying their loans and have thus additionally intensified the crisis.

However, it is not only the housing bubble that has led to the economic crisis in Southern European countries. Serraos et al. (in this volume) conclude that the crisis in Greece, for example, emerges as a consequence of the massive budget deficit and the simultaneous inability of the state to attract further external finances. They further argue that the economic growth and prosperity of the last decades were based on increases in government expenditures and debt-fuelling government spending, mainly based on the above mentioned capital flows from North Europe. When capital flows suddenly stopped, due to the overall crisis, this led to major imbalances between state expenses and financing abilities as well as between borrowing and repayment abilities.

In addition, many authors in this volume (see for instance Mourão & Marat-Mendes; Seixas et al.; Papaioannou & Nikolakopoulou) have emphasised that the economic crisis has also been triggered by pre-crisis urban developments. The neoliberal policies and models followed in the last decades have promoted territorial competitiveness, outsourcing of public services, and privatisation of public space. The different national strands of neoliberalisation in Southern European countries have created conditions that favour large-scale events and projects, the planning by projects and not by plans, and the undermining of participatory processes (see Romero, Melo, & Brandis; Caruso, Cotella, & Pede; Seixas et al., in this volume, for instance). Furthermore, as various examples highlight (e.g. Papaioannou & Nikolakopoulou; Seixas et al.; Rodrigez Álvarez), the Southern European context is characterised by institutional particularities and the existence of internal factors, such as the mistrust in public institutions and corruption, that influence the development paths of the countries but also their ability to enforce and implement targeted policies to mitigate the impacts of the crisis. As argued by Papaioannou and Nikolakopoulou, Greece for instance has experienced decades of short-term policies and plans that have not been focusing on real local needs. This shows that along with the economic crisis, Southern European cities witness also a crisis of territorial governance and of traditional tools.

It could be concluded that the financial crisis, the economic downturn as a result of it, and the austerity politics promoted in response to the financial deficits have had widespread impacts on the territories and societies in Southern Europe. Both developed and less developed cities and regions have experienced a decline in employment and in economic output and have been strongly affected by the shrinking GDP and the increasing public debt. Yet, the stagnation of the real estate property market and the contraction of the building sector have been higher in certain urban and Metropolitan Areas such as Madrid and Athens as well as in coastal areas strongly focused on the tourism industry and dependent on the construction sector. This might result in new patterns of regional polarisation and brings the discussion to the fore why some cities are more resilient to crisis events, why others deal better with the crisis' impacts, and what factors could mitigate these impacts.

The economic contractions from the last years, the explosive increase in unemployment, and the daily evictions have created hardship for millions of people. As shown in many of the contributions in this volume this has led to a significant increase in the number of people at risk of poverty and exclusion as well as to the re-emergence of low living standards (see for instance Papaioannou & Nikolakopoulou; Serraos et al.; Romero, Melo, & Brandis; Chuliá, Guillen, & Santolino). Many authors have also documented that the crisis has severely affected exactly the most vulnerable groups of the population. Rodrigez Álvarez (in this volume) even points to the emergence of two lost generations due to the crisis – the young people that are unable to enter the labour market and the elderly ones that are excluded with limited chances for reintegration. In addition, the crisis has affected the different economic sectors unequally leading to highest percentage of job losses in the construction, real estate, and tourism sectors. The shrinking of the economy, the rising inequalities in income distribution, and the threat of social segregation have resulted in change in the concerns of people and in lack of confidence in the future. As a consequence, many Southern European cities witness today net emigration and brain drain that might have long-term effects on their future development. As argued by Caruso, Cotella, & Pede (in this volume) all these recent trends add a further dimension to the increasing social and economic complexities of contemporary urban life in Southern European cities.

Responses and reactions to the crisis

The economic crisis and the prospects of a prolonged period of high unemployment, negative economic growth, and threatened social cohesion have called in question the institutional mechanisms and the urban policies applied by Southern European cities prior to the crisis. The need for new approaches and developments for the years ahead has affected the policy priorities of the Southern European states and has resulted in a series of institutional and regulatory restructuring as well as welfare and budget reforms both on the national and the local level. While witnessing the reorientation of territorial and urban governance, recent years have also seen the emergence of new forms of self-organisation. In addition, the opposition against austerity politics has given rise to instances of social mobilisation and the emergence of new socio-political cultures.

New institutional settings for territorial governance, regulatory restructuring, and policy reorientation

The current economic crisis has directly affected the financial scope of the public budgets and has set in motion new socio-political trends and processes of institutional restructuring. Since the crisis is contextually determined and has partly intervened in ongoing developments, these processes differ according to each specific context's particularities and the existing structural frameworks. Yet, some major similarities might be identified in the recent developments in Southern European countries. These have been largely characterised by financially driven state policies and territorially driven urban development strategies.

Since the outburst of the crisis there has been a strong tendency in Southern European countries towards decentralisation of public responsibilities. This has resulted in new freedoms, rights, and responsibilities for the local governments. The administrative reforms towards more decentralisation aimed at transferring power and authority to the local level and have been combined with changes in the normative framework (see also Cotella et al. in this volume). Portugal, for instance, which is still one of the most centralised states in Europe, has adopted a new law for the delegation of competences from the national level to the municipal and inter-municipal one as well as a law on administrative reorganisation and restructuring of municipalities. By reducing the number of existing parishes and transferring more management competences to them an attempt has been made to increase local government capacities. Yet, as argued by Seixas et al. (in this volume) the pressure for austerity localism in Portugal has been mainly a result of financially driven central state policies that aimed at expenditure and institutional cuts rather than actual decentralisation. The combination of top-down institutional approaches and local territorially driven political strategies has shown different outcomes in different municipalities. This clearly points to the fact that local structural determinants play a central role in restructuring processes and political lock-ins could slow down the processes and indirectly hamper the development of indigenous potential. The latter aspect also suggests that the performance of cities and municipalities during the crisis should be seen in the light of path dependent development. A cornerstone in the establishment of new development paths is the change of established practices and rules (see contribution of Knieling et al. in this volume).

The reforms of the administrative systems of Southern European countries have been initiated to respond to reduced public expenditures, to existing institutional weaknesses, and to improve the public administration's efficiency. Various approaches towards the implementation of the reforms can be identified in different countries. In Spain and Italy, for instance, the reforms envisage the introduction of Metropolitan Areas, respectively metropolitan cities, as a new territorial level (see contributions of Boira & Marrades, and Caruso, Cotella, & Pede, this volume). As shown at the example of the Metropolitan Area of Barcelona (see Rodrigez Álvarez), the introduction of this new territorial level has been meant to avoid duplications and simplify administrative procedures, yet its effectiveness has not been evaluated. In contrast to the Spanish case, the introduction of metropolitan governments in Italy mainly follows the logic of public expenditure rationalisation, but pays no specific attention to actual territorial governance needs, which may lead to competition between local political arenas (see Caruso, Cotella, & Pede, this volume).

Various examples in this volume highlight that the rescaling of competences has also found its expression in a process of recentralisation of public policies (see for instance contributions of Caruso, Cotella, & Pede; or Seixas et al.). Central functions in important policy areas such as major infrastructure investments have been strengthened. In the course of this process the planning powers at the central level have been strengthened as well, which, as argued by Caruso, Cotella, and Pede (this volume), has contributed to the recentralisation of decision-making. This has resulted in the revision of main urban and regional planning laws in most of the Southern European countries hit by the crisis (see also Cotella et al. in this volume). In the majority of the cases the revision of planning laws and regulations has aimed at promoting market-oriented strategies and has led to the emergence of a pro-growth planning agenda. In Greece, for instance, new regulations to facilitate private investments of strategic importance have been adopted, which are to bypass the traditional statutory planning and to promote privatisation and the outsourcing of services such as the Environmental Impact Assessment (see Serraos et al., this volume; see also Reimer, Getimis & Blotevogel, 2014). A Special Spatial Development Plan of Strategic Investments has recently been adopted in Greece, which enables landowners and investors to override possible restrictions imposed by existing spatial plans. In addition, legislation changes in recent years have inserted tools to avoid costly administrative procedures, to accelerate them with the introduction of so-called fast-track processes for strategic investment projects, and to privatise former public organisations (see contributions of Papaioannou & Nikolakopoulou; Serraos et al.; Crespo, Mendes, & Nicolau, this volume). Thus, the new planning regulations have strengthened non-institutional and private actors in the production of space. At the same time, the promotion of market interests and private initiatives has raised concerns about insufficient consideration of social and environmental aspects in the planning process. It could be argued that these concerns might open space for rethinking terms such as social cohesion and for discussing new concepts such as low carbon territories (see Mourão & Marat-Mendes, this volume).

A topic identified by many authors in this volume is that the recent administrative and legislative changes in response to the economic crisis have mainly been state driven. At the same time it is actually the urban level that has come to the fore and is best placed to deal with the manifold impacts of the crisis. The crisis' effects, various in their nature, require flexibility and open possibilities for the local level to apply place-based approaches in order to recover and trigger development and cohesion (see contributions of Salone, Besana, & Janin Rivolin; Caruso, Cotella, & Pede, this volume). This results in new responsibilities for the urban level in activating local stakeholders and intensifying the coordination between various policy fields. At the same time, the consideration of national political, institutional, and economic frameworks as well as the implementation of EU legislation emphasises the need for strengthened cooperation between initiatives and actors situated at different territorial levels. This points to the importance of new forms of territorial governance and calls for urban policies that combine multi-sectoral visions and are developed in constant negotiations between diverse actors and through compromise (see also Cotella et al., this volume).

Moreover, the severe effects of the crisis require policies that are oriented much more towards the diverse scales of contemporary urban problems and that ensure permanent structures for citizen empowerment and social innovation (see Knieling et al., this volume). In this line it could be argued that the crisis has played an influential role in diminishing the role of landowners, private developers, and real estate companies, which have been the main development agents in the pre-crisis time (see Romero, Melo, & Brandis, this volume), and has given more emphasis to spatial planning and public participation in Southern European countries. In recent years, different tools for civil participation and new participatory processes have been introduced in many Southern European cities (see for instance Rodrigez Álvarez, this volume, who refers to the public referendum La Diagonal and the new Open Governance project in Barcelona). Although their success is still uncertain they are a clear expression of the growing demand of citizens for more direct involvement in planning processes and urban politics (see also contribution of Othengrafen, Romero, & Kokkali, in this volume).

Challenged to tackle the negative effects of the economic crisis many Southern European cities have faced the need to launch new planning initiatives and to adopt new spatial policies and plans. As evidenced by Portuguese experience, a number of programmes for regeneration of deprived areas, e.g. introducing priority intervention neighbourhoods, have been developed (see Seixas et al., this volume). Regeneration policies have been initiated for the central districts of Greek cities as well and a new Plan for Integrated Urban Intervention for Athens has been elaborated recently, which addresses the spatial implications of the crisis and promotes integrated strategies (see Papaioannou & Nikolakopoulou and Serraos et al., this volume). Although it might be assumed critically that the regeneration policies may boost new gentrification trends, their introduction quite recently has not yet allowed the evaluation of their effects.

It is important to stress that the influence of the crisis on Southern European countries should be seen in the context of their planning practices and systems (see for instance Salone, Besana, & Janin Rivolin, and Knieling et al., this volume, on 'conformative' planning systems). Additionally, urban policies in Southern European countries seem to focus on 'economic competitiveness' as dominant rationale since the 2000s. Many of the authors in this volume (e.g. Serraos et al.; Boira & Marrades; Mourão & Marat-Mendes) emphasise that urban policies during the crisis have continued to focus on the boost of economic activities and growth of revenues. Thus they have strengthened the market orientation of planning and the finance-dominated models of development. It should also be noted that since the outburst of the crisis the discussion on how policies contribute to improve the quality of life in cities (see Papaioannou & Nikolakopoulou, this volume) and how they may foster social and economic resilience is gaining significance (see Lang, this volume).

Welfare reforms, budget, and structural adjustments

The recent economic crisis and the radical austerity policy responses to mitigate its impacts have led to the deterioration of the fiscal positions of the Southern European governments. As various contributions in this volume show (e.g. Serraos et al.; Seixas et al.), the Southern European countries have placed a priority on the cuts of government spending and have imposed serious constraints on local budgets. This, along with the low revenue collection rates due to the weak economic climate, has resulted in a growing scarcity of local public resources, in local government fiscal indebtedness and in the need for local budgetary reforms. Furthermore, the drastic reduction of funds for providing the public services has become an assault on the welfare state, which has been dramatically shrinking while the social needs have been increasing. To fill the existing budgetary gaps and to meet the growing demands of their residents Southern European cities are challenged to identify new revenue sources, to test innovative collaboration forms for the provision of services and the administration of facilities, and to set budget priorities.

In response to the deteriorating revenue collections and the increased needs for expenditures many of the central governments in Southern Europe have voted to introduce new taxes and fees or to increase the rates of existing ones. In Portugal, for instance, a mix of tax increases has been imposed on work and pension revenues and consumption (see Seixas et al., this volume). To ensure the growth of its revenues, the Greek government has followed a similar track. In recent years, it has attempted to impose a new fee for the 'regularisation' of illegal buildings and new taxes on real estate property. These were initially meant as a 'temporary' measure, but are to be replaced by a permanent property tax with no tax-free threshold (see Serraos et al., this volume). Local governments, in turn, have enforced a series of local taxes and have increased fees for public services such as public transport and electricity. While it might be argued that fees and taxes related to specific expenses are more acceptable to the public, it might also be true that the raised prices of electricity, heating oil, and gas could lead to a new 'energy poverty' (see Serraos et al., this volume), characterised by the inability of many households to pay their bills and to meet their everyday needs.

The socio-economic environment in the crisis years, characterised by high unemployment rates and lower incomes, has made the rise of taxes a difficult practice. As all contributions in this volume consistently show, many of the attempts for further tax increases in Southern Europe have faced the reluctance of the population, which found its expression in reduced political support, different forms of social unrest, and the blockade of political decisions. Similar reactions have followed the insertion of public administration cost reduction programmes. In recent years changes in the normative framework of many Southern European countries have been made aiming at the reduction of the number of local and regional governments' staff. As highlighted by Crespo, Mendes, and Nicolau (in this volume) these legislative changes might have serious effects on the performance of the local governments, particularly when the scope and quality of provided services are concerned. The case of Portugal, for instance, shows that the new laws directly influence the municipalities' capacity of providing municipal services. The process of administrative decentralisation gives more competences to the local authorities but, at the same time, reduces the organisational structures for the provision of services and the overall number of employees. New organisational norms weaken the scope of public services provided to the population and threaten their quality (see Crespo, Mendes, & Nicolau, this volume).

As a result of the economic crisis and the process of restructuring, local governments gained ground with regard to the rationalisation of public services. In recent years, there has been a clear change towards more strategic governance, operating through networks and other forms of public–private partnerships (Crespo, Mendes, & Nicolau, this volume). The need to find more efficient ways for managing private property and interests has forced local governments to promote new forms of governance and has led to the establishment of partnerships with neighbouring municipalities or other private or public entities (see also Cotella et al., in this volume). Furthermore, responsibilities have been delegated to private companies also in domains such as the planning and implementation of public works, which have been traditionally controlled by the public administration. In many cases this has resulted in shared responsibility between city governments and private companies in the construction and implementation of facilities (see for instance Rodrigez Álvarez, this volume). Along with the development of a new commitment of local companies to the city, however, new public–private partnerships might also raise mistrust by the citizens. In particular, large-scale urban development projects might raise concerns that they mark a trend towards governmental withdrawal from the public sphere and limit the opportunity for dialogue with the civil society (see Othengrafen, Romero, & Kokkali, and Rodrigez Álvarez). Thus, while the importance of new collaborative forms has been emphasised by many authors (see Crespo, Mendes, & Nicolau; Serraos et al.; Seixas et al., this volume) their restrictions, effectiveness, legitimacy, and applicability in a certain context need further examination.

In line with the above discussion many local authorities in Southern Europe, which face the need for acquisition of additional resources, have established new public–private partnerships for the implementation of already started projects. Looking for alternative revenue possibilities city administrations have also tested new forms of urban enhancement. In Spain for instance unused public buildings have been sold out and public works under construction have been cancelled. Furthermore, city venues, such as public squares and stations of the public transport, have been sold or rented to private companies for marketing and advertisement purposes (see Rodrigez Álvarez, this volume). As several contributions in this volume show, the number of these new approaches for revenue collection is increasing, yet their effectiveness and what they mean for the future use of public spaces is still to be evaluated.

The sharp increase in deficits and debt over the last years has called for changes in the allocation of financial resources and has forced local authorities to prioritise and better target their expenditures. As shown on the basis of concrete examples, the focus of many Southern European cities' budgets has been gradually moved towards increased funding of social policies when compared to the pre-crisis years. Rodrigez Álvarez has illustrated the implications of this change for the city of Barcelona. In 2014, a significant part of the city's budget has been allocated to security measures and social services, such as the provision of food subsidies for children from poorer families. In many Greek cities relief actions such as the reintegration of homeless people have been initiated. These, however, have been fragmented in their nature and, as argued by Serraos et al. (in this volume), may not cope with the serious impacts of the crisis if not integrated into comprehensive policies of the central state. In this line it should also be noted that in several cases the provision of new social services has gone in parallel with the abolishment of existing ones such as the housing provision or inequality reduction, or has led to the worsening of welfare services such as education and health care (see Serraos et al.; Seixas et al.; Romero, Melo, & Brandis; Chuliá, Guillen, & Santolino, this volume). This has resulted in the re-emergence of basic needs among the most vulnerable parts of the population and has given birth to civic uproar as well as new forms of social solidarity and self-organisation.

New forms of self-organisation and emerging socio-political cultures

Since the outburst of the economic crisis many public services and facilities in Southern European cities, most particularly health care and education, have been experiencing ongoing downgrading. As documented by most of the authors in this volume the dramatic reduction of public expenditure has threatened the fundamentals of inclusive and sustainable driven societies in a disruptive way (see for instance Seixas et al.). As a response to this threat, new self-organised civic groups and forms of social solidarity have been gradually gaining importance. The empirical evidence has shown that in recent years the social networks for support of the most vulnerable groups of the population have been continuously reinforced. Examples of such networks show that the prime field of struggle is everyday life. These developments can be found in almost all Southern European countries. Greek cities for instance have seen the establishment of pharmacies, social groceries, and school support centres for poor children, which are all functioning on a volunteer basis (see Papaioannou & Nikolakopoulou, this volume). Social services based on volunteerism had not been a practice in Greece in the past. In this line the new grass-root solidarity groups, the increased volunteerism, and the establishment of stable structures might be seen as a rescue mechanism for the endangered social cohesion.

The strong rejection of welfare cuts and austerity policies has not only resulted in the organisation of collective action and local initiatives for support of the weakest part of the society, but has also found its expression in large grass-root mobilisations and new social movements. In the majority of the cases these movements have been a reaction against the applied austerity politics and an opposition towards the promoted neoliberal trends that have been largely presented as the only alternative for most of the Southern European cities. The dissatisfaction with the current neoliberal agendas and the existing democratic deficits in cities such as Madrid and Valencia has resulted in the organisation of massive demonstrations and public protests (see Othengrafen, Romero, & Kokkali, this volume). The mobilisation of large masses of people demanding changes of current politics and requiring alternative reading for existing development paths as in the case of the 'Indignados' movement in Spain are clear evidence of a changing social structure.

The emergence of new landscapes of public protest movements has been accompanied by the emergence of new political orientations. The recent years have seen the political activation of young and educated people and the ascension of new independent political parties, such as the 'Podemos' party in Spain and the Coalition of the Radical Left in Greece. As argued by Seixas et al. and Rodrigez Álvarez (in this volume) these latest developments are a phenomenon for many of the Southern European states that did not exist in the pre-crisis times. It might be assumed that they are first signs for the emergence of a new socio-political culture. In the short term, they could result in significant political changes at the city level, in the orientation of national policies, and in the economic and political model of the European Union. Yet, as discussed by

Othengrafen, Romero, and Kokkali (in this volume), conflicting interests of political parties as well as public protests that take the form of violent manifestations might endanger urban politics both at the national and the local level with polarisation. Hence, an emphasis should be placed on the elaboration of new public strategies which could contribute to social cohesion in the long run. These should be based on better understanding of the emerging socio-political cultures and the rationales behind protest movements and should open new ways of cooperation to include the protest into developing revised urban futures.

Outlook: chances for reflecting urban futures of 'cities in crisis'?

As the contributions in this volume have shown the recent crisis has resulted in a number of social, economic, and institutional reforms and experiments. While the crisis has necessitated fast reactions to deal with unemployment and economic decline, it has also created conditions for changes in existing practices. Additionally, it has set the ground for initiatives that can open up new perspectives and can point into directions that would not have been accessible in a saturated environment. From a theoretical point of view a crisis opens up the regulative framework and institutional restrictions, and forces people to think beyond their routines. Arguing with the words of transition theory crisis-related change on the higher level can create 'windows of opportunity' on the regime and niche level allowing niche innovations to mainstream or at least to have an impact on the routines that are organised on the regime level (see also Knieling et al., this volume). What do those abstract considerations mean for cities that experience financial and economic crisis for several years now? Which sort of niche innovations can be identified or have come to the fore that could prove the hypothesis of 'crisis as chance'?

   This discussion is not meant in a cynical way to trivialise the dramatic situation of millions of people in Southern European countries and cities. It tries to contribute to the development of future scenarios that take the crisis as an initial point and aim at identifying solutions to better understand the crisis' roots and to overcome its impacts (also Panayotakis, 2014). In the following paragraphs selected future scenarios will be discussed. A particular focus will be placed on the approaches and initiatives that are directly related to urban and regional development, namely:

- local economy initiatives that make use of local and regional cycles of production and consumption, sometimes including elements of a countertrade economy;
- civil self-organisation that brings people together who find solutions in cooperative structures, e.g. housing, agricultural, or food cooperatives;
- post-growth initiatives, sometimes experimenting with the concept of self-sufficiency;
- revival of the 'commons' that include appreciation of public goods.

Local economy initiatives

One of the main reasons for the occurrence of the crisis, its duration, depth, and dimension, is to be found in the globalisation of the economic system. When in Spain the housing bubble burst, the risky game of internationally floating finances had come to an end. For sure, the investors were struck hard and lost a huge amount of money. However, the crisis struck even harder the people that were not able to pay down their loans anymore, and quite often had to even quit their homes. In addition, many of them are still heavily loaded with remaining debts. A counter-reaction to this situation is experimenting with localised economical approaches. Cities offer a 'laboratory' for economic cycles in various fields of production, processing, and services. As a result of the crisis many grass-root businesses have been set up producing specialised products and directly delivering them to regionally located traders or even individual clients. For sure, those initiatives will not turn around the globalised economy. However, they demonstrate a changed pattern of economic development that is strongly connected to the theoretical concepts of resilience (see contribution of Lang, this volume). Local and regional economy is no more a losing rest category in a more and more centralising economy but wins new self-confidence as a complementary sector. This development correlates with complementary trends from recent years such as the appreciation of regional products, the strengthening of the links between producer and consumer, or the wish of people to set up an own sustainable business.

Civil self-organisation and participatory economy

The protests in recent years in many cities and regions in Southern Europe have brought many more people on the streets than ever expected. Many of those did not only want to criticise their governments, but to contribute to the establishment of a new path of development. This became obvious when new local civil society groups as well as new political groups recently occurred in Spain, Italy, or Greece. It might be argued that while trying to critically counterweigh to the interests of the ruling political parties these groups also try to bring a radical change in the rules that govern social life and thus to influence future development paths.

The exploration of alternative ways of future development has also found its expression in the establishment of cooperatives that tackle economic and social topics in the regional context. Many European countries have had a long tradition of participatory respectively cooperative economy. However, cooperatives had lost their attraction in the decades prior to the crisis since cooperative economies were often criticised as not efficient and competitive enough on a liberalised global market. The crisis brought their advantages back to the fore: the joint responsibility of the members, the solidarity within the organisation, and the regional orientation of many cooperatives diminishing their dependence on global economic structures and developments. Fields of action can be housing, agricultural, or food cooperatives etc. Certainly, cooperatives are not the only and ideal way of economic recovery for Southern European cities. Nevertheless, many new initiatives like the 'Cooperativa integral' in Barcelona[1] have shown that bringing people together, taking over responsibility for new employment, and integrating this in the regional economic structure offers strong advantages in times of crisis.

Post-growth initiatives

A more radical way of criticising the economic system are approaches that try to establish ways of living and working that go beyond the growth-related paradigm and lead to the development of a post-growth economy. There are several approaches that claim to contributing to the post-growth concept. These range from initiatives aiming at a change from quality oriented growth to ones targeting a sufficiency related development. The latter is based on a fundamental change of individual behaviour and needs. In times of crisis such an approach can offer ways of living that are less dependent on central politics and offer a more sustainable development path. However, the post-growth concept still needs to prove in which way it can contribute to solving basic problems, such as unemployment, lack of housing, or of enough money to live, that dominate the discussion in many Southern European cities.

Revival of the 'commons'

The twentieth century can be described as a cultural phase of a 'neglect of the commons' (Ostrom, 1990). Common goods, like open spaces, waterways or lakes, forests, or farming land, that are owned by the city and are used by the people have been a characterising element of many cities. During the last decades there has been a tendency towards privatisation that has been strongly pushed by neoliberal politics up from the 1980s. In recent years, however, privatisation has been heavily criticised due to its social impacts and negative consequences for individuals and communities.

The economic crisis could contribute to a renaissance of the commons in many cities (e.g. Ferguson & Urban Drift Project, 2014; Ostrom & Hess, 2007). Public-owned infrastructures, land, and real estate offer the chance to launch social or built environment experiments and bottom-up initiatives that contribute to sustainable urban development (e.g. Tonkiss, 2014; Till, 2014). However, the use of the commons has to prove that it fulfils high qualitative expectations and certainly needs innovative forms of urban governance that go far beyond the routines. Moreover, it needs to establish new forms of cooperation between politics, administration, businesses, and citizens for creating the future vision of the citizen community.

The contributions in this book offer a wide range of insights into the origins of the crisis, its impacts on Southern European cities and urban regions and the challenges these face. Furthermore, they discuss a variety of possible solutions and identify various approaches. However, it becomes clear that the crisis in different countries has different consequences for the people and the cities. Due to this differentiation the topic 'cities in crisis' offers a broad and important field for further research. This book may set a frame and hopes to contribute with useful additional aspects and ideas enriching the multiple efforts that have already been undertaken in recent years to help cities and their citizens to tackle the impacts of the crisis and to set up modernised governance for future sustainable and resilient urban development.

Note

1 For more details see www.cooperativa.cat/en.

References

Ferguson, F. & Urban Drift Project (2014) *Make_shift city: Renegotiating the urban commons.* Berlin, Jovis.
Ostrom, E. (1990) *Governing the commons: The evolution of institutions for collective action.* Cambridge, Cambridge University Press.
Ostrom, E. & Hess, C. (eds) (2007) *Understanding knowledge as a commons: From theory to practice.* Cambridge, MIT Press.
Panayotakis, C. (2014) Scarcity at a time of capitalist crisis. *dérive*, 55, 10–14.
Reimer, M., Getimis, P., & Blotevogel, H. H. (2014) *Spatial planning systems and practices in Europe: A comparative perspective on continuity and changes.* New York, Routledge.
Till, J. (2014) From objects of austerity to processes of scarcity. *archithese. International Thematic Review on Architecture*, 44 (6), 44–55.
Tonkiss, F. (2014) From austerity to audacity: Make-shift urbanism and the post-crisis city. In: Ferguson, F. & Urban Drift Project (2014) *Make_shift city: Renegotiating the urban Commons.* Berlin, Jovis, pp. 165–167.

Index

Page numbers in *italics* denote tables, those in **bold** denote figures.